THE GREAT HISTORIES

A series under the general editorship of

Hugh R. Trevor-Roper,

REGIUS PROFESSOR OF MODERN HISTORY, OXFORD UNIVERSITY

HISTORY OF ITALY and
HISTORY OF FLORENCE

GUICCIARDINI

HISTORY OF ITALY
and
HISTORY OF FLORENCE

Translated by Cecil Grayson

Edited and Abridged with an Introduction by

JOHN R. HALE

FELLOW OF JESUS COLLEGE, OXFORD UNIVERSITY

TWAYNE PUBLISHERS, INC.
31 Union Square, N. Y. 3

Library of Congress Catalog Card Number: 64-16737

The first edition of *Storia d'Italia* (History of Italy) was
published in Italian by Agnolo Guicciardini in 1561 in Florence.

The first edition of *Storia Fiorentina* (History of Florence)
was published in Italian by Barbèra, Bianchi e Comp. in 1859 in Florence as
volume three of Guicciardini's *Opere Inedite* (Unpublished Works).

Contents

Contents

Introduction

Except to Renaissance scholars, Guicciardini is virtually unknown. Yet he is the greatest historian between Tacitus in the first century and Voltaire and Gibbon in the eighteenth and he is one of the greatest of all writers of contemporary history.

His reputation has been the victim of circumstance and fashion. The *History of Italy* was published posthumously in 1561. Its rational, anti-clerical monotone was out of place in a world of richly orchestrated Counter Reformation and its treatment of the peninsula as a whole was irrelevant to an Italy where, with any move to federation or unity blocked by foreign domination, the several states drowsed in a listless provincialism. Regarded as a warehouse of information, it was translated before the end of the sixteenth century into Latin, French, German, Dutch, Spanish and English, but it was not valued as a work of art, and little interest was felt in its author. The eighteenth century, with its interest in philosophic history and its partial relinquishment of religious and rational bias, was better able to read it with sympathy; and in England, indeed, a year after Viscount Bolingbroke had declared in his influential *Letters on the Study and Use of History* (1752) that he preferred Guicciardini to Thucydides "in every respect," a new translation of the *History of Italy* appeared. But the vogue was short-lived, smothered by a feeling that the time spent in reading a massive work (such as the *History of Italy*) was misdirected unless it involved the past of a reader's own country or a common classical past.

A second chance came in the middle of the nineteenth century with the publication in Italy between 1857 and 1867 of ten volumes containing Guicciardini's hitherto unpublished works, including the youthful, vigorous *History of Florence* and various autobiographical writings.

Once more, however, the timing of his appearance was disastrous. The dislike of the Counter Reformation for the historian was pale beside the loathing of the Risorgimento for the man. It was expressed by the most widely respected of Italian critics, Francesco de Sanctis, in a brilliantly written article, "The Guicciardinian Man" (1869), which took at once a prominent place in the sad annals of invective. For de Sanctis, Guicciardini was a symbol of the state of mind that had cost Italy her independence during the Renaissance and was threatening to impede the recovery of her greatness now. Generalizing chiefly from the *Ricordi,* a series of reflections on political life that is the saddest and most cynical item in the Guicciardini canon, he constructed the image of a man selfish, shifty and defeatist, a monument of sour intelligence, the antithesis of the generous, self-sacrificing patriot of whom Italy stood in such need. He ended his attack by warning his audience that the Guicciardinian man is still abroad, active in politics, and unless he is sought out and slain his sterile wisdom will bar the way to freedom and unity.

In spite of the overtly polemical character of de Sanctis' article, the validity of his portrait was widely accepted—in part, at least, because it provided a clue to the puzzling co-existence of intellectual mastery and political beggary during the Renaissance. It passed almost whole, for instance, into the article on Guicciardini which the foremost English student of Italian Renaissance history, John Addington Symonds, wrote for the *Encyclopædia Britannica* in 1885: "[Guicciardini was] a man whose moral nature inspires a sentiment of liveliest repugnance. It is not merely that he was ambitious, cruel, revengeful and avaricious, for these vices have existed in men far less antipathetic than Guicciardini. Over and above those faults, which made him odious to his fellow-citizens, we trace in him a meanness that our century is less willing to condone. His phlegmatic and persistent egotism, his sacrifice of truth and honor to self-interest, his acquiescence in the worst conditions of the world, if only he could use them for his own advantage, combined with the glaring discord between his opinions and his practice, form a character which would be contemptible in our eyes were it not so sinister." For nineteenth-century taste, the Renaissance villain was less the poisoner, the pagan or the pederast than the cold intellectual who was indifferent both to the riot of the senses which (it was held) characterized the Italian's liberation from the prison of the Middle Ages, and to the generous dreams of political unity which (it was believed) made Machiavelli the prophet of the Risorgimento. Confronted by such a portrait, and warned by no less an authority than Leopold von Ranke that the *History of Italy* could be faulted for inaccuracy, credulity and a regressive annalistic treatment,[1] it is small wonder that the nineteenth century failed to give Guicciardini, once more, the niche of honor he deserved.

We can see more clearly today. We have his correspondence; we have a magistral biography by Roberto Ridolfi. Study of his manuscript notes has shown him to be the first historian to have based his work on original documents and to have treated his sources in a critical manner. We can feel, as previous generations could not easily feel, a sympathy for his subject matter: we too have witnessed the collapse of a state system and witnessed the writhing expedients of a diplomacy dealing with forces it did not properly understand; we too are grimly aware of the connection between political and military events on the one hand and constitutional forms and civic morale on the other; we too have come to pay a special attention to the technical problems and the moral implications of writing the history of our own times. Looking back, we can see Guicciardini for the master that he was. Perhaps he will always remain a historian's historian—his mature work, for reasons that we shall explore, is ponderous, immensely detailed and without purple patches or anthology pieces—but we can at last bring a full understanding to bear on what is still (in de Sanctis' words) "from the point of view of

intellectual power, the most important work to have issued from an Italian mind."

II

Guicciardini lived in an age of continual political and
military crisis. He was eleven in 1494 when Charles
VIII of France invaded the closed and more or less
tranquil world of the Italian states. Charles brought "the
seeds of innumerable disasters, terrible events, and
change in almost everything," Guicciardini wrote later.
"His invasion was not only the origin of changes of
government, subversion of kingdoms, devastation of the
countryside, slaughter of cities, cruel murders, but also
of new habits, new customs, new and bloody methods of
warfare, diseases unknown until that day [syphilis]; and
the instruments of peace and harmony in Italy were
thrown into such confusion that they have never since
been able to be reconstituted, so that other foreign nations and barbarian armies have been able to devastate
and trample wretchedly upon her."[2] Thus by 1540, when
Guicciardini died, Milan and Naples were Spanish col-
onies and his own city of Florence was neither free nor
independent, her republican constitution replaced by
princely rule, and her fortresses held by an Imperial
lieutenant. Rome and the pope remained, but only thir-
teen years before the city had been sacked by an army of
foreigners and the pope held to ransom. In the meantime no state, and few large cities, had gone unscathed.
In 1509 Venice had been cut back to her lagoons by
the greatest military defeat of her history and her mainland possessions had been divided among the victors.
The French had taken the Duchy of Milan in 1499, had
lost it and regained it again in 1500, lost nearly all of it
in 1512, regained it in 1515, lost nearly all of it again
in 1522, regained much of it in 1524, and finally lost
it all in 1525. Florence had been taken by arms and a
new constitution forced upon her in 1512 and again in
1530, while her internal history from 1494 to 1540 provides a series of constitutional changes not to be paral-

leled until the English civil wars and the French Revolution.

We can see, now, how all this came about: how France and Spain, hitherto preoccupied with wars against the English and the Moors respectively, were finally able at the end of the fifteenth century to turn and take up their old marriage and kinship interests in Italy—the richest and, through division, the weakest country in Europe. We can see that because the Franco-Spanish rivalry impelled these two powers to seek allies among the Italian states, their greed could not be expressed in simple terms of smash and grab. Italy was doomed to be a battleground as well as a source of supply. This became more than ever true in 1519 when Charles V became ruler of both Spain and the German Empire, and used Italy as a pier to support the flimsy bridge between his wide-spaced dominions. We can see, too, how centuries of independence made it difficult for the Italian states to present a united front or even to comprehend the reserves of power which enabled their enemies (whom they called in scorn "barbari") to come back again, campaign after campaign. And we can see why they continually changed sides in order to gain immediate advantages, making Dante's description of Florence as a sick woman tossing and turning on a bed prickly with faction and constitutional experiment applicable to Italy as a whole.

But contemporaries could see little of this. They saw "innumerable disasters, terrible events and change in almost everything"; they felt the humiliation of defeat and loss of liberty; they asked themselves why this was happening. The wars of Italy provided a compulsory education in politics. Nowhere was the curriculum more stringent than in Florence, where the connection between war and constitutional change was so close; and in that school few pupils had a better chance to learn than Francesco Guicciardini.

"Thucydides and Guicciardini," noted Gibbon, "occupied the true station for historians of their own times. Both were acquainted with the business of peace and war—their characters procured them every information

—had studied the greatest men of their times—were better acquainted with them all, than each of them was
with the other—and had personal knowledge of great
men, the chief advantage of their personal memoirs."3
Guicciardini came from a family of patricians. From the
early fourteenth century his ancestors had served the
Florentine Republic in high offices of state, as gonfaloniers and ambassadors. Their power increased when they
helped Cosimo de' Medici to return from exile in 1434,
and identified themselves with his successors, Piero de'
Medici and Lorenzo the Magnificent. Guicciardini's father was exceptional in that a scholarly and retiring nature made him shrink from active political service; but
it was thanks to this restraint that when Piero was banished for betraying Florentine interests to Charles VIII
in 1494 the Guicciardini family remained unmolested,
and Francesco was able to grow up and make his early
career in his native city.

After the routine classical schooling of his social class,
Francesco decided in 1498 to study law. He studied at
Ferrara and Padua, changing from university to university and from teacher to teacher as ambition prompted
him. He emerges (from his autobiographical jottings)
as a young man whose head was in firm control of his
heart. In 1504, still without a vocation, he almost entered the Church after the death of his uncle, the
bishop of Cortona, seeing this as a short cut to the
cardinalate; but he was finally dissuaded by his father.
In 1508 he married Maria Salviati—not for love, not
for money, but for position; her father was one of the
weightiest opponents of Piero Soderini who, as Life Gonfalonier, was the nominal head of the Republic. By this
time Guicciardini had returned to Florence and was
building up a legal practice so lucrative that when he
was chosen ambassador to Ferdinand of Aragon in 1511
he hesitated to accept.

To Spain he went, however, and began a lifelong career of political activity. While he was away, the Medici
returned to Florence and Soderini was banished; the Republic, under the pressure first of one Medici pope, Leo
X, then of another, Clement VII, slowly lost its popular

character and became more and more of a princely state; and Guicciardini himself became an official of the Medici. In 1515, after his return from Spain, he was made a member of the *Signoria*, the governing body of Florence; and the next year he was sent by Leo X as papal governor to Modena.

This was no easy task. Like all papal cities on the northern fringe of the papal states, Modena was disputed territory, cut off from the south by the Apennine Mountains and within both the historical and geographical sphere of the powerful Duchy of Ferrara. It had, indeed, changed masters four times in the past six years, for throughout the Italian wars papal politics added secondary themes to the major clashes of peninsular disharmonies. Guicciardini dealt promptly and fiercely with discord within the city and organizational chaos in its surrounding territory. In 1517 his administrative ability and (a rarer quality) his resistance to bribes earned him the addition of Reggio, another problem city recently taken back from Ferrara, to his governorship. An even more strenuous task was handed to him in 1521, when the French withdrew from Parma and he was sent to hold that city, with its blasted walls and defeatist council, for the pope. A French counterattack soon came, and its failure was due to the competence with which Guicciardini raised the morale of the citizens, browbeat and cajoled their council into action, and kept the few professional troops from downright mutiny.

In 1524 Guicciardini was made President of the Romagna, responsible for such trouble spots as Ravenna, Cesena, Rimini, Imola and Forlì, the last of which had only recently been (literally) a football ground for human heads. This whole area—now in, now out of effective papal control—was the most divided and factious of all the provinces of Italy; nowhere else had civic violence brought such confusion to agriculture and trade. With a justice leveled at lay and ecclesiastic offender alike, Guicciardini worked ruthlessly for order and for the encouragement of peaceful trade. So successful was he that in 1526 he was called to Rome to become one

of Clement VII's principal advisers; he was, to his own
bitter subsequent regret, among the most persuasive ad-
vocates of the papal *rapprochement* with France which
provoked the Imperialist sack of Rome. When the papal
army assembled, he was sent north as its Lieutenant General and was at least able to save Florence from being
put to sack as the two armies shifted slowly south from
Lombardy to Rome.

After the sack of Rome and the papal surrender Guicciardini's lieutenancy was at an end and he returned to
Florence, now once again a real republic. But his position in his native city was equivocal. Many of the leading citizens of the Republic distrusted him for his long
service with the Medici and he was persecuted with vin-
dictive taxes; on the other hand, the gonfalonier, Niccolò Capponi, trusted him and constantly sought his advice. In 1530 the Florentines finally surrendered to an
Imperial army (fighting now *for* the pope); the fine
flicker of the Last Republic was over; the Medici returned once more, and Guicciardini was charged by
Clement VII with preserving order while the machinery
of popular government was dismantled. For the next ten
years he continued to advise Florence's Medici rulers,
first Alessandro, then Cosimo, and, as their power hardened towards absolutism, the scorn of exiles and friends
of the old broad Republic rose up in execration against
him. He died in 1540.

This, then, was the experience through which Guicciardini had become "acquainted with the business of
peace and war." He had lived at close quarters through
the shifts of theory, faction and outside pressure which
had taken Florence all the way from a popular government under God (Christ is King of Florence, as Savonarola had proclaimed) to the rule of dukes in the interest
of a single family. In Spain he had seen the Italian
peninsula from afar and intimately observed one of its
foremost adversaries: the wily Ferdinand. In Italy he
saw the wars and changing alliances from the center,
from positions that kept him in touch both with the
little men who thronged his law courts and filled his
armies and with the great men who made the laws and

started the wars. Above all, he knew the world where decisions were taken—"You have lost a pope," he reminded himself in 1527, "who had a special affection for you, and even more confidence in you, who wanted you to be always at his side to discuss and decide all important responsibilities and secrets of state and who in wartime sent you to the army with as much authority as he wielded himself"[4]—and he knew that decisions were often reached timorously, selfishly, fumblingly. And he knew, from the baffling vagueness of his instructions when he was sent to Spain and from the fatal hesitations of the Duke of Urbino when commanding the papal forces in 1526-1527, that rule did not necessarily bring authority. He knew that however high the level at which decisions were taken, it could never be assumed that logic or principle would count more than guesswork or ambition or fear. This disillusion came to be diffused throughout his historical work, in which episodes are brought to life because they had been paralleled in his own experience. For instance, when he came to write of Lodovico Sforza's betrayal by the castellan of Milan he would do so with special feeling because he had been betrayed himself by the castellan he had left at Reggio in 1523. Throughout, as actor as well as observer, Guicciardini was uniquely fitted to describe the events of that turbulent period between 1494 and 1540.

Guicciardini wrote three separate histories. The first, the *History of Florence*, was begun in 1508 and left unfinished in 1509. It was published for the first time in 1859 when its editor, Canestrini, divided the continuous narrative of the original into chapters and invented a title, *Storia Fiorentina*, which the original lacked. This work contains conjecture and confessions of ignorance about events, and suspensions of judgment (of Savonarola, for instance, Guicciardini admitted, "I have not been able to make up my mind at all; I must wait . . ."); it is likely that he hoped to revise it for publication.[5] It begins with the revolt of the Ciompi in 1378, hastily sketches the events leading to the establishment of Medici rule in 1434, and hurries to 1454, when, with the Peace of Lodi, the influence of Florence becomes the guarantee of political stability in Italy. Thereafter, the treatment becomes fuller, though only with the arrival of the French does it become minutely detailed; the events of 1494-1509 occupy twenty-three of the thirty-three chapters into which Canestrini divided the work.

Partly because the tone of the work was openly anti-Medicean, partly because his approach to the writing of history was changing, Guicciardini let the manuscript of the *History of Florence* lie unrevised, and when he next turned to Florentine history, in 1527 or 1528, he began afresh. In this interval his pen had not been idle. An inveterate self-communer, he had written a series of essays on contemporary political events. These essays were in pairs: in the manner now of defense counsel, now of prosecutor, he had presented the arguments both for and against a particular course of action. He had also written an account of his impressions of Spain, an essay on the Florentine constitution and, at much greater length, a *Dialogue on the Government of Florence*. Finally, he had written a great number of his *Ricordi*. All these works were composed without thought of publication in the intervals of a busy administrative career. In them he had worked out a philosophy of man and of politics, and now, when Clement's fall brought him leisure, he set out to show, in a second major work, this philosophy working through examples. The new work, first published in 1945, was called by its editor Roberto Ridolfi *Cose Fiorentine (Florentine Affairs)*.

Guicciardini's experience of men and events, and the detailed paper work of careful bureaucracy, had left little taste for the racy style and easy judgments of the early *History*, and the new work was a painful, dogged search among records and conflicting narratives for what had actually happened in Florence before the catastrophe. It begins in 1375 and was perhaps intended to reach 1494; but in fact the narrative peters out before the middle of the fifteenth century. In 1534 Guicciardini laid it aside, and when he resumed his pen, two years later, it was to begin another historical work, a *History of Italy*, in which Florence played no greater part than was needed to understand the fortunes of the peninsula as a whole.

For this change of direction three reasons can be suggested (Guicciardini himself gives none). As its editor points out, the manuscript of the *Cose Fiorentine* shows the author becoming absorbed by the writing of history based largely on documents. As his narrative comes nearer to the present, the text, which is taken from other historians, becomes increasingly crowded by notes and queries relating to source material, and finally dwindles to a mere thread. This appetite for documents could best be sated from the history of his own time. In the second place, Guicciardini had told Iacopo Nardi in about 1528 that he wanted to write an account of his lieutenancy, and by 1535 he had made copious notes for the years 1525 and 1526. Finally, the death of Clement VII in 1534 was not only a turning point in his own career, ending any chance of further service with the papacy: it was also a turning point for Florence and for Italy. Without the support of a Medici pope, Florentine history blended into the story of Spanish domination in Italy. That story was now complete. Independent in 1494, Italy forty years later had become merely an appendix to the history of the great European powers.

In 1536, then, Guicciardini began to draft the introduction to a history of Italy from the death of one of the Medici, Lorenzo the Magnificent, who had striven to preserve Florence in the balance of Italian powers, to the death of another, Clement VII, who had striven to preserve Italy in the balance of European power. This, the first attempt to write in a critical spirit the history of Italy as a geographical whole, provided at last an adequate canvas for the display of Guicciardini's knowledge of man and events. Though this work too was left without a title and a little short of completion on the author's death in 1540, his determination to be known by it is shown by the minute care he lavished on draft after draft of the text. Moreover, when Guicciardini sat for his portrait he instructed the artist, Bugiardini, to show him, pen in hand, looking up for a moment from a page on which is written: "I have decided to write about the events which have taken place in Italy within living memory since the time when French armies called by our own princes began to trouble her peace with great upheavals." These words begin the opening paragraph of the *History of Italy*.

III

A historian must possess an instinctive pleasure in writing careful narrative, a zeal for the collection of facts and a concern with causation. If he possesses each of these qualities to an advanced degree he will be a good historian. If they are allied to a profound personal commitment to his subject matter, he may be a great one. Guicciardini had all these qualities.

In a man who wrote so much purely for his own pleasure, and who worked out his opinions of human behavior and political events on paper with such devoted exactness as Guicciardini, the instinctive pleasure in writing is self-evident. From the youthful, stock-taking "Francesco Guicciardini to himself" on, it is clear that he wrote, as others talk or. read, compulsively. His zeal for facts, too, needs no emphasis. It even moved Montaigne, seeing the trees but not the forest, to comment that "endeavoring to omit nothing that might be spoken, having so large and full a subject, and almost infinite, he proveth somewhat languishing, and giveth a taste of a kind of scholasticall tedious babbling."[6] His concern with causation, too, is evident in his naïve zest for explanation as part of the historian's business. "In these events," he wrote in the *History of Florence*, "I will endeavor to show not only the general causes and effects but also in as much detail as possible the origins and sources of all these ills." And of the Medici conspiracy of 1497 he noted, "In August came an event of great importance . . . and so that it may be better understood, I will go back to its origins." Later, in one of the *Ricordi*, he wrote, "Small and almost imperceptible beginnings are often the occasion of great disaster or of great prosperity. The highest prudence, therefore, lies in noting and weighing well all circumstances, even the most trifling." This treatment of events as circumstances accreting round an accident informs not only minor happenings—like the cry of "Back, back!" with which a soldier hoped to gain room to swing an axe but which was interpreted as an order to retreat[7]—but also the many links of chance which Guicciardini, in the first chapters of the *History of Italy,* forges into the great chain of causation whereby the French were drawn down into Italy. In fact for Guicciardini the impulse to explain the causation of individual events is matched with an even greater desire—almost a psychological need—to explain the causation of the tragedy of Italy as a whole.

His interest in history was further sustained by the scope it offered for moral judgment and general reflection on human nature. Many of the *Ricordi* are embedded, almost intact, in the *History of Italy.* Far from being a dry-as-dust relator of the facts and nothing but the facts, he constantly appears with monitory finger and Savonarolan frown. (His father, indeed, had been a follower of Savonarola, and his own youthful admiration for him is shown both by a collection of notes which he made from the friar's sermons and by his use of the portrait of a tyrant in Savonarola's *Treatise on the government of Florence* as his model for the portrait of Lorenzo de' Medici in his *History of Florence.*) Guicciardini feels, for example, that the Italians' failure to keep out the French armies of Charles VIII on their humiliating stroll down the peninsula to Naples was caused by weaknesses of character as well as by political and military ineptitude, and his denunciation of the lack of spirit and faith shown by the Neapolitans recalls Savonarola's scornful abuse of the "tepid" citizens of Florence. He also denounced the Italian habit of having one foot in both camps for safety's sake. While in the *History of Florence* he noted without comment that Paolantonio Soderini, an eager supporter of Savonarola, made his son join the most perfervid group of the friar's enemies "in order to have a stake on their side in case of misfortune," in the *History of Italy* he remarked grimly of another example of such a precaution that it caused "astonishment to the French, who were unused to these subtle distinctions of the Italians," and when the Duke of Ferrara, while refusing to oppose France himself, encouraged his son to do so, he referred to this as "typical Italian caution."

Guicciardini did not believe, however, that the morality of private and public life could be one and the same. "He who has to exercise authority over others," runs one of the *Ricordi,* "must not be too nice or scrupulous in issuing his commands. I do not say that he is to lay aside all scruples, but that in excess they are harmful." On this point he takes precisely the same view as Machiavelli, but he does so without relish. When Gonzalo de Córdoba breaks his oath to free the captured Duke of Calabria in 1501, Guicciardini comments that "neither the fear of God nor concern for reputation were of any avail against *ragione di stato* [reason of state]"; when Charles V's ministers are discussing whether to release Francis I from captivity after the battle of Pavia in 1525, he makes one of them remark that "we all know but too well what value is to be set on the word of honor when interests of state are involved." He is more outspoken in his regret that selfish concern for private affairs often brings great public concerns to nought. He regrets the damage to the Italian cause after the retreat of the French in 1495, when Milan and Venice were "blinded by private greed"; he regrets the failure of a European crusade against the Turks in 1518 through "negligence of public, and immoderate concern for private affairs." And further fuel for his indignation was not lacking. There is an assassination plot in Padua in 1514. Down thumps the moralist's fist: "So little resemblance is there between the methods of war in our day and those of the virtuous ancients." Late that year he describes the triumphal entrance into Rome of an elephant, a gift from the King of Portugal. After describing the enthusiastic reception given to this beast he looks at once across the Alps. "At this juncture the King of France, who had his mind employed on other objects than on pomp and shows, was ardently intent on making all possible preparations for war." In 1509

France and Spain are prepared to leave Pisa to the mercy of Florence in spite of treaty obligations; "so great is the power of gold in our days as to outweigh all regard to honor and decency." After this it does not seem altogether quaint when he tells how Gilbert de Montpensier's son fell dead from grief on beholding his father's monument, and justifies the anecdote with the observation that the occurrence was "the more rare, as the love of children for their father has become so uncommon in our time." A regard for Guicciardini as the first historian who can be called in any significant sense "modern" must not play down the extent to which he was moralist and preacher.

A still less modern aspect of this vein in his work is the theme of the Fall of Princes, or Time's Revenges. Reflect on the fortune of the great! See Lodovico Sforza, the great Duke of Milan, a refugee fleeing to Germany "through all those places where not long before, in the midst of his glory, and at the height of his prosperity, he had made so magnificent an appearance." We see him again the following year, captive "in a narrow prison which just provided room enough to hold the man whose thoughts and ambitions all Italy was scarce large enough to circumscribe." We see that when the tricky Cesare Borgia decided to trust the pope, his father's successor, although the two men had been enemies, the gamble failed. "Thus fell Valentino [Cesare was Duke of Valentinois] from the height of the greatness to which he had hastened his ascent by steps of fraud and cruelty no less than by the arms and power of the Church; and thus did the speedy increase of his grandeur terminate in his more speedy ruin, after having experienced the same delusive arts practiced upon himself, with which he and his father had plagued so many others." The flesh even of princes is as grass. An extension of this theme is Guicciardini's delight in startling contrasts—for instance, Clement VII's catastrophic fall from greatness in 1527 followed by his equally remarkable recovery, or Milan's sudden dive to poverty and distress in 1526 after having been the most prosperous and luxury-loving city in Italy. Pursued furthere, the vein exhibits a naïve pleasure in coincidence: Lodovico's treacherous governor of Valenza, for instance, let in the French on the same day of the year in which he had previously betrayed Tortona to Lodovico, and Alviano was made Captain-General of the Venetian army "on the same day that four years before he fell into the hands of his enemies."

Just as history satisfied the moralist as well as the analyst in Guicciardini, so it gratified the egotist, allowing not only the frequent deployment of his own wisdom but also an element of straightforward autobiography. His family pride was strong. The opening words of the *History of Florence* are: "In 1378, when Luigi di Messer Piero Guicciardini was Gonfalonier, the revolt of the Ciompi took place." He wrote this *History*, in fact, in conjunction with a family memoir, the *Memorie di Famiglia*. Both drew on documents in the family archive, the *History* representing the public, the *Memorie* the private side of the same story. In the *History*, he treated with restraint the parts played by members of the family, and this is a tribute to the maturity of his sense of historical decorum, but there is little doubt that his interest was quickened by the presence of his kin in the wings.

There was also his own personal part to chronicle—or to justify. In 1522 he wrote an account of his defense of Parma. In 1527 he called forth trickier self-defenses. That was a bad year for his self-esteem: it was bruised by a sense of his responsibility for the catastrophic effects of the League of Cognac, and he was subject to a double attack both from the Medici and from their opponents in Florence. The former claimed that he had preserved order in Florence more out of regard for his brother, Luigi, who was Gonfalonier, than for them; the latter maintained that by exaggerating the threat from the League of Cognac he had persuaded them to postpone their ejection of the Medici. In these essays (*Oratio accusatoria, Oratio defensoria, Consolatoria*) he reviewed all the arguments, both for and against his actions, and by giving form to his distress drew from it what comfort he could. The *Defensoria* was left unfinished, possibly because the precise significance of his advice to the pope in 1526 and its consequences could only be demonstrated by showing, in detailed historical form, what exactly had happened. It was shortly after this that he mentioned a plan to write an account of his lieutenancy.

The writing of these overtly autobiographical pieces and, in the following years, a concentration on the technical problems involved in writing history, helped Guicciardini to play down the autobiographical element when he came to write the *History of Italy*, though the sense of his own presence in the wings still acted as a stimulant. There are traces of family pride (in 1509 Maximilian I gave audience at Verona to the Florentine ambassadors, "among whom was Piero Guicciardini, my father") and a desire not only to appear in person, but to shine. Mentioning his selection as ambassador to Spain in 1511 he adds that he was "at that time so young that he was by the laws of his country incapable of exercising any public employment on account of his age," implying that a flattering exception was made in his case. Mentioning his appointment as Commissary-General of the papal troops in 1521 he adds that he had "a very ample authority, above what is usually conferred on commissaries." His defense of Parma against the French siege that year is gone into with a regard to detail unusual even for him, and at one point he goes out of his way to show that he could understand the Spanish of one of the papal commanders. When the enemy finally withdrew, Guicciardini represents the leader of the foiled attack as confessing that "he had thought it incredible that a governor who was not a man of war, and had only just arrived in the city, should choose rather to expose himself to danger without hope of profit, since the pontiff [Leo X] was dead, than to take the easy measures for his own preservation which he might have done without bringing on himself any dishonor or disgrace"—incredible, that is, that Guicciardini should not have behaved like a normal dishonest Italian! And coming to his pacific influence in Florence in April, 1527, he writes that "it would very likely have been a most bitter and unfortunate day for the Florentines if the Lieutenant [Guicciardini himself] had not at that instant been ready with his counsel to settle that complex and urgent affair."

Brought up at a time when much history was already being written and when constitutional issues (of deep concern to men of his class) were discussed with constant reference to the past, he found that the writing of history satisfied his own deepest needs: to commemorate his family and his career, to comment and moralize, and to explain.

IV

A private satisfaction, yes; but what did Guicciardini think of the ulterior purpose of history, of its utility to the public? His attitude seems plain from a statement at the beginning of the *History of Italy:* "From the understanding of these events, so diverse and grave, all men will be able to draw many useful lessons both for themselves and for the public good." The same point was put, rather more guardedly, in one of the *Ricordi:* "Past events throw light on future, because the world has always been the same as it now is, and all that is now, or shall be hereafter, has been in time past. Things accordingly repeat themselves, but under changed names and colors so that it is not everyone who can recognize them but only he who is discerning and who notes and considers them diligently."[8] When the remarks made by Guicciardini on the possibility of learning from history are seen as a whole the tone is more guarded yet.

The question of historical parallels had been raised in an extreme form by Machiavelli in his *Discourses on Livy.* He believed that the history of Rome provided a mine of instruction for the modern statesman, a mine that had not yet been properly worked. Given proper guidance, wrote Machiavelli, "it is easy, by diligent study of the past, to foresee what is likely to happen in the future in any republic, and to apply those remedies that were used by the ancients, or, not finding any that were used by them, to divine new ones from the similarity of events." Guicciardini knew both the *Discourses,* upon which he had written a series of reflections *(Considerazioni intorno ai discorsi del Machiavelli),* and Machiavelli himself, whom he found sympathetic as a man and stimulating as a thinker. Much of Guicciardini's thought is the result of an unacknowledged mental dialogue with Machiavelli, the trenchancy of whose opinions was a constant challenge to his own caution and fastidiousness. Guicciardini did not share Machiavelli's unstinted admiration for ancient Rome, partly because he thought Machiavelli had misunderstood the true nature of the Roman state and partly because he had—exceptionally at this time—a notion of progress, of history waiting neither for a spiritual millennium nor for the re-attainment of classical wisdom, but proceeding by secular laws, sometimes falling short of the ancients, sometimes (as in the case of the exploration of the New World and of tropical Africa) going well beyond them. He could thus look more coolly at the storehouse of ancient examples from which Machiavelli compiled his fervent inventory. "What a mistake is theirs," he commented in the *Ricordi,* "who cite on all occasions the example of the Romans!" And elsewhere in the same work he explained why. "It is most misleading to judge by examples; for unless these be in all respects parallel they are of no force, the least divergence in the circumstances giving rise to the widest possible divergence in the conclusions."[9] It was difficult enough to see these differences within a generation, let alone after fifteen centuries. And in the *History of Italy* he comments on Piero de' Medici's disastrous attempt in 1494 to meet and come to terms with Charles VIII in the same way in which his father had come to terms with the Neapolitan threat to Florence in 1479: "It is certainly very dangerous to imitate the example of others, if the same conditions do not apply, not only in general but in every particular, and if in addition to everything else the same good fortune does not play its part." In fact not only must the past case resemble the present case in minute detail, but the sum of trivia—the stomach-aches, the quarrels, the weather, the accidents which the great military theorist Clausewitz summed up in the term "friction"—has to coincide as well. For Guicciardini lessons of history exist not as a fund of useful parallel situations but as a casebook of man's folly. History should be studied for evidence of how individuals behave, not ("so full are our mortal affairs of dark obscurities") for evidence of recurring patterns.

These patterns may exist, but, says Guicciardini, we shall never know them, "for if you note it well, you will perceive that we have no true knowledge even of the present, and of what goes on from day to day in our own town."[10] Our ability to foretell the future from knowledge of the past or wise reflection on the present is as hit-or-miss as the astrologer's. Nor is it helped by abstract notions of right or wrong; "he who has a just cause cannot anticipate victory, for every day you see victory going to injustice." Knowledge, wisdom, faith: all are fallible guides. In the *Consolatoria* Guicciardini reviews the advice he gave the pope, and the factors he had not foreseen. He consoles himself with the reflection that he gave the best advice he could, admitting that some aspects of the truth will always be hidden from reason—and, by implication, from history, which is reason's explanation of the world.

Therefore if history is to teach, its subject must be not patterns, but man. Man, too, must be the central preoccupation of the historian's search into causes. A first cause, God's purpose, existed, but it was inscrutable. There was an agent, Chance or Fortune, which operated midway between God's will and man's choice, but it was, apparently, capricious. Thus secondary causes must be the staple of a historian's search for explanation because only man could be known. And in man there was one quality above all others which was relevant to the study of causation—ambition.

Guicciardini's historical outlook was essentially dynamic. Nothing was stable, because no power was based on right. From the usurpations of the Romans onwards, all government was based on violence. The Holy Roman Empire was based on a rule established by violence in antiquity. Papal power was based on violence and main-

tained by violence, both spiritual and temporal. Stability
in individual states was based on violence, because the
interests of ruler and subject were irreconcilable. There
was no morally justified pattern of historical development, which might be expected to receive God's support.
Rulers could not behave, therefore, as though justice
were part of the scheme of things. "States cannot be established or maintained by conforming to the moral law.
For if you look to their beginnings, all will be seen to
have had their origin in violence."[11]

Political life was improvisation and conflict: state
against state, faction against faction, subject against
ruler. And the main cause of this conflict was ambition.
It figures in judgment after judgment on the protagonists
of the *Histories*. In the *History of Florence*, Lodovico
Sforza's virtues, for instance, were more than balanced
by *una ambizione infinita,* and in Alexander VI *fu infinita la ambizione.* In the *History of Italy*, when the
French had withdrawn in 1495 and peace seemed possible, Guicciardini discusses the diplomacy of Milan and
Venice and concludes that "ambition, which would not
allow them to remain content within their due bounds,
was the reason Italy was soon involved in new disorders."
Human affairs are never long in a state of rest, because
"the ambition of princes makes them ever ready to
embrace all pretenses to empire, however frivolous."
These examples could be easily multiplied.

The emphasis on ambition is all the greater in that
Guicciardini did not use it simply as a term of abuse.
To him the cardinal sin in politics is inactivity. He distrusted neutrality as roundly as did Machiavelli. He devoted one of the *Ricordi* to a gloss on the tag *Ducunt
volentes fata, nolentes trahunt* (Fate guides the heeding
man, and drags the unheeding).[12] Move one must, and it
is better to keep step than be pushed, because only by
keeping in step with fate can a man hope to preserve
some measure of self-determination. In the *History of
Italy* Domenico Morone is described as drawn to his
fate "by that necessity which drags along those who will
not suffer themselves to be led." Guicciardini shared
Machiavelli's view that the politician must be constantly

testing the wind in order to take advantage of any change in its direction. Even a bad decision, he advised Clement VII in 1526, is better than no decision, and he elaborated the point in a speech put into the mouth of the Venetian senator Antonio Grimaldi, in 1498, when the chance of alliance with Milan had offered itself: "Opportunities like this are rare and transient, and it is the part of prudence and a generous resolution to lay hold of them, as on the contrary it would be folly and meanness of spirit to reject them. Wisdom that is over-curious, and too nicely ponders events, is often blame-able; for human affairs are so subject to vicissitudes that the success of an enterprise rarely answers the end of the wisest projectors, and the person who dares not em-brace a present good for fear of a dubious and distant evil will in vain repent his lost opportunity of acquiring wealth and glory, out of fear of an approaching danger which he found afterwards vanished."

The coldness and caution of Guicciardini's own tem-perament has been emphasized so often that it is worth stressing this concern with action. In the *Ricordi* he repeatedly makes the point that while a mere desire for self-aggrandizement is bad, "he who is not touched by the passion for fame is a frigid soul"; what prompts am-bition "even in pure hearts is the longing we all have to surpass our fellows, for this reason more than any other: that in nothing else can we resemble God."[13] The phrase is echoed in the *Consolatoria* when his comforter persuades him not to regret his own ambition, for "there seems no other way in which we can resemble God." In one of his essays he asks: if one's personal liberty, or the liberty of one's country, seems hopelessly threat-ened, is it justifiable to commit suicide? He answers, no: you must carry on, to mitigate hardship for others and to wait for a change for the better. Suicide is the supreme symbol of indecision—the final inaction—for the individual, as neutrality is for the state.

Thus Guicciardini is in fact far from de Sanctis' "Guicciardinian Man"—passive, calculating, sour. When Guicciardini inserted a long digression on the voyages of discovery in the *History of Italy* it was not so much

to illustrate their effect on the spice-trade of Venice as
to celebrate the daring and resolution of the navigators.
If there are heroes in his book they are the soldiers, the
men of action and decision. He celebrates the great
Spaniard, Gonzalo de Córdoba, brave, energetic and
single-minded, the man who cried, "Better a step taken
forward against an enemy, and death, than retreat and
a hundred added years of life!" He celebrates Bartolommeo Alviano, a soldier whose rashness cost him repeated
defeats but who was "of vast boldness and courage,"
and describes how Alviano's men kept his body with
them for twenty-five days, and when the time came to
take it across enemy country to be buried in Venice, refused to beg for a safe-conduct because it was shameful
that a man who had never shown fear of his foes in his
lifetime should truckle to them in death. He commends,
in the most brilliant of his battle pieces, the quixotic
bravery of the Swiss who fought at Novara in 1513
against great odds from no need, not for survival but
for glory, and he dwells on the reputation they gained
from this victory. "The Swiss returned in a triumphant
manner the same day to Novara, with such universal
honor and renown that many who considered the magnanimity of the resolution, the most magnificent contempt of death, the fierceness of the fight, and the felicity
of the success, did not hesitate to prefer this action to
almost all the memorable feats that are recorded of the
ancient Greeks and Romans." When every allowance has
been made for the influence of humanist literary tradition and for Guicciardini's desire to shame the traitors
and trimmers of Italy by contrasting them with selfless
and dedicated heroes, there remains this special admiration felt for professional men of action by a historian
who, tracing the course and causes of affairs in terms
of human actions, found most of these timid and inglorious.

Guicciardini's emphasis on the individual and his
choices as the chief element in historical explanation did
not lead him to any interest in the ordinary man. As a
historian of diplomatic and military affairs, his concern
was with the leaders. The few move the many, bear the

burden of administration and government and initiate actions. His own aristocratic bias led him to see the mob—the common people—as an envious, changeable blur, and he spoke of them with steady contempt. But as the citizen of a republic who believed that God held republics especially dear (another trace of Savonarola), his influential few were more numerous than they might have been had he been brought up in a state where the decision-making was largely in the hands of one man. He knew that republics had their disadvantages—they came to decisions slowly, they encouraged faction—but in his constitutional writings and his Florentine histories (especially in the *Cose Fiorentine*) he came out strongly against the rule of one man, and in favor of a constitution where all responsible men had a say in the choice of their governors and where most of the decisions were made by a small senate of responsible aristocrats, under the chairmanship of a Life Gonfalonier.

One result of his immersion in a republican atmosphere was to see the quarrels between the Italian states in terms of the inner dissensions of a republic. He projected his knowledge of Florentine politics on to the screen of Italian politics and saw it as an unruly mass of ambitions and fears, with governments, just like individuals, ready to pounce or retreat, hedge or ensure, at each new crisis. The Italians had for so long been used to undisastrous wars, to taking risks in a drama that was always on the hither side of tragedy, that the habit of gambling and working against one another continued even when there was a need for dogged cooperation, when wars might actually be ruinous and a political mistake a disaster.

Just as in civic affairs it is necessary to know an opponent's character and interests in order to anticipate his decisions, so it is necessary to understand the characteristics and interests of opposing nations. "In arguments of state," Guicciardini noted in the *Ricordi*, "I have often found that men judge wrongly from looking to what this or the other prince ought in reason to do, and not to what his temper and character will prompt him to do. He, for instance, who will form a just opinion as to how the King of France will act ought rather to consider what are the habits and disposition of a Frenchman than what course a prudent man might be expected to take."[14] And from the *History of Italy* a composite portrait of the European nations can be built up. The French are unreliable, restless, arrogant, self-infatuated, both bold and negligent in planning and quickly discouraged by reverses; the Spanish emerge as avaricious, feckless, unreliable, mercenary and courageous; the Germans are brutal but ineffective. The Italian states, too, have their characteristics: the Neapolitans, for instance, being "famous among all the peoples of Italy for instability and eagerness for change." From a concern for individual psychology it is natural to move to the psychology of nations, though the larger the unit described, the less useful the definition.

Guicciardini's national portraits are crude, and when dealing with individuals who are not first and foremost political men his touch can be equally crude; at one point he even suggests that Luther could have been bought off with a benefice (though on the causes for Luther's support from princes and people Guicciardini is hard-headed enough). But when dealing with the sort of man he knew, he is far from such simplicity. He discusses five distinct motives that may have moved Leo X to break the peace in 1521 and concludes that "whatever was his motive, whether one, or more, or all these reasons, he turned all his thoughts upon war." Throughout the *History of Italy* is the vivid presence of individuals, reappraising each turn of events in the light of their own natures and interests, influenced a little by traditional attitudes but not at all by supernatural prompting. Complex and various, they are actors, not puppets; they write the script as they go along. History provides some rough and ready themes; with these the actors improvise. Guicciardini's chosen technique—to move with the actors scene by scene, year by year—and his deep interest in psychology and motive make these actors come alive. Here, of course, he was assisted by his own career. The historian who is mainly interested in results need never move from his desk. The historian who is concerned with motive is helped by having moved among men and watched them make up their minds. Conversely, it is natural that a man who has played a major part in political life will resent the implication that the decisions he has made, and watched others make, were influenced by some hidden power.

Does Providence, then, play no part in Guicciardini's eyes in shaping the affairs of man? If man hews his own destiny, why does Guicciardini show, on the eve of the French invasion, statues sweating, monsters being born, armed men on enormous horses fighting in the sky? Why, if revolutions are man-made, was the return of the Medici in 1512 prefaced by a thunderbolt which hit the Palazzo della Signoria, penetrated into the chamber of the Gonfalonier, and touching only the large silver box containing the balls used to elect the chief magistrate, descended to the bottom, where it struck a great stone that was at the foot of the stairs and supported the building, in such a way that being forced out of its place without being damaged, it seemed to be removed by some dextrous and skillful architect? Were these signs from God? And, if so, were they clues to the divine direction of human affairs, or merely extracts from a ghostly commentary, parallel to, but not conditioning, these affairs?

Certainly Guicciardini was no brusque rationalist. He believed in lucky days. He believed in ghosts and saw them as "secret powers of nature, or rather of that higher agent by whom all things are set in motion, revealed to Him, but hidden from us."[15] Though prone to mock at astrologers, he believed in astrology enough to have his own horoscope cast in great detail; this qualified belief in the stars and cautious faith in prophecy implied that there was something to be foreknown, something that limited freedom of choice. That man had to bow before some power of fate was clear from the story of the past, and the consciousness of this produced the most nobly fatalistic of his dicta: "All cities, states and kingdoms are mortal, since either by nature or accident everything in this world must sometime have an end. Accordingly, the citizen who happens to be living when his country is in its decline should not so much lament over its unhappy fortunes as over his own. For his country only suffers what it was fated to suffer. His is the infelicity of being born at the moment when his country has to fulfil its doom."[16]

But how far were these secular patterns designed by God? Guicciardini's attitude to religion, while not skeptical, was cool. His disgust at corruption in the Church made him harshly anticlerical. He had no illusions about the popes he served, saying of Leo X in the *History of Italy* that he passed as a good prince, "I dare not say of an apostolical goodness, for in our corrupt times the goodness of a pontiff is commended when it does not surpass the wickedness of other men." But he spoke bitterly of Luther as a heretic and proudly of the fact that the Florentines were more religious than the other Italians, as the number and magnificence of their churches showed. For Guicciardini the practice of religion was not far from a sign of breeding. It stood for a way of life in which certain things were not done. It was not done, for instance, to ally with infidels, as the French allied with the Turks; it was not done to annex new territories out of sheer greed, as the early discoverers did. The practice of religion involved, or should involve, a certain fastidiousness of values, supported by a supernaturally devised handbook of moral etiquette.

Guicciardini did not doubt the existence of God, or that He judged men. The trouble was that His judgments were not made in the sight of man. On earth the good action was often punished, the evil deed crowned by success. "Yet we are not therefore to pronounce that the justice of God falls short, since his counsels are so deep as rightly to be spoken of as unfathomable."[17] If the side with a just cause gets the victory, this is because it has a sense of conviction that cuts through the irresolution of its opponents. "In this way it may now and then indirectly help you that your cause is just. But it is a mistake to suppose that directly any such effect is produced."[18] Even when a man seems especially qualified to interpret the will of God, it is hazardous to follow his advice. When Piero de' Medici fled in 1494 and the principal citizens were debating what form the new constitution should take, the party that favored a restricted executive on the Venetian model would have won the day—and their proposal was the one favored in retrospect by Guicciardini himself—"if in the deliberations of men there had not intervened divine authority speaking through Girolamo Savonarola of Ferrara, a friar of the Preachers' order." This swung the decision to that broader form of government whose irresolution and inefficiency brought the Medici back in 1512 and prevented Florence from playing her proper part in the Italian wars. The statesman and the historian of contemporary events, therefore, could look neither to God's book, nor to his agents, for guidance. Conscious of Providence, and aware, through a prophecy that came true (as did several of Savonarola's), or the fall of a thunderbolt at an appropriate moment, that God was concerned with events on earth, they could only shrug their shoulders and turn aside to tackle the task in hand by the light of reason alone.

However, having decided to leave God out of his calculations, Guicciardini was faced by much that reason unassisted could not explain. So he invoked Chance, and when Chance (or Fortune) is invoked frequently, and to explain important events, it comes to take on the appearance of a pagan alternative to Providence, the goddess Fortuna.

Speaking in the *History of Florence* of a Florentine defeat (at Poggibonsi, in 1479), Guicciardini wrote that Fortune gave the enemy a victory that according to reason should have gone to the Florentines. Fortune (or Fate) is frequently used in the *History of Italy* as an alternative to a national explanation. When Julius II recovered from his serious illness in 1511, this "proceeded either from the great robustness of his constitution, or because he was reserved by the fates to be the author and principal cause of longer and greater calamities to Italy." Alviano lost so many battles "either through the malice of Fortune, or, as many thought, because he was rash." New disturbances broke out in Italy in 1517

"either through the unhappiness of our fate, or because
Italy, being divided into so many principalities and
states, it was next to impossible . . . that she should not
be subjected to continual alarms." Although Guicciardini frequently used Fortune as a portmanteau term to
contain the little accidental, unforeseeable slips 'twixt
cup and lip, in these instances she has become a full-
scale Power, and he had worked out the best means of
dealing with her, aided here as, one suspects, in so
many other respects, by contact with the ideas of
Machiavelli. Talking of the army of the League, in 1525,
he points out the disadvantage of having so many separate contingents, for in such an army "you will never
find among them that promptness and alacrity for pursuing the favor of Fortune when she shows herself kind,
nor a firm disposition to make a resolute and constant
resistance when she looks on them with a frowning
aspect." Secular-minded historians were to invoke Fortune to eke out their grasp of causation until the days
of Vico, Hegel, Marx and Freud; and it is remarkable
that Guicciardini withstood her allure as stoutly as he
did, for while he shows her frequently present on the
battlefield, she seldom appears in the council chamber,
and never without Reason as an escort. Supernatural
though she is, Fortune is invoked by Guicciardini as a
last resort: the result of his determination to see human
affairs in terms of man.

v

In turning to Guicciardini's technique as a historian
the first thing to emphasize is the unprecedented use he
made of original sources. Other historians had used the
communal archives of Florence, and it had become almost a tradition for chancery officials to turn historian
(among them Leonardo Bruni and Machiavelli), but no
historian had used source material so copiously or so
open-mindedly. With no overriding literary model in
mind (here he differed from Bruni) and no axe to grind
(here he differed from Machiavelli), Guicciardini let
documents tell their own tale. Using them more and

more in successive works, in the *History of Italy* he became the first historian of modern times to *recreate* the past, rather than to tell a story about it.

The *History of Florence* was based to a large extent on public documents in the Guicciardini family archive which Dr. Rubinstein, in his study of the work, describes as being "in certain aspects, miniature State archives." They contained instructions to members of the Guicciardini family who had gone on embassies and copies of letters sent back from them to the government. In theory, official notes and correspondence should have been handed in to the government department concerned; but in practice ambassadors and commissioners frequently took them home, where they remained to nourish family pride. From these, from his own experience and from conversations with his father and father-in-law, who could give him an account of the *pratiche* (committees called *ad hoc* to discuss issues of special importance or urgency) they had attended, Guicciardini was able to provide a full narrative of Florentine history, although he left many details blank, intending to check them later. This he never did and, as we have seen, when he turned to Florentine history again, he left the youthful *History of Florence* to one side.

The *Cose Fiorentine* was far fuller in its treatment of late fourteenth- and early fifteenth-century affairs than the *History of Florence,* which sketched this period in a few rapid pages. It was based largely, not on documents, but on histories, some published, some not. Guicciardini did use the manuscript letter-books of two diplomats, Rinaldo degli Albizzi and Michele Castellani, and material from the Guicciardini archive, but the core of the book was a narrative compiled, after close comparative scrutiny, from such Florentine historians as Villani, Marchionne Stefani, Bruni, Poggio, Gino and Neri Capponi, Domenico Buoninsegni, Goro Dati and Machiavelli, and such non-Florentines as Biondo, Platina, Sabellico and Froissart. This narrative was written on large sheets, leaving a wide margin for corrections, doubts and conflicting opinions. Guicciardini referred to his authorities by an initial letter and filled these margins with com-

ments on their reliability and points which he intended
to follow up had he not also left this second work unfinished.

The *History of Italy* was based, once more, primarily
on documents. Here Guicciardini was helped by the fact
that when he entered Florence in 1530, charged by the
pope with patrolling the change of government and re-
viewing the events of the previous years, he removed
the whole of the archives of the *Dieci*—the committee
of ten concerned with external affairs—to his own home.
This gave him the correspondence between the Florentine government and its agents not only in Naples,
Venice, Ferrara, Genoa, Rome and other Italian states,
but also in France, Spain and Germany. He also used
material in the communal archives relating to other
government departments—especially those which threw
light on events outside Florence. To this mass of first-
hand evidence he added letters from correspondents describing particular events, and, of course, his own records of the events with which he had been directly concerned. In addition he made extracts from contemporary
accounts of the major episodes of recent history including Bernardo Rucellai's *De bello italico* for Charles
VIII's invasion, and Galeazzo Capra's *Commentarii* for
the battle of Pavia. Ranke's accusation that he followed
these and other narratives even where documentary evidence was available, thus falling into needless error,
has not been seriously investigated, and most historians
who have turned to the *History of Italy* have been impressed by its accuracy.

Certainly Guicciardini took immense pains to make
it a satisfactory record of events. Ridolfi's analysis of
his notebooks and of the successive drafts of his narrative makes this abundantly clear. Working from large
collections of notes—some written by himself, some dictated to a secretary—Guicciardini began with the first
book, revised it and added the second, then revised both
and went on. When he had a complete first draft he
made a list of doubts and queries, and as he followed
these up he settled down to a close study of language
and orthography, so that style and spelling would con-

form with the ruling of those pundits (like Pietro Bembo) who were trying to regulate the written language of Italy. The resulting second draft was then checked, more factual queries answered, and a fair copy was sent to Giovanni Corsi—the most learned of his old friends—for his opinion. A third version then followed, incorporating some radical changes of style and incorporating much new matter, and then another fair copy was made. "For some parts of the text," Ridolfi notes, "this was the seventh revision!" From first to last, Guicciardini was concerned to make his history—and the very language in which it was written—a faithful portrait of Italy as a whole.

This cosmopolitanism of the *History of Italy* represents a striking change from the parochialism of the *History of Florence,* in which the taking of Pietrasanta is gloatingly welcomed as thrusting "a bit in the mouth of the Lucchese" (old enemies of Florence), Venice is referred to as a "pest and calamity," and a tiny diplomatic triumph over Milan in 1495 is recounted with unseemly glee. The earlier history sees events firmly from the point of view of *nostra città,* and in terms of the actions of *la gente nostra.* In 1508-9, with Italy's fate still undecided, Guicciardini could afford to clap hands when the French marched into Genoa and evicted "the vile plebeian" who had got himself made doge; to applaud the justice of Lodovico Sforza's fall, even though this was brought about by France and served the purpose of Venice; and to deplore the slackening of Spanish influence in Naples because Spain would thence have kept Venice in her place.

In the *History of Italy* the tone is quite different. Service first in Spain and then with the papacy had drawn Guicciardini away from straightforward local patriotism, and the intervening years had shown that the events of 1494 had initiated permanent changes in the condition and status of the whole peninsula. Every Italian knew in his bones that however much he disliked his neighbor, all Italians had something in common which distinguished them from mere barbarians. But this something, compounded of a common language

and a sense of shared descent from the glories of ancient Rome, was too vague a concept to come to the sur-
face of a historical work (save a purely descriptive,
antiquarian one) unless its author had been forced to
reflect on it by brutal circumstance. Guicciardini had reflected on it, but his nostalgia for the time when the
peninsula was still independent did not lead him to blur
his picture of inter-state rivalry by projecting back on it
any yearning for Italian unity. While he deplored the
selfishness of the Italian states and their inability to
combine against the common enemy, he believed that
their rivalry had produced a healthy spirit of competi-
tion. What had happened to the Italian states system
was tragic, but he took the system for granted and recorded its decay imperturbably, objectively. His tone of
"would it had been otherwise!" is reserved for men.

From the *History of Italy* it would be hard to guess
the author's native city: perhaps one would guess Venice,
rather than Florence; so many of the great discourses
are set in Venice, and no Florentine is allowed the long
rapturous praise of his own city that Guicciardini puts
into the mouth of a Venetian doge of 1509. The space
given to Florence herself in the *History of Italy* is large,
but it is not disproportionate. For Florence underwent
a number of important constitutional changes under the
shock of war, and these determined the role she played
in the politics of the peninsula—and what side she
played it on. Moreover the two Medici popes, Leo and
Clement, were directly concerned with Florence, and
there were two moments—in 1512 and 1530—when the
city was the direct concern of the great non-Italian powers, as well as of their Italian allies.

But what about the case of Pisa? This small Florentine
city certainly plays a most prominent part in Guicciardini's *History:* a part whose prominence and prolixity
have been made famous by Macaulay.[19] However, the attention can be justified. For reasons of prestige as well as
commerce, Florence was vitally concerned with recovering Pisa, which had refused to return to its allegiance
when the French garrison was recalled in 1495: and it
was not until 1509 that the Florentines were able to bring

the recalcitrant city to heel. The *History of Florence* makes the obsessive nature of this problem clear: Guicciardini comments that of the two main Florentine events of 1494—the gaining of liberty and the loss of Pisa—men found it difficult to decide which was the more important. Then, in the following year "we were pressed to join the League, whose princes hoped to unite Italians to discourage Charles from ever returning. This was rejected because they would not return Pisa to us, and if we did not have Pisa back, *the unity of Italy was no use to the city.*" In the *History of Italy*, however, Pisa is stressed because it was a perfect example of those diplomatic pressure points which, when touched, cause the whole body politic to wince and lunge. Florence had rejoiced at slipping a bit into Lucca's mouth by taking Pietrasanta; but Pisa was the bit in Florence's mouth and Venice, Milan, the German emperor, and the pope tried in turns to control her by jerking it. On the other hand, it was the conviction that only through an alliance with France could she recover Pisa that made Florence the odd man out in Italy and colored the city's relations with the other states. What is more, the struggle to find loyal and efficient armies with which to take Pisa, and the tensions that arose from the raising of money to pay for them, affected domestic politics: and these in turn, as we have seen, affected the role Florence played in inter-state affairs. Florentine history without Pisa would be like that' of Egypt without the Suez Canal.

If Guicciardini understood the significance of the minute pressure point—like Pisa—how did he treat the great threats to Italy from outside her frontiers? Already in an essay written in Spain in 1512 "On the changes that followed the battle of Ravenna" (when the French won a pyrrhic victory over a papal-Spanish army) he had noted that "Italian affairs can hardly be judged on their own. They . . . depend to an important extent on the actions of the Emperor, the Catholic King [of Spain], England and the Swiss." In the *History of Italy* Guicciardini recognized that Italy was being forced into European history: dealing with this same year, he turns to domestic events in France, with the excuse that "the dependence of the state of affairs in our own country upon that beyond the mountains, and the connection of events (so often observed) in one, with the resolutions and events in the other, oblige me not to pass them quite over in silence." Throughout the *History* he attempts to explain foreign initiative, as well as the reactions of foreign powers to Italian prompting. He describes Maximilian's preoccupation with Hungary, for instance, in order to explain his uncertain attitude to Italian affairs in 1506; and for the same reason he goes into the Swiss-French quarrel in 1510, and the background of Anglo-French relations in 1513. At times he even gives rather more information about a foreign power than is needed to explain Italian events—as when he provides a long account of recent Turkish wars in Egypt and the Mameluke kingdom as background to the plans for a crusade in 1518. If his treatment of foreign powers is inadequate by modern standards, this is largely due to faulty and inadequate information. Europe is a thin, fitful presence in the *History of Italy,* but that it should be conjured up at all is a tribute to Guicciardini's originality and strength of mind.

This strength, this steady genius for including all matters of importance, is what de Sanctis had in mind when he called Guicciardini's *History of Italy* the supreme work—from the point of view of intellectual power —to have issued from an Italian mind. Each event, however trivial, receives the same determined investigation. For Guicciardini did not plan his book merely in terms of great events and things accomplished—he was interested in suspicions, second thoughts, changes of plan; his story is littered with the *disjecta membra* of decisions. He explained this concentration on detail, this desire to show exactly what happened year by year (and not only what led to great happenings) in the *Ricordi,* and it is worth quoting the explanation in full: "All historians, without, it seems to me, a single exception, are at fault in omitting to relate many things known in their times as being matters of universal notoriety. Whence it happens that in the histories of the Greeks, the Romans and all other nations we are at the present day in the dark concerning many matters of fact. For instance, the authority and distinctions of their magistrates, their systems of government, their methods of warfare, the size of their towns and many like matters, which, being very well known at the date they wrote, they, in consequence, passed over. But had they reflected that in the course of time cities disappear and the memory of things is lost, and that histories are written for no other reason than that these may be perpetuated, they would have been more careful *to write in such a way that men born in a distant age should have every event as much before their eyes as those in whose presence it happened; for this is the true object of history.*"[20]

This conviction, plus an interest in motive that made him note an impulse even if it led to no action, made him, as year by year he scanned the full circle of the Italian scene, less like an artist than a radar screen. What was there, showed up; and complex trivial things might register more insistently than simple crucial things. This is his way of bringing us into the presence of what happened. The size of the pile in a diplomat's, or an administrator's, in-tray suggests the sheer intricacy—rather than the importance—of a year's work; such are the annual reports of this ex-administrator, ex-diplomatist.

To do this year by year involved an annalistic treatment. To say (it has been often said, by Ranke and others) that this makes the *History of Italy* old-fashioned is totally to misconceive Guicciardini's aim. He is the Virgil to the reader's Dante and he has to describe his earthly tragedy stage by stage. Interested in the motives behind a decision as well as the decision itself, he has to keep in step with his characters. If he had never read a medieval chronicle he would still have written annalistically. His was an age of short-term, hand-to-mouth planning. Alliances changed so rapidly that statesmen faced each year with the possibility of a clean board and a fresh approach. The concept of strategy hardly existed; each campaign was expected to achieve its aims before the troops retired into winter quarters. Starting each year afresh may have led Guicciardini to underplay

such continuity of policy as there was; but the gain in
verisimilitude far outweighed this loss. Guicciardini was
not attempting the synthesizing, selective history of hind-
sight: he was writing the diplomatic history of his own
times, and to this day the writers of recent diplomatic
history use the annal form; political and military man
has not yet freed himself from the calendar.

The annal form also enabled Guicciardini to make the
most of his gift for psychological portraiture. Events were
largely man-made, and could only be understood in terms
of their makers. But men changed. Just as it was un-
satisfactory to wait till a man died and then compose an
obituary (Lorenzo de' Medici's for instance, in the *History
of Florence*), so it was misleading to portray him in the
round at the start of his career (Savonarola, in the same
work). In the *History of Italy* the fullest portraits are
not put down in one piece, but *seriatim;* Guicciardini
describes a statesman as he faces one crisis after another, building up a character in a manner remarkable
both for psychological penetration and a natural sense
of development. The extent to which his mastery developed can be seen by contrasting the set-piece portrait of
Lorenzo in the *History of Florence*—with its traditional
vice-virtue contrasts, and its humanist apology for the
lack of feats of arms "which confer such fame on the
ancients"—with the portrait of Clement VII in the *History of Italy*. The pope is shown being greeted with the
liveliest expectations on account of his energy and single-
mindedness; but as his career unfolds, Guicciardini
shows the steady disintegration of his good qualities and
the emergence of craft, greed and irresolution. He anat-
omizes the special quality of this irresolution. "It happened that both in his resolving as well as in the execution of what he had resolved, every trifling concern that
happened then to occur to him, every slight impediment
that crossed his way, seemed sufficient to make him re-
lapse into the same confusion in which he had stood
hesitating before he made up his mind, for he always
fancied, after making a resolution, that the advice he had
rejected had been the best. And this was because, remembering at the moment only the reasons he had re-

jected, he never examined afresh the ones which had moved him to make his choice, by comparison with which the opposing arguments would have had their force weakened. Nor could the memory of his being often under the power of vain fears teach him to avoid giving way to this weakness for the future." From a conventional religious upbringing Guicciardini retained a tendency to moralize, to see a man's character in terms of vices and virtues. But he also had a lawyer's grasp of the complexity of human motivation, while his own career had often involved the serving of two masters and obeying his head at the expense of his instincts, so he knew that no decision was simple, no judgment could be straightforward. As a result his characters emerge not as personifications, but as temperaments—temperaments encountering events to create the decisions out of which history is made.

His annalistic treatment of the portrait is a device that helps the reader recreate the past and live it through. In addition he is given background information from which to take his bearings. Time after time Guicciardini breaks through the annal form to sketch the history of some town, form of government, or political connection, which only then assumes its full significance for the year in question. He is restrained on these occasions, only launching into a veritable digression when he describes the growth of the temporal power of the papacy and when he dwells on the triumphs of the Portuguese and Spanish voyagers, drawn on in the first case by anticlericalism and in the second by genuine enthusiasm and scientific interest. These, and the more frequent brief flashbacks that occur throughout his texts, reveal him as a master of synthesis as well as of analysis. And there are no passages in Renaissance historiography that can rival the swift sufficiency with which he describes the origin of the Guelf-Ghibelline, Nobility-*popolo*, Bianchi-Neri feuds at the beginning of the *Cose Fiorentine*, or sketches the situation in Italy at the start of the *History of Italy*.

Nor is there any serious rival to his use of the "set discourse," the device developed in antiquity by which a speech is used to sum up points of view in a way more dramatic and more psychologically true than would be possible by simply reporting them in the text. There are some thirty of them in the *History of Italy,* and the finest (especially the debate between Giorgio Cornaro and Andrea Gritti on the question of Venice's allying herself with Charles V in 1523, and the debates between the Bishop of Osma and the Duke of Alva, and between the Chancellor Gattinara and the Viceroy of Naples on the course of action to be taken in 1525 after the victory of Pavia and the capture of Francis I) provide the best of all introductions to the temper of sixteenth-century political life. And here is the proof—if the dry, stately, cumbered periods of his narrative at its best do not provide it—of Guicciardini's mastery as a writer. An austere mastery: Guicciardini showed no interest in the arts, only once in his life did he break, flatly, into verse. There are few images in his prose, and these in the main relate to medicine and to fire: "the disorders of Italy were of such a nature . . . as not to be recovered by slight remedies." And so on. "While these things were being done in Rome and the Kingdom of Naples, in another part of Italy the sparks were growing of a small fire which was destined in the end to turn into a vast conflagration." And so on. It is a style without flute or buskin, sparing of epigram; a ministerial style, free from the crass vitality of the people, whom he despised, and from the rhetoric of professional orators, whose insincerity he more than once denounced. But it is everywhere equal to the change of pace or analytical subtlety demanded of it, and its unself-consciousness (in spite of Guicciardini's care to Italianize it) gives these superb debates the ring of truth as well as the permanence of art.

Guicciardini was so much the greatest historian of the Renaissance that there is no point in trying to labor his originality; the finest exponent of an art form is never its pioneer. Since the time of Petrarch, concern with classical textual criticism had helped historians to criticize their sources. Cæsar's decision to leave a record of current affairs for the benefit of posterity was taken up by fifteenth-century historians like Leonardo Bruni, who wrote of his own *Commentaries:* "I feel that I have an obligation to this age of mine to give some notice of it to posterity in whatever light it may appear to the future. If only those who lived before us and had some literary ability had done this, we would not find ourselves today in such a state of darkness and ignorance."[21] We have seen this sentiment echoed and elaborated by Guicciardini. From the fourteenth-century cult of Cicero, the dictum that history is the guide of life had encouraged historians to stress the political and the moral lessons of their narrative. And, again, from the fourteenth century, histories had frequently been written by men with experience of public affairs, for an audience which was increasingly assumed to be one of politicians, statesmen and warriors, stressed (with various degrees of lip-service to a First Cause) the extent to which history was determined by the decisions of men. Fifteenth-century historians, following classical models, had used devices like the set speech. Interest in the writing of history indeed reached a climax during the century before Guicciardini wrote the *History of Italy.* Its importance was stressed, its varieties analyzed, its subject matter debated. Guicciardini was influenced, moreover, by an environment in which the study of history and of politics was united as never before, and he had, as a historian, the advantage of contact with the most radical and challenging of the historically minded students of politics: Machiavelli. He learned much, but he improved on the lessons. Just as his debates drew strength from his lifelong habit of writing essays *pro* and *contra,* so his entire cast of thought and his experience—Florentine and Italian, constitutional, diplomatic and military—enabled him to exploit these previous developments to the utmost in his writing of contemporary history, and to go far beyond them in the ruminative decorum of his narrative, and in his subordination of a vast mass of petty circumstance to a tragic vision of greatness humbled and liberty lost.

J. R. Hale

1. *Zur Kritik neuerer Geschichtschreiber*, 1824.

2. Above, p. x.

3. *Miscellaneous Works, 1796-1815*, Vol. III, p. 550.

4. *Consolatoria*, in *Scritti Autobiografici e rari*, ed. R. Palmarocchi, Bari, 1936, p. 165.

5. E.g., his careful explanation that the party cry *Palle, Palle* referred to the balls in the Medici coat of arms seems designed to enlighten posterity about a family which had been banished (apparently for good) in 1494.

6. "Of Bookes," Florio's translation. He anticipates Gibbon's point: "He is a diligent Historiographer, and from whom in my conceit, a man may as exactly learne the truth of such affaires as passed in his time as of any other writer whatsoever: and the rather because himselfe hath been an Actor of most part of them, and in verie honourable place."

7. Above, p. xix.

8. Series 1, no. 114.

9. Ser. 2, no. 110; ser. 2, no. 117.

10. *Ricordi*, ser. 2, no. 141.

11. Ibid., ser. 2, no. 48.

12. Ibid., ser. 2, no. 80.

13. Ibid., ser. 2, no. 32; ser. 1, no. 60.

14. Ibid., ser. 2, no. 97.

15. Ibid., ser. 2, no. 211.

16. Ibid., ser. 2, no. 189.

17. Ibid., ser. 2, no. 92.

18. Ibid., ser. 2, no. 147.

19. "There was, it is said, a criminal in Italy who was suffered to make his choice between Guicciardini and the galleys. He chose the history. But the war of Pisa was too much for him. He changed his mind and went to the oar." Macaulay, *Essays*, "Burleigh and his Times," 1832.

20. Series 2, no. 143. [Italics mine]

21. Quoted by Myron Gilmore in his article "The Renaissance conception of the lessons of history," in *Facets of the Renaissance*, ed. W. H. Werkmeister, 1959, p. 79.

There is no work in English on Guicciardini.

Roberto Ridolfi's *Vita di Francesco Guicciardini* (Rome, 1960) is a definitive biography. The same scholar has edited the *Cose Fiorentine* (Florence, 1945), and this is the only edition of this work. It has not been translated. He has also elaborated the description of Guicciardini's preparatory work on the *History of Italy* which was given by A. Gherardi (edition of the *Storia d'Italia*, Florence, 1919) in a monograph, *Genesi della Storia d'Italia Guicciardiniana*, Florence, 1939. There has been no translation of the *History of Italy* since that by A. P. Goddard, London, 1753-6. The most recent Italian edition was edited by C. Panigada, and published, in five volumes, by Laterza of Bari in 1929. A stout volume of extracts (in Italian) from Guicciardini's writings, which contains a good part of the *History of Italy* is *Francesco Guicciardini: Opere*, edited by Vittorio de Caprariis, Milan, 1961. There is no translation of the *History of Florence*. The best study of it is the article by Nicolai Rubinstein. "The *Storie Fiorentine* and the *Memorie di Famiglia* by Francesco Guicciardini," in *Rinascimento*, 1953. The most recent Italian edition is the Laterza, Bari, edition of 1931. The best account of the books written about Guicciardini is to be found in V. Luciani, *Francesco Guicciardini e la fortuna dell'opera sua*, Florence, 1949.

Sections have been chosen from Guicciardini's histories which cover the same years, 1492 to 1498, from the death of Lorenzo the Magnificent to the death of Savonarola. To contemporary Italians the invasion of Charles VIII of France in 1494 seemed a break between a period of greatness and independence and a period of humiliation and servitude. Even today, in spite of a healthy reluctance to see watersheds in history, the year has a special significance; from the point of view of diplomacy, international affairs and developments in the art of war it is the crucial date in a series of revolutionary changes, and no source can compare with Guicciardini in his portrayal of what happened in the years that followed. The narrative given here stops in 1498. In that year occurred not only the death of Savonarola but also that of Charles VIII: it seemed that Italy might after all be spared. The invasion of his successor Louis XII in the following summer destroyed these hopes. The years 1494 to 1498 thus form the first and the most important phase of those Italian wars which only ceased in the middle of the sixteenth century. It is of particular interest that Guicciardini treated them in both his history of Florence and of Italy. The reader can compare youthful with mature work, and see how events in Florence came to be fitted into an account of the peninsula as a whole.

The texts are uncut. This means that the reader is confronted with a mass of details: sieges, skirmishes, the names of obscure captains and political agents. To have "simplified" the text by omitting what appears in retrospect to be unimportant would have ruined the flavor as well as maimed the intention of these narratives. It would also have destroyed their value as a source. In this first appearance in a modern English guise, it is just that Guicciardini should speak, uncensored, in his own voice.

For general background a reader unfamiliar with the

period would be much assisted by the chapters by C. M. Ady in Vol. I of the New Cambridge Modern History (1957) and by E. Armstrong, "Florence: Savonarola" in Vol. I of the old Cambridge Modern History (1902).

The translation is based on the following editions: *Storie Fiorentine dal 1378 al 1509*, a cura di Roberto Palmarocchi, Bari, Laterza, 1931, pp. 72-159.

Storia d'Italia, a cura di Costantino Panigada, Vol. I, Bari, Laterza, 1929, pp. 1-298.

I have adopted not only these editors' division of the texts into chapters but also their introduction of chapter headings to facilitate reading and consultation (the original manuscripts, apart from the division of the *History of Italy* into books, present a continuous narrative). Within the chapters, however, while generally following their division into paragraphs, I have felt myself free to introduce fresh paragraphs wherever it seemed expedient to make the text more easily readable.

With regard to the translation itself, the prime object has been to provide an accurate and legible English text for the modern reader rather than to reproduce the style and periods of the original. So that while following the original text as closely as possible, I have not hesitated, where necessary, to break up the longer and more involved sentences (occasionally filling a whole page in the above editions) in the interests of greater clarity and legibility. It was also considered desirable to modernize the forms of names in accordance with the generally accepted practice of modern historical usage, to introduce uniformity where Guicciardini varies in his spelling (e.g. Virginio-Verginio), and to establish a distinction between the names of the Kings of Naples and Spain (Ferrando-Ferdinand; see note 1 to text).

C. G.

April	1492	Death of Lorenzo de' Medici. Succeeded by Piero, his son.
Aug.	1492	Alexander VI (Borgia) becomes Pope.
Sept.	1494	Charles VIII of France invades Italy.
Nov.	1494	Piero expelled from Florence.
March	1495	League of Venice. Spain intervenes to check French progress in Italy.
July	1495	Battle of Fornovo. French retire, leaving garrisons in Naples.
April	1498	Charles VIII dies, succeeded by Louis XII.
May	1498	Savonarola executed.
Aug.	1499	French invade Italy.
Nov.	1500	Treaty of Grenada. Spain cooperates with France in Naples and sends army under Gonzalo de Córdoba.
Nov.	1503	Julius II becomes Pope.
Dec.	1508	League of Cambrai against Venice.
Sept.	1512	Medici return to Florence by force of arms.
Mar.	1513	Leo X (Medici) becomes Pope.
Jan.	1515	Louis XII succeeded by Francis I.
Sept.	1515	Marignano. French victory in Lombàrdy.
Jan.	1519	Death of Maximilian of Germany. Charles V, since 1516 King of Spain, becomes Emperor.
June	1521	Franco-Imperial rivalry for Lombardy begins.
Dec.	1521	Leo X dies. Adrian VI becomes Pope in Jan. 1522.
Nov.	1523	Clement VII (Medici) succeeds Adrian.
Feb.	1525	Francis I taken prisoner at the battle of Pavia.
Jan.	1526	Francis freed by Charles V. Franco-Imperialist wars in Italy recommence.
May	1527	Sack of Rome. Medici expelled from Florence, "Last Republic" instituted.
Aug.	1530	Medici back in Florence.

The History of Florence

Chapter IX

Florence in 1492. [Death of Lorenzo de' Medici. His portrait. Comparison with Cosimo, his grandfather.]

The city enjoyed perfect peace, the citizens were united and in harmony, and the government so powerful that no one dared oppose it. The people every day delighted in shows, revelries and other novelties; they were well fed, as the city was plentifully supplied with victuals, and all its activities flourished. Men of intellect and ability were contented, for all letters, all arts, all talents were welcomed and recognized. While the city within was universally enjoying the most perfect peace and quiet, without her glory and reputation were supreme because she had a government and a leader of the highest authority, her territory had recently been extended, she had been largely responsible for the rescue of Ferrara and then of King Ferdinand,[1] she enjoyed the wholehearted support of Pope Innocent, she was allied with Naples and Milan, and she had become virtually the counterpoise of the whole of Italy. There then occurred an event which turned everything upside down not only for the city but for the rest of Italy. In the year 1491 Lorenzo, who had long suffered from an illness thought at first by the doctors to be of no great importance, slowly got worse, perhaps because he was not given proper treatment, and finally on the ——[2] day of April 1492 he departed this life.

This death was recognized by many prophets as being of the greatest significance. Shortly before, the comet had appeared, wolves were heard to howl, a madwoman had cried out in Santa Maria Novella that a bull with horns

1

of fire was burning the whole city, lions had fought together and killed one of the finest of their number, and finally, a day or two before his death, a thunderbolt had fallen at night on the lantern of the dome of Santa Liperata[3] and brought down several very large blocks of stone which fell toward the Medici house. Some also thought it a portent that Maestro Piero Leone da Spoleto, reputed the first doctor in Italy, who had treated Lorenzo, threw himself in despair down a well and drowned, although some said that he had been thrown in.

Lorenzo de' Medici was forty-three when he died, and he had been in power for twenty-three years, as he was twenty when his father Piero died in 1469. Although he was then so young and practically under the guardianship of Messer Tommaso Soderini and other elder statesmen, nonetheless in a short time he acquired such a standing and so great a reputation that he governed the city on his own. His authority grew daily, and subsequently became immense as a result of the events of 1478, and then after his return from Naples,[4] so that until his death he ruled and disposed of the city as completely at his own whim as if he had been its absolute overlord. Because his greatness was extraordinary and Florence had never had a citizen like him, and because his fame was universal both during his lifetime and after his death, I do not think it will be irrelevant, but rather most useful to give a detailed description of his manners and character, which I have known not at first hand—because I was a child when he died—but from people and sources which are authentic and worthy of belief, and of such a kind that, if I am not mistaken, what I shall write will be the simple truth.

Lorenzo possessed many outstanding qualities. He also had certain vices—some natural, others induced by necessity. He had such great authority that one may say that the city was not free in his time, even though it was rich in all those glories and good fortunes which a city may enjoy when free in name but in fact ruled as a tyrant by one of its citizens. The things he did—although some of them can be criticized—were nevertheless full of greatness, so much so that they arouse our admiration far more when we consider them than when we hear them enumerated, for they are lacking, through no fault of his but because of the nature of the times, in feats of arms and in military art and discipline which confer such fame on the ancients. We shall not read in his case of the brilliant defense of a city, the memorable taking of a stronghold, a stratagem in battle or a victory over the enemy. The story of his deeds does not shine with the glitter of arms. But we shall find in him all the signs and indications of virtues that are apparent and of value in civic life. No one even of his enemies and critics denies that he had a brilliant and outstanding mind; and the proof is that for twenty-three years he ruled the city and constantly increased her power and glory, and he would be a fool who denied it. This is all the more remarkable since Florence is a city accustomed to the greatest freedom of speech, full of the most volatile and restless spirits, and at the same time a small state incapable of supporting all its citizens from its own resources, so that it is necessary if the needs of one section are satisfied that the rest should suffer exclusion. A further proof is to be seen in the friendship and great credit which he enjoyed with many of the princes of Italy and outside Italy: with Innocent, with King Ferdinand, with Duke Galeazzo [Visconti of Milan], with King Louis of France and even the Grand Turk and the Sultan, from whom in the last years of his life he received a present of a giraffe, a lion and some geldings. All this arose simply from his ability to treat with these princes with great brilliance and skill. Furthermore, those who heard him can bear witness to his acumen and wit when speaking in public or in private, through which on many occasions and in many places, and especially at the Diet of Cremona, he achieved a considerable reputation. And there is proof too in the letters he dictated, so full of genius that they leave nothing to be desired; and they seemed all the finer as they were accompanied by great eloquence and a most elegant style.

His judgment was good and full of wisdom, though not to be compared with the qualities of his intellect. He committed more than one rash action, such as the war

3

over Volterra [in 1472], when in his desire to eject the people of Volterra from the alum mines, he forced them to revolt and started a conflagration which set all Italy in disarray, although it ended well. After the events of 1478, if he had behaved circumspectly with the Pope and the King, they might not have declared war on him, but his insistence on acting as a man with a grievance and his unwillingness to dissimulate the provocation he had received might have been the cause of a war involving great harm and danger to the city and to himself. His going to Naples was regarded as too bold and rash a decision, for he put himself in the hands of a king by nature treacherous, unstable and bitterly opposed to him. Although it was justified by his and the city's need for peace, nevertheless it was felt he might have achieved his object without leaving Florence, with greater safety and no less profit.

He desired glory and success more than any man. One may criticize him for carrying this passion even into things of small importance, so that even in poetry, in games and other pursuits he would not permit any to imitate or compete with him, and was angry with those who did so. Even in greater things his ambition was excessive, for he wished to rival and compete with all the princes of Italy in everything, which displeased Lodovico Sforza a great deal. Nevertheless, on the whole this ambition was praiseworthy and made him famous everywhere even outside Italy, for he strove to ensure that all the arts and talents should flourish more brilliantly in Florence than in any other city in Italy. Principally for the study of letters he set up a university in Pisa, and when people argued that for many reasons there could never be as many students there as there had been at Pavia and Padua, he said it was enough for him if the teachers were the best in Italy. So in his lifetime all the best and most famous men in Italy taught there and were very highly paid, for no expense or trouble was spared to get hold of them. Thus the study of the humanities flourished in Florence under Messer Agnolo Poliziano, Greek studies under Messer Demetrio [Calcondila] and later under Lascaris, philosophy and arts had Marsilio

Ficino, Maestro Giorgio Benigno, Count Pico della Mirandola and other eminent men. He also equally favored poetry in the vernacular, music, architecture, painting, sculpture, and all the arts of the mind and hand, so that the city abounded in all such ornaments of life. And they flourished all the more because he was able, with his universal taste, to appreciate them and favor their authors accordingly, so that everyone competed in their works to please him. Another factor was his infinite liberality, making abundant provision for able men and providing all the necessary instruments for their work. For example, to set up a Greek library he sent Lascaris, a most learned man then teaching Greek in Florence, to search for ancient and valuable books in Greece.

This same liberality helped to maintain his fame and friendships with the princes of Italy and rulers abroad, since he neglected no form of magnificence that might gain him the good will of the great, despite the enormous and ruinous expense. At Lyons, Milan, and Bruges and in the places where he had trading and banking interests, his expenditure on lavish entertainment and gifts increased, while his income diminished because his affairs were managed by men who were not really capable—Lionetto de' Rossi, Tommaso Portinari and so forth. Furthermore they did not render proper accounts, because he knew nothing about business and paid little attention to it, so that his affairs on many occasions fell into such disorder that he was on the point of bankruptcy and had to fall back on his friends' money and on public funds. Thus in 1478 he borrowed 60,000 ducats from the sons of Pierfrancesco de' Medici, and being unable to repay them, he made restitution over a period of years by assigning to them Caffagiuolo and the property he owned in Mugello. In the war of that year he arranged that the soldiers should be paid by the Bartolini bank in which he had shares. By his orders they held back in their payments about eight per cent, which was to the detriment of the commune since the condottieri kept so many fewer men and the commune had to pay for extra commissions. At other times, too, he used public funds to supply his own needs, which were often so great that in 1484 in

5

order not to go bankrupt he was forced to borrow 4,000 ducats from Lodovico Sforza [of Milan] and sell a house he had in Milan for another 4,000. This had been given by the Duke Francesco [Sforza] to his grandfather Cosimo, and one cannot but imagine, in view of his generous and magnificent nature, that he parted with it with tears in his eyes. Finding his commercial interests no longer prosperous, he decided to ensure himself an income of 15 or 20,000 ducats from property, and beyond his hereditary possessions he extended his holdings in the area of Pisa, which must have been worth about 10,000.

He was by nature very arrogant, so that, besides not allowing others to oppose him, he also wished them to understand him by allusions, using in important affairs few and ambiguous words. In ordinary conversation he was pleasant and witty; in his domestic life rather plain and decent than sumptuous—except in the magnificent feasts which he gave in honor of noble foreigners who came to Florence. He was libidinous, amorous and faithful in his loves, which would last for a number of years. In the opinion of many he was so weakened by his amorous excesses that he died relatively young. His last love, which lasted for many years, was for Bartolomea de' Nasi, wife of Donato Benci. Though she was not beautiful, she was gracious and charming, and he was so obsessed with her that one winter when she was in the country he would leave Florence at the fifth or sixth hour of the night on horseback with several companions to go and see her, and would start back so early that he was in Florence again by morning. Luigi della Stufa and Butta de' Medici, who went with him, grumbled about these excursions; Bartolomea overheard them and put them so much in disfavor with Lorenzo that to satisfy her he sent Luigi as ambassador to the Sultan and Butta to the Grand Turk. It seems absurd that a man of such greatness, reputation and prudence should be so infatuated in his fortieth year with a woman who was neither young nor beautiful that he could do things which would have been unworthy in a boy.

Some held that he had a cruel and revengeful nature because of the harsh way he dealt with the Pazzi conspiracy, imprisoning innocent young men and refusing to allow the girls to marry, after so many had been killed. Yet that event was so bitter for him that it is not surprising if his revenge was extraordinary. Later on his anger was appeased, and he allowed the girls to marry and the Pazzi were released from prison and permitted to leave the country. We see also that in his other actions he was not a cruel or blood-thirsty man. His worst fault was his mistrust, which was not perhaps natural to him but brought about by the knowledge that he had to dominate a free city, where whatever needed to be done had to be done by the magistrates both according to the laws of the city and under the forms and shows of liberty. In his early days, when he first began to assert his power, he sought to gain a hold as far as possible over all those citizens whom he recognized must be esteemed for their noble birth or their wealth or their power or their reputation. Although such men, if they were by birth and family faithful to the state, were given ample share in the government of the city, in embassies, commissions of state and similar honors, yet he did not trust them; and as officers in charge of taxes and voting and confidants of his closest secrets, he chose men whose reputation depended upon him and who were of such quality that without his support they would have had no power. Such were Messer Bernardo Buongirolami, Antonio di Puccio, Giovanni Lanfredini, Girolamo Morelli (though the latter became so powerful that in 1479 Lorenzo grew afraid of him), Messer Agnolo Niccolini, Bernardo del Nero, Messer Piero Alamanni, Pierfilippo Pandolfini, Giovanni Bonsi, Cosimo Bartoli and others like them, though at different times. This at times offended Messer Tommaso Soderini, Messers Luigi and Iacopo Guicciardini, Messer Antonio Ridolfi, Messer Bongianni Gianfigliazzi, Messer Giovanni Canigiani; and then Francesco Valori, Bernardo Rucellai, Piero Vettori, Girolamo degli Albizzi, Piero Capponi, Paolantonio Soderini and others. This was how Antonio di Bernardo achieved his position, for he was an artisan promoted to the running of the Municipal Pawnshop with so much power that one may say he governed two thirds of the city. Ser Giovanni, notary in charge of drafting

7

legislation, was the son of a notary from Pratovecchio, and enjoyed so much of Lorenzo's favor that, after holding all the other government offices, he might well have become Gonfalonier of Justice. Messer Bartolomeo della Scala was the son of a miller from Colle, who became Chief Secretary of the Signoria, and was then made Gonfalonier of Justice to the great indignation of all right-minded citizens. In fact, although men of the highest quality such as we have named above took part in the affairs of state, nevertheless in the Council of a Hundred, in elections and taxes, Lorenzo mixed with them so many other mediocre men of whose support he was sure so that he was master of the situation.

This same mistrust made him careful that men already powerful on their own account should not acquire ties of marriage, and he sought to marry them in such a way that he need not be jealous of them. Sometimes in order to prevent such ties he forced young men of quality to take wives whom they would not otherwise have married. In fact things went so far that no alliance could be made beyond the most ordinary sort without his permission and interference. This same mistrust caused him to establish in Rome, Naples and Milan a permanent secretary paid from public funds to be at the service of the respective ambassadors, so that they might do only what he wanted and he should be kept informed of everything that went on. I would not place under the heading of mistrust the fact that he took with him everywhere a large number of armed guards, to whom he showed great favor, giving to some of them hospitals and holy places, because the origin of that was the Pazzi conspiracy. Nevertheless, it was not the mark of a free city or of a private citizen but of a tyrant and a city in subjection. In short, one must conclude that under him the city was not free, although it would be impossible to find a better and more agreeable tyrant. Through his natural goodness and inclinations he brought great benefits to the city. The evils which inevitably followed from tyrannical rule were moderate and limited as far as possible, and very few abuses arose from his wilfulness and arbitrary rule. Although those who were repressed were glad when he died, statesmen and even those who had sometimes been offended by him were grieved, not knowing what might become of them from a change of government. It was also a great sorrow to the population of the city, and especially to the lower classes, always kept by him in abundance, with many pleasures, entertainments and feasts. It grieved all those in Italy who excelled in letters, painting, sculpture and similar arts, because either they were commissioned by him with lavish salaries or they were held in higher esteem by the other princes who feared that if they did not make much of them they would go off to Lorenzo.

He left three sons: Piero, the eldest, about twenty-one years of age; Messer Giovanni, the second, who a few weeks before Lorenzo's death had been given the red hat and installed as cardinal; and Giuliano, the third, who was still a child. He was of medium height, his face dark-skinned and ugly though with an expression of gravity; his speech and voice rough and unpleasing for he seemed to talk through his nose.

Many people inquire whether he or Cosimo was the greater, for Piero,[5] though he had far more piety and clemency than either of them, was undoubtedly less well endowed than they with other qualities. In this matter it seems right to conclude that Cosimo had greater wisdom and better judgment, because he built up the state and after he had done so, he enjoyed it in safety for thirty years without opposition, tolerating the Neri and others of whom he entertained suspicions without breaking with them and yet without weakening his own position. And although he had many cares of state, he did not neglect commerce and his private affairs; rather he managed them with so much diligence and skill that his wealth was always greater than the state, which was enormous, and he was never forced to manipulate the income of the state or to usurp private fortunes. In Lorenzo there was not so much good judgment, although his only task was to hold the state, as he found it already made. Nevertheless he did hold it through many dangers, such as the Pazzi conspiracy and the journey to Naples. In private affairs and commerce he had very little aptitude, so that when they went badly, he was forced to use public money

9

and on occasions probably also other people's private fortunes, which brought him considerable reproach and blame. But he was endowed with great eloquence, ability and universal talent, so that he delighted in all noble activities and was their patron. Cosimo lacked this capacity entirely and is said to have been, particularly in his youth, rather inept in his speech.

The generosity of both was immense, but in different fields. Cosimo was lavish in building palaces and churches in and outside Florence, and things which should last and perpetuate his fame. Lorenzo began a most sumptuous building at Poggio a Caiano and died before it could be finished. This was a great enterprise in itself, but compared with the innumerable works of Cosimo it seems next to nothing. However he was a great patron and with his gifts and liberality he achieved great friendships with princes and with men who served them. On these grounds I conclude that when everything is weighed, Cosimo was a more able man; nevertheless both were so eminent in virtue and fortune that perhaps since the fall of Rome Italy has had no private citizen to compare with them.

When the death of Lorenzo was known in Florence—for he died in his house at Careggi—at once a multitude of citizens hastened to call on Piero his son, who, being the eldest, was entitled to inherit his position in the government. Then the funeral took place in Florence without pomp and splendor but attended by all the citizens, all of them with some sign of mourning showing that a father of the people and master of the city had died. And as, taking everything into consideration, the city had been happy in his time, and after his death fell into such calamities and misfortunes, this greatly increased his reputation and people's regret at losing him.

Chapter X

[*Succession of Piero di Lorenzo. His character and policy. Death of Innocent VIII and election of Alexander VI. Piero allied with the Orsini and the*

With Lorenzo dead the citizens met together and resolved that the state should pass into Piero's hands, and in the councils they voted him the honors, offices and prerogatives formerly held by his father, Lorenzo. In effect they transferred to him all Lorenzo's status and authority. The Pope, Naples, Milan, and the other princes and potentates of Italy showed their grief at Lorenzo's death and sent ambassadors to Florence to express their condolences, to commend his sons to the people and to urge that Piero should be confirmed in his father's position for the sake of the good government of the city. In fact all competed for Piero's favor. Among the others, the demonstrations of esteem and friendship of Lodovico Sforza were especially remarkable. He sent as his ambassador Messer Antonio Maria da Sanseverino, the son of Signor Ruberto, whom he held in high regard and affection. Piero's beginnings were so great, uniting so powerfully in his favor the unanimous will of the city and the benevolence of the princes, that if his prudence had corresponded in the smallest degree to his good fortune he would have been so confirmed in his authority that it would have been almost impossible to dislodge him. But his lack of intelligence and the city's ill-luck achieved with the greatest ease what had seemed impossible. In these events I will endeavor to show not only the general causes and effects but also in as much detail as possible the origins and sources of all these ills.

When the eminence of his father was thus transferred to—or rather perpetuated in—Piero, it seemed at first that he should take counsel with his father's friends and those of the state, as it was said Lorenzo had recommended him to do on his deathbed. Accordingly there came together Bernardo Rucellai, who had married a sister of Lorenzo, and Paolantonio Soderini, who was Lorenzo's first cousin, being the son of his mother's sister. Both of them had been much used in Lorenzo's time, though with due reserve since they were the kind of men

11

who without Lorenzo's support seemed fitted to acquire authority in the city. I believe they had the sincere intention of maintaining Piero in power, but wished him to limit and moderate some of those things which in Lorenzo's time had been irksome to the citizens and which even then Bernardo Rucellai had criticized on occasion. Together these two began to urge him to use his authority with moderation, and while maintaining his power, to adapt his state to a more constitutional government rather than continue those practices that suggested tyranny which had made Lorenzo unpopular with many citizens. They tried to show him that this would in effect result in a strengthening of his position through the gratitude and popularity it would bring him in the city.

Piero's mind was not naturally inclined to accept such advice since, as his behavior daily proved, his nature was haughty and tyrannical. Further, when they heard of this approach, at once Ser Piero da Bibbiena, his chancellor, and certain citizens—most vehement among whom, it is said, was Francesco Valori—told him that this would not be in his interests, and that anyone who advised him thus wished him to fall from power. Not only, therefore, did he not accept this advice of Bernardo and Paolantonio, but filled with silent mistrust of them he began to keep them at a distance. When they realized this, they did not proceed cautiously as they should, but shortly afterward formed alliances (without Piero's knowledge until it was done) between their families and the Strozzi. Bernardo gave a little daughter of his in marriage to Lorenzo, Filippo Strozzi's son, then still a boy, and Paolantonio gave in marriage to Tommaso, his eldest son, a daughter of Filippo Strozzi with a large dowry.

This alliance could not have displeased Piero more, as he felt that the joining of two men of such authority with a family which, though not in power, was both important—because noble, rich and numerous—and hostile to his regime, was the beginning of an attempt to oppose him and wrest power from him. In the light of this he interpreted those first remonstrances of theirs as having had a treacherous object. He was therefore angry and mistrustful of them, and urged on by Ser Piero and

12

others who worked on his suspicions to gain favor, he broke with Rucellai and Soderini and removed them from all share in government, showing openly that he regarded them as enemies. When they found themselves rejected by Piero, each behaved differently. Paolantonio showed regret for what he had done, and with patience and the help of his brother-in-law Niccolò Ridolfi contrived to regain favor. Bernardo, whose nature was more inclined to break than to bend, daily exacerbated Piero's hostility toward him, and showed quite clearly that he disliked the present government.

This rift between them and Piero not only left him suspicious of them but almost ready to believe that all or nearly all men of quality were of the same mind; and so he allowed Ser Piero, Messer Agnolo Niccolini and other troublemakers to persuade him not to trust his father's friends. Thus, although he did not openly alienate these friends and even maintained them in their former positions and honors—except for Bernardo and Paolantonio— yet he did not trust them entirely and relied more on his own judgment and on Messer Agnolo and Ser Piero, who in consequence controlled almost everything and achieved great power, as they had treacherously planned from the first, to Piero's great detriment. Anyone who considers it must see that persuading Piero not to trust the wise citizens and friends of the government was the origin of his downfall.

In the same year in the month of ——6 Pope Innocent died and in his place was elected Roderigo Borgia of Valencia, the nephew of Pope Calixtus, who rose to this eminence with the favor of Signor Lodovico [Sforza] and Monsignor Ascanio [Sforza], who as a reward was made Vice-Chancellor. But his principal means to this end was simony, because with money, offices, benefices, promises, and all his powers and resources he suborned and bought the votes of the cardinals and the college: a hideous and abominable thing, and a most apt beginning to his future deplorable proceedings and behavior. At once representatives were elected by the city [Florence] to go and swear obedience to him according to the common custom of the Christian world. These ambassadors were Messer Gentile,

13

bishop of Arezzo, a native of Urbino, and a learned and virtuous man who had been Lorenzo's teacher and raised to this eminence by Lorenzo's favor; Messer Puccio di Antonio Pucci, Doctor of Law; Tommaso Minerbetti, who went to be knighted by the Pope; Francesco Valori, Pierfilippo Pandolfini, and Piero de' Medici. As they were preparing to leave, Signor Lodovico proposed that since Naples, Milan and Florence were allies, it would be a good thing for the reputation of the league if the ambassadors all met at some place outside Rome and then made their entry together, and one of their number spoke for all three. This was agreed to in Florence and in Naples. Subsequently Messer Gentile, who wanted to deliver the oration and knew that this would be the privilege of the King's orator, persuaded Piero that it would be better for each to enter and speak separately. They wrote to Naples to the King to ask him to put this suggestion to Lodovico, and he did so, explaining however that it was to please the Florentines. Signor Lodovico was annoyed at the change and foresaw that Piero was not likely to get on with him very well. When this second plan was put into effect, another difference arose: those who were elected as orators for Milan were Messer Ermes, the Duke's brother, and certain other leading citizens, and although their preparations were extremely sumptuous, those of Piero were more lavish and indeed infinitely more brilliant. Signor Lodovico was also annoyed by this, feeling that Piero had meant to compete with him and wished not merely to equal himself and the other princes of Italy, but to outdo them. These small things, although they did not make him Piero's enemy, yet prepared the way for greater matters to anger him more easily, and from these would ultimately follow their common downfall.

Signor Francesco Cibo, the son of Pope Innocent and Piero de' Medici's brother-in-law, had held in his father's lifetime some lands in the Roman territory which belonged to the Church, and now he feared that he might lose them by the creation of the new pontiff. He therefore sold them through Piero to Virginio Orsino, a relative of Piero whose mother and wife were of the Orsini family. The whole thing was done with the approval of King Ferdinand, in whose service Virginio was a captain. As the King could see that the Pope had been created by the support of Milan, he wished these lands to be an embarrassment to the Pope and a means whereby the Orsini might influence him at the King's pleasure. With the same purpose he supported Giuliano, cardinal of San Piero in Vinculi, who held Ostia and was refusing to surrender it to the Pope. The Pope was very displeased by this, and Signor Lodovico no less so, for he felt that it was to his own advantage, because of his friendship with the Pope, to keep him in power and high regard, and so he took it ill that the King should assume greater power and authority. He suspected that if he could, the King would drive him out of Milan so that the state should remain in the hands of the Duke. In addition to these considerations regarding the Pope and the King, he did not like Piero throwing himself into the King's arms, and being convinced that the King through the Orsini would always have Piero at his disposal while he himself would never be able to make use of him, he became very angry and determined not to submit to this offense. He many times signified to Messer Antonio di Gennaro, the King's orator, and to Messer Agnolo Niccolini and later to Piero Guicciardini, who were successively Florentine ambassadors to Milan, how displeased he was at the Pope's being ill-treated, and said that if Virginio did not restore the lands, he would not be patient forever. Seeing the affair dragging on and ending only in words, he concluded a pact with the Pope and the Venetians early in 1493, whereby in addition to general obligations of mutual defense between the states, he and the Venetians agreed to supply the Pope with certain forces to help him to recover the lands that Virginio held. Shortly after, when he felt that the Venetians were being rather slow to support the Pope and move their troops, having broken completely with the King and the Florentines, and feeling angry and wishing to have his revenge and make his own position secure, he began to negotiate with Charles, King of France, to persuade him to enter Italy to conquer the Kingdom of Naples which Charles claimed as his own as heir to the Angevins: he promised financial help for the enterprise. As the King was young and bold and naturally disposed to the enterprise, Lodovico found a more willing audience in the court for his proposal than he expected. When this was rumored and spread abroad in Italy, and as the King was determined to invade and he and his court were saying so openly, ambassadors were sent to France by Florence to treat but not to make any firm proposals. These were Messer Gentile, bishop of Arezzo, and Piero Soderini, whom Piero had begun to favor in order to annoy his elder brother Paolantonio.

These were the beginnings and the origins of the ruin of Italy and particularly of Piero de' Medici. Besides losing the support of some part of the city he completely alienated the state of Milan, from which alliance, ever since it had been in the hands of the Sforzas, the city and his family in particular had always drawn advantage for their reputation and security. As every day the rumors grew that the King intended to invade Italy, King Ferdinand made Virginio come to an agreement with the Pope, not however restoring the lands, but buying them again and taking them in fee from the Church for a certain sum of money. But by now feelings were high between Naples and Milan and full of suspicion and violent hatred; and Signor Lodovico went on with his negotiations with the French. These no longer merely spoke of invading, but were making ready to do so at the earliest moment. When they pressed the Florentines to declare for them and make a pact, the city, in order to gain time and deal only in words, recalled the earlier ambassadors, and Messer Guidantonio Vespucci and Piero Capponi were sent as the new representatives.

At the end of the year King Ferdinand died[7] and was succeeded by Alfonso Duke of Calabria, his eldest son, who wrote a letter in his own hand to Signor Lodovico, which was so friendly and full of kind words and promises that he wished to be his ally, that Lodovico was greatly moved and encouraged to attempt to pacify the affairs of Italy and dissuade the French from their intentions. Later, however, through some minor incident tempers were again roused, and the French enterprise continued to gain momentum; and the Pope, fearing that a great calamity might befall Italy, came to an agreement with King Alfonso and the Florentines. This further enraged Signor Lodovico, now entirely at enmity with the King and Piero de' Medici, and being persuaded that his own security depended on their downfall, he omitted nothing to promote his purpose.

Chapter XI

[Piero de' Medici shows himself more and more friendly to Naples and against France. Attempt of King Alfonso against Genoa. Invasion of Charles VIII. New policies of the Italian states and new methods of warfare introduced by the French. Charles VIII at Milan. Piero goes to meet him and surrenders the strongholds of the Republic. On his return to Florence the city rises against him and compels him to flee. Pisa regains her freedom. Reflections on the house of the Medici and the present state of Florence.]

1494. Lorenzo and Giovanni, the two sons of Pierfrancesco de' Medici, were very rich young men and generally loved as they had not had a hand in anything unpopular. They were not satisfied with Piero, especially Giovanni, who was of a restless nature and stirred up Lorenzo, an easy-going man. They began to intrigue with Signor Lodovico through Cosimo, the son of Bernardo Rucellai, who being Piero's enemy had left Florence. While they were yet in the early stages of negotiations and had not done anything important, the affair became known and they were both detained in April 1494. When they confessed what they had done, although Piero was very angry with them, nevertheless the citizens were not willing to execute a bloody punishment, and the young men were released and banished from Florence to their possessions at Castello, and Cosimo Rucellai in his absence was declared a rebel.

In those very days four French ambassadors entered

Florence on their way to Rome, and in passing they communicated the King's decision and the preparations he was making to invade Italy, requesting the city's support or at least their safe conduct for his troops and supplies. Both requests were refused by Piero against the advice of all the wise citizens, because through the influence of the Orsini he had entirely ranged himself on the side of the King of Naples. His pretext was that he could not agree to do these things because of his treaty with King Alfonso. As things grew more urgent every day, Giovan Batista Ridolfi and Paolantonio Soderini were sent as ambassadors to Venice to find out their intentions with regard to these developments and to persuade them that they should not permit the ruin of Italy to go forward unchecked. Thus the city came out more and more openly on the side of Naples against France, to the universal displeasure of the Florentines, who were naturally inimical to the house of Aragon and friendly to France, and against the will of the citizens involved in government, who seeing Piero so determined on this course did not dare to oppose him, particularly as Messer Agnolo Niccolini and his closest associates always spoke in council without paying any heed to the others.

Piero had created an inner council of citizens with whom these political matters were discussed: Messer Piero Alamanni, Messer Tommaso Minerbetti, Messer Agnolo Niccolini, Messer Antonio Malegonnelle, Messer Puccio Pucci, Bernardo del Nero, Giovanni Serristori, Pierfilippo Pandolfini, Francesco Valori, Niccolò Ridolfi, Piero Guicciardini, Piero de' Medici and Antonio di Bernardo. All these with few exceptions disliked Piero's policy, and yet as it was favored by those closest to him none opposed it except occasionally and not very forcefully Francesco Valori and Piero Guicciardini. But as Piero sensed their dissatisfaction, he did not show them all the letters and reports but only those which minimized the threat and were to the discredit of the King of France, who meantime continued to make preparations, while at Genoa ships were being got ready for him and placed on a war footing.

18

King Alfonso thought how useful it would be to deprive him of the assistance of Genoa, and with the support of some Genoese exiles he sought to overthrow the government there, and sent to Pisa his brother Don Federigo with a large army. The latter went to La Spezia and landed forces which were repulsed and defeated; so failing in his enterprise, Don Federigo returned to Pisa. The King and Piero thought that keeping Sarzana well manned would prevent King Charles from getting through, as the pass was extremely strong at that place. To block his way through Romagna they sent Ferrando Duke of Calabria, the King's eldest son, to Romagna with a large army, so that with Cesena, which was Church land, and Faenza, which was under Florentine protection, at his back, he should face the French. During this time King Charles, hoping to pass peacefully through our territory, again sent a representative to Florence to ask for free passage, promising friendship and all the favors and assistance in his power. When this was still refused, he ejected all our merchants from his kingdom. This did not lessen Piero's obstinacy. He continued to persist on the course of his downfall, inspired partly by his friendship for King Alfonso and the Orsini, and partly by his suspicions of Signor Lodovico, with whose support the King was able to invade, and with whom Lorenzo and Giovanni, the sons of Pierfrancesco, had taken refuge. In order to fortify and make Pisa a base for operations at Sarzana and the rest of that area, Pierfilippo Pandolfini and Piero Guicciardini were sent out as commissioners for the whole of the campaign.

Part of King Charles' army had already crossed the Alps, and he followed in person with the rest of his troops. It was a very large force both of infantry and artillery, though I do not know the details. With them a flame and a plague had entered Italy which not only overthrew the states, but changed their forms of government and the methods of warfare. Before, Italy had been principally divided into five states: the Papacy, Naples, Venice, Milan and Florence, each seeking to preserve its own possessions, watchful lest any should usurp what belonged to another and grow so strong that the rest should fear him; and so they watched the slightest movement that was made, and raised a commotion even at the least change in some unimportant castle. And when matters came to war, the support on both sides was so balanced and the infantry and artillery so slow in operations and movements, that the taking of one castle by siege occupied nearly a whole summer, so that wars were very long and battles commonly ended with few or no casualties. Now owing to this invasion of the French everything was turned upside down as if by a sudden storm; the unity of Italy was broken and shattered, and so was the consideration and care which all used to give to their common affairs. Seeing cities, duchies and kingdoms attacked and overthrown, each began to look fearfully to his own affairs, not daring to move lest a nearby fire or the collapse of a nearby place should burn or ruin his own state. Sudden and violent wars broke out, ending with the conquest of a state in less time than it used to take to occupy a villa. The siege and taking of a city became extremely rapid and achieved not in months but in days and hours. Battles became savage and bloody in the extreme. In fact states were now saved or ruined, given and taken, not by plans made in the chancery but by feats of arms in the field.

When the King entered Italy and was approaching Milan, Signor Lodovico—although the French had come through his agency and were bound to him in friendship, nonetheless, considering the faithlessness of princes and particularly of the French, who in matters of their own interest think little of faith and honor—began to wonder whether the King under color of wishing the government to be entirely in the hands of the Duke Giovan Galeazzo his nephew, might not for some purpose of his own remove him from power. To make sure the Duke could not stand in his way he poisoned him. When that innocent young man was dead, Signor Lodovico called together the citizens of Milan, some of whom on his instructions proposed him as Duke; and he was elected, although the dead prince had left an heir, a most beautiful child. King Charles then entered Milan, where he was received with great pomp, and proceeded with part of his forces down the Pontremoli road, having sent another part to meet the Duke of Calabria. Because the castle of Sarzana was very strong and well furnished with artillery and everything needed for its defense, he did not waste time there, but turned off to Fivizzano, which he took and sacked to the great terror of all that province.

In Florence things were in a bad way and Piero's power considerably weakened. Seeing themselves involved in a terrible war which they would not be able to sustain, without the slightest need or purpose, but in favor of the Aragonese who were universally hated, and against the French who were very popular, the people began to criticize Piero openly, especially as it was known that this policy of his had been against the will of the principal citizens. Besides there were all those things which make the populace hostile to those in power: the natural desire for change, envy and resentment against those in office. Furthermore all those who were hostile to the government and repressed by it, aroused and filled again with the hope that the city might regain her ancient freedom and that they might attain the position they felt they deserved, contributed to make this disaffection the more perilous. It was strengthened by the fact that Piero's rule and his own nature were such that he was not only hated by his enemies but displeased even his friends, who found him hard to bear. He was a haughty and cruel man, who preferred being feared rather than loved. Savage and bloodthirsty, he had on occasion attacked and wounded men by night and been present at the deaths of several. He lacked that gravity which was necessary to anyone in such a position, for amid these dangers to the city and to himself he was out every day in the streets publicly playing football. He was obstinate and, not understanding affairs, either he was determined to manage them according to his own ideas, believing only in himself, or if he trusted and took counsel with anyone, it was not with those citizens who had long experience of the city's affairs and of government and were reputed to be wise and had an

21

interest in public success or failure and were by nature his friends and friends of his father and of his family; no, it was with Ser Piero da Bibbiena, with Messer Agnolo Niccolini and such ambitious and wicked men, who advised him in everything according to their own blind ambitions and greed, and to please him and ingratiate themselves, nearly always led him in the direction in which they saw he was already inclined to go.

Nevertheless, when Piero found himself in great danger because of disorders without and unrest within the city, he decided that he must come to an agreement with the French—judging quite rightly that, if this problem were solved, everyone in the city would calm down either out of fear or for some other reason. Therefore, following the example of his father Lorenzo when he went to Naples, though in different and less opportune circumstances, he rode out one evening in great haste accompanied by Iacopo Gianfigliazzi, Giannozzo Pucci and other friends of his, and went to find the King at Sarzana where Duke Lodovico, too, had come from Milan. There after much discussion and negotiation it was agreed to give into the King's hands for his security the fortresses of Pisa, Sarzana, Pietrasanta and Leghorn. And at once, without any further permission from the city and without confirmation, those of Sarzana and Pietrasanta were handed over by Piero di Lionardo Tornabuoni and Piero di Giuliano Ridolfi.

When Piero left Florence everyone felt bolder and freer to criticize him publicly; and also in official circles there was open disaffection. Messer Luca Corsini (who was one of the Signori,[8] and had been appointed by Piero as entirely reliable and devoted to the government, to please his brother Piero Corsini) and Iacopo di Tanai de' Nerli and Gualterotto Gualterotti who were gonfaloniers, together, led on it is believed by Piero Capponi who was very hostile to the government, began to speak ill of Piero in the councils, and to say that the city was being ruined by his leadership, and that it would be a good thing to remove the city from his hands and from tyranny, and restore free and democratic institutions. When they heard that he had agreed to give up the fortresses to the King—and that Sarzana had already been handed over—there was a loud clamor in the city that they should be given in the name of the people and not of the tyrant; and so ambassadors were elected who at once rode off to see the King. These were Fra Girolamo Savonarola of Ferrara (who was preaching in Florence and of whom I shall say more later), Tanai de' Nerli, Pandolfo Rucellai, Piero Capponi and Giovanni Cavalcanti.

Francesco della Scarfa was Gonfalonier of Justice, and the Signori were all men who had been chosen as great and close friends of the government. Nevertheless Messer Luca had come out openly on the other side and was supported by Chimenti Cerpellone, and the Gonfalonier seemed likely to let things take their course. On the other hand Antonio Lorini, Francesco d'Antonio di Taddeo and Francesco Niccolini were all strongly on Piero's side; so that one evening when the two sides had had words, Messer Luca ran to ring the great bell,⁹ and as he was restrained by those who pursued him, he was only able to ring it two or three times. This was heard in the city, being about the third hour of the night, and the whole population ran into the main square; but then, not hearing the bell again nor seeing any movement inside or outside the palace, all went home wondering what it had been about. With the city in this state of commotion and suspense, Piero, having been warned by his friends how things stood in Florence and that everyone in his absence had become bold and outspoken, took leave of the King and returned to Florence on the 8th of November. It was a return very unlike that of his father when he had come back from Naples, when all the population of the city had gone out to meet him, and he had been received with the greatest joy, having brought with him peace and the preservation of the city. Only a few of his friends went out to meet Piero, and he was received with little enthusiasm, as he returned without any final settlement except for having weakened and dismembered Pisa and Leghorn, the principal treasures of our state, and Pietrasanta and Sarzana which had been taken by his father at great cost and with great glory.

On his return he went at once to see the Signoria; and when he had explained what he had done, his enemies and those who had come out against him were greatly afraid and decided that they must take desperate steps. The next day, November 9, 1494, the day of Saint Savior, it was heard that Paolo Orsino, a captain in our pay, had come with five hundred horsemen to the gates to support Piero. As most of the Signoria had turned against Piero, Iacopo de' Nerli followed by some other colleagues had gone armed to the palace and had the doors locked and stood guard. Then Piero, to encourage those in the palace who were his friends, thinking that no one would have the courage to bar his way, came there with his henchmen and a large number of armed men, and bearing arms himself beneath his cloak. There he was told that if he wished to enter he should do so alone and through the wicket; whereupon he was completely taken aback, and seeing his power lost, he returned home. When he got home he heard how the Signori who were against him were appealing to the people, who were beginning to rise crying "people and liberty." Later he was notified by a mace-bearer of the Signori that they had declared him a rebel, and this decision had received the support even of his friends, who were afraid and practically coerced into it by their colleagues. Piero thereupon mounted his horse and rode towards Bologna. When it was known that Piero had been rejected from the palace, only the cardinal and Pierantonio Carnesecchi acted in his support, and moved up to the square with armed men. But hearing that popular feeling against Piero had increased and that he had been declared a rebel and was fleeing the city, they all went home. The cardinal left Florence disguised in a friar's habit. Their brother Giuliano also fled with Ser Piero da Bibbiena and his brother Bernardo, who were greatly hated by the people.

During this upheaval Francesco Valori returned from his mission to the King, to whom he had again been sent as ambassador together with several other citizens.

Because he was well liked by the people, having always been an upright man and a lover of justice with the reputation of having opposed Piero, he was received with great rejoicing by the populace and practically carried into the palace on the shoulders of the citizens. The mob ran in a frenzy to Piero's house and put it to the sack; and then turning to the houses of Antonio di Bernardo and Ser Giovanni da Pratovecchio, notary to the government, they sacked and burnt them too. These two, although they had hidden in churches and convents, were eventually found and taken prisoner to the gaol. The mob then went to the house of Messer Agnolo Niccolini, and had already set fire to the door and would have burnt the house down if Messer Francesco Gualterotti and some other worthy men had not hurried to the spot fearing that this outbreak might go too far. They restrained the crowd and led it back to the square with loud shouts of "people and liberty." Here on behalf of the Signoria, Messer Francesco Gualterotti went up on the balcony and announced that the "white money" had been withdrawn.[10]

When they saw that Piero's rule was overthrown, Bernardo del Nero and Niccolò Ridolfi came into the square on horseback shouting "people and liberty"; but they were driven away again as suspect, and in danger of their lives they returned home. In the evening they came to the palace well guarded by order of the Signoria. And so did Pierfilippo Pandolfini, who had that evening returned from Pisa without permission, either because he was afraid for the fate of Pisa, or because he had heard that he was being spoken ill of in Florence and wished to protect his interests as far as he could. Messer Agnolo Niccolini, another of the ambassadors to the King, feeling that this was the end of Piero and fearing Lorenzo and Giovanni di Pierfrancesco whose great enemy he had been (he had incited Piero against them), left Pisa and traveled through the mountains of Pistoia into Lombardy. With Piero ejected and the tumult somewhat abated (although day and night the people mounted armed guard on the city), it was decided by the Signoria that the offices of the Eight and the Seventy[11] should be suspended and not allowed to meet until further notice.

On this same Saint Savior's day, November 9th, King Charles had received the fortresses of Leghorn, Pietrasanta and Sarzana, and had entered Pisa where the citadels were handed over to him. These according to the agreement were to be held by the King to guarantee his safety, while the city of Pisa itself and the other territories were to be held and ruled by the Florentines as before. However, the Pisans banded together the same evening and went to ask the King to give them back their freedom. This was granted, and shouting "liberty" they marched off to do mischief to the Florentine officials (who, having heard the tumult, had taken refuge in the Capponi bank): Tanai de' Nerli, Piero Capponi, Piero Corsini, Piero Guicciardini and a few others. There they obtained a guard from the King and so were saved from the malice and perfidy of the Pisans. The Florentines, seeing the city entirely in revolt and fearing that when the King left they would not be safe, set out with him the next day and left him on their way to Florence. Thus on the same Saint Savior's day there were two extremely important events: the change of our government and the rebellion of Pisa— the two most vital things in the city's existence that could possibly be altered.

It was certainly astonishing that the rule of the Medici, which had prevailed with such authority for sixty years and was thought to be supported by nearly all the principal citizens, should be overthrown so suddenly by the agency of Messer Luca Corsini and Iacopo de' Nerli, frivolous young men without reputation, without authority or good counsel. This all arose simply from the fact that the attitude and behavior of Piero and the insolence of those around him had alienated all men's affections. It was particularly resented that he had stupidly brought upon Florence a most serious war which they could not sustain, and without the slightest need or cause had laid all our territory open to plunder and depredation. Thus those who first came out against him found the position such that after the first push it went on of its own accord. This was how the Medici house ended and how it fell from power, a most noble and wealthy house, held in the highest repute throughout Italy and in the past greatly loved in Florence. The heads of the family —and particularly Cosimo and Lorenzo—had with the greatest difficulty and talent, with time and opportunity, created, preserved and increased the state, not only extending their own power, but adding as well to the public possessions of the city, with Borgo a San Sepolcro, Pietrasanta and Sarzana, Fivizzano, and that part of Lunigiana, the Casentino, Pietramala, and Val di Bagno: all possessions which came to the city under the rule of that house. The ultimate downfall of the house occurred in the briefest possible time under the rule of a rash young man, who found himself so well grounded in power and authority and so well supported and favored, that if he had not made an effort and deliberately sought to lose them, he could not have failed to keep them. His folly was not only his own ruin but the city's too. Within a week Florence was stripped of Pisa, Leghorn, Sarzana and Pietrasanta—places on which our power, safety, authority and reputation depended, as later events more clearly showed. So that we may say that one day wiped out, or rather, completely outweighed all the benefits which the city had ever received from that house. The loss of Pisa especially was so great and did such incalculable harm to the city that many have wondered which was the greater on that Saint Savior's day: the regaining of our freedom or the loss of Pisa. My own conclusion, leaving aside many possible arguments, is that one is to be more valued than the other, inasmuch as it is more natural for men to seek their own liberty than to rule over others; and particularly so, since in truth those who have not their own freedom cannot be said to rule over others.

Once Piero was removed, the Signoria decided to have restored to their rights all the citizens who had been imprisoned or exiled for political reasons from the year 1434 to November 9, 1494. Although these measures pleased everyone, nevertheless so many dangers threatened all around that people could not really enjoy their

27

good fortune. I certainly believe that for a very long time the city had not been in worse trouble. Internally, a most powerful house had been removed from power after sixty years of government and all its enemies had been brought to power. Through these changes all the methods of government were altered. All those who had held office under Lorenzo or Piero were terrified—and so were all those who had ever harmed, or whose ancestors had ever harmed, the exiles or their forefathers. So were all those who had bought or seized property belonging to anyone who had been declared a rebel. Externally, so many lands had been lost and practically the whole of our dominion broken up, that the city was greatly weakened, its income and power diminished, its people involved in a most difficult and dangerous war not only with the Pisans but with many others who would oppose our reoccupation of that city. Furthermore we had on our territory a king of France with a great army, our enemy; recently offended by us, full of cruelty and greed, he gave cause to fear that he would not only lay waste our lands, and incite our other possessions to rebel, but even sack the city, restore Piero de' Medici, and possibly take over the government of Florence himself. If he went away, the best one could hope was that we would have to pay him a very large sum of money and drain the city of her substance and life blood.

Chapter XII

[*Charles VIII in Florence. His agreement with the Republic. Reorganization of the government. Fra Girolamo Savonarola. Internal reforms inspired by him. Beginning of the Pisan campaign.*]

King Charles left Pisa, as we have said above, and set off towards Florence in a hostile mood—and, it was thought, intending to put the city to the sack. He had heard of the change of government and how at Piero's departure all the population had taken arms and had still not laid them down; and realizing that it was a

great nation, he not only began to think he would not
be able to force an entry and sack the city, but to wonder whether, when he entered Florence, the people in
arms might not set upon him. For this reason he stopped
on the road and sent to say that his wish was to enter
the city peacefully, but that he had in his army many
men of different nations and languages, and having
heard that our people were up in arms he feared that
disorders might arise. He would therefore remain where
he was until the people were disarmed, so that he might
enter Florence in friendship and without tumult. When
this was agreed to, he went on to Signa and there took
up his lodging in the house of Battista Pandolfini and
remained for many days waiting for things to calm
down. At the same time he ordered cloths and garments
for his horses and men to make a rich and magnificent
entry into the city. Although he had almost given up the
idea of sacking the city and decided instead to extract
as much money as possible from them, he sent for
Piero de' Medici, calculating that he would pay a great
deal to get back into the city, or would at least be a
good stick to threaten the citizens with. When he left
Florence, Piero had fled to Bologna and thence to Venice.
There he received the King's request that he should return, and wishing on the one hand to go, and on the
other fearing that the King might sell him to the
Florentines, he took counsel with the Venetians who
worked on his suspicions and persuaded him not to
go. They were not concerned about Piero's interests, but
feared he might be the means by which King Charles
would take over possession and control of Florence.
They would not have liked that, in spite of their hatred
for us, because they did not want the King to gain so
much power in Italy, with which they and others would
have to reckon. When the King had remained for many
days at Signa, whither the city had sent many ambassadors to do him honor, he entered Florence on Sunday,
the ——12 of November.

This entry into Florence was as magnificent, honorable
and splendid an affair as any seen in the city for a very
long time. On the city's side no honor was omitted of

all those it was possible to offer to so great a prince. A
great number of richly liveried young men went out to
meet him. All the men of quality went out, the Signoria,
according to custom, going on foot as far as the gate of
San Friano. At Santa Liperata, where he was first to dis-
mount, all possible preparations had been made. But the
greatest magnificence and splendor were displayed by the
King. He entered Florence with all his forces in arms:
first the foot soldiers in ranks with pikes, crossbows and
firearms, most of them being Swiss; then the cavalry and
the men at arms in full dress, a most handsome sight
because of their great number, the bearing of the men
and the beauty of the arms and horses with very rich
trappings of cloth and gold brocade. Finally came the
King in armor under the baldaquin as conqueror in
triumph over the city, a sight in itself very beautiful but
scarcely appreciated, as all men were full of terror and
alarm. He showed a certain kindness in that, when the
Signoria, according to their custom on the entry of pope,
emperor or king, wished to take his horse's bridle, he
would by no means consent to this. He rode with this
great display from the gate of San Friano to the Fon-
daccio and Borgo San Iacopo, and then having crossed
the Ponte Vecchio, through Porta Santa Maria he went
into the main square, and thence to Santa Liperata and
on to the house of Piero de' Medici where his lodging
had been made ready. All his soldiers, both horse and
foot, were quartered throughout the city and divided up
between the citizens' houses—a thing unheard of for
them who were used to sending soldiers around to other
people's houses, not keeping them in their own.

The King remained in Florence —— days.[13] When
the agreement was discussed, he demanded possession
of the city, advancing among other reasons that it belonged to him according to the laws of France since he
had entered it arms in hand. He also demanded the return of Piero. The citizens were absolutely determined
to refuse these requests, and sent Bernardo Rucellai riding post to Milan to tell the Duke all this, thinking,
quite rightly, that he would not like the King to have
a hold over Florence. Hence the Duke charged the

Count of Gaiazzo and Messer Galeazzo da Sanseverino, who were with the King on his behalf, to do their utmost to discourage him from these demands and employ their best efforts to further the city's cause.

Several days passed amid these debates, and the citizens were greatly afraid because they were not accustomed to seeing arms and having a powerful army in their midst. On the other hand, the French saw that the population was very large and knew that when Piero was ejected the whole people at the ringing of the great bell had taken arms, and that the country districts would do likewise; so they too were afraid and sent out patrols and took precautions to see that bells should not be rung. So the fear was mutual. On two or three occasions there was uproar in the city and the French ran to arms; yet because these alarms arose from fear, they never went further.

Francesco Valori, Piero Capponi, Braccio Martelli, and several other citizens were elected to negotiate with the King; and when they were ready to make a settlement, they brought to the King a draft of the terms to which the city would agree. The King did not approve of these and put forward another draft on the basis of which he wished to make the agreement. As this contained unreasonable demands, Piero Capponi took it and boldly tore it up in the King's presence adding that as the King did not want to reach agreement things would be settled in some other way: he could blow his trumpets and we would ring the bells. Certainly these were the words of a great and courageous man, uttered in the presence of a King of France, who was haughty and barbarous, and where there was the danger that brutal deeds might follow angry words. As a result the King and his men were alarmed, seeing such courage and being already afraid of the number of the population and the great bell, for they had heard that at its sound more than 30,000 men in the city and the surrounding places could take up arms. They were so fearful, it is thought, at these threats that they gave up their unreasonable demands and arrived at more reasonable conditions of agreement. Finally after much debate, on the —— day of

31

December[14] 1494, a treaty was made. It was ratified in
Santa Liperata in the presence of the King, the Signoria
and the whole people. He personally swore on the sacred
altar stone that he would honor the provisions of the
treaty. Peace, friendship, and alliance were sworn between us and the King of France according to the common form of other alliances, friendship to friends, enmity to enemies. A condition was that the city should
pay King Charles 120,000 gold ducats in reparations, of
which he was to receive 50,000 at once before leaving
the city and the remaining 70,000 in two installments
at different though brief intervals. The King was to hold
for his security during the war and the expedition
against Naples, the fortresses of Pisa, Leghorn, Pietrasanta and Sarzana, leaving nonetheless the civil government of the rest of these territories as it was before his
invasion in the hands of the Florentines. When the
Naples expedition was over, he was to restore them
freely and without exception.

When the treaty was made and 50,000 ducats paid
over, the King left Florence within two days and set
out towards Rome. After he had gone, as the city was
disorganized, the citizens turned their attention to reforming the government. A plan was drawn up by some
of the principal citizens, among whom the leaders were
Tanai de' Nerli, Piero Capponi, Francesco Valori, Lorenzo di Pierfrancesco and Bernardo Rucellai. When they
were agreed, the bells were rung for a "parliament,"[15]
and a great concourse of citizens then approved the new
framework of government. These provisions were in effect the following: the councils of Eight and Seventy
should be dismissed; there should be a scrutiny to appoint the Signoria, and all the magistrates and officers
within and without the city, and when this was accomplished, everything else should be done by drawing lots.
To this end the present Signori and colleges [councils]
should at once elect twenty *accoppiatori* [election dele-
gates] who should carry out the scrutiny within a year,
which would also be the duration of their appointment.
During this period they should elect the Signoria by
show of hands. These *accoppiatori* were to be forty years

old except for one who could be below that age; and this was done so that Lorenzo di Pierfrancesco could hold office. In the same way they removed the ban on Francesco dello Scarfa, Gonfalonier of Justice, so that he could be an *accoppiatore*. The "white money" taxes were no longer to be levied; the *dieci della balia*[16] should be created to conduct the Pisan war, with the usual authority according to the laws of the city, their tenure to be for six months. The "parliament" was held without disorder, and on the next day the following men were elected: Messer Domenico Bonsi, Ridolfo di Pagnozzo Ridolfi, Tanai de' Nerli, Piero Capponi, Antonio di Sasso, Bardo Corsi, Bartolomeo Giugni, Niccolò di Andreuolo Sacchetti, Giuliano Salviati, Iacopo del Zaccheria, Francesco dello Scarfa, Messer Guidantonio Vespucci, Piero Popoleschi, Bernardo Rucellai, Francesco Valori, Guglielmo de' Pazzi, Braccio Martelli, and Lorenzo di Pierfrancesco. It caused some astonishment among the people that Paolantonio Soderini had not been elected, being a man of great authority who had been injured by Piero de' Medici; and it was attributed to Piero Capponi, a powerful man who was his enemy. It was later said openly that because of this affront Paolantonio, to change the government, persuaded Fra Girolamo and used him as his instrument to preach the foundation of a popular government. Then the Ten were created: Piero Vettori, Piero Corsini, Paolantonio Soderini, Piero Guicciardini, Piero Pieri, Lorenzo Morelli, Lorenzo Lenzi, Francesco degli Albizzi, Iacopo Pandolfini and Lorenzo Benintendi. Also the new *otto di balia*[17] were created: Guido Mannelli, Andrea Strozzi and others. These spent so much of the committee's funds on entertaining that they were later commonly called the "good time Eight."

When these magistrates had been elected, Antonio di Bernardo was hanged from the windows of the Bargello to satisfy public opinion. He was a clever man and knew as much as anyone could about the affairs of the *Monte*[18] and other sources of the city's income, and furthermore as regards his position and powers he had not been corrupt. But having held for so long an office hateful in itself, and the fact of his not belonging to a noble family,

33

which made people all the more jealous of him, combined with his rough nature which was attributed by those who had dealings with him to arrogance and cruelty towards the poor, had made him so hated by the majority that they thirsted for his blood. It was proposed to do likewise with Ser Giovanni, the government notary, who was greatly hated and was besides a man of little worth; but Fra Girolamo saved him, crying from the pulpit that it was no longer the time for justice but for mercy. He was reprieved from execution and sent to life imprisonment at Volterra, whence he was released a few years later and pardoned.

There were many in the city who would have liked to take revenge on Bernardo del Nero, Niccolò Ridolfi, Pierfilippo, Messer Agnolo, Lorenzo Tornabuoni, Iacopo Salviati and the other citizens of the former government. But many respectable men opposed this, particularly Piero Capponi and Francesco Valori, partly out of consideration for the public good, because the city would really suffer serious harm thereby, and partly from private motives. As they and their forefathers had naturally been friends of the Medici, and had restored Cosimo in 1434, they feared lest, if the other men of the former government, popularly known as the *bigi*, were destroyed, they themselves might remain at the mercy of those who had suffered in 1434, who naturally were their enemies. For this reason, in the election of the Ten and the Twenty they had also included some of those who had never been offended by Piero—like Giuliano Salviati, Lorenzo Morelli, Piero Guicciardini and men like them, who were less unpopular than others. Nevertheless, although they were supporting a just and reasonable cause and their authority was then at its highest, it would have been almost impossible for them to withstand this pressure for revenge, inspired by so many enemies of the former government and pleasing to the populace who like all forms of novelty and upheaval. At this moment help came from an unexpected quarter—from Fra Girolamo; and because he was a great man and the author of great things and changes in our city, I shall give such an account of him as seems necessary to explain the events in which we shall have to mention his name.

Fra Girolamo was from Ferrara, and belonged to the Savonarolas, a lower-class family of moderate means. He studied at the university and entered the Dominican Order. Having done very well in philosophy and even better in divinity, he came to Florence, where he began to preach in public, in Lorenzo's time, predicting in his sermons with some subtlety that great scourges and tribulations were to come. This preaching did not much please Lorenzo. Nevertheless, partly because it did not touch him on the raw, and partly because he had once made himself unpopular by driving out of Florence Fra Bernardino da Feltre, who was reputed a very saintly man, and perhaps also because he felt a certain respect for Fra Girolamo, whom he knew to be a man of saintly life, he did not forbid him to preach, although he did occasionally urge him through Messer Agnolo Niccolini and Pierfilippo and others, to preach less about the future. When Lorenzo died, Fra Girolamo had already acquired a popular reputation for holiness and learning, and he went on as before in Piero's time, now however widening the range of his sermons and prophesying the renewal of the Church and a scourge soon to fall upon Italy, in which barbarous nations would come and take the fortresses without effort and overcome all defenses. He also obtained a brief from Pope Alexander, although with the greatest difficulty, allowing the congregation of teaching friars of Florence and other convents of Tuscany to separate from those of Lombardy and become autonomous. This kept him in Florence and meant that he did not have to move every year as the friars usually have to do. He warmed more and more to his prophecies, and acquired a great following and the reputation of a prophet and holy man. All manner of people came to hear him, among them Giovanni Pico, count of Mirandola, as learned a man as our age ever had, who it was thought, if he had not died soon after, would have become a friar. In this way Fra Girolamo achieved such a reputation that when Piero went to Sarzana, he was sent, as we have said, as ambassador to King Charles in the hope that his great virtues would have a good effect. The King always heard him with pleasure and showed that he revered him, so that on that occasion and later when the King was in Florence, he was of assistance to the city and labored always for its good.

When Piero was driven out, he spoke up openly and said that he had from God these future events he preached about. He had an enormous following in whom he inspired great faith. Then he turned to saving some of the citizens and recommending mercy, and got a reprieve for Ser Giovanni who was a friend of his. He preached that it was God's doing, not man's, that had freed the city from tyranny; and God wanted her to remain free and institute a popular government like the Venetian, which was more natural than any other to our peoples. His efforts in this direction were so successful either through his own talents or by divine inspiration that, although it was very much disliked by Bernardo Rucellai, Francesco Valori, Piero Capponi, Lorenzo di Pierfrancesco, the Nerlis and the other leading men in the government, they did not oppose it; and as the project was favored by the Signoria, discussions were begun on the subject. Finally it gained so much favor that the Gonfaloniers, the Twelve,[19] the Twenty, the Ten and the Eight were each commissioned to draw up a form of popular government. When this was done and the constitution proposed by the Ten was the most favored, Fra Girolamo was sent for and it was read out to him in the presence of the Signoria. He approved it with wise words and showed that at this moment it was enough to arrive at a system which was good in principle, because it would be easier to see in time what the defects might be in matters of detail, and they could then be corrected and perfected at leisure. And then, when the council of the people and the commune was called, it was voted and approved. The provision was that a council should be called of all the citizens not in the city's black book who were over twenty-nine years of age, and whose father, grandfather or great-grandfather had belonged to the three main councils.[20] In this council should be elected the holders of all the offices

36

and magistratures in the city and abroad, except the Signoria, which was to be chosen by the Twenty for that year, and when their term came to an end, by the grand council. The method of election was to be that for each appointment a certain number of electors should be drawn from a bag, and they should each name one candidate, though no one could nominate anyone from his own family. Those so nominated should then be voted on, and whoever received most black beans and won the election by at least half the votes plus one more was to be declared elected to that office. This was apart from certain outside offices below a certain salary, where they simply voted on the ones who were drawn from the general bag and the ones with the most beans were successful. So that the electors should have cause to make good nominations, it was arranged that anyone whose nominee got elected should receive a certain sum according to the importance of the office. The above grand council was to form a council of eighty men of over forty, to be changed every six months, though they were to be re-eligible. Their function would be to advise the Signoria, elect ambassadors and commissioners. All decisions of any kind made by the Signoria were to pass through their hands, but were to receive their final confirmation in the grand council, which had no authority unless there were at least a thousand members present. In the palace there was no room where so many could meet together, so it was decided that a great hall should be built for them over the customs house. Until that was done all those qualified for the council did not belong to it, but only a thousand at a time, which were drawn by lot for a period of four or six months.

When the constitution was approved and the council elected, Fra Girolamo went on with his preaching and showed that God had been merciful to the city and preserved her from the hands of a most powerful king, and said that they should do likewise with the citizens of the old régime. And to show mercy and preserve the city in peace he urged that a decree should be passed whereby any act of government before Piero's departure should be forgiven and peace and unity among the

37

citizens should be established. Furthermore, so that each might enjoy his own more securely now and in the future, and it should not be within the power of six Signori[21] to trouble the city at their pleasure, and banish or execute citizens as they liked (as was often done in the past), and by this means make themselves absolute, he persuaded them to remove such great powers from the six beans [votes] and to provide that whenever a citizen was condemned on behalf of the state to any punishment by the Signoria or by any other magistrates, he could appeal to the grand council; and any magistrate who did not admit such an appeal should incur the same penalty as the appellant. Many men of authority greatly disliked these decrees, but finally after many days of argument they were put to the vote in council and passed by a large majority, for it seemed that anything put forward by him possessed more than human power.

With the city's affairs thus settled for the time being, the Ten commissioned captains, levied special taxes, and sent our troops into the territory of Pisa, still obstinately in rebellion. Our captains with greatest authority were Messer Francesco Secco, Count Rinuccio da Marciano and Messer Ercole Bentivoglio, with Piero Capponi as commissioner. They took Palaia, Peccioli, Marti, Buti, and a few castles of small value, not forcing an entry into Vico, Cascina, Librafatta and Verrucola. The other places were a prey to constant change, and alternately were taken and lost again. Two ambassadors were sent to Milan to bear congratulations to the new Duke. These were Messer Luca Corsini and Giovanni Cavalcanti. A very poor beginning, which greatly lowered the city's reputation with that prince, who thought that it was ruled by the mob, which failed to distinguish the proper worth of men. At this point a new problem arose when Montepulciano rebelled and went over to Siena. War thus broke out between us and the Sienese, and part of our forces had to be sent to Montepulciano to attempt, though without success, to retake it, and to protect Ponte a Valiano and our other possessions. We also lost Fivizzano and our other possessions in Lunigiana which fell into the hands of the Marchesi Malespini; and we gave up the protection of Faenza, as we were in no condition even to defend ourselves.

Chapter XIII

[*Charles VIII in Naples. Popular government consolidated in Florence. League against Charles. The French driven out of Italy. Failure to return the Florentine fortresses. Internal divisions in Florence between partisans and enemies of Savonarola.*]

1495. While our state was thus in peril, Cardinal Saint Malo, the French King's principal minister came to Florence; and when he had collected 40,000 ducats, he went to Pisa with the declared intention of restoring it to us, or at least the city itself. After remaining there a short time without concluding anything in our favor, he returned to King Charles, who had brought his expedition to Naples to a victorious conclusion with remarkable speed. When he left Florence and entered Roman territory, Pope Alexander had been unable to resist, and so had made an agreement with him, handing over certain lands for his security and one of his sons as a hostage. He also gave him the Grand Turk's brother who was a prisoner in Rome, and who died soon after. It was thought that the Pope had given him poison beforehand. King Charles entered Rome for Holy Week, and having had the bishop of St. Malo made cardinal, he went on his way to Naples. When King Alfonso heard this, he despaired of being able to defend himself, and giving up his throne to Ferrando, Duke of Calabria, his eldest son, he had him made king. No longer calling himself king, but simply Don Alfonso, he fled to Sicily into a monastery of friars where he died a few months later. The new King Ferrando was not long in following him in flight; for King Charles, meeting no opposition whatever, and gaining territory as fast as he could ride, on account of the universal uprising of the people, took possession of the entire Kingdom of Naples within a few days—a thing almost beyond belief. The King fled to Spain. Virginio Orsino and Count Niccola da Pitigliano of the Orsini family were captured at Nola. Only the fortresses of Naples remained in the hands of the Aragonese, and soon surrendered.

In Florence they rang the bells and there were great demonstrations of joy at this news, although in fact everyone was very much displeased. However, we were forced to celebrate because of our dependence on Charles, and because he held our fortresses. There were sent as ambassadors to him Messer Guidantonio Vespucci, Lorenzo Morelli, Bernardo Rucellai and Lorenzo di Pierfrancesco, to congratulate him on so great a victory and ask him to return our possessions, as he was pledged to do once the war with Naples was over, particularly since we had paid over all that sum of money which we had agreed.

This victory over Naples, which came so swiftly and more completely than anyone expected, caused grave alarm everywhere, for it seemed that, with so great a realm added to his own state of France and a victorious army at his disposal, the whole of Italy must lie at his mercy. This displeased not only the Italian rulers, but also Maximilian, King of the Romans[22] and Ferdinand, King of Spain, to whom any increase of French power was suspect and harmful because she was their neighbor and because of ancient enmity. Therefore, for the common safety of the states a general defensive league was formed against France, between the Pope, the Emperor, the King of Spain, the Venetians and the Duke of Milan. They gave the leadership of their forces to Francesco Gonzaga, Marquis of Mantua, who was a soldier of the Venetians. In Lombardy a great deal of money was contributed by the Duke and the Venetians, and on all sides forces were collected to oppose King Charles. At the time of the conclusion of the league, the Pope's son secretly fled from the King. Although they were approached, the Florentines did not wish to join the league

or give up the King because they were waiting for the
restitution of the fortresses as had been promised.

At that time the constitution of the popular government was still being founded and strengthened in Florence to the displeasure of the Twenty and many other
citizens of authority. Fearing lest they, seeing the end
of their tenure of office drawing near when they would
be equal with the rest of the citizens, should appoint a
Signoria after their own fashion and overthrow the popular government, Fra Girolamo began to preach cleverly
against them, pointing out that it would be a good thing
if that body were dissolved. Their name and office were
hated by the people as much from fear that they might
change the council, as for their manners and behavior,
which had been ungracious, foolish and inconsistent.
The first time they elected the Signoria, they had made
Filippo Corbizzi Gonfalonier of Justice, a man of little
authority and talent but strongly supported by Tanai de'
Nerli. Francesco Valori had strongly opposed his appointment and favored Pagolo Falconieri, a man of even
lower degree than Filippo (a quality sought after at that
time to please the populace), though of more brains and
talent. Differences of opinion arose then and agreement
could not be reached, and the Twenty were obliged to
take the one with more votes although he had not really
won the election. Then they made Tanai de' Nerli Gonfalonier, a noble man and very rich and powerful because of the number of his children, and especially
since Iacopo had been so prominent in getting rid of
Piero; but in matters of government he was not of
much worth. This displeased everyone very much as it
seemed a bad thing that an elector should elect himself,
and particularly as he had been Gonfalonier before in
Lorenzo's time, and it appeared that he must be moved
only by ambition. After him they elected Bardo Corsi,
another of the Twenty. This choice did not offend in
itself, because he was old and had been repressed and
barred from office by the Medici. In all these elections
the Twenty were of such diverse opinions and so much
in disagreement that there was neither trust nor unity
among them; and although they often tried to reach

agreement, it was useless, and when it was known that there was this division, everyone censured them for it, and their authority too diminished. As Fra Girolamo's authority and reputation increased, the people began to threaten and insult the Twenty, and they found themselves in the greatest difficulties. With feelings running higher, Giuliano Salviati, either frightened or persuaded by Fra Girolamo, spontaneously refused office. Hence his colleagues, finding themselves not only divided but very unpopular, and feeling their reputation was being damaged, put forward a motion in council for them all to resign, which was passed with great enthusiasm, and they at once gave up office. This was in May 1495, and the authority to elect the Signoria was handed over to the people, who appointed Lorenzo Lenzi first Gonfalonier of Justice.

When King Charles heard about the league, he decided to return to France. He left behind part of his French troops under a few of his own captains and some Italians under Camillo Vitelli, and came with the rest into Tuscany. He had always refused the restitution of our possessions to our envoys, and they had reported that he was very ill disposed toward all Italians, and in particular some of his chief advisers hated our city. As a result our citizens so universally suspected Charles that, warned by past dangers, they all provided themselves with arms, filled their houses with troops from the country districts, and fortified the city with every means for her defense; so that, if he again sought to stay in Florence like the last time, they might safely let him in. When Charles heard all this, partly so as to avoid possible danger here and partly because he could not afford to delay—knowing that the Venetians and the Duke of Milan had collected against him a huge army in the province of Parma—he went from Siena to Pisa without touching our city. At Poggibonsi he met Fra Girolamo and talked with him, showing him great respect, but without any result as regards our affairs in Pisa. Then he went on to Pisa and from there toward Lombardy. While he was in Pisa, or about that time, he received news that Louis Duke of Orléans had taken

Novara in the Duke of Milan's territory. On his departure
from Pisa he left our fortresses guarded by his troops,
and went through Lunigiana, sacked Pontremoli which
belonged to Milan, and arrived in the province of Parma,
where he found the armies of the Venetians and the
Duke camped on the Taro. They were far greater than
his own in number, so much so that the Venetian army
alone was larger than his.

When he reached this place with the intention of returning to France if he were not stopped, there was
some argument in the Italian camp as to what should be
done. Signor Ridolfo da Gonzaga, the Marquis' uncle, and
some of the older captains thought that they should not
join battle but follow the enemy closely while they were
in the state of Milan, to ensure that the French would
not plunder that territory; besides it might be that the
scarcity of victuals would force them either to fight at
a great disadvantage or accept the conditions offered
by the league. The Marquis, who wanted to fight, thought
otherwise; and I believe Messer Marchionne Trevisano,
the Venetian commissioner, was of the same opinion.
Finally they joined battle and there was a fierce struggle which lasted many hours; and though the French
were greatly outnumbered, they made very good use of
their artillery. The result was that at nightfall the combatants parted and each side retired to its own camp,
so that as neither side had fled, neither can be said to
have been beaten. But the losses of the French were not
high, while those of the Italians were very considerable,
for they lost four or five thousand men and many officers, among them Signor Ridolfo da Gonzaga; and all
these were suffered by the Marquis' force, because the
Duke's army under the Count of Gaiazzo, on the Duke's
orders hardly took part in the fighting at all. The reason
was that—as the Duke saw the Venetians had many
more men than he and they were on his territory—he
was afraid that if the King of France were defeated, he
would be at the mercy of the Venetians who were his
natural enemies and think nothing of alliances and keeping faith. He may also have thought that if he risked
his own men and they were defeated, he stood in greater

danger than the Venetians, because the French were on his territory and he would be the first to lose his state. He may have calculated that if the King were defeated, this would be an offense which would prevent peace being made with the French—a fact he had to consider more than anyone else as he was their neighbor, and they would think themselves more injured by him because he had been the first to call them into Italy, and then when he had made himself Duke of Milan he had turned against them. These considerations may have inspired him to wish that in any eventuality his own and the King's forces should survive.

After the battle the French, meeting no further opposition, moved to Asti where they made a short truce with the league, which was welcome to both sides. The Duke of Milan encamped outside Novara with his own forces and some of the Venetians, and took it more by hunger than by force of arms.

About the time that the King reached Asti the people of the Kingdom of Naples, who were very discontented with French rule and encouraged by the King's departure and the new league, revolted in Naples and many other places, and King Ferrando, otherwise known as Ferrandino, returned to Naples. In the kingdom there were strong forces for the King of France and many towns remained faithful to him, so wishing to recover the whole kingdom and being without money, Ferrandino borrowed from the Venetians through the King of Spain and the Duke of Milan a certain sum, giving them as guarantee Otranto, Brindisi, and other ports of the realm. In return the Venetians promised him and the King of Spain that they would give back these ports as soon as they received their money. When this had been agreed, the Marquis of Mantua as the Venetians' general entered the kingdom to fight the French. Here after a few months the French were beaten and starved out of Atella; Camillo Vitelli was killed, and with their numbers gravely reduced and little hope of further help from King Charles, who callously allowed them to perish, they were forced to leave the kingdom. The few who remained made an agreement with King Ferrando restoring to him all his state, and left by sea for France.

When the King went to Asti our spokesmen, Messer Guidantonio Vespucci and Neri Capponi, and possibly also Soderini, bishop of Volterra, made a new agreement giving him certain sums of money, and he promised absolutely the restitution of our possessions. This seemed quite likely, as he would be out of Italy and no longer have any use for them, and we on the other hand had kept faith with him and remained the only friends he had in Italy. While these negotiations were in progress our armies were sent to Vicopisano in August 1495, and having been there many days without any success, while many of our men were lost or wounded, the siege was raised, to our shame. Then came the orders from France to those who held our fortresses to hand them back to us, together with the passwords to the citadels. Our troops were accordingly mustered, and Francesco Valori and Paolantonio Soderini were sent as commissioners. Making a sudden attack on Borgo San Marco, they took it at once, and finding the gate open, they began to pour in without meeting any resistance, while the Pisans withdrew in terror beyond the Arno. Then the French commander of the new citadel began to fire his artillery at us; and when the commissioners heard this, not knowing of the success of our troops and the flight of the Pisans, they at once ordered the retreat, and thus was lost a wonderful chance to retake Pisa. If we had followed up our victory, Pisa would have been completely in our hands that day. The commissioners were much criticized by the people for this, though unjustifiably, because it was reasonable that when the citadel opened fire they should have done what they did. Although to have acted otherwise would have brought victory, this would have been a matter of chance rather than of reasonable deliberation. After remaining a few days in Borgo San Marco, and seeing that the commander of the citadel did not intend to give it up either because he had secret orders from the King or for some other reason, our army withdrew without achieving any result. Thus all the efforts of that summer were wasted.

So great a sum of money had been spent on them that the Ten in office were commonly referred to as "the spending Ten." They were the first Ten elected by the people, and most of them were old men of good reputation, but they had little experience of governing the state. Their leaders were Messer Francesco Pepi and Filippo Buondelmonti.

M. de Lille then came from France to supervise the restitution. Our city was in great hopes over his coming when, as our fate would have it, he fell ill and died in Florence where he was buried with great public honors. At last, after many envoys and letters sent to and fro, only Leghorn was restored, where M. de Beaumont was in charge. The keeper of the citadel at Pisa had been given a certain sum of money by the Pisans (who had got it from the Duke of Milan), and he handed over to them the new citadel which had been built by the Florentines. The Pisans at once dismantled it, keeping the old one which was there formerly. Pietrasanta fell into the hands of the Luccans, who had to give the King a large sum of money to buy it back. Sarzana was taken by the Genoese; and thus our territory was broken up and divided among our neighbors. It is sad to think that the Genoese, the Sienese, and the Luccans, who such a short time before feared our arms, now, without any respect whatever, broke up our territory and seized portions of it—not through force of arms and reputation but by means of the King of France. He ignored the treaty made with us in Florence and sworn so solemnly on the altar, ignored the agreement reached at Asti and the fact that we had kept faith with him so completely, giving him so much money and remaining his only allies in all Italy, and he perfidiously sold us and our possessions to our enemies.

The Pisans, who would have had difficulty in defending themselves against us, appealed to the league, and on their being admitted, troops of the Duke and the Venetians entered the town in the name of the league. Shortly after, the Duke asked the Venetians to occupy the town alone, either to involve the Venetians in more military undertakings and thus dissipate their resources

in heavy expenditure, or for some other reason. When
this was discussed in Venice, it was opposed by Messer
Filippo Trono and many other elderly noblemen who
did not like the idea of being involved in many compli-
cations, and supported on the other hand by Messer
Augustino Barbarigo, the doge, and his followers, who
were numerous and younger men. It was decided in the
end to accept; and so the Venetians, when the Duke left,
remained alone in Pisa with the object of holding it for
the league. In theory they were preserving the liberty of
the Pisans; in fact they took over the fortresses and did
as they liked with them. We were then pressed to join
the league, whose princes hoped to unite Italy to discourage Charles from ever returning. This was rejected
because they would not return Pisa to us, and if we did
not have Pisa back, the unity of Italy was no use to
Florence. Disunity was indeed more to our purpose, as
well as the King's return to Italy and any upheaval; the
more so as King Charles was daily telling our envoys
(Bishop Soderini and Giovacchino Guasconi) that he intended returning to Italy, and that having had such
proof of our fidelity and of the perfidy of the Venetians
and the Duke, he wanted to reward us for all our
troubles and punish them for the injuries they had done
him.

This attitude was strengthened by the sermons of
Fra Girolamo, who after Piero's removal and the setting
up of the grand council went on preaching in Santa
Liperata to a larger congregation than any preacher
had ever had there, openly declaring that he had been
sent by God to announce the things to come. He had
repeatedly made statements as to the future of the
Christian religion as well as that of our city: the Church
was to be renewed and reformed to lead a better life,
and this would come about not through temporal blessings and benefits, but with scourging and terrible tribulations. Italy was first to be struck and troubled with
famine, plague and war. Many foreign barbarians would
invade who would flay her to the bones. Her governments must first be changed, since neither wisdom,
wealth, nor armed strength would avail. Our city must

suffer great tribulations and come very near to losing all she possessed. Nevertheless, because Florence had been chosen by God as the place where such great events were to be prophesied—and as it was from here that the light of the renewal of the Church was to be spread over the whole world—she would not perish; and even if all her dominions were lost, the city itself should still be saved, and at last return, under the scourge, to a life of true Christian simplicity, when she would regain Pisa and all else that had been lost. This was not to be through human aid and agency, but by the power of God—and at a moment when no one expected it and in a manner that no one should be able to deny was due to divine intervention. Florence would then acquire possessions which had never before been hers, and would become much more prosperous, glorious and powerful than ever before. The popular government and grand council had been brought in by God's will, and therefore should not be changed. Rather, anyone who attacked it would come to a bad end. He added that these events were to occur so soon that among his hearers there was no one so old that if he fulfilled his natural span, he should not see them come to pass. He also gave many other details, and spoke of the persecution both spiritual and temporal that he must suffer. I leave out all this as not being relevant to the matter in hand, and because his sermons are available in print and give all the necessary information.

This manner of preaching had earned him the hatred of the Pope, because in predicting the renovation of the Church he expressed his loathing for, and openly attacked the rule and behavior of the priests. His sermons had also brought him the hatred of the Venetians and the Duke of Milan, who felt that he favored the French and was the cause for the city not allying itself with the league. They also caused divisions in the city. Many citizens either naturally disbelieved such prophecies or disliked the popular government which they saw warmly approved of and supported by him; and yet others were devotees of the Franciscans and other religious orders, who all opposed Fra Girolamo out of jealousy for the devotion accorded to the friars of San Marco; and yet again many vicious men were displeased that he, in his hatred for sodomy and other vices and gambling, had greatly restricted licentious living. All these had risen fiercely against him, persecuting him in public and opposing his works as far as they were able. The leaders of this faction were Piero Capponi (though, seeing the power of the other side, he sometimes wavered and sometimes dissimulated), Tanai de' Nerli and his sons, especially Benedetto and Iacopo, Lorenzo di Pierfrancesco, Braccio Martelli, the Pazzi, Messer Guidantonio Vespucci, Bernardo Rucellai, and Cosimo his son. Behind them were Piero degli Alberti, Bartolomeo Giugni, Giovanni Canacci, Piero Popoleschi, Bernardo da Diacceto and many like them.

On the other hand many citizens strongly approved and supported Fra Girolamo's work. Some were naturally led to believe by the goodness of their natures and their religious inclinations, and thought that his work was good and that what he predicted was constantly being fulfilled. Others—evil men of bad repute—sought to cover up their ill deeds and acquire the fame of good men by hiding beneath a cloak of holiness. Still others, men of decent reputation, seeing the popularity and power of this faction, supported it, as men will, to further their ambitions for place and to gain public favor. The leaders of this party were Francesco Valori, Giovan Battista Ridolfi and Paolantonio Soderini, Messer Domenico Bonsi, Messer Francesco Gualterotti, Giuliano Salviati, Bernardo Nasi, and Antonio Canigiani. Pierfilippo Pandolfini and Piero Guicciardini were also with them, but they behaved with moderation in the controversies which arose, and so were not entirely regarded as of their number. The party also had as followers Lorenzo and Piero Lenzi, Pierfrancesco and Tommaso Tosinghi, Luca d'Antonio degli Albizzi, Domenico Mazzinghi, Matteo del Caccia, Michele Niccolini, Batista Serristori, Alamanno and Iacopo Salviati, Lanfredino Lanfredini; Messer Antonio Malegonnelle too, but he could not take a leading part on account of his role in the former government—although Pierfilippo Pandolfini had already

49

been elected to the Ten and recovered his reputation. Then there were Francesco d'Antonio di Taddeo, Amerigo Corsini, Alessandro Acciaiuoli, Carlo Strozzi, Luigi della Stufa, Giovacchino Guasconi, Gino Ginori and many others. To these were added the majority of the people, many of whom were favorable to these things, so that, his persecutors being hated and in ill repute while conversely his supporters were popular and much favored, the honors and positions in the city were given far oftener to the men of this party than to the other. Fra Girolamo's partisans were thus very powerful and believed that according to his prophecy the princes of Italy must meet disaster, and the King of France would again be victorious. This was the reason, along with others, for the city not joining the league. Thus a great division and violent hatred had grown up in the hearts of the citizens, so that between brothers or between fathers and sons there was dissension over the question of the friar. Now there was yet another deep division: all those who favored the friar supported France, while those who were against him would have liked to come to terms with the league.

At the end of the year 1495 the great hall of the council was built over the customs house, and there all the people met to elect the new Signoria—after first hearing a sermon by Fra Girolamo. Domenico Mazzinghi was chosen Gonfalonier of Justice to take up office at the beginning of March; and thus the popular régime grew and prospered daily.

Chapter XIV

[*Conspiracy against the popular government. Death of Piero Capponi. The league turns to the Emperor Maximilian who enters Italy. Failure of his expedition. Francesco Valori as Gonfalonier.*]

The year 1496 began with turbulence and danger inside and outside the city. At the beginning of the year, toward the end of April, a conspiracy was discovered of many citizens who were all opposed to the friar and men of little authority. Their intention was to band together in council and support one another for office. When they were successful in this they would attempt some bolder purpose. This movement was gaining strength daily when it was uncovered; and on the morning of the council meeting to elect the new Signoria in place of Domenico Mazzinghi, three of the conspirators —Filippo Corbizzi, Giovanni Benizzi, and Giovanni da Tignano—were arrested by order of the Signoria and the Eight and taken to the Bargello. When they had been interrogated and the whole plan revealed, it seemed not to be a matter of a mere understanding among them, but a sort of coup d'état, although not such as to deserve the death penalty. So these three were sentenced by the Signoria and the Eight to loss of political rights and life imprisonment in the Stinche. Schiatta Bagnesi, a man of the lower class, and some others like him were deprived of political rights for a period; and so this danger was averted, which would have done great harm if it had not been remedied in good time. This affair was the reason why Francesco degli Albizzi, who expected to be the next Gonfalonier of Justice, was passed over by the council, because that conspiracy had been among men who were enemies of the friar and of the council, and Francesco, although not suspected of conspiracy, was yet thought to dislike both friar and council. The council instead elected Piero di Lucantonio degli Albizzi, his kinsman, who was elderly, amiable and not very capable. During his tenure, according to the law passed in 1494 the prisoners in the Stinche appealed to the council, and because they were in prison and could not appear in person, first the case for the prosecution was read out and then what they had written in their own defense. Francesco Rinuccini, who had been one of the Signori or one of the Eight, spoke last justifying what had been done; and when it was put to the vote they were not reprieved.

After this affair was settled our troops were around Pisa retaking the country districts. But at the siege of Soiana, a castle of small importance, the commissioner

Piero Capponi was killed by a shot from an arquebus.
Thus Piero Capponi met his end, a man of great worth
and of remarkable intelligence and ability in speaking,
but a trifle changeable and not very dependable in
his judgments; a man of the greatest courage, great ambitions and considerable reputation. Even in Lorenzo's
time, though he was not often given office, he had great
reputation as a wise and worthy man, and was even
feared by Lorenzo for his abilities and standing. In
Piero's time he was a principal cause of the change of
government, and hence rose to great authority and popularity. At the time when the King of France was in
Florence, he made great efforts in the interests of the
city both in drawing up the treaty and in finding the
sum of money which had to be paid to Charles. Then,
being elected to the Twenty, he was prominent in the
saving of the citizens of the old government, and for a
few months he was more powerful in the city than anyone else. Later he became the friar's enemy, and it was
believed that he did not like the council and was plotting
with princes to change it—and so he was hated by the
people. Although the friar's enemies and their leaders
were all behind him, yet opposed and feared by the
other side, he did not achieve anything in council. Although he was highly esteemed for his great reputation and following, his death was universally welcome
and pleasing to the people.

At this juncture the city was disunited and divided
within, while without the expedition against Pisa continued to make little progress as we had no outside
help, while the Pisans were being defended by the Venetians. The Pisans held Vicopisano, Cascina, Librafatta, la
Verrucola, and the river mouth; the other castles were
held now by one side now by the other, because when
they were in our hands they rebelled against us as soon
as they had the opportunity. The city was in a bad way,
and every day there seemed less hope that King Charles
would invade Italy. It was hard to see how Florence
could regain her possessions and stability, being out of
favor with all the princes of Italy. The Pope did not
want us to regain our possessions, because when that

was settled it seemed likely that the affairs of Italy
would quiet down, and that would be against his plans
which were full of ambition and directed to extending
his territory, and these would not be successful if Italy
were suddenly united. The Venetians were not in favor
either, because they held Pisa and had no wish to abandon it, as they hoped that city might be the means of
extending their dominion over the whole of Italy. Duke
Lodovico did not want it to happen because he had
planned to make himself powerful amid the troubles of
Italy; and if he had to form an alliance with the city,
he would have wished to bring in a government of one
man or an oligarchy, hoping that it would be easier to
rely on them and make use of them than on a government of many with whom it is difficult to form friendship and trust or negotiate anything in secret. Always
in his conversations with his ministers and in the presence of Messer Francesco Gualterotti our ambassador,
he expressed his dislike of our government, making fun
now of the city's methods of electing its magistrates and
now of the common men who took part in the council.
To these attacks Messer Francesco, according to his
nature, always replied promptly and with dignity.

Since the city was now clearly aware that we should
not be restored to our dominions through the help of
these princes, she continued to refuse to join the league
and abandon King Charles, although constantly pressed
to do so with many threats. Indeed, she showed con-
sistently that she intended to remain on France's side,
and continually urged the King to return to Italy. Because of this, the princes of the league, in order to dissuade the King from re-entering Italy at our instance—
and to undermine any plan he might have with regard to
our affairs—brought in at the end of September, Maximilian, King of the Romans, promising him assistance
with men and money to obtain the imperial crown, so
that we might be forced to enter the league. When he
was on the borders of Italy he sent ambassadors to Florence, who besides asking for victuals and safe passage
were to urge the city to be good Italians. The answer
they were given was that ambassadors would be sent to

His Majesty; and hearing shortly afterward that he was in the state of Milan, there were sent as spokesmen Messer Cosimo de' Pazzi, bishop of Arezzo and Messer Francesco Pepi—after Piero Guicciardini and then Pierfilippo Pandolfini had refused.

When they reached Lombardy, they found that Maximilian had already gone to Genoa to take ship for Pisa. Following him there, they explained their mission, showing how much the city wished to please him, and how useful her friendship might be to him if he asked only for things which concerned his interests. However, his demand that Florence should enter the league was improper as it would be betraying her word; and those who had unjustly robbed her were unwilling to return their spoils. This matter touched His Majesty too, since every day he could see the numbers grow of those who were his natural enemies. The Emperor realized that what they said was the truth, yet he could only reply what the league had told him. The day he embarked for Pisa he told the envoys that he had been too busy to give them a definite answer, but that the Pope's legate who was in Genoa would reply to them. They went to the legate, who informed them that the Duke of Milan would give them their answer. They left Genoa therefore, and on reaching Milan sought an audience with the Duke, who received them in the presence of the papal legate and all the envoys of the league. He expected them to seek his answer, but they said that, having orders to return to Florence and taking the same way back by which they had come, they had wished to visit the Duke out of courtesy and to offer and commend the city to him. The Duke thought he was being made a fool of and asked them if they wished to hear his answer; to which they replied that their commission did not extend to that. He then said that the Emperor had referred them to him and so they should repeat what they had said to the Emperor so that he might reply; but they said there was no need and they had no instructions to do so. When he added that he did not know whether this manner of proceeding was occasioned by excess of caution or lack of good will, Gualterotto, our resident envoy in Milan, re-

plied that it arose from lack of good will, but on the part
of others. And so the Duke and the envoys of the league
were made fools of, and our envoys, taking their leave,
returned to Florence.

Maximilian had received money in Genoa on behalf of
the league and then embarked for Pisa; but he was many
days at sea, held up by winds and bad weather. So when
he reached Leghorn he had used up his money and it
was time for the next installment to be paid. After a few
days in Leghorn, the money had not been sent by the
Venetians, so he went on to Pisa leaving some ships behind in Leghorn. There at the end of October French
galleys came to our assistance. The Emperor's ships,
which had against them not only the French but the
winds too, were defeated. The Emperor, now without
money and without any hope of victory, turned back
and retired ignominiously to Germany.

The reason why the Venetians did not send him money
was that, as the Emperor was much more the Duke's
man than theirs, they had begun to suspect the Duke
of wanting to take Pisa out of their hands, and so, not
trusting him, they did not wish at their own expense to
support an instrument which might do everything the
Duke wanted. This break was more to the city's benefit
and advantage than one can possibly say. The citizens,
finding themselves without assistance and with the whole
of Italy against them, believed their situation hopeless,
so that our preservation was regarded by many as being
due to a miracle rather than to human agency. It appeared that the Emperor's having had to stay at sea
because of the bad weather, his forces being divided so
opportunely, and then the winds favoring our cause, were
acts of divine providence, particularly since Fra Girolamo had at that time preached and encouraged the
citizens not to fear, saying that God would set them
free.

When the Emperor had departed, Francesco Valori was
made Gonfalonier of Justice from the beginning of January, in spite of the fact that about two months before he
had failed to get into the Ten and had been beaten not
only by Pierfilippo Pandolfini but also by Taddeo Gaddi.

It is a striking example of the changeable temper of the people, who rejected him and then a little later put him into such an important office when Pierfilippo Pandolfini was also a candidate. He got in through the support of the friar's party, of which he was made absolute leader. Hence he tried during his tenure to favor the friar as far as possible, even going so far as to drive out of Florence many Franciscan preachers who openly attacked him. And because the Medici cause had reached such a point that it was openly discussed abroad and many Florentine priests and courtiers had gone to Rome to join Cardinal de' Medici, Valori introduced very harsh laws recalling them and forbidding all contact with the Medici. He had so much difficulty in getting these laws passed—though he used all his power and authority to do so—that sometimes he would have been glad not to have begun the attempt. This arose not so much from the Medici being favored in Florence as from the friar's enemies and those who were discontented with the government. He also strengthened the council, making a law that anyone on the debtors' list could not be elected; and as the numbers remained small, he brought in the young men over twenty-four years of age where before no one under thirty was eligible. He also removed many who should not have been there according to the rules, but had got in during the confusion at the beginning, under the names of different families and other false colors. For these actions and because he was regarded as a good citizen and above corruption, his reputation stood extremely high. The friar's enemies had no leader of like authority to set against him since the death of Piero Capponi, and they turned to Bernardo del Nero, who, although he had belonged to the old régime, had already been elected to the Ten and recovered public esteem. He was an old man with a great reputation for wisdom and of such experience and authority that there seemed to be no other man who could oppose Francesco Valori. They made him Gonfalonier of Justice after Francesco, and thus, as he was already named head of the other party, there arose between Francesco and him great rivalry and hatred.

Chapter XV

[*Failure of Piero de' Medici's attempt to return to Florence. Alexander VI excommunicates Savonarola. Conspiracy in favor of Piero. Five citizens put to death. Savonarola takes up his sermons again.*]

The next year, 1497, was one of great changes and movement. At the end of April, while Bernardo del Nero was still Gonfalonier, Piero de' Medici with Bartolommeo d'Alviano and many troops came to Siena at the instigation of the Venetians, who in order to secure their hold on Pisa supported his attempt to overthrow the government. This seeemed easy to him, knowing that the lower classes were discontented because of the great scarcity of food, with corn at five lire the bushel. Further, he knew that there were many important men in the city who were his friends. There were others too, with whom he already had dealings; of these we shall speak below. Bernardo del Nero was Gonfalonier of Justice and Battista Serristori and Francesco di Lorenzo Davanzati were of the Signori—all men who had once been strongly on his side. With this belief he left Siena on April 27 and came in the evening to Tavernelle intending to be at the gates of Florence by dawn the next day. He failed to do so because during the night it rained so hard that he could not ride at the hour appointed.

In Florence it was known that Piero had reached Siena and had then set out again, but it was not thought he would come so near. Paolo Vitelli had been commissioned for the defense of the city: he had recently come from Mantua where he had been held prisoner after being captured in the Kingdom of Naples where he had been with his brother Camillo. Then on the morning of the 28th, when it was learned that Piero was moving towards the city, the new Signoria was elected in the early hours with Piero degli Alberti as Gonfalonier. They were all enemies of the Medici and supporters of the new government. As Piero came nearer, Paolantonio Soderini

and Piero Guicciardini were sent to give Paolo his orders
and ride with him. They were chosen—particularly Piero
—more because they were friends of Vitelli than because
they were enemies of the Medici. He rode with them to
the gate of San Piero Gattolini, and when he heard that
Piero was a mile or two away, he stopped there and had
the gate barred. As it was suspected that Piero had
collaborators within, nearly two hundred citizens were
arrested in the palace, those most suspected of holding to the old government. Nevertheless no one took up
arms in the city until it was heard that Piero was going
away, except a few of his special enemies—and those
not very promptly—like the Nerli, the Capponi, the Pazzi,
Lorenzo di Pierfrancesco, the Strozzi and so forth. Piero
stayed at the gate for several hours and seeing no uprising in the city and realizing that his remaining there
was dangerous, he turned back, and by the same road,
without any attack being made on him, he returned to
Siena.

When Piero had gone and the new Signoria came into
office, there was a great dispute over the friar, because
the Gonfalonier Giovanni Canacci and Benedetto de'
Nerli, who were members of the Signoria and his deadly
enemies, wanted to drive him out. On the other side
Messer Antonio Canigiani and Messer Baldo Inghirlani
supported him, managing to keep four votes in his favor,
though with the utmost difficulty. In this controversy the
passions of the citizens were inflamed and they were
deeply divided among themselves. The following were
nominated by both parties to pacify the city and settle
the dispute: Bernardo del Nero, Tanai de' Nerli, Niccolò
Ridolfi, Paolantonio Soderini, Piero Guicciardini, Messer
Agnolo Niccolini, Messer Guidantonio Vespucci, Bernardo
Rucellai, Francesco Valori, Pierfilippo Pandolfini and
Lorenzo di Pierfrancesco. They had no success whatever,
and every day tempers rose in such a manner that it was
generally felt that there must be some outbreak; and
as the friar was preaching on Ascension Day in Santa
Liperata, there arose a tremendous outcry for which
there seemed no good reason. As the noise was tremendous, he showed signs of great fear, and in the end he

could not go on with his sermon and retired to San Marco accompanied by many armed citizens, among them Giovan Batista Ridolfi with a lance over his shoulder.

The dissensions among the citizens did not cease here but increased daily, until in the month of June Pope Alexander published the excommunication of the friar in Florence, accusing him of having publicly preached heretical doctrines and of having refused to appear before him when summoned. It is believed that the Pope was glad to do this on his own account, but he did it all the more gladly when urged on by the friar's enemies in Florence. Yet to attest to his innocence a petition was drawn up in San Marco by citizens who all testified that he was a true and good Catholic. Around five hundred signed, and hardly any of the known supporters of his party failed to do so. As the friar refrained from preaching because of the excommunication, and his enemies were satisfied, it seemed as though the dispute would die down.

It was observed that the morning the excommunication of Fra Girolamo was published, the news reached Florence that the Duke of Gandia, the Pope's favorite son, had been killed in Rome. It was said that this was the doing of the Cardinal of Valencia, the Pope's other son, who was jealous of his brother's greater favor with their father. This seemed to the friar's party a sign that God wished to show the Pope his error in excommunicating Fra Girolamo. Then in August came an event of great importance, while Domenico Bartoli was Gonfalonier of Justice; and so that it may be better understood, I will go back to its origins.

The internal government of the city was in great disorder, as all the magistrates were elected in the grand council which at first favored good men of the people who knew nothing about government, rather than those who had most authority and experience. Then it was gradually realized that government needed to be carried on by wise and experienced men. So when the city was purged of its jealousy of a large number of those who had previously held office, they began to behave more reasonably in the elections to the more important offices—especially the Gonfalonier and the Ten. Hence, where formerly men like Antonio Manetti had been preferred for gonfalonier to Paolantonio Soderini and others like him, and where formerly Piero del Benino, Pandolfo Rucellai and Andrea Giugni had enjoyed more favor in the elections for the Ten than the most worthy men in the city, the council's judgment now became keener and Francesco Valori and Bernardo del Nero had been made Gonfalonier of Justice in succession; while to the office of the Ten they were always elected together with Guidantonio Vespucci, Pierfilippo Pandolfini, Paolantonio Soderini, Bernardo Rucellai and men like them.

As a result, even for the most important appointments abroad—in Arezzo, Pistoia, Volterra, Cortona and so on —very sensible elections were made. In this respect the council was much improved and one could see that if elections continued on the basis of a simple majority the government would not go out of the hands of the few best qualified men. Nevertheless, as the friar's men enjoyed more influence than his enemies, which derived partly from his personal reputation and partly from the fact that, apart from Bernardo del Nero, Messer Guidantonio, Bernardo Rucellai and a few others, they were better men, all the friar's adversaries desired a change of government. Many of them, and particularly Bernardo del Nero, wished, not to recall Piero de' Medici to Florence, but to form a government of a small group of worthy men with Lorenzo and Giovanni di Pierfrancesco at its head. With the secret support of the Duke of Milan, Giovanni had gone at his orders to Imola and there secretly married the Countess of Imola and Forlì (she was the bastard daughter of Duke Galeazzo, and thus the niece of Duke Ludovico, and had been the wife of Count Girolamo, on behalf of whose sons she now governed that state). This may have been done in the hope of having troops behind him when he was ready to change the government of Florence.

As it seemed to the council's enemies that the daily improvement made in the elections would cause many worthy men to accustom themselves willingly to this

form of government, and so it would grow continually
stronger, they thought it would be a good idea to introduce broader elections and change the method of the
majority vote. They believed that the broader the elections were, the more disorganized the council would be
and the more displeasing to worthy men who would dislike seeing offices in the hands of people who either by
low birth or by their vices or for some other reason did
not deserve them. To achieve this object—as they had
not the strength to do so openly—they began, when an
outside office was being voted on, to give white beans[23]
for every candidate so that no one could be elected.
Thus some other method had to be found. In this they
were helped by many people who did not realize what
their purpose was, but who lent their support not to
destroy the council but to stop the system of election by
a simple majority of votes.

Many months passed amid negotiations until finally
those who did not want disorder introduced a motion for
a law that when an office had been voted on three times
in council and no one had been elected, it should be
given to the man who had most beans in those three bal-
lots although he had not in fact won the election. Thus
those who, in order to create confusion, tried to get no
one elected, would have been thwarted, seeing that although no one was successful, the offices would be filled.
When they were about to reach agreement on this point,
Bernardo del Nero, realizing that it prevented their plan
from working, opposed it so strongly that nothing was
decided. Finally as a lesser evil it was necessary to make
a law changing the method of electing to outside offices.
Where before a certain number of nominees were voted
on and they took the one with the most beans, now they
were to vote on candidates chosen by lot—that is, drawn
from a general bag containing all the names of those
eligible for the office. Then all those who won the ballot
by half the beans plus one more were to be put in the
bag and the name drawn out would have the job. The
result of this was that the elections began to get much
worse and take in a wider field, because with the drawing
of names less suitable men than the nominations pro-

61

duced came to be voted on. Furthermore, all those who had half the beans and one more were regarded as equal even though some had far more than others, and had an equal chance in the draw. Not only was there this drawback with the outside appointments, but it was also introduced in consequence, as we shall see, in the internal ones. Nevertheless those who were its authors did not succeed in their object. Before, the appointments went around among a few and were restricted to a number of two hundred citizens or a few more, so that these were all supporters of the council, while all outsiders were its enemies and far more numerous. Now that the number of possible appointees was greatly increased to include many who were against the council, they began to be on its side; so it had far more friends than formerly.

Their designs did not stop here, however. All the time they interfered in and opposed what was done. A pernicious freedom developed of publicly criticizing the council among citizens of all parties, and of saying that we were better governed under the Medici. These things went unpunished because that is what happens in divided cities where the citizens cannot attend to everything, being too absorbed in their contentions. Further, whoever is in disfavor with one side may have favor with the other, and as everyone felt that the government and the city were not the property of one or a few but of many, there was no one willing to face up to this public attack and hostility. As this license grew worse every day, it seemed to Niccolò Ridolfi, Lorenzo Tornabuoni, Giannozzo di Antonio Pucci and others who desired the return of Piero, that he would command a strong following in the city. Drawing encouragement from public expressions of discontent and seeing many citizens disaffected, they began to negotiate with Piero. He was encouraged by this and being assured by the league that they would support him as a means of detaching the city from her alliance with France, he sent to Florence, to prepare the ground, Maestro Mariano da Ghinazzano, general of the Augustinians, who formerly in Lorenzo's time had preached to large numbers in the city. He came to preach under color of opposing Fra Girolamo; but he hinted cleverly from the pulpit that the city should come to agreement with the league, and in private he negotiated with Piero's friends. Although his arrival and his contacts with these citizens while he was in Florence aroused almost universal suspicion of what he was doing, nevertheless the divisions of the city prevented his activities from being investigated and punished.

Piero was emboldened by all this and asked the league for its support; but at this point the Duke of Milan backed out. There may have been two reasons for this: first, the Duke may have thought that to restore Piero now would merely establish the Venetians more firmly in Pisa; secondly, as he himself had been a principal cause of Piero's fall, he doubted, even if he helped him, that he would ever be able to trust him. So, lacking the Duke's help, Piero was supported only by the Venetians, and not with the forces he would have liked. Still, he put his trust in the friends with whom he had had communication, in having a Signoria of men who had been benefited by his house, and above all in the fact that so many citizens were discontented and the populace and the peasants longed for a change of government because they were starving. He hoped that when he drew near the gates the multitude would rise and acclaim him. (These were all plans in the air, based on the hopes all exiles nurture, forever persuading themselves that they have friends and strong support within the city.) So he came bravely to the gates, as we have described above, at the time when Bernardo del Nero was Gonfalonier. It was commonly believed that he had contacts in Florence; yet because there was no certainty about it and people were absorbed in the affairs of Fra Girolamo, the whole thing died down until the following August.

At that time Lamberto della Antella,. who had been banished several years before for corresponding with Piero and was then living in Rome, had got to know something about Piero's negotiations with people in Florence; and either because he bore Piero a grudge or hoped to have his exile ended and make some profit out of it, he wrote to Florence to some private citizen (I believe it was to Francesco Gualterotti) that if he were given a safe conduct, he would come and furnish information of great importance. As there was delay in replying, he eventually came into Florentine territory; and when this was known, he was arrested and tortured with the *strappado;* whereupon he let fall hints as to how all the details of the plot might be known. As this seemed a matter of the greatest importance, the Signoria named a committee of some twenty citizens who should have all its own powers to summon and examine witnesses and investigate the affair.

When they began their work they summoned and arrested Bernardo del Nero, Niccolò Ridolfi, Lorenzo Tornabuoni, Giannozzo Pucci and Giovanni Cambi. Many others were summoned who did not appear as they were away in the country—such as Pandolfo Corbinelli, Gino di Lodovico Capponi, Piero di Messer Luca Pitti, Francesco di Ruberto Martelli otherwise known as el Tinca, Galeazzo Sassetti, and Jacopo di Messer Bongianni Gianfigliazzi. Madonna Lucrezia, daughter of Lorenzo de' Medici and wife of Jacopo Salviati was also summoned and held in the house of Guglielmo de' Pazzi. Proceeding then to examination of the witnesses, the five I have mentioned were given the *strappado;* and from them it was learned that Giannozzo and Lorenzo Tornabuoni had exchanged many letters with Piero, informing him of the city's affairs, and had encouraged him to make an attempt to re-enter Florence with the help of the league; when Fra Mariano was here, Niccolò Ridolfi had been much concerned with these same plans and discussed them with him; and he also told Bernardo del Nero, who had only this information, but had not written or advised or spoken or done anything: Madonna Lucrezia had been told and acted in the same way, without the knowledge of Jacopo her husband, with whom she had been very discreet. Giovanni Cambi and others who had fled had also erred in some of these ways.

When all these things had been verified and confirmed, a special council[24] of about two hundred citizens was called, and they began to discuss the matter. There were many varied ideas and opinions among them. Some who would have liked the Medici back in Florence wished to see the conspirators' lives preserved; but these were few and mostly men of little standing, and if there were any influential men among them, they would not dare to speak. Some thought that it was a serious matter to lay hands on so many worthy citizens, and that if their blood were shed, it might be the beginning of the ruin of the city. Others moved by pity or by personal friendship with some of the accused would have liked to save them; and among these were Messer Guidantonio Vespucci and the Nerli who would have been grieved to lose Bernardo del Nero, the head of their faction against the friar. On the other side all those who in the past had come out openly as enemies of the Medici—except the Nerli— and who feared their possible return, together with all those who liked the popular government and the present way of life, were united in great numbers in wishing to see them executed. Francesco Valori was made the leader of this group; and he, either because he was notoriously an enemy of the Medici or because he wished to preserve the council in which he thought he ruled the city or, as rumor later had it, because he wanted to get rid of Bernardo del Nero, the only man capable of opposing him and hindering his rise to power, spoke vigorously against the prisoners. Although he would grieve at the death of Lorenzo Tornabuoni and would have been glad to save him, nevertheless considering that Lorenzo was more incriminated almost than any other and that if he were saved all the others would have to be, his determination was such that he had quite made up his mind to see them dead.

When the council met Messer Antonio Strozzi spoke very strongly on behalf of the Gonfaloniers of companies, showing that conspiracies against the liberty of the city were such that according to the law, not only those active in them must lose their lives, but also those who knew of them and kept silent. He was followed by Bernardo di Inghilese Ridolfi who spoke in the same vein on behalf of the Twelve, although Piero di Giuliano Ridolfi, one of the Twelve, was Niccolò's kinsman. Then closely following the other magistrates, Messer Guido ably assisted their cause by showing that the prisoners' crimes were all different and some had done more and some less and in various ways, while some had only known and not taken active part: for this reason they should compare the laws and statutes of the city and consider thoroughly what punishment they deserved and whether it should be the same for all or different. He reminded the council that in a matter of irrevocable punishment involving a man's life, plenty of time should be allowed.

The result of this council was an almost unanimous decision to have them all beheaded. When on the following day they had been condemned by a vote of the Signoria and, on its orders, also by the Eight, an appeal was lodged by their relatives in accordance with the law of 1494, which had been observed in the cases of Filippo Corbizzi, Giovanni Benizzi, and the others. The Signoria could not agree over this request and the council was recalled: some advised that the law should be observed, but the great majority took the opposite view, saying that it would be dangerous to delay as there might be a popular rising and when a tumult is feared, according to common law, all appeals are abolished. The leaders of this opinion were Francesco Valori (most important of them all), Guglielmo de' Pazzi, Messer Francesco Gualterotti, Messer Luca and Piero Corsini, Lorenzo Morelli, Pierfrancesco and Tommaso Tosinghi, Bernardo Nasi, Antonio Canigiani, Luca d'Antonio degli Albizzi and Carlo Strozzi.

The council finally adopted this resolution and it was proposed several times in the Signoria by Luca Martini who was presiding. In the voting there were only four black beans, from the Gonfalonier, Luca di Tommaso, Niccolò Giovanni and Francesco Girolami. The other five, who were Piero Guicciardini, Piero d'Antonio di Taddeo, Niccolò Zati, Michele Berti and Bernardo Neretti, openly opposed it. The motion therefore was not carried, and after a great deal had been said in the council in a vain attempt to persuade the Signoria to agree, Francesco Valori at last jumped up in a rage saying that either he would die or they would, and with his authority he roused such a tumult that many were emboldened to insult and threaten the Signoria. Carlo Strozzi seized Piero Guicciardini by his gown and threatened to throw him out of the window—for he thought that as Piero had more authority than any of his colleagues the thing would be done if he were out of the way. Seeing therefore so great a commotion, the decision was again put to the vote and succeeded with six black beans, because Niccolò Zati and one of the artisans gave way, either fearing for their own safety or lest there might be even greater disorders. Piero Guicciardini, Piero d'Antonio di Taddeo and the other artisan still stood firm and constant. The motion being thus carried, a few hours later that same night all five were first visited by confessors and then beheaded.

This was the unexpected end of these five citizens, some of whom were among the leaders of our city. Giovanni Cambi was a man of little account and a friend of the Medici not because of hereditary interests or because he owed any position to them, but because he had been with them in the Pisa expedition; later, having been impoverished by the rebellion of Pisa, he had been smitten with this madness. Giannozzo was a young man of great intelligence, very able and of excellent parts, but devoted to Piero on account of his father Antonio di Puccio and his other forbears, and because he had been Piero's companion. Further, because his family was not noble and he was unpopular with the masses because of his father's evil actions, he saw that he could have no advancement with this government and so desired the return of Piero. Lorenzo Tornabuoni's motives had been different. He was a young man all nobility and grace, and universally beloved by all the people more than any other man of his age. But besides his relationship with Piero, who was his first cousin, and the influence he appeared to enjoy in that government, the fact that he was a generous man and a lavish spender and that his financial affairs were bound up with the Medici company had involved him in such difficulties that he must soon have gone bankrupt. Therefore he looked to a change of government to restore his fortunes. Furthermore, as he believed that the council would not last, he feared that Lorenzo and Giovanni di Pierfrancesco might become leaders of the city; and as they were his enemies he was afraid of them and so wished to provide against the event.

Niccolò did not lack talent; nor, had he been willing to conform like Pierfilippo and others, would he have lacked honors and reputation in the natural course of his life. But his son Piero was married to Contessina, Piero de' Medici's sister, and he had on this account been extremely powerful under the old government. So, moved by ambition and not content with what he might have had under the present government, he sought something better and met an end unworthy of a man of his wisdom and manners, unworthy of the nobility of his family, and of the honors, dignity, authority and power he had enjoyed, which were as great as those of any other citizen of his time.

Bernardo del Nero was very old, childless, and a man of many parts; for these qualities and the great honors he had received, as well as for the prudence he was deservedly held to possess, he was regarded as the only man capable of leading a party in opposition to Francesco Valori. Although he enjoyed such a high reputation under this régime, he did not like the council, either because he had had a tax of 400 ducats levied on him (a scandalous thing), or because he was too used to the old government and could not adapt himself to the equality and democracy that are needed in a government like the new one, or because he was obliged to conform to the wishes of his followers. Nevertheless his aim was to have as leaders the sons of Pierfrancesco and not to restore Piero de' Medici. Although he had recently lent an ear to the persuasions of Niccolò, and, thinking that his original plan was too difficult to carry out, he had come to prefer, as an easy solution, the return of Piero to the prospect of going on forever in the present manner. Nonetheless his fault was so slight that he would certainly have survived had it not been for the hatred between himself and Francesco Valori—and Francesco's desire to get rid of his rival. This was the reason why Francesco so vehemently opposed the appeal, fearing that his reputation and favor with the people, together with the insignificance of his offense, might suffice to secure his acquittal.

The death of these men who had wealth, power, authority and distinguished family connections—and who were universally popular—may serve as an example to all citizens, that when they are prosperous and have a reasonable share of things, they should be content with that and not try for more, because in most cases they will suffer a heavy fall. If they still wish to attempt new ventures, they should be careful to choose enterprises likely to succeed, and ones that are not against the people, for one cannot win against so many enemies. They should always bear in mind that the result of such enterprises must be either to achieve their purpose or to lose their lives—or at least their home and city. They should reflect that when they have been discovered and are in danger, universal grace and favor is but a dream: the people begin to hear everything against them, some things true, many false; and when they try to justify themselves, they are either not listened to or not believed. And so good will turns to hatred and everyone wants to crucify them. All their friends and relations abandon them and will not put themselves in danger for them; rather, to justify themselves, they take an active part in persecuting them. The power and authority such a man once enjoyed now do him harm, for everyone says: "It serves him right, what did he lack? What was he trying to achieve?" Thus it was with these five, against whom the populace was so enraged that there is no doubt whatever that they would never have succeeded in their appeal. Yet a few months later, when their fury had passed, everyone regretted their deaths; but this was not enough to give them back their lives. Certainly if the magistrates of the city had dared to allow them the benefit of the law, there would have been a judgment that was fully justified, of great reputation for the city and of no blame to the Signoria. But those who desire a thing too strongly are always afraid and suspicious.

When these citizens had been executed, those who had fled were banished to their possessions in the country, some for ten years and some for five, according to their crimes. Nevertheless most of them were pardoned within a year or two, providing an example for those who have committed crimes—that it is better to flee than to show up, because if they had appeared they would have lost their lives, and conversely, the others, if they had fled would not only have saved their lives, but would not even have been declared rebels or lost their property. Madonna Lucrezia, wife of Jacopo Salviati, was freed thanks to Francesco Valori, who was fond of Jacopo and thought it wrong to punish a woman. And so after this judgment and with Bernardo del Nero dead, Francesco Valori remained absolute head of the city until his death. He was supported especially by the friar's party, and in particular by a number of citizens who were always ready to do his bidding: Messer Francesco Gualterotti, Bernardo and Alessandro Nasi, Antonio Canigiani, Pierfrancesco and Tommaso Tosinghi, Alessandro Acciaiuoli and others. His enemy Pierfilippo Pandolfini was overawed by the greatness of this following and even more horrified and terrified by the death of these five. He fell ill and died a few days later. The popular régime was confirmed in power by this severe judgment, and for the security of the state a guard of foot soldiers was placed in the Piazza de' Signori, which remained there until the friar's troubles started.

In the same year—1497—in January or February when Giuliano Salviati was Gonfalonier of Justice, Fra Girolamo, who had not preached since June because of the excommunication—though he had continued to say mass in San Marco and shown that he did not fear this ban—saw that enthusiasm for his work was waning; and so finding himself with a gonfalonier and a Signoria to his purpose who would not prevent him, he began to preach publicly in Santa Liperata, asserting with many specious arguments that he was not obliged to observe or fear this excommunication. Whereupon feelings and dissensions

which had died down slightly while he had not been
preaching again rose high. When he heard of this disobedience the Pope was angry and, urged on also by many
of our priests and citizens, he sent a more severe letter
and an order that no one should go to hear the friar
under pain of the same excommunication. His congregation was therefore greatly diminished and the chapter of
Santa Liperata would no longer allow him to preach
there; so to avoid scandal he went back to preaching in
San Marco. While he was preaching there, the new
Signoria was elected for March and April with Piero
Popoleschi as Gonfalonier, and the friar had little support in it, although two of his followers, Lanfredino
Lanfredini and Alessandro di Papi degli Alessandri, w͟re
members. Then the Pope sent to the Signoria very insist-
ent letters asking them to forbid the friar to preach. A
great council was held on this subject and there were
much argument and controversy. At last a great majority
advised that he should not be allowed to preach. And so
the Signoria commanded him and he obeyed, leaving Fra
Domenico da Pescia to preach instead of him in San
Marco and others of his friars in other churches.

His opponents were much stronger than usual for
several reasons: first, because it is the habit of the
masses—when they have supported something for a
while—to turn their coat for no good reason. Then the
excommunication had alienated from him many who had
been his followers, and made enemies of those who used
to be neutral and indifferent, as they thought it a serious
matter, and improper for good Christians not to obey the
Pope's commands. The leaders of the opposing faction,
seeing that many high-spirited young men of quality
bearing arms were enemies of the friar, had gathered
them together in a band called the *compagnacci;* their
leader was Doffo Spini, and they often met and dined
together. As they were men of good family and bore
arms, they kept everyone in fear of them; so much so that
Paolantonio Soderini, who was passionately for the friar,
had his son Tommaso enter their company in order to
have a stake on their side in case of misfortune. For

these reasons Fra Girolamo's cause declined until his career came to an end in an extraordinary manner as I shall go on to relate.

Chapter XVI

[*The ordeal by fire. Death of Francesco Valori and popular riots. Arrest of Savonarola, his trial and execution. Judgment on him.*]

The year 1498 was full of many grave and varied events which opened with the downfall of Fra Girolamo. He had stopped preaching on the orders of the Signoria, and just when the violent persecution he suffered from both clerics and laymen seemed to have died down, a small incident gave rise to a complete reversal of his fortunes. About two years before, when preaching in Santa Liperata, Fra Domenico da Pescia, his companion in the Order of San Marco, who was a simple man with a reputation for living a saintly life and who followed Fra Girolamo's style in predicting future events in his sermons, had said that if it were necessary to prove the truth of what they foretold, they would revive a corpse and walk through fire unharmed through God's grace; and Fra Girolamo had later repeated this. Nothing had been said about this since, until one Fra Francesco of the Franciscan Order, who preached in Santa Croce and loathed Fra Girolamo and all his works, began to say in his sermons that to prove how false these were he was willing to walk through fire in the Piazza de' Signori if Fra Girolamo would do so too. He added that he was sure he would burn, but so would Fra Girolamo, and this would prove that there was no truth in him, as he had so often boasted that he would issue unhurt from the fire. Fra Domenico was told of this while he was preaching instead of Fra Girolamo; and so he accepted the challenge in the pulpit, offering not Fra Girolamo but himself for this experiment.

This pleased many citizens of both parties who wished these divisions to end and all the uncertainties to be settled once and for all. They began to negotiate with the two preachers about putting the trial into effect. Finally after much argument all the friars agreed that a fire should be lit, and for Fra Girolamo a friar of his Order should enter it, the choice of the representative being left to him. Likewise for the other side a Franciscan friar should be nominated by his superiors. Having decided also on the date, Fra Girolamo had permission from the Signoria to preach; and preaching in San Marco he showed the great importance of miracles and said that they should not be used except in dire necessity when reasoning and experience proved insufficient; as the Christian faith had been proved in infinitely varied ways, and the truth of the things he had predicted had been shown with such effect and reason that anyone who was not hardened in wickedness could understand them, he had not had recourse to miracles so as not to tempt God. Nevertheless, since they had now been challenged, they willingly accepted, and all could be sure that on entering the fire the result would be that their friar would come out alive and unharmed while the other would be burned. If the opposite happened, they might freely say that he had preached lies. He added that not only his friars but anyone who entered the fire in defense of this truth would have the same experience. And then he asked them whether, if need be, they would go through fire to support the cause of so great a work ordered by God. With a great cry nearly everyone present answered that they would. An amazing thing to think of, because without any doubt, if Fra Girolamo had told them to, very many would indeed have gone through fire. Finally on the appointed day, the ——[25] of April, which was the Saturday before Palm Sunday, a platform was set up in the middle of the Piazza de' Signori with a great bonfire of faggots. The Franciscans came at the appointed time and went into the loggia of the Signoria; and then the Dominican friars arrived, many of them robed, singing the psalm *Exurgat Dominus et dissipentur inimici eius*, and with them Fra Girolamo bearing the Host, in honor of which some friars and many lay-followers carried lighted torches. Their procession was so devout and

73

showed so clearly that they came to the trial with the highest courage, that it not only reassured their own followers but even made their enemies flinch.

When they had entered the loggia, separated however from the Franciscans by a wooden partition, some difficulty arose about the clothes Fra Domenico da Pescia was to wear to walk through he fire. The Franciscans were afraid they might be enchanted. As they could not agree, the Signoria repeatedly sent two citizens from each party to discuss their differences: Messer Francesco Gualterotti, Giovan Batista Ridolfi, Tommaso Antinori and Piero degli Alberti. When they had so arranged matters that agreement was near, they took the leaders of the friars into the palace and here resolved their difficulties and agreed on terms. But when they were about to start the ordeal, it came to the knowledge of the Franciscans that Fra Domenico was to enter the fire bearing the Host. They began vehemently to reject this proposal, arguing that if the Host were burned it would be a scandal and a grave danger to the whole Christian faith. On the other side Fra Girolamo continued to insist that he should carry it; and in the end after much argument, with both sides persisting in their own views and there being no way of reconciling them, they all went home without even lighting the bonfire. And although Fra Girolamo went at once into the pulpit and showed how the failure of the ordeal was due to the Franciscans and that the victory was his, many people thought that the question of the Host was a quibble rather than a genuine reason; he lost many of his friends that day and public opinion became very hostile to him. In consequence, on the following day his supporters were disillusioned, and were insulted in the streets by the populace, while his adversaries were much emboldened by popular support, and by having the backing of the Compagnacci under arms and a sympathetic Signoria in the palace. A friar of San Marco was to preach in Santa Liperata after dinner that day, when a great tumult arose as if by chance, spreading rapidly throughout the city as happens when people are excited and minds are full of doubt and suspicion. The enemies of the friar and the Compagnacci took up arms and be-

gan to drive the mob toward San Marco. Many of the
friar's followers were there at vespers, and they began to
defend the convent with weapons and stones although it
was not besieged. The fury of the mob then turned toward the house of Francesco Valori, which they attacked
while it was defended by those within. Francesco's wife,
the daughter of Messer Giovanni Canigiani, appeared at
a window and was struck in the head by a spear which
killed her instantly. Then the mob broke into the house
and found Francesco in an attic; he begged to be taken
alive to the palace and was brought outside. As he was
accompanied on his way by a guard, he had gone only a
few steps when he was attacked and killed by Vincenzio
Ridolfi and Simone Tornabuoni in revenge for their kinsmen, Niccolò Ridolfi and Lorenzo Tornabuoni. He was
also attacked by Jacopo di Messer Luca Pitti, a violent
supporter of the opposite party; but when he struck him
he was already dead.

Thus was shown in Francesco Valori a great example
of the reversal of fate. But a short time before he had
been undoubtedly the city's most important figure in
authority, following and popularity: then suddenly all
was changed. In the same day his house was sacked, his
wife killed before his eyes, and he himself almost at the
same moment basely murdered by his enemies; so that
many thought God had wished to punish him for having,
a few months earlier, refused the right to appeal against
their death sentence to Bernardo del Nero and the other
citizens of great authority who had long been his friends
and colleagues in government. This was a benefit introduced by a new law, and had been allowed to Filippo
Corbizzi, Giovanni Benizzi, and others, from whom it
might have been withheld with more justification considering their relative merits. And so, when circumstances
changed, Francesco was killed by their relatives. Yet they,
though executed without appeal, had been allowed to
state their case and had been condemned by judgment of
the magistrates and in a civil way; they had had time at
the end to take the sacrament and die like Christians.
But Francesco was killed in a skirmish by private hands
without being able to utter a word—and in such sharp

tumult and sudden calamity that he had no time to recognize let alone to reflect on his tragic downfall.

Francesco was a very ambitious and haughty man, so vehement and obstinate in his opinions that he pursued them without scruple, attacking and insulting all who opposed him. On the other hand he was a clever man and so free of corruption or the taint of taking other men's goods, that there have been few citizens in Florentine politics who can compare with him; and he was greatly and uncompromisingly devoted to the public good. Because of these virtues, added to the nobility of his family and the fact that he was childless, he enjoyed immense popularity for a time; but later his violent manner and his excessively free criticism and sharp words in a free city came to displease the people, and his popularity changed to blame which made it easier for the friar's enemies and the relatives of the five who had been beheaded to murder him.

When Francesco Valori had been killed and his house sacked, the fury of the mob turned toward the house of Paolantonio Soderini, who after Francesco was with Giovan Batista Ridolfi the leader of that party. However, many men of authority hurried thither who did not hate Paolantonio as they did Francesco, and the Signoria sent guards so that their impetus was checked. If it had not been it would have resulted in great damage to the city in general and the ruin of all the leaders of the friar's party in particular. Then the mob returned to San Marco, where a spirited defense was put up, and Jacopo de' Nerli had his eye put out with (I believe) a shot from a crossbow while leading all this disturbance against the friar with a great following of armed youths and disaffected citizens. At last, after many hours of fighting, they forced their way into San Marco and took as prisoners to the palace Fra Girolamo, Fra Domenico, and Fra Silvestro ——[26] of Florence, who, although he did not preach, was one of Fra Girolamo's intimates and was believed to know all his secrets.

When arms had been laid down after this victory and popular favor and power of government had been transferred to the Friar's enemies, they began to concern themselves with consolidating the present state of affairs. As this party did not trust the Ten and the Eight, regarding them as *piagnoni* (which was the name given to the friar's supporters at that time), they summoned the great council and elected a new Eight and Ten, all men trusted by those in power. Doffo Spini, leader of the Compagnacci, was made one of the Eight, and Benedetto de' Nerli, Piero degli Alberti, Piero Popoleschi, Jacopo Pandolfini and other devoted members of that faction were elected to the Ten. Here one should note that although Messer Guido and Bernardo Rucellai were their leaders and had more authority and following than any others—and had also secretly directed this revolt against the friar's party —neither of them got in when the Ten was elected. In their own districts they were beaten by Giovanni Canacci and Piero Popoleschi. So that, considering how fallacious the judgment of the people is and how much trouble and danger they had undergone without result, they were understandably more determined to save the citizens of the other party—as we shall presently explain.

About twenty citizens were then entrusted with the task of examining Fra Girolamo and his companions—all of them his direst enemies. Eventually, after they had given him a few drops on the *strappado*, without the Pope's permission, a few days later they drew up a document and published in the great council what they said they had extracted from him. This was signed by the vicars of Florence and Fiesole and by some of the principal friars of San Marco in whose presence the document had been read to Fra Girolamo; and when he was asked if it were true, he agreed that what was written down was true. The most important conclusions were to this effect: the things he had predicted he had not had from God or from revelation or any other divine means—they had been his own invention without the participation or knowledge of any other person lay or cleric; he had acted out of pride and ambition, and his purpose had been to provoke a general council of the Christian princes which should depose the Pope and reform the Church, and if he had been elected Pope he would have accepted; nevertheless he was much more desirous that the great reform should be carried out by his agency than that he should become Pope, because any man may be Pope—even one of little worth—but only a great man could be author and leader of such an endeavor; he had himself planned that to strengthen the government of the city a gonfalonier of justice should be created for life or for a long period, and he thought Francesco Valori more suitable than anyone else—though he disliked his character and overbearing manners. And after him he preferred Giovan Batista Ridolfi, though he disapproved of his high family connections; he had not proposed the ordeal by fire, but Fra Domenico had done so without his knowledge, and he had consented as he could not honorably withdraw and hoping that the Franciscans would be frightened into giving way; and yet he was sure that, if the ordeal were carried out, the Host borne in his friar's hands would save him. These were the conclusions against him; the rest were rather in his favor, for they showed that apart from pride there had been no vice of any kind in him, and that he was absolutely innocent of lust, avarice, and such sins. And further, that he had not had any political dealings either with princes abroad or citizens within.

When these proceedings had been published, his punishment was delayed for a few days because the Pope, having heard of his arrest and his confession, which were most pleasing to him, had sent his absolution not only to the citizens who had examined him without ecclesiastical license, but to those who had attended his sermons in defiance of the apostolic order. He had then asked that Fra Girolamo should be sent to Rome. This was refused, as it seemed dishonorable that our city should serve as a gaol. In the end he sent the general of the Dominicans and a certain Messer Romolino, a Spaniard whom he later created cardinal, as apostolic commissioners to Florence to examine Fra Girolamo and his companions. While awaiting their arrival, the Florentines began to deal with the case of the citizens who had been his followers. Although no fault could be discovered in them from Fra Girolamo's examination, nor any conspiracy of theirs against the state, nevertheless the voice of the mob was against them. Besides, many wicked citi-

zens who were in the palace and the councils wanted
to lay hands on them. Among them was Franceschino
degli Albizzi, who, the day Francesco Valori was killed,
came to the Signoria and said: "Your Worships have
heard what has happened to Francesco Valori; what do
you desire should be done now with Giovan Batista
Ridolfi and Paolantonio?" As if to say: if you wish, we
will go and kill them. On the other hand Messer Guido,
Bernardo Rucellai, the Nerli and those who in fact were
the leaders, were strongly in favor of preserving their
lives—mainly because, as many thought, they had believed that by overthrowing the friar the great council
would be destroyed, and that was why they had worked
so vigorously against him. But they were later disillusioned in this, for they saw that many of their followers
—the Compagnacci in particular—and all the people
wanted to keep the council. So they did not want to lay
hands on those citizens without any profit or increase of
power, especially as Messer Guido and Bernardo had had
the proof in the elections to the Ten of how much reliance they could place on popular favor. It was Bernardo's phrase that all the wrongs in this affair should be
taken off the citizens and loaded on the friar. It was
therefore decided after some argument and disagreement
that they should be spared; although, to satisfy the people, Giovan Batista, Paolantonio and a few other leaders
were condemned to make a loan of certain sums of
money. In this way the faction was quieted and Giovan
Batista and Paolantonio, who had gone away on their
friends' advice to allow popular hostility to die down, returned to Florence.

After that the new Signoria was elected with Vieri de'
Medici as Gonfalonier; and the Signoria included Messer Ormannozzo Deti, Pippo Giugni, Tommasi Gianni and
others. During this time the commissioners from Rome
arrived, and having re-examined Fra Girolamo and the
others, all three were condemned to be burned at the
stake. On the ——[27] day of May they were first degraded
in the Piazza de' Signori and then hanged and burned
before a greater crowd than used to come to their sermons. It was thought an astonishing thing that none

of them, particularly Fra Girolamo, should have said anything publicly on that occasion to accuse or excuse themselves.

Thus Girolamo Savonarola came to a shameful end; and perhaps it will not be out of place here to speak at greater length about his qualities, for we have not seen in our times—nor did our fathers and grandfathers in theirs—a monk so full of many virtues or with so much credit and authority as he enjoyed. Even his enemies admit that he was extremely learned in several branches of knowledge, especially philosophy, which he possessed so thoroughly and could use so aptly for all his own purposes as if he had invented it himself—but more particularly in Holy Scripture in which it is believed there had not been anyone to compare with him for several centuries. He had wonderfully sound judgment not only in scholarship but also in worldly affairs, in the principles of which he had great understanding, as in my opinion his sermons show. In this art of preaching he far excelled all others of his time with these qualities of his; for he also possessed an eloquence neither artificial nor forced, but natural and easy. In this he had a quite remarkable reputation and following, for he had preached not only the Lenten sermons but also for many feast days of the year for so many years on end, in a city full of most subtle and fastidious minds, where even excellent preachers tend to bore after a Lenten season or two at most. These qualities of his were so clear and manifest that his adversaries as well as his supporters and followers agree in their recognition of them.

But doubt and difference remain regarding the saintliness of his life. All that one can say about this is that if there was any vice in him it was simply that of inventing things out of pride and ambition. Those who long observed his life and habits found in them not the slightest trace of avarice or lust or any other sort of greed or weakness; on the contrary they saw in him a most religious life, full of charity and prayer and strict observance not of the outward forms of religion but of its very essence. And so, although in his trials his calumniators made every effort to discover faults in him, not the least trace of that kind of thing could be found. His endeavors in securing decent behavior were most holy and wonderfully successful; and there was never in Florence so much virtue and religion as in his time. After his death manners decayed to such an extent that it proved that what good was done had been brought in by and depended upon him. There was no public gambling, and only with restraint in private houses. The taverns, where all the vicious and ill-conducted youths tend to gather, were closed. Sodomy was suppressed and punished severely. Women to a great extent gave up indecent and lascivious dress. Boys were almost all reformed from many wicked ways and led to a decent and God-fearing life. They were gathered together in companies under the care of Fra Domenico, attended church, wore their hair short, and pursued with stones and insults wicked men and gamblers and immodestly dressed women. At carnival time they went about collecting dice, cards, cosmetics, indecent pictures and books, which they burned publicly in the Piazza de' Signori after a religious procession full of devotion on the day which used to be one of a thousand iniquities. Old men were all turned to religion, attending mass, vespers and sermons, and often going to confession and communion. At carnival time a vast number of people went to confession, and there was much giving of alms and charity. Every day he urged men to give up pomp and vanity and adopt a simplicity of living proper to devout Christians. To this effect he proposed laws to regulate dress and ornament in women and boys. These were so strongly opposed by his enemies that they were never passed by the council. At least the one about boys was; but it was never observed. Through his preaching a great number of friars entered his order—of every age and class, many noble youths from the leading families of the city, many men of advanced years and great reputation: Pandolfo Rucellai, who belonged to the Ten and was nominated ambassador to King Charles; Messer Giorgio Antonio Vespucci and Messer Malatesta, canons of Santa Liperata, good men of learning and gravity; Maestro Pietro

81

Paolo of Urbino, a doctor of great reputation and virtuous life; Zanobi Acciaiuoli, very learned in Greek and Latin letters; and many others like them. The result was that there was no convent like it in Italy; and he so directed the young men in their studies—not only of Greek and Latin but also of Hebrew—that they gave promise of being the very ornaments of religion. While he thus made a great contribution to spiritual affairs, he did no less good to the affairs of the city and to the public weal.

When Piero was driven out and the "parliament" called, the city was badly shaken and the friends of the former government were in such disrepute and danger that it seemed impossible to save a great number of them from violence, Francesco Valori and Piero Capponi being powerless to defend them. This would have been a great disaster for the city, as there were among them many good, wise and rich men of great families and connections. If that had happened, there would have been violent divisions among those who ruled the city—as was seen in the example of the Twenty—and they would have been divided because there were many of almost equal reputation who desired to be leader; innovations and "parliaments" would follow, expulsions of citizens, and several changes of government, and perhaps in the end the violent return of Piero with infinite destruction and slaughter. Fra Girolamo alone stopped these tendencies and impulses, introduced the great council, and so put a bridle on all those with ambitions; he imposed the appeal to the Signoria, which was a restraint to preserve the lives of the citizens. He secured universal peace, which was simply done by removing the opportunity for punishing the Medici adherents under color of going back to the old institutions.

Without any doubt these actions saved Florence; and as he very truly said, they benefited those who now ruled the city, as well as those who had ruled in the past. Indeed his works were so good, while in particular some of his prophecies turned out to be true, that many have continued for long to believe that he was really sent by God and a true prophet in spite of the excommunication, his trial and death. I am doubtful and I have not been able to make up my mind at all; I must wait—if I live long enough—for time to reveal the truth. But I draw this conclusion: if he were really a good man, then we have seen in our days a great prophet; if he were wicked, then we have seen a great man, because, apart from his learning, if he were able to feign in public for so many years so great a mission without ever being caught out in a falsehood, one must admit that he had a most remarkable judgment, talent, and power of invention.

With him were executed, as I have said, Fra Domenico and Fra Silvestro, of whom Fra Domenico was a most simple and holy man, such that, if he erred, it was from ingenuousness and not malice. Fra Silvestro was regarded as more astute and more in contact with the townspeople—and yet, according to the trials, unaware of any fraud. But they were killed to satisfy the rage of their enemies, who were commonly called at that time the Arrabbiati.

The History of Italy

BOOK I

Chapter I

[Aim and purpose of the work. Prosperity of Italy around 1490. The policy of Lorenzo de' Medici and the desire for peace among the princes of Italy. The alliance of the princes and the ambitions of Venice.]

I have decided to write about the events which have taken place in Italy within living memory since the time when French armies called in by our own princes began to trouble her peace with great upheavals. A very rich theme for its variety and extent, and full of appalling disasters, for Italy has suffered for many years every kind of calamity that may vex wretched mortals either through the just wrath of God or through the impious and wicked actions of their fellow men. From the understanding of these events, so diverse and grave, all men will be able to draw many useful lessons both for themselves and for the public good. It will appear from countless examples how unstable are human affairs—like a sea driven by the winds; how pernicious, nearly always to themselves but invariably to the common people, are the ill-judged actions of rulers when they pursue only vain error or present greed. And forgetting how often fortunate changes, and converting to other peoples harm the power vested in them for the public good, they become through lack of prudence or excess of ambition the authors of fresh upheavals.

The calamities of Italy began (and I say this so that I may make known what was her condition before, and the causes from which so many evils arose), to the greater sorrow and terror of all men, at a time when circumstances seemed universally most propitious and fortunate. It is indisputable that since the Roman Empire, weakened largely by the decay of her ancient customs, began to decline more than a thousand years ago from that greatness to which it had risen with marvelous virtue and good fortune, Italy had never known such prosperity or such a desirable condition as that which it enjoyed in all tranquillity in the year of Our Lord 1490 and the years immediately before and after. For, all at peace and quietness, cultivated no less in the mountainous and sterile places than in the fertile regions and plains, knowing no other rule than that of its own people, Italy was not only rich in population, merchandise and wealth, but she was adorned to the highest degree by the magnificence of many princes, by the splendor of innumerable noble and beautiful cities, by the throne and majesty of religion; full of men most able in the administration of public affairs, and of noble minds learned in every branch of study and versed in every worthy art and skill. Nor did she lack military glory according to the standards of those times; and being so richly endowed, she deservedly enjoyed among all other nations a most brilliant reputation.

Italy was preserved in this happy state, which had been attained through a variety of causes, by a number of circumstances, but among these by common consent no little credit was due to the industry and virtue of Lorenzo de' Medici, a citizen so far above the rank of private citizen in Florence that all the affairs of the Republic were decided by his advice. Florence was at that time powerful by virtue of her geographical position, the intelligence of her people and the readiness of her wealth rather than for the extent of her dominion. Lorenzo had lately allied himself through marriage to Pope Innocent VIII (who listened readily to his counsels); his name was respected throughout Italy and his authority was great in all discussions on matters of common interest. Knowing that it would be very dangerous to himself and to the Florentine Republic if any of the larger states increased their power, he diligently sought to maintain the affairs of Italy in such a balance that they might not favor one side more than another. This would not have been possible without the preservation of peace and without the most careful watch over any disturbance, however small. Ferdinand of Aragon, King of Naples,[28] shared his desire for universal peace—undoubtedly a most prudent and respected prince; though in the past he had often shown ambitious designs contrary to the counsels of peace, and at this time was being egged on by Alfonso, Duke of Calabria, his eldest son, who resented seeing his son-in-law, Giovan Galeazzo Sforza, Duke of Milan—now over twenty years of age though quite lacking in ability—merely keeping the title of duke and being overborne and crushed by Lodovico Sforza, his uncle. The latter, more than ten years earlier, had taken over the guardianship of the young Duke because of the imprudence and lewd habits of his mother Madonna Bona, and thus little by little had taken into his own hands the fortresses, soldiers, treasury, and all the instruments of power; and he now continued to govern, no longer as guardian or regent, but in everything except the title of Duke of Milan, with all the outward shows and actions of a prince. Nevertheless Ferdinand did not desire any upheaval in Italy, having more regard for present benefits than past ambitions or for his son's indignation, however well-founded. Perhaps because a few years earlier he had experienced, with the gravest danger, the hatred of his barons and his common subjects, and knowing the affection which many of his people still held for the name of the royal house of France, he was afraid that discord in Italy might give the French an opportunity to attack the Kingdom of Naples. Or perhaps he realized that to balance the power of the Venetians, which was then a threat to the whole of Italy, he must remain allied with the other states— particularly Milan and Florence. Lodovico Sforza, though of a restless and ambitious nature, must have shared this view, because the danger from the Venetian senate threatened the rulers of Milan no less than the others and because it was easier for him to maintain the power he had usurped in the tranquillity of peace than

87

in the vicissitudes of war. He always suspected the intentions of Ferdinand and Alfonso of Aragon, but knowing Lorenzo de' Medici's desire for peace and his fear of their power—and believing that because of the difference of attitude and ancient hatred between Ferdinand and the Venetians there was no fear that they might form an alliance—he felt fairly sure that the Aragonese would not find allies to attempt against him what they could not do alone.

Since there was the same will for peace in Ferdinand, Lodovico, and Lorenzo—partly for the same and partly for different reasons—it was easy to maintain an alliance in the name of Ferdinand, King of Naples, Giovan Galeazzo, Duke of Milan, and the Florentine Republic for the mutual defense of their states. This treaty, which was entered into many years before and subsequently interrupted for various reasons, had been renewed in 1480 for twenty-five years with the adherence of nearly all the small states of Italy. Its principal object was to prevent the Venetians from increasing their power, for they were undoubtedly greater than any one of the confederates, but much less so than all of them put together. They kept their own counsel, hoping to increase their power through friction and disunity among others, and stood ready to profit by any event which might open the way for them to the domination of the whole of Italy. It had been clear on more than one occasion that this was what they sought, especially when, on the death of Filippo Maria Visconti, Duke of Milan, they attempted to seize that state under color of defending the freedom of the Milanese; and more recently when in open war they tried to occupy the Duchy of Ferrara. It was easy for the confederation to curb the greed of the Venetian senate, but it did not unite the allies in sincere and faithful friendship, because—full of jealousy and rivalry —they constantly watched one another's movements, mutually thwarting every design whereby any one of them might increase its power or reputation. This did not make the peace any less stable, but rather inspired each with a greater promptness to put out any sparks which might be the origin of a new outbreak.

Chapter II

[*Death of Lorenzo de' Medici. Death of Pope Innocent VIII and election of Alexander VI. The policy of friendship of Piero de' Medici toward Ferdinand of Aragon and the first fears of Lodovico Sforza.*]

Such was the state of things, such the foundation of the peace of Italy, so arranged and juxtaposed that not only was there no fear of any present disorder but it was difficult to imagine how, by what plots, incidents or forces, such tranquillity might be destroyed. Then, in the month of April 1492 there occurred the death of Lorenzo de' Medici. It was bitter for him, because he was not quite forty-four years of age, and bitter for his republic, which, because of his prudence, reputation and intellect in everything honorable and excellent, flourished marvelously with riches and all those ornaments and advantages with which a long peace is usually accompanied. But it was also a most untimely death for the rest of Italy, both because of the work he constantly did for the common safety and because he was the means by which the disagreements and suspicions that frequently arose between Ferdinand and Lodovico—two princes almost equal in power and ambition—were moderated and held in check.

The death of Lorenzo was followed a few months later by that of the Pope, as day by day things moved toward the coming disaster. The pontiff, though otherwise of no value to the common weal, was at least useful in that— having laid down the arms he had unsuccessfully taken up against Ferdinand at the instigation of many barons of the Kingdom of Naples at the beginning of his tenure —he turned his attention entirely to idle pleasures, and had no longer either any ambitions for himself or his family which might disturb the peace of Italy. Innocent was followed by Rodrigo Borgia of Valencia, one of the royal cities of Spain. A senior cardinal and a leading figure at the court of Rome, he was raised to the papacy, however, by the disagreements between the cardinals Ascanio Sforza and Giuliano di San Piero in Vincoli, and much more by the fact that, setting a new example in that age, he openly bought, partly with money and partly with promises of offices and favors he would bestow, many of the cardinals' votes. These cardinals, despising the teachings of the Gospels, were not ashamed to sell the power to traffic with sacred treasures in God's holy name, in the highest part of the temple. Cardinal Ascanio led many of them into this abominable contract, no less by his own example than by persuasion and pleading. Corrupted by an insatiable appetite for riches, he got for himself as the price of such wickedness the vice-chancellery, the principal office of the Roman court, churches, castles and his own palace in Rome, full of furniture of enormous value. But for all that he did not escape either divine judgment later or the just hatred and contempt of the men of his time, who were full of horror and alarm at an election conducted with such wicked devices, no less so because the character and habits of the man elected were in great part known to many. It is well known that the King of Naples, though in public he hid his grief, told his wife with tears— which he was unaccustomed to shed even at the death of his children—that a pope had been elected who would be fatal to Italy and the whole Christian world: truly a prophecy not unworthy of the wisdom of Ferdinand. For Alexander VI (as the new Pope wished to be called) possessed remarkable sagacity and acumen, excellent counsel, marvelous powers of persuasion and incredible ability and application in all difficult enterprises; but these virtues were far outweighed by his vices: utterly obscene habits, neither sincerity nor shame nor truth nor faith nor religion, insatiable avarice, immoderate ambition, more than barbarous cruelty and a burning desire to advance his many children in any possible way. Some of them—so that to execute his depraved designs a depraved instrument should not be lacking—were in no way less abominable than their father.

Such were the changes brought about in the state of

the Church by the death of Innocent VIII. Yet the affairs of Florence had suffered no less a change by the death of Lorenzo de' Medici. Piero, the eldest of his three sons, had succeeded him without meeting any opposition. He was still very young and, both by age and other qualities unfit to carry such a burden; and he was unable to proceed with that moderation by which his father—in internal and foreign affairs, while prudently temporizing with the allied princes—had in his lifetime extended his public and private estate, and at his death left among all men the firm opinion that, principally through his efforts, the peace of Italy had been preserved. For hardly had Piero entered the administration of the Republic than, in direct opposition to his father's advice and without informing the principal citizens whose advice was always sought in grave matters—induced by Virginio Orsino his kinsman (both Piero's mother and his wife were of the Orsini family)—he so closely allied himself with Ferdinand and Alfonso, on whom Virginio was dependent, that Lodovico Sforza had just cause to fear that, whenever the Aragonese wished to attack him, they would have the forces of the Florentine Republic with them by authority of Piero de' Medici. This alliance, the germ and origin of so many evils, though it was at first negotiated and concluded with great secrecy, was almost immediately by obscure conjecture suspected by Lodovico Sforza, a most vigilant prince and of very acute intelligence.

When, according to the age-old custom of all Christendom, ambassadors were to be sent to pay homage to the new Pope as the Vicar of Christ on earth, Lodovico Sforza suggested that all the ambassadors of the allies should enter Rome together, and together present themselves at the public consistory before the Pope, and that one of them should speak for all so that in this way, and with great increase of reputation to all, the whole of Italy should see that there existed between them not merely friendship and alliance, but rather such unity that they seemed as one prince and one state. It was typical of Lodovico to endeavor to appear superior to everyone else in prudence by putting forward ideas no one else had thought of. The value of this plan, he said, was evident, because it had been believed that the late Pope had been encouraged to attack the Kingdom of Naples by the apparent disunity of the allies in having sworn obedience to him at different times and with different orations. Ferdinand made no difficulties about accepting Lodovico's suggestion, and the Florentines approved it on the authority of both, while Piero de' Medici said nothing against it in public council. Privately, however, he disagreed strongly, because as he himself was one of the representatives elected by the Republic and he had planned to make his own train most brilliant with fine and almost regal trappings, he realized that entering Rome and presenting himself before the Pope with the other ambassadors of the allies, he would not be able in such a crowd to display the splendor of his magnificent preparations. He was supported in this youthful vanity by the ambitious counsels of Gentile, bishop of Arezzo, likewise one of the chosen ambassadors. As it was to be his duty, on account of his episcopal office and his having professed those studies which are called the Humanities, to speak in the name of the Florentines, he was disappointed beyond measure to lose in this unexpected and unusual way the opportunity to show off his eloquence on an occasion so honorable and solemn. Therefore Piero, inspired partly by his own frivolity and partly by the ambition of others, and yet unwilling that Lodovico Sforza should learn that he was against his plan, asked the King to suggest that each party should act separately as had been done in the past, and to explain that he had thought it over and now felt that these proceedings could not be carried out together without great confusion, The King was anxious to please him, but not so anxious that he would incur Lodovico's displeasure; and so he complied more in the result than in the manner, for he did not hide the fact that it was only at Piero de' Medici's request that he went back on what he had at first agreed to do. Lodovico was angrier at this sudden change than the importance of the occasion merited in itself, complaining bitterly that as the Pope and the entire Roman court already knew of the first plan and who had put it forward, it was now being withdrawn on purpose to damage his reputation. He was even more displeased when he began to realize, through this small and really unimportant incident, that Piero de' Medici had a secret understanding with Ferdinand. And this became more evident every day from the events which followed.

Chapter III

[*Franceschetto Cibo sells his castles in Lazio to Virginio Orsino. The Pope's anger, stirred up by Lodovico Sforza. He tries to detach Piero de' Medici from his friendship with Ferdinand of Aragon. Alliance of Lodovico with the Pope and the Venetians. His plans to ensure his safety by means of foreign arms.*]

Franceschetto Cibo, a Genoese and the natural son of Pope Innocent, owned Anguillara, Cervetri, and a few other small castles near Rome. After his father's death he went to live in Florence under the protection of Piero de' Medici, who was the brother of his wife Maddalena. Soon after his arrival in that city, at Piero's instance, he sold those castles to Virginio Orsino for 40,000 ducats. This was negotiated primarily with Ferdinand, who secretly lent most of the money in the belief that it was to his advantage for Virginio, who was his own captain, supporter and kinsman, to extend his power in the neighborhood of Rome. The King thought that the papal power was an instrument very likely to disturb the Kingdom of Naples, an ancient fee of the Roman Church with an immensely long common frontier with the Church lands; and remembering the disputes he and his father had often had with the popes, and that there was always material at hand for fresh disagreements over frontier demarcation, levying of taxes, conferring of benefices, the petitions of the barons and many other differences which often arise between neighboring states and no less often between the feudal lord and his vassal, he always regarded as one of the bases of his own security that all or most of the most powerful barons of the Roman territory should be dependent on him. At this moment he pursued this aim the more readily, as it was thought that Lodovico Sforza's influence with the Pope would be very great through Cardinal Ascanio, his brother. Also perhaps, as many people thought, he was no less moved by fear that the hatred and greed of his uncle Pope Calixtus III might prove to be hereditary in Alexander. Calixtus, out of an overweening desire for the aggrandizement of his nephew Pietro Borgia, would have sent an army to occupy the Kingdom of Naples at the death of Ferdinand's father Alfonso, if his own death had not interrupted these plans. He claimed that Naples then reverted to the Church and forgot (so short is man's memory of the favors he has received) that it was through Alfonso himself, in whose dominions he was born and whose minister he had been for a long time, that he had obtained his other ecclesiastical preferments and considerable help in attaining the papacy. But it is all too true that wise men do not always discern or judge correctly: inevitably evidence of the weakness of the human mind must often appear. The King, though he was reputed to be a prince of great prudence, did not consider how much blame could be attached to that decision—which at best held hopes of small profit and at the worst could be the origin of serious trouble. For the sale of those insignificant castles aroused the desire for innovations in those very people who shared the common unity and harmony and in whose interests it would have been to ensure its preservation. The Pope asserted that, as they had been transferred without his knowledge, the lands had reverted to the Holy See according to the provisions of the law; feeling that a severe blow had been dealt to papal authority and considering moreover what Ferdinand's motives were, he filled the whole of Italy with complaints against him, against Piero de' Medici, and against Virginio. He swore that wherever his power reached, he would leave nothing undone to promote the dignity and interests of the Holy See.

Lodovico Sforza, who was always suspicious of Ferdinand's actions, was no less agitated; because having vainly deluded himself that the Pope would act according to the advice he and Ascanio gave, he felt that any diminution of Alexander's power would be his own loss. But above all he was worried by the fact that there was no longer room for doubt that the Aragonese and Piero de' Medici, since they worked together in matters of this kind, must have contracted a close alliance. He urged the pontiff as strongly as he could to preserve his own dignity in order to thwart their plans, which were a danger to his affairs, and to draw Alexander more closely to him. And he pointed out to him that he should bear in mind not so much the nature of the present incident, as the importance of the dignity of his high office having been thus openly insulted in the earliest days of his tenure of the Holy See by his own vassals. He should not believe that it was just Virginio's greed or the importance of the castles or any other motive which had inspired Ferdinand, but the desire to try his patience and his temper with insults which might at first seem small. After these, if the Pope put up with them, he would make bold from day to day to attempt something bigger. His ambitions were just the same as those of the other kings of Naples, who were perpetual enemies of the Roman Church; and they had repeatedly attacked the popes and several times occupied Rome. Had not this same King twice sent his armies against two popes under his son's command, right to the walls of Rome? Had he not always been in open enmity with his predecessors? Ferdinand was moved now not only by the example of former kings and by his natural desire for domination, but even more by his desire for revenge for the injury done him by the Pope's uncle Calixtus. The Pope should pay careful heed to these facts and consider that if he bore these early offenses with patience, honored only with outward shows and hollow deference, he would in fact be despised by everyone and give encouragement to more dangerous projects. But if he reacted strongly he would easily preserve the ancient majesty and greatness and the true veneration owed by all the world to the Roman pontiffs. To these powerful arguments he added even more efficacious deeds; for he promptly lent the Pope 40,000 ducats, and recruited 300 soldiers at their common expense, which should however be stationed wherever the Pope wished. Nevertheless, wishing to avoid the need to enter into fresh difficulties, he urged Ferdinand to persuade Virginio to pacify the Pope with some respectful gesture, pointing out that otherwise serious disturbances might arise from these small beginnings. More freely and with greater insistence he several times advised Piero de' Medici that, considering how expedient for the preservation of the peace of Italy had been his father Lorenzo's policy of acting as mediator and common friend between Ferdinand and himself, he should follow this domestic example and imitate a great man rather than, believing new counsel, give others cause or need to make plans which in the end must be harmful to all. He should remember how the long friendship between the houses of Sforza and Medici had ensured the security and reputation of both, and how many offenses and injuries his father and forefathers and the Florentine Republic had suffered at the hands of the house of Aragon—how often Ferdinand and Alfonso his father before him had attempted, sometimes by force, sometimes by treachery, to occupy the state of Tuscany.

These persuasions and counsels did more harm than good, because Ferdinand, thinking it undignified to give way to Lodovico and Ascanio, whose incitements he considered responsible for the Pope's anger, and urged on by his son Alfonso, secretly advised Virginio not to delay taking possession of the castles in accordance with the contract, and promised to protect him from any attack that might be made on him. On the other hand, with his natural cunning he suggested various kinds of settlement with the Pope, though meanwhile secretly advising Virginio only to agree to terms which would leave him the castles and compensate the Pope with sums of money. Thus Virginio was emboldened to refuse repeatedly the settlements which Ferdinand, so as not to offend the Pope unduly, pressed him to accept. It was evident that

in these negotiations Piero de' Medici followed the King's
line and that it was useless to try to make him change
his mind. Lodovico Sforza, therefore, realizing how serious it was that Florence should be influenced by his
enemies, since its attitude had in the past constituted
the principal basis of his security, and feeling that the
future held many dangers for him, decided to make
fresh provisions for his security. He knew how strongly
the Aragonese desired his removal from the management of his nephew's affairs. Although Ferdinand, who
brought to all his actions unbelievable guile and dissimulation, had tried to keep this feeling hidden, Alfonso, a man of a very open nature, had never refrained from lamenting openly the oppression of his
son-in-law, uttering, with more freedom than prudence,
threats and insults. Besides this Lodovico knew that Isabella, Giovan Galeazzo's wife, a vigorous young woman,
constantly stirred up her grandfather and her father,
saying that if they were not moved by the dishonor of
seeing her and her husband in such a position, they
should at least be moved by the danger to their lives
in which they stood together with their children. But
what most frightened Lodovico was the knowledge that
his name was loathed by all the people of the Duchy of
Milan, both because of the many unusual taxes he had
levied on them and because of the sympathy everyone
felt for Giovan Galeazzo, the legitimate prince. He tried
to make people believe that the Aragonese wanted to
take possession of the state of Milan and laid claim to
it through the ancient provisions of the will of Filippo
Maria Visconti who had made Alfonso, Ferdinand's father, his heir; and that to further this plan they wanted
to deprive his nephew of his title. Nevertheless he did
not succeed by these wiles in moderating the hatred
they had conceived of him, nor did he prevent them from
reflecting on the wickedness to which men are led by the
pestilential greed for power.

Therefore, after he had considered at length the state
of his affairs and the imminent dangers, setting aside
all other concerns, he gave all his attention to seeking
fresh alliances and support. Seeing a great opportunity

in the Pope's anger against Ferdinand and the desire
the Venetian senate was supposed to entertain that the
former alliance should be broken up (which had for so
long stood in the way of its ambitions), he proposed to
the Pope and the Venetians a new alliance for their
mutual advantage. However, the Pope's ruling passion,
over and above anger or any other feeling, was a bound-
less greed for the advancement of his sons. He loved
them excessively, and unlike the former popes who to
cover up their sinfulness somewhat, used to call them
nephews, he always called them sons and showed them
to everyone as such. Finding as yet no other opportunity
to begin his efforts in this direction, he was negotiating
to obtain as a bride for one of his sons one of Alfonso's
illegitimate daughters, with a dowry of some rich territory in the Kingdom of Naples. Until he finally lost all
hope of this, he lent his ear rather than his mind to the
alliance proposed by Lodovico. If he had achieved this
ambition, the peace of Italy might not have been destroyed so soon. Although Ferdinand was not against it,
Alfonso hated the ambition and pomp of the popes and
always refused to agree; and therefore, not showing
their distaste for the marriage but putting difficulties in
the way of the dowry, they failed to satisfy Alexander.
For this reason he was angry and decided to follow
Lodovico's advice, driven to it by greed and indignation
and in part by fear; for not only was Virginio Orsino
in the pay of Ferdinand and at that time extremely
powerful in all the Church territories through the excessive favors he enjoyed from the Florentines and from
Ferdinand and through the following of the Guelph
faction, but also Prospero and Fabrizio, the heads of the
Colonna family. Furthermore the cardinal of San Piero
in Vincoli, a cardinal of the highest reputation who had
withdrawn to the fort of Ostia which he held as bishop
of that place, out of fear that the Pope might have designs on his life, had become very friendly with Ferdinand after having been his dire enemy and incited against
him in the past first his uncle Pope Sixtus and later
Pope Innocent. The Venetian senate, however, was not
as ready as had been supposed for this confederation;

because although the disunity of others might please
them well, they were given pause by the unreliability
of the Pope, who grew daily more suspect to all, and by
the memory of the leagues they had made with Sixtus
and Innocent his immediate predecessors. From the former they had got much trouble without any advantage;
and Sixtus, when the war against the Duke of Ferrara
was at its height—which he at first had urged them to
undertake—had then changed his mind and turned
against them with spiritual arms, and also had taken up
temporal arms against them together with the rest of
Italy. But Lodovico's diligence and industry overcame
all the difficulties with the senate and privately with
many of the senators. Finally in April 1493 there was
signed between the Pope, the Venetian senate and
Giovan Galeazzo Duke of Milan (all the decisions of
that state were taken in his name) a new league for
mutual defense and specifically for the maintenance of
Lodovico's rule, with the provision that the Venetians
and the Duke of Milan each were to send at once to
Rome two hundred men at arms for the safety of the
ecclesiastical state and the Pope, and help him with
these and if need be with larger forces to retake the
castles occupied by Virginio.

These new deliberations had a notable effect throughout the whole of Italy because the Duke of Milan was
now cut off from the alliance which for twelve years
had maintained common security—although by it, it was
expressly forbidden for any of the members to make new
alliances without the consent of the others. Therefore,
seeing that union on which the balance of power depended broken into unequal parts and the minds of the
princes full of suspicion and anger, what else could
one expect but that from such seeds like fruits must
grow to the detriment of all Italy? The Duke of Calabria
and Piero de' Medici, thinking it was safer to forestall
than be forestalled, were inclined to listen to Prospero
and Fabrizio Colonna. They, secretly encouraged by the
Cardinal of San Piero in Vincoli, offered to occupy Rome
by surprise with the men at arms of their companies and
the men of the Ghibelline faction—provided the Orsini

forces followed them, and the Duke took up a position whence, three days after they entered the city, he could come to their assistance. However, Ferdinand wished not to irritate the Pope further but to pacify him and to put right what had been done imprudently up to that time; and he absolutely rejected these counsels which he thought would engender not safety but greater trials and dangers. He made up his mind to do all he could, no longer merely in appearance but in fact, to make up the quarrel over the castles, believing that if that cause of so much discord were removed, Italy would easily and almost of herself return to her earlier condition. But one may not always remove the effects by removing their causes. For, as it often happens that decisions taken through fear seem unequal to the danger to those who fear, Lodovico was not sure he had found adequate support for his security. Doubting, because the purposes of the Venetian senate and the Pope were so different from his own, that he could rely for very long on the alliance with them, and that therefore his affairs might for various reasons meet with many difficulties, he applied his mind more to curing from the roots the first ill which appeared than to those which might in consequence arise later. He forgot how dangerous it may be to use medicine more powerful than the nature of the disease and the constitution of the patient warranted. As though embarking on greater risks was the sole remedy to present dangers, he decided, in order to ensure his own security with foreign arms—as he could not rely on his own forces and his Italian allies—to do everything he could to persuade Charles VIII King of France to attack the Kingdom of Naples, to which he laid claim through the ancient rights of the Angevins.

Chapter IV

[*The Kingdom of Naples up to the time of Ferdinand and the rights of succession of the House of Anjou. Charles VIII's claims on the Kingdom encouraged by Lodovico Sforza. The great nobles of*

the Kingdom of France oppose the expedition.
Pacts concluded between Charles VIII and Lodo-
vico Sforza. The author's views.]

The Kingdom of Naples is absurdly described in the
investitures and bulls of the Roman Church—of which
it is an ancient fee—as the Kingdom of Sicily east of
the Punto del Faro. After it had been unjustly occupied
by Manfred, the natural son of the Emperor Frederick
II, it was conceded in fee together with the island of
Sicily, under the title of the Two Sicilies, from the year
1264, by Pope Urban IV to Charles, Count of Provence
and Anjou. He was the brother of that King Louis of
France who, famous for his power but even more so for
the saintliness of his life, deserved after his death to be
numbered among the saints. The Count of Provence effectively obtained by armed force what had been bestowed on him by title with legal authority; and after
his death the Kingdom of Naples passed to his son
Charles, whom the Italians called Charles II to distinguish him from his father; and after him to his
grandson Robert. After that, Robert, having died without sons, was succeeded by Giovanna daughter of Charles
Duke of Calabria who had pre-deceased his father. Her
authority was soon held in contempt no less for her
immoral conduct than for the weakness of her sex. On
this account many disputes and wars arose over the
years, but only among the descendants of Charles I, the
children of various sons of Charles II. Giovanna, deciding it was the only way of defending her kingdom,
adopted as her son Louis Duke of Anjou, the brother of
Charles V of France whom the French called The Wise
because he had suffered little misfortune and gained
many victories. Giovanna met a violent death and the
kingdom passed to Charles of Durazzo, who was also
a descendant of Charles I. When Louis entered Italy with
a very powerful army and victory was almost in his
grasp, he died of fever in Puglia, so that the Angevins
gained nothing from this adoption but the County of
Provence which had been continuously in the possession
of the descendants of Charles I. Nevertheless this was

the origin of the claim by virtue of which Louis of Anjou, the son of the first Louis, and later his grandson of the same name, encouraged by the popes when they quarreled with the kings of Naples, repeatedly attacked the kingdom, though with little success. However, Charles of Durazzo had been succeeded by his son Ladislao; and when he died childless in 1414, the crown passed to his sister Giovanna II. This was an unlucky name for that kingdom, and unlucky too to both those who bore it, for they were alike in imprudence and the lewdness of their habits. Giovanna placed the government of her kingdom in the hands of those to whom she shamelessly abandoned her body, and soon fell into such difficulties that, harassed by the third Louis of Anjou with the help of Pope Martin V, she was forced as a last resort to adopt as her son Alfonso, King of Aragon and Sicily. Soon, however, she quarreled with him and canceled the adoption on grounds of ingratitude. Then she adopted and called to her aid that same Louis for fear of whose attack she had been obliged to make the first adoption. Alfonso was driven out of the realm by armed force, and Giovanna enjoyed her kingdom in peace for the rest of her life.

When she died childless, she made (it was said) René Duke of Anjou and Count of Provence her heir. This was the brother of her adopted son Louis who happened to die in the same year. Many of the barons of the kingdom disapproved of the succession of René, and it was rumored that her will was a forgery of the Neapolitans, so Alfonso was called in by some of the barons and the people. This was the origin of the wars between Alfonso and René, which afflicted that noble kingdom for many years, and were waged by them with the resources of the kingdom itself rather than with their own. From this arose the factions of the Aragonese and Angevins, which are still not entirely extinct in our own day. In the course of the years the titles and appearances of right varied because the popes, following their own greedy impulses or the needs of the times rather than considerations of justice, accorded the investiture now to one and now to the other side. However, Alfonso, a more able and powerful prince, was victorious in the war with René, and when he died without legitimate issue, he forgot his brother John who had succeeded to the Kingdoms of Sicily and Aragon, and left the Kingdom of Naples as his personal acquisition and therefore not the property of the crown of Aragon to his natural son Ferdinand. Almost immediately after his father's death he was attacked by Jean, René's son, supported by the principal barons of the realm, but not only did he defend himself with great success and courage, but he defeated his enemies so soundly that never again in René's lifetime (and he survived his son by several years) did he have to fear the Angevins or fight them. In the end René died; and being without male heirs he made Charles his brother's son heir to all his states and rights. The latter died shortly after without children and willed his inheritance to Louis XI King of France, who not only acquired by reversion as its feudal overlord the Duchy of Anjou, where, being crown lands, women may not inherit, but (although the Duke of Lorraine, who was the son of a daughter of René, asserted that the succession of the other states should be his) he also took possession of Provence, and could, by the terms of the will, claim that the Angevins' rights in the Kingdom of Naples reverted to him. These passed on his death to his son Charles VIII, in whom Ferdinand gained a considerable adversary, and a great opportunity was thus available to anyone who wished to attack him.

The Kingdom of France was at that time richer in men, in military glory, in power, in wealth, in authority among other kingdoms, than perhaps it had ever been since Charlemagne. She had recently extended her power in each of those three parts into which, according to the ancient writers, Gaul was divided. Only forty years before, under Charles VII—a king called The Fortunate on account of the many victories he gained in the face of grave dangers—Normandy and the Duchy of Guienne, which formerly belonged to the English, were added to the kingdom; and in the last years of Louis XI the County of Provence, the Duchy of Burgundy and nearly all Picardy; and after that, by a marriage of Charles VIII,

the Duchy of Brittany. Charles was not at all unwilling
to attempt to acquire by force the Kingdom of Naples
as his own rightful property. The idea had been with
him almost instinctively since childhood, and had been
nourished by the encouragement of certain people who
were very close to him. They filled him up with
vain ideas and made him believe this was an opportunity to surpass the glory of his predecessors, as,
once he had conquered the Kingdom of Naples, he could
easily defeat the empire of the Turks. These plans, already known to many, gave Lodovico Sforza the hope of
easily persuading him to do what he wished. Besides, he
could rely on the reputation of his family with the
French court, because he and his brother Galeazzo before him had kept up the friendship founded by Francesco Sforza their father, with many good offices and
tokens of good will. Thirty years earlier Francesco Sforza
had received in fee from Louis XI—who always loathed
everything Italian—the city of Savona and the rights he
claimed over Genoa, which had formerly been held by
his father, and he had never failed the King in time of
danger with assistance and good advice. Nevertheless
Lodovico thought it was dangerous to be the only one to
start a movement of such gravity; and so, in order to
negotiate the affair in France with more credit and
authority, he sought first to win over the Pope to this
cause with the spur of ambition and anger. He pointed
out to him that he would never, either with the support
of the Italian princes or their forces, have any hope of
revenging himself on Ferdinand or of acquiring worthy
states for his children. Having found him well disposed
either through a desire for innovations or to obtain from
the Aragonese through fear what they refused to give
spontaneously, they secretly sent trusted men to France
to sound the King and those who were in his confidence.[29] When they showed themselves not unwilling,
Lodovico, full of enthusiasm for this plan, openly sent
to France as ambassador Carlo da Barbiano Count of
Belgioioso, although the purpose of his mission was given
as something quite different. After he had been at court
several days and had exercised his persuasions with

Charles in private and with the most important people, he was at last brought into the royal council in the King's presence, where besides the royal ministers there were present all the lords and many prelates and nobles of the court. And there he is said to have spoken as follows:

"If anyone for any reason, most Christian King, should mistrust the good faith and sincerity with which Lodovico Sforza urges you to the conquest of the Kingdom of Naples, offering also money and the assistance of his forces, he will easily dispel such ill-founded suspicions when he remembers the long-standing loyalty of Lodovico himself and his brother Galeazzo, and before that of Francesco his father, toward Louis XI your father, and then toward your own most glorious name; and all the more, considering that Lodovico may sustain grievous loss from this enterprise without hope of any profit, while for you yourself the chances are just the opposite. Victory would bring you a fine kingdom with infinite glory and the chance of still greater things; but Lodovico would gain nothing but a just revenge against the intrigues and offenses of the Aragonese. If, on the other hand, the attempt should prove unsuccessful, your greatness would not be diminished at all. But who does not realize that in that event Lodovico, hated by many and despised by all, would have no remedy for the danger he would be in? Therefore, how can there be mistrust of the counsel of one who in any event stands to gain less or to lose more than yourself? Yet the arguments in favor of your embarking on so honorable an expedition are so clear and powerful in themselves that they admit of no doubt, for all the foundations are abundantly there, which must principally be considered in deciding on such enterprises: the justice of the cause, the ease of success, the rich reward of victory. For it is well known to all how strong are the claims of the House of Anjou to the Kingdom of Naples, to which you are the legitimate heir, and how just is the succession which claims it for the descendants of Charles. He first of the royal blood of France obtained that kingdom with the authority of the Roman pontiffs and the prowess of his own arms. The ease of conquest is no less than the justice of the cause. Who does not know how much weaker in armed strength and authority is the King of Naples than the first and most powerful of all Christian monarchs? How great and terrible the name of the French throughout the world, how much feared your arms among all nations? The petty Dukes of Anjou never attacked the Kingdom of Naples without reducing it to the gravest danger. It is in recent memory how Jean son of René had victory in his grasp against the present Ferdinand, if it had not been taken from him by Pope Pius and even more by Francesco Sforza who acted in this, as is well known, in accordance with the wishes of Louis XI your father. What then will the armies of so great a king not accomplish, when the opportunities are so much greater than those René and Jean enjoyed and the difficulties so much less, and now that those princes are allied with you, who prevented their victory, and who can attack the Kingdom of Naples with the utmost ease? The Pope can do so by land because of the proximity of the Church estates, and the Duke of Milan by sea from Genoa. No one in Italy will oppose you, for the Venetians will not want to face the expense and danger nor lose the friendship they have long held for the kings of France, to preserve Ferdinand who is their enemy; while it is impossible that the Florentines should abandon their natural affection for the House of France. And even if they wanted to oppose you, what could they do against such power? How often has your most warlike nation crossed the Alps against the will of all Italy, and still with inestimable glory and success carried off great victories and triumphs! When was the Kingdom of France happier, more glorious, more powerful than now? And when was it easier for her to make lasting peace with all her neighbors? If all these factors had come together in the past, your father would perhaps have been ready to undertake this same expedition.

"The enemy's difficulties are increased in the same proportion as your advantages, because the Angevin party is still powerful in that realm, the followers are strong of the many princes and nobles unjustly driven out a few years ago, and because such grievous harm has been continually done by Ferdinand to the barons and the people and even to those of the Aragonese faction. So great is his treachery, his avarice so immoderate, so horrible and frequent the instances of his cruelty and that of Alfonso his eldest son, that it is well known that the entire kingdom, moved by incredible hatred of them and remembering from recent experience the liberality, the kindness, the generosity, the humanity and the justice of the French, will rise with unbounded joy at the rumor of your coming, so that the mere decision to make the expedition will be enough to secure your victory. For when your armies have crossed the mountains, when the navy has gathered at Genoa, Ferdinand and his sons, terrified by the thought of their own wickedness, will think rather of flight than of defending themselves. So with the greatest of ease you will have recovered a kingdom which, though it may not be compared with the greatness of France, is yet a large and wealthy state, and one to be valued all the more for the profit and infinite usefulness it will bring to this kingdom. I would describe all these benefits, were it not well known that French generosity has higher aims, that so magnanimous and glorious a King has worthier and more noble thoughts, aimed not at his own gain but at the universal greatness of the entire Christian republic. What better opportunity could be found for this? What greater occasion? What place more convenient, more suitable for waging war against the enemies of our faith? It is well known that in some places the sea between the Kingdom of Naples and Greece is only seventy miles wide. From that province torn and oppressed by the Turks, its only desire to see the Christian banners, how easy it would be to penetrate the vitals of that nation, to strike at Constantinople, heart and head of that empire! Who better than you, most powerful King, should turn his thoughts and spirit to this holy enterprise because of the marvelous power which God has given you, the most Christian name you bear, and the example of your glorious predecessors? Often issuing forth in arms from this kingdom now to free God's Holy Church oppressed

107

by tyrants, now to attack the infidel, now to recover the
Holy Sepulchre, they raised to the skies the fame and
majesty of the Kings of France. With these counsels,
with these devices, these actions, these purposes, the
great and glorious Charles became Roman Emperor. And
as you bear his name, now is your opportunity to acquire his glory and title. But why do I waste more time
on these arguments, as though it were not more natural
an instinct to preserve than to acquire? For who does
not know what infamy it would be—especially when so
great an opportunity invites you—to allow any longer
that Ferdinand should occupy a kingdom of yours, which
has been in the possession of kings of your blood by
continuous succession for little less than two hundred
years, and is clearly yours by law? Who does not know
how much your dignity demands that you retake it, and
what a pious action it would be to free those peoples,
who revere your glorious name and are by rights your
subjects, from the bitter tyranny of the Catalans? Therefore the enterprise is most just, most easy, and necessary.
And it is no less glorious and holy, both in itself and
because it opens the way to deeds worthy of a Most
Christian King of France. To these not only men but
God openly calls you, O great King; it is God who leads
you with such wonderful and obvious opportunities, offering you the greatest success before you even begin.
What greater happiness can any prince know than that
the designs from which his own glory and greatness are
to grow are accompanied by circumstances and consequences such that they appear to be undertaken equally
for the benefit and safety of all men, and even more
for the glorification of the whole Christian republic?"

This proposal was not heard with pleasure by the
great lords of France, particularly by those who for their
rank and reputation for wisdom enjoyed the greatest
authority. They thought it could only be a war of infinite difficulty and danger, as the armies would have
to go into a foreign country so far away from France
against highly respected and powerful enemies. Ferdinand's reputation for sagacity was enormous, and no
less was Alfonso's for skill in military affairs. It was

believed that Ferdinand, having ruled for thirty years and dispossessed at various times so many barons, must have accumulated vast quantities of treasure. They thought that the King was incapable of bearing by himself so heavy a burden, and that the counsel and experience of those who had influence with him more from favoritism than good reason, were inadequate for the management of wars and states. Furthermore he lacked money, of which they calculated a vast amount would be required. It had to be remembered how cunning and artful the Italians were, and borne firmly in mind that not only the other princes but Sforza himself—who was well known in Italy for faithlessness besides other things —could not really want the Kingdom of Naples in the hands of a King of France. Hence conquest would be hard, and holding it even harder. For this reason Louis, Charles' father, a prince who had always pursued the substance rather than the shadow of things, had never accepted the lures offered him in Italy nor valued the rights he had inherited in the Kingdom of Naples, but had always maintained that to send armies across the mountains was merely to buy trouble and danger at the cost of infinite blood and treasure of the Kingdom of France. It was essential before all else, if one were going to undertake this expedition, to compose their differences with neighboring kings. For there was no lack of causes for disagreement and distrust with Ferdinand King of Spain, and there were not only rivalries but many grievances with Maximilian King of the Romans and Philip Archduke of Austria, his son; and they could not be reconciled to friendship without concessions harmful to the French crown. Even so they might be reconciled more in appearance than in fact; for what agreement could ensure that, if the royal armies met with some difficulties in Italy, they would not attack France? It was not to be expected either that Henry VII King of England would not be influenced more by the natural hatred of the English for the French than by the peace they had made with him a few months earlier. It was clear that he had been persuaded to make it, more than anything else, by the fact that the preparations of the

King of the Romans did not match the promises with which he had induced him to lay siege to Boulogne.

These and other arguments like them were used by the great nobles, among themselves and to the King, to dissuade him from the new war. Among its opponents whose influence was strongest, was Iacopo Gravilla, Admiral of France, whose long-standing reputation for wisdom throughout the kingdom preserved his authority, though his greatness was somewhat diminished. Nevertheless Charles listened greedily to the other view. He was only twenty-two, little gifted by nature with understanding of human affairs, and carried away by a burning desire for conquest and the appetite for glory, based more on whim and impulse than on mature thought. Either of his own inclination or because of his father's example and advice he placed little reliance on the princes and nobles of his kingdom after he had outgrown the tutelage of the Duchess Anne of Burgundy, his sister; and no longer paying heed to the advice of the Admiral and others who had been influential in that government, he managed his affairs with the counsel of some men of low rank, almost all of them raised in his personal service. His favorites among them strongly urged him to undertake the expedition; some because— as the counsellors of princes are often venal—they had been corrupted by the gifts and promises of Lodovico's ambassador who neglected no art or effort to win over those who could influence the decision; and some because they had hopes either of obtaining lands in the Kingdom of Naples or of receiving from the Pope ecclesiastical preferment and revenues. The chief of all these was Etienne de Vesc of Languedoc, a man of low birth brought up for many years in the King's chamber and created by him Seneschal of Beaucaire. Another supporter was Guillaume Briçonnet, who from being a merchant had become first General of France, and then bishop of St. Malo. He was not only head of the administration of the royal revenues, which the French call the finances, but together with Etienne and through his influence, he had a hand in all the most important affairs, although he had very little talent for matters of state. They were also supported by Antonello da San Severino, Prince of Salerno, and by Bernardino of the same family, Prince of Bisignano, and many other barons in exile from the Kingdom of Naples. They had taken refuge in France many years earlier and had constantly pressed Charles to undertake this expedition, urging that the kingdom was in a bad way, in fact practically desperate, and that they would receive strong support and following there. Amid these differences of opinion the decision remained in suspense for several days. Not only were the others doubtful as to what should be done, but Charles himself was vacillating and uncertain. Sometimes he was urged on by the desire for glory and empire, now he was held back by fear; sometimes he was undecided, sometimes he decided the very opposite of what he seemed at first to have resolved. Yet in the end his first impulse proved stronger than any opposition, and so did the unhappy destiny of Italy. He rejected all counsels of peace and concluded an agreement with Lodovico's ambassador, but kept it secret from all but the bishop of St. Malo and the Seneschal of Beaucaire. The terms of this agreement were kept hidden for several months, but the substance was that, when Charles entered Italy or sent an army to conquer Naples, the Duke of Milan was bound to give him passage through his state and contribute 500 paid soldiers, allow him to fit out as many ships as he liked at Genoa, and lend him, before he left France, 200,000 ducats. On the other hand the King pledged himself to defend the Duchy of Milan against all comers, with particular mention of preserving Lodovico's authority, and to keep in Asti, the Duke of Orléans' city, while the war lasted, 200 lances[31] which should be ready if necessary to defend that state. Either then or not long after, in a document signed by his own hand, he promised that when he had taken the Kingdom of Naples, he would cede to Lodovico the Principality of Taranto.

It is certainly not wasted or unrewarding effort to consider how times and things change. Francesco Sforza, Lodovico's father, a prince of rare prudence and ability, was an enemy of the Aragonese because of the grave injuries he received at the hands of Alfonso, Ferdinand's father, and an old friend of the Angevins. Nevertheless, in 1457, when Jean the son of René attacked the Kingdom of Naples, he supported Ferdinand so promptly that final victory was largely due to him. His only reason for doing so was that it seemed to him too dangerous to his own Duchy of Milan for his close neighbors the French to occupy a state so powerful in the affairs of Italy. The same motive had earlier led Filippo Maria Visconti to abandon the Angevins—whom he had hitherto favored— and to free Alfonso his enemy. The latter had been captured by the Genoese in a naval battle off Gaeta and had been brought a prisoner to Filippo Maria in Milan with all the nobles of his kingdom. On the other hand Charles' father Louis, though many had often urged him with strong chances of success to conquer Naples and although the Genoese had insistently invited him to rule their state which had been held by his father Charles, had always refused to become involved in the affairs of Italy, regarding it as full of expense and difficulty and in the end harmful to the kingdom of France. Now men's opinions had changed, though not perhaps the logic of things. Lodovico was calling on the French to cross the mountains, unafraid of a most powerful King of France holding Naples, where his own father, most valiant in arms, had feared to let it fall into the hands of a little count of Provence; while Charles burned with ambition to make war in Italy, preferring the temerity of low-born unqualified men to the counsels of his father, a king of great prudence and long experience. It is certain that Lodovico, likewise, was encouraged in his action by his father-in-law, Ercole d'Este Duke of Ferrara, who was longing to recover the Polesine of Rovigo —lands bordering on Ferrara and most vital to her security, which had been taken from him by the Venetians in his war with them ten years before. He realized that the only way of recovering it was a complete upheaval of the whole of Italy. Many believed, however, that Ercole, though he feigned great friendship for his son-in-law, nevertheless secretly loathed him because in the war we have mentioned—whereas the rest of Italy which had taken up arms on his behalf was far superior in strength to the Venetians—Lodovico, who was already ruling the state of Milan, moved by his own interests, forced the others to make peace with the condition that the Venetians should keep the Polesine. So Ercole, who could not revenge himself by force of arms, now perhaps sought to do so by giving him fatal advice.

Chapter V

[*Public declarations of preparedness for defense and secret worries of Ferdinand of Aragon. His action to avert the danger and reconcile himself with the Pope and Lodovico Sforza. The King of France makes up his differences with the King of Spain, the King of the Romans and the Archduke of Austria. The investiture of Lodovico Sforza as Duke of Milan. Embassy of Perron de Baschi to the Pope, the Venetian senate and the Florentines. Piero de' Medici and the demands of the King of France. The alliance between the Pope and Ferdinand of Aragon begins to weaken.*]

As rumors of what was being planned beyond the Alps were already beginning to spread in Italy—though at first from unreliable sources—people took up a wide variety of attitudes. Many thought it a matter of the greatest significance, because of the power of the Kingdom of France, the readiness of that nation for new enterprises and the divisions among the Italian peoples. Others regarded it more as a youthful impulse than a considered decision, and thought that when it had boiled up for a while, it would easily pass off. Their reasons for thinking so were the age and character of the King, the natural unreliability of the French and the difficulties which always beset great enterprises. Ferdinand, against whom all this was being contrived, did not show much fear, saying that it would be a very difficult campaign because if they intended to attack him from the sea they would find him provided with a fleet large enough to fight them in the open sea, and the ports well

113

fortified and all in his hands: there was no baron in the country who could let them in as Jean d'Anjou had been by the Prince of Rossano and other great nobles. The expedition by land would be difficult, long and risky, since the whole length of Italy had to be traversed, so that every state would have cause to fear, and perhaps Lodovico Sforza most of all—although he pretended that the common danger applied only to others, because Milan was so near to France, and the King would find it easier and probably be more anxious to occupy it. As the Duke of Milan was so closely related to him, how could Lodovico be sure that the King did not intend to free him from Lodovico's oppression? Especially as just a few years before the King had openly stated that he would not allow his cousin Giovan Galeazzo to be so unjustly oppressed. The affairs of the Aragonese were not in such straits that the hope of their weakness should give the French courage to attack them, as he was well supplied with many fine troops, plenty of chargers, munitions, artillery, and all provisions needed for war, and so much money that he could easily obtain further supplies of anything he needed. Besides numerous able captains in his service, he had at the head of his armies his eldest son the Duke of Calabria, an officer of great renown and no less courage, with many years of experience in all the wars of Italy. To his own resources must be added the ready assistance of his relatives, since it was not likely that he would lack the help of the King of Spain, his cousin and his wife's brother, both on account of their close kinship and because he would not care to have the French so near to Sicily.

This was what Ferdinand was saying in public, exaggerating his own power and belittling as far as he could the strength and chances of his enemies. But as he was a king of remarkable prudence and very great experience, inwardly he was tormented by serious doubts, remembering the difficulties he had had with France at the beginning of his reign. He really believed that the war would involve him with an enemy who was extremely aggressive and powerful, far superior to himself in cavalry, foot soldiers, navies, artillery, money, and men full of ambition to expose themselves to any danger for the glory and greatness of their king. He on the other hand could rely on nothing, as his kingdom was full of hatred for the name of Aragon or strong sympathy for the rebels, and the majority of his people in any case always eager for a change. Fortune would weigh more than fidelity with them, and common opinion of his situation more than reality. The funds he had amassed would not cover the expenses of defense, and as rebellion and tumult would break out everywhere because of the war, in a flash all his revenues would vanish. He had many enemies in Italy, and not one reliable and constant friendship. Who had not been damaged at one time or another by his arms or intrigues? From Spain, as past experience and the conditions of that kingdom showed, he could hope for no other assistance in his peril than generous promises and great talk of preparations—but only small and tardy results. His fear was increased by many predictions of misfortune to his house, which had come to his notice at different times, partly through newly discovered ancient writings, partly through the words of men who, often unsure of the present, claim certain knowledge of the future: things which in prosperous times are little believed, but gain all too much credence when adversity comes. Anguished by these considerations, and fear seeming incomparably greater to him than hope, he realized that the only remedy to these dangers was either to dispel such thoughts from the mind of the King of France by making an agreement as soon as possible, or to remove some of the causes which incited him to war. He already had ambassadors in France, sent there to negotiate the betrothal of Ciarlotta, the daughter of his second son Don Federigo, to the King of Scotland. As this girl was the daughter of a sister of Charles' mother and had been brought up at the French court, the matter was being handled there. Ferdinand gave these ambassadors further instructions in these affairs, and sent out in addition Cammillo Pandone who had been to France before for him. He was secretly to offer the nobles great gifts and bribes, and if there were no other way of pacifying him, he was to do all he could to make peace with the King by offering him terms of tribute and other tokens of submission. Furthermore, not only did he intervene with all his energy and authority to settle the quarrel over the castles bought by Virginio Orsino, whose obstinacy he lamented as having been the cause of all the upheavals, but he also reopened with the Pope their former negotiations for a marriage alliance. But his main care and attention was directed toward mollifying and reassuring Lodovico Sforza, the origin and prime instigator of all the trouble, for he believed that it was fear more than anything else that had led him to so dangerous a step. So placing his own safety before the interests of his granddaughter and the safety of her child, he offered Lodovico through various channels to accept anything he liked to do in the affairs of Giovan Galeazzo and the Duchy of Milan. He ignored Alfonso's opinion, who, taking heart from Lodovico's natural timidity, and forgetting that the timid man is inclined to rash decisions through fear no less easily than the bold man through temerity, felt that the best way to make him withdraw from these plans of his was to frighten and threaten him.

In the end, after many difficulties arising more on Virginio's side than the Pope's, the dispute over the castles was settled. Don Federigo had a hand in the agreement, having been sent to Rome by his father for this purpose. It was agreed that Virginio should keep the castles, paying the Pope as much as he had paid Franceschettó Cibo for their purchase. The betrothal of Sancia Alfonso's natural daughter to Don Gioffredo the Pope's younger son was also concluded, though both were too young for the marriage to be consummated. The conditions were that Don Gioffredo should go to live in Naples in a few months time, and should receive in dowry the Principality of Squillace with an income of 10,000 ducats a year, and be given command of a hundred men at arms at Ferdinand's expense. This confirmed the belief held by many that what the Pope had negotiated in France had been done largely to frighten the Aragonese into submitting to these conditions. Ferdinand also tried to ally himself with the Pope for their common defense, but the Pope raised many difficulties, and he obtained only a promise given by brief in strict secret, to help him defend the Kingdom of Naples if Ferdinand promised to do likewise for the papal state. When this was settled, the Pope dismissed from his territory the forces which the Venetians and the Duke of Milan had sent to help him. Ferdinand had equal hopes of success in the negotiations. He then began with Lodovico Sforza, who showed consummate art in soothing the other princes' fears and encouraging their hopes. Sometimes he expressed his disapproval of the French king's intentions as dangerous to all Italy; sometimes he put forward as his excuse that he had been obliged to listen to the demands made on him, as he said, by that king, because he held Genoa in fee and because of the ancient alliance with the house of France: sometimes he promised Ferdinand—and sometimes the Pope and Piero de' Medici separately—to do all in his power to discourage Charles, his object being to deter them from uniting against him before the French affair was decided and planned. He was believed the more easily because it was considered that bringing the King of France into Italy would be so unsafe for himself as well that it seemed impossible that he would not draw back in the end when he realized the danger.

The whole summer passed amid these discussions. Lodovico behaved in such a way that, while he avoided offending the King of France, neither Ferdinand nor the Pope nor the Florentines despaired of his promises nor entirely relied upon them. But all this time the preparations were being diligently made in France for the new expedition, for which the King's enthusiasm grew daily against the advice of nearly all the great nobles. To make his way easier, he made up his quarrel with Ferdinand and Isabella, King and Queen of Spain, who were rulers at that time very celebrated and renowned for their wisdom, for having brought their kingdoms out of great turbulence into the greatest peace and obedience, and because they had recently, in a war lasting ten years, regained for Christendom the Kingdom of Granada which had been held by the Moors of Africa for

117

almost eight hundred years. Because of that victory they received from the Pope, with great approbation from all Christians, the title of Catholic Monarchs. In this treaty[32] with Charles—which was confirmed with the greatest solemnity and with public oaths sworn by both parties in church—it was provided that Ferdinand and Isabella (Spain was ruled jointly in their names) would not help the Aragonese either directly or indirectly, would not form new ties of marriage with them or in any way oppose Charles by defending Naples. To obtain these pledges, Charles, beginning with certain loss in exchange for uncertain gain, returned without any payment whatever Perpignan and the whole County of Roussillon, which had been pledged many years before to his father Louis by King John of Aragon, Ferdinand's father. This was most harmful to the whole Kingdom of France, because that county, situated at the foot of the Pyrenees and therefore, according to the ancient frontiers, part of Gaul, prevented the Spaniards from invading on that side. For the same reason Charles made peace[33] with Maximilian King of the Romans, and with Philip Archduke of Austria his son, who had serious differences with him both old and new, their origin being that Louis his father had, on the death of Charles, Duke of Burgundy and Count of Flanders and of many other neighboring lands, occupied the Duchy of Burgundy, the County of Artois and many other lands possessed by him. As a result there had been a war between Louis and Marie, the Duke's only child, who shortly after her father's death had married Maximilian. Then Marie being dead and Philip her son by Maximilian having succeeded to his mother's inheritance, peace had been made with Louis of France—more at the wish of the people of Flanders than that of Maximilian. To cement this peace Louis' son Charles was married to Marguerite, Philip's sister, and although she was a minor she was brought to live in France. After she had been there a number of years, Charles repudiated her and took as his wife Anne, who held the Duchy of Brittany since her father Francis had died without male issue. Thus Maximilian received a double insult: being deprived at once of his daughter's marriage and of his own bride, because earlier he had himself married Anne by proxy. Nevertheless, as he was not powerful enough to carry on by himself the war which had broken out again as a result of this offense; and as the Flemish people, who were ruling themselves during Philip's minority, refused to be at war with the French, and because the kings of Spain and England had made peace with them, he agreed to do the same. By this peace Charles restored to Philip his sister Marguerite, who had been kept in France until then, together with the County of Artois, but retaining the fortresses with the obligation to give them back at the end of four years when Philip would attain his majority and so be able to ratify the agreement. These lands had been designated as Marguerite's dowry in the earlier peace made with Louis.

When France had made peace with all her neighbors, the war against Naples was fixed for the following year, and in the interval all the necessary preparations were to be made, which were constantly being urged by Lodovico Sforza. He (as men's ambitions grow by degrees) no longer thought only of making himself safe in power, but aiming at higher things, had in mind to transfer the Duchy of Milan entirely into his own hands through the opportunity offered by the difficulties of the Aragonese. To give some color of justice to so great an injustice and establish his position more firmly against all eventualities, he married Bianca Maria, his niece and Giovan Galeazzo's sister, to Maximilian who had lately succeeded to the Roman Empire through the death of his father Frederick. As a dowry he promised him in intallments 400,000 ducats in cash, and 40,000 ducats in jewels and other goods. In return Maximilian, who was more eager for the money than for the family alliance, undertook to give Lodovico, at the expense of his new brother-in-law Giovan Galeazzo, the investiture of the Duchy of Milan for himself, his children and descendants, as though that duchy had always lacked a legitimate duke since the death of Filippo Maria Visconti. He promised to send him the privileges drawn up in complete form as soon as the last installment was paid.

The Visconti, who were noblemen of Milan, during the most bloody factions of the Guelphs and Ghibellines in Italy, when the Guelphs were finally driven out, became (for this is nearly always the outcome of civil war) from being leaders of one part of Milan, masters of it all. When they had been in this position of power for many years, they sought, according to the usual course of tyrannies (so that what was usurpation might seem theirs of right), to give their fortunes the color of legality and later to illustrate them with fine titles. So they obtained from the emperors—of whom Italy was beginning to know the name more than the power—first the title of Captains and then of Imperial Vicars; and finally Giovan Galeazzo, who, having received the County of Virtus from his father-in-law, King John of France, called himself Conte di Virtù, obtained from Wenceslas King of the Romans for himself and his male descendants the title of Duke of Milan—in which he was succeeded in turn by Giovan Maria and Filippo Maria his sons. The male line failed on the death of Filippo who, in his will named as his heir Alfonso King of Aragon and Naples on account of the great friendship the latter had formed for him after he had set him free, and even more in order to ensure that the Duchy of Milan, with so powerful a defender, would not be occupied by the Venetians, who were already visibly aspiring to do so. However, Francesco Sforza, a most distinguished captain of that time and no less gifted in the arts of peace than in those of war, helped by a combination of circumstances and no less by his own determination to rule rather than to keep faith, seized the Duchy by armed force and claimed it for his wife Bianca Maria, the natural daughter of Filippo Maria. It is said that afterward he could have had the investiture from the Emperor Frederick quite cheaply; but he scorned it, being sure that he could retain the Duchy with the same arts by which he had first acquired it. Galeazzo his son went on without investiture, and so did Giovan Galeazzo, his grandson. Hence Lodovico was not only criminal toward his living nephew, but insulted the memory of his dead father and brother by inferring that none of them had been legitimate Dukes of Milan, and he obtained the investiture from Maximilian as though the state had reverted to the Empire, taking the title of fourth Duke of Milan instead of seventh. However these actions were known only to very few while his nephew was alive. Besides he used to say—taking as his example Cyrus the younger brother of Ataxerxes King of Persia, and supporting it with the opinions of many legal authorities— that he had precedence over his brother, not in age, but in being their father's first son born after he had become Duke of Milan. These two arguments (leaving out the example of Cyrus) were stated in the Imperial Privilege. In order to cover up Lodovico's greed, though in a ridiculous manner, it was added in separate letters that it was not customary for the Holy Empire to give a state to anyone who had previously held it on the authority of others; and therefore Maximilian had turned down Lodovico's requests that Giovan Galeazzo should have the investiture, as the latter had already held the Duchy from the Milanese people. Lodovico's new family ties with Maximilian led Ferdinand to hope that he might be cooling off in his friendship for the King of France, supposing that his alliance with a rival—and an enemy for so many good reasons—together with his handing over so much money, would generate mistrust between them; and that Lodovico, taking courage from this new connection, would be bolder to separate himself from the French. Lodovico nourished these hopes with the greatest skill, and nonetheless (such was his sagacity and dexterity) at the same time he kept up relations with Ferdinand and the other rulers of Italy while remaining on good terms with the King of the Romans and the King of France. Ferdinand also hoped that the Venetian senate, to whom he had sent ambassadors, would object to a prince so much greater than themselves entering Italy where they held the highest position in power and authority. The Spanish monarchs too gave him hope and encouragement, promising him powerful assistance in case they were unable to prevent the expedition by their authority and persuasion.

On the other hand the King of France was making an

121

effort to remove the obstacles and difficulties he might
meet on this side of the mountains now that he had
dealt with those on the other side. Therefore he sent Perron de Baschi, a man not unskilled in the affairs of
Italy where he had been under Jean d'Anjou. He communicated to the Pope, to the Venetians and to the
Florentines the King's decision to regain the Kingdom of
Naples and urged them all to join him in an alliance.
But all he took away were hopes and replies in general
terms, because as the war was planned only for the
following year, none was willing to reveal his intentions
so early. The King also summoned the Florentine
spokesmen who had been sent to him with Ferdinand's
consent to reassure him that they were not supporting
the Aragonese, and requested them to promise him free
passage and victuals for his army through their territory
against due payment, and to send with it a hundred soldiers which he demanded, he said, as a token of the
Florentine Republic's continuing friendship. Although
it was pointed out to him that they could not make such
a declaration without grave danger before his army was
actually in Italy, and that he could in any case rely on
the city for anything that was in accord with their long
friendship and fidelity to the crown of France, nevertheless they were forced by French impetuosity to promise—being threatened otherwise with the closing down
of Florentine trade which was very considerable in that
kingdom. As it was later evident, this was done on the
advice of Lodovico Sforza, who was then the guide and
director of all their negotiations with the Italians. Piero
de' Medici endeavored to persuade Ferdinand that these
demands would matter so little to the result of the war
that it might be more useful to him for Piero and the
Republic to remain friends with Charles and so perhaps
be in a position to mediate in some settlement. Besides
this he also pointed out the terrible blame and hatred
which would fall on him in Florence if the Florentine
merchants were expelled from France. It was, he said, a
matter of good faith, the principal basis of alliances,
that each of the allies should bear with patience a certain degree of inconvenience so that the other might

not incur graver losses. But Ferdinand, considering how much his security and credit would be diminished if the Florentines abandoned him, did not accept these arguments and complained bitterly that Piero's constancy and faith should begin so soon to fall below what he had hoped of him. Therefore Piero, who was determined to keep the friendship of the Aragonese before all else, contrived to make the French wait for the answer they were urgently demanding, finally saying that the intentions of the Republic would be communicated through fresh ambassadors.

At the end of this year the alliance between the Pope and Ferdinand began to weaken, either because the Pope hoped by causing fresh difficulties to obtain from him greater concessions, or because he thought he could induce him in this way to force the Cardinal of San Piero in Vincoli to obey him. The Pope was extremely anxious for the cardinal to come to Rome, and offered as guarantors of his safety the College of Cardinals, Ferdinand and the Venetians. He was uneasy about his absence because of the importance of the fortress of Ostia (for around Rome he held Ronciglione and Grottaferrata), the considerable following and authority he enjoyed at the court, and finally because of his natural fondness for change and his obstinacy in affronting any danger rather than give way in the smallest degree over anything he had decided. Ferdinand argued effectively that he could not force Vincoli to return, as he was so full of mistrust that no surety seemed appropriate to the risk he ran. Ferdinand also complained of his ill luck with the Pope, who always blamed him for what was really the fault of others. The Pope had thought Virginio had bought the castles on Ferdinand's advice and with his money, and yet the purchase had been carried out without his participation; whereas it was he who had got Virginio to come to an agreement with the Pope and put up the money which was paid in compensation for the castles. The Pope did not accept these excuses, but went on complaining about Ferdinand with bitter and almost threatening words, so that it seemed that there could be no lasting basis to their reconciliation.

Chapter VI

[*The King of France expels the ambassadors of Ferdinand of Aragon. Death of Ferdinand. Author's judgment on him. Alliance between the Pope and Alfonso of Aragon. Attempts to reconcile Alfonso with Lodovico Sforza and the latter's dissimulation. The King of France's ambassadors attempt to secure from the Florentines an assurance of their alliance or at least friendly help for the French army. Charles VIII asks the Pope to proclaim him King of Naples. The Pope's reply. The Florentine government's reply to the orators of the King of France. The King's indignation with Piero. Venice's neutrality.*]

In this mood and amid this confusion of affairs so clearly tending toward fresh troubles the year 1494 began (I count the beginning according to the Roman style), a most unhappy year for Italy, and truly the beginning of years of wretchedness, because it opened the way for innumerable horrible calamities which later for various reasons affected a great part of the rest of the world. At the beginning of that year Charles, who had no wish to come to any agreement with Ferdinand, ordered his ambassadors to leave the Kingdom of France as representatives of an enemy power. Practically at the same time Ferdinand died of a sudden catarrh, worn out more by worry than by old age. He was a king famous for the prudence and industry by which, with the help of good fortune, he kept his kingdom that had been recaptured by his father, in the face of great difficulties which arose at the beginning of his reign, and brought it to such greatness as few kings had enjoyed for many years past. He would have been a good king if he had gone on ruling with the same methods with which he began; but as time went on, either, like most princes, he had been unable to resist the violence which power brings and had changed his ways or, as most

124

people thought, his true nature showed itself which he had earlier concealed with great skill. And he became notorious for treachery and cruelty such that his own supporters judged it worthy rather of the name of bestiality.

Ferdinand's death seemed sure to harm the common cause. Besides the fact that he would certainly have attempted anything to stop the French crossing the Alps, there is no doubt that it would have been more difficult to get Lodovico Sforza to reconcile himself with the haughty and intemperate nature of Alfonso than to persuade him to renew his friendship with Ferdinand, who in the past had often been inclined to let Sforza have his way so as to have no cause for quarrel with the state of Milan. Apart from anything else it is well known that when Isabella, Alfonso's daughter, went to join her husband, Lodovico fell in love with her at sight and wished to get her from her father for his own wife. To this end he worked with spells and magic—so it was believed throughout Italy—so that Giovan Galeazzo was incapable for many months of consummating the marriage. Ferdinand would have agreed, but Alfonso was against it; so Lodovico, deprived of that hope, took another wife. And when he had had children with her, he turned all his thoughts to handing on the Duchy of Milan to them. Some have also written that Ferdinand was ready to put up with any trial and indignity to avoid the coming war, and had decided, as soon as the weather permitted, to embark in light galleys for Genoa and go thence by land to Milan to give satisfaction to Lodovico in anything he wished and bring his granddaughter back to Naples. His hope was that, besides the practical results, this public confession that his safety depended entirely on Lodovico would soften his heart, as it was well known what an unbounded ambition he had to appear the arbiter and practically the oracle of Italy.

However, Alfonso, as soon as his father was dead, sent four ambassadors to the Pope. The latter was showing signs of wishing to go back to his first idea of friendship with France. In a bull signed by the college of cardinals he had recently promised, at the request of the

125

King of France, the rank of cardinal for the bishop of
St. Malo, and at the joint expense of himself and the
Duke of Milan he had recruited Prospero Colonna, who
used to be the King's captain, and some other military
commanders. Nevertheless he was ready to reach an
agreement because of the great concessions which Alfonso offered him in the hope of making sure of him and
of binding him to his defense. They therefore openly
agreed that there should be an alliance between them
for the common defense of their states with a determined
number of troops on each side. The Pope was to grant
Alfonso the investiture of the kingdom with the reduction of the tribute which Ferdinand had obtained from
previous popes for his lifetime only, and should send a
papal legate to crown him. He should make Lodovico,
the son of Don Enrico who was Alfonso's natural brother,
a cardinal—he was later called the Cardinal of Aragon.
The King was to pay the Pope 30,000 ducats immediately, and he was to give the Duke of Gandia[34] lands
in the kingdom with an income of 12,000 ducats a year
and the first of the seven principal offices which fell
vacant. During the Pope's lifetime the Duke should be
commissioned at the King's expense with 300 men at
arms with which he should be at the service of both of
them. Don Gioffredo, who was to go and live with his
father-in-law virtually as a pledge of his father's good
faith, was to receive, besides all the things promised
him in the first agreement, the protonotariate, which
was likewise one of the said seven offices. Income from
benefices in the kingdom was to go to the Pope's son
Cesare Borgia, recently promoted by his father to the
rank of cardinal. It was not normal to promote a bastard
to such a dignity, so the Pope, to remove this obstacle,
had proved with false witnesses that he was the legitimate son of someone else. Furthermore, Virginio Orsino,
who represented the King in these negotiations, promised
that the King would help the Pope to retake the fortress
of Ostia if the Cardinal of San Piero in Vincoli refused
to go to Rome; but the King stated that this promise had
been made without his knowledge or consent. He felt
that in such dangerous times it was imprudent to make an

enemy of this cardinal, who was powerful in the affairs of Genoa—on which, with his encouragement, Alfonso planned to make an attempt—and also as in all these upheavals there might arise questions of a general council or other matters prejudicial to the Holy See, he did his best to reconcile the cardinal with the Pope. However, as the latter would not agree to anything if Vincoli did not return to Rome, and as the Cardinal was absolutely determined never to trust his life to the word of a lot of Catalans, as he used to say, Alfonso's wishes and efforts were in vain. The cardinal, after he had pretended to be almost certain to accept the conditions which were being negotiated, suddenly left Ostia by night aboard an armed brigantine, leaving the fortress well-guarded. He spent a few days at Savona and then at Avignon—of which city he was the legate—and finally went to Lyons where Charles had recently gone to prepare for the war with greater ease and publicity. He was already openly declaring his intention of going to the war in person. The cardinal was received by the King with great honor and ceremony, and then joined forces with the rest of those who were planning the upheaval of Italy.

Alfonso, to whom fear had become a good teacher, pursued with Lodovico Sforza the efforts begun by his father, offering him the same concessions. Sforza, in his usual way, ingeniously fed him with various hopes, but gave him to understand that he was forced to proceed with the greatest skill and care so that the war planned against others should not begin against himself. On the other hand he never ceased pressing on the preparations in France. To do this more effectively and the better to establish all the details of what had to be arranged, and also so that there should be no delay in the execution of those plans, he sent to France—saying he had been summoned by the King—Galeazzo da Sanseverino, the husband of his natural daughter, who was greatly favored and trusted by him.

On Lodovico's advice Charles sent to the Pope four representatives with a commission to ask on their way through Florence for a declaration of the Republic's intentions. These were Béraud Aubigny, a Scottish captain, the General of France, the President of the Parliament of Provence and the same Perron de Baschi whom he had sent the year before. These, according to their instructions drawn up mostly in Milan, explained in Florence and Rome the reasons why the King of France was the heir of the House of Anjou and because the line of Charles I had failed, pretended to the Kingdom of Naples, and they communicated his decision to enter Italy himself that very year—not to occupy anything which belonged to others, but only to take possession of what was rightly his. His ultimate aim, however, was not so much the Kingdom of Naples as the opportunity to turn his armies afterward against the Turks for the greater glory and fame of Christianity. In Florence they explained how much the King relied on that city which had been rebuilt by Charlemagne, and had been always favored by the King's forebears and recently by Louis his father in the war unjustly waged against them by Pope Sixtus, by the late King Ferdinand and the present King Alfonso. They recalled the great benefits which accrued to the Florentines through commerce in the Kingdom of France, where they were well received and privileged as though they were Frenchmen. Likewise, when the King ruled Naples, they could expect the same benefits and advantages there; whereas they had never had anything from the Aragonese but harm and offense. The ambassadors asked that they should give some indication of co-operation with the King in this enterprise; and if they were prevented from doing so by some just cause, they should at least allow passage and victualing through their territory, for which the French army would pay. They discussed these matters with the Republic. Privately they reminded Piero de' Medici of the many benefits and honors bestowed on his father and his ancestors by Louis XI—making many efforts in times of danger to preserve their greatness, and as a token of friendship, honoring their arms with the device of the house of France. On the other hand Ferdinand, not satisfied with having openly attacked them by force of arms, had wickedly taken part in the local conspiracies in which his uncle Giuliano had been killed and his father Lorenzo gravely injured.[35]

They reminded the Pope of the long services and constant devotion of the house of France toward the Apostolic See—to which all histories ancient and modern bore ample witness—and at the same time the obstinacy and frequent disobedience of the Aragonese. They asked for the investiture of the Kingdom of Naples for Charles as legally due to him, and offered the Pope great prospects and rewards if he would favor this expedition which had been decided upon as much through his encouragement and on his authority as for any other reason. The Pope replied that, as so many of his predecessors had given the investiture of that kingdom to three kings of Aragon in succession, because in Ferdinand's investiture Alfonso was included by name, it was not possible to grant it to Charles until it had been declared by legal authority that his title was the better one. The investiture of Alfonso had not prejudiced the issue because, with this in mind, it had been specified in it that it should be understood without prejudice. He reminded them that the Kingdom of Naples was in the absolute ownership of the Apostolic See, saying that he did not believe that the King wished to do violence to this authority—as he would if he attacked the kingdom, contrary to the custom of his predecessors who had always been its steadfast defenders. It was more fitting to his dignity and virtue—if he had a claim—to seek to substantiate it through legal processes, which he (the Pope) as feudal overlord and sole judge of this cause was ready to administer. A Most Christian King should not demand anything more of a Roman pontiff whose office it was to forbid, not foment wars and violence between Christian princes. He pointed out that, even if the King wished to do otherwise, it would be extremely difficult and dangerous because of the nearness of Alfonso and the Florentines, whose alliance drew the whole of Tuscany with it, and because so many barons owed allegiance to the King of Naples, whose territories reached right up to the gates of Rome. Nevertheless he sought not to remove all their hopes, although he him-

129

self had decided not to give up the alliance he had made with Alfonso.

In Florence there was strong feeling in favor of the French: so many Florentines traded in that kingdom; there was the ancient but untrue legend that Charlemagne had rebuilt the city after its destruction by Totila King of the Goths; there was the close and long-standing alliance of their ancestors, as Guelphs, with Charles I King of Naples and with many of his descendants who had been protectors of the Guelph party in Italy; and finally there was the memory of the wars which had been made on the city first by the old Alfonso and then in 1478 by Ferdinand, who sent his son Alfonso to fight in person. For these reasons the entire populace desired that the French should be allowed free passage. It was desired no less by the wisest and most eminent citizens of the Republic, who thought it the height of imprudence to bring into Florentine territory—for other people's quarrels—so dangerous a war by opposing the person of the King of France and so powerful an army, which would enter Italy with the support of the state of Milan and, if without the actual consent of the Venetian senate. at least not opposed by them. They supported their opinion with the example of Cosimo de' Medici who had in his time been considered one of the wisest men in Italy. In the war between Jean d'Anjou and Ferdinand, although the latter was supported by the Pope and the Duke of Milan, Cosimo had always counseled that the city should not oppose Anjou. They recalled the example of Lorenzo, Piero's father, who had always supported the same policy whenever there was a rumor of the Angevins' return. They recalled the words he often used when alarmed by the power of the French, especially after this king had acquired Brittany: that the Italians would face terrible ills if the French king ever realized his own power. But Piero de' Medici—judging affairs more by his own desires than by prudence and placing too much reliance on his own opinion, convinced that this affair would end with more noise than practical effect, and encouraged by some of his ministers, corrupted, it was said, by Alfonso's gifts—decided to persist

in the friendship with the Aragonese. With the result
that, because of his power, all the other citizens had to
agree. I have it on respectable authority that Piero, not
satisfied with the power his father had obtained in the
Republic—although it was such that all the magistrates
were chosen according to his wishes, and they did not
decide the more important affairs without asking his
opinion—aspired to more absolute power and the title
of prince. In this he did not wisely consider the state
of the city, which was then powerful and rich, and had
been nourished for centuries on republican institutions
with the principal citizens accustomed to take part in
government more as equals than as subjects. It was
therefore likely that the city would not tolerate so great
and sudden a change without considerable violence. For
this reason Piero, knowing that some unusual basis must
be found to sustain his ambition, had allied himself
closely with the Aragonese and decided to link his fortune with theirs so as to create a powerful support for
the preservation of his new principality.

It happened by chance that a few days before the
French ambassadors reached Florence, there came to
light certain negotiations which Lorenzo and Giovanni
de' Medici—extremely wealthy young men closely related to Piero and hostile to him because of differences
they had had in their youth—had opened through Cosimo
Rucellai, half-brother of Piero, with Lodovico Sforza and
through him with the King of France, and which were
directed against Piero's rule. They were arrested by the
magistrates, but let off lightly and exiled to their houses
in the country because the most experienced citizens
persuaded Piero, though not without great difficulty, that
the utmost severity of the law should not be used against
his own family. But as this incident confirmed to him
that Lodovico Sforza was determined on his downfall, he
thought himself all the more obliged to persevere in his
earlier decision. The French envoys therefore received
an answer in elaborate and respectful words but lacking
the conclusion they had desired. They were told on the
one hand of the natural friendship of the Florentines for

131

the house of France and their strong desire to please so
glorious a king; on the other of the obstacles preventing
them. Nothing was more unworthy of princes and republics than to fail in their promises, and without doing
this they could not consent to his wishes, as the alliance
was still in force which they had made with Ferdinand
on the authority of King Louis his father,[36] with a clause
that after Ferdinand's death it should hold good for Alfonso, and with the express condition that they should
not only assist in the defense of Naples, but refuse passage through their territory to anyone going to attack
it. They were extremely sorry that they could not do
otherwise, but hoped that the King, most wise and most
just, knowing their friendly disposition, would attribute
their not being able to help him to these obstacles, and
recognize them as just. The King was furious at this
reply; he immediately dismissed the Florentine ambassadors from France, and deported from Lyons on Lodovico Sforza's advice, not the other merchants, but only
the officials of Piero de' Medici's bank; so that in Florence
it should be understood that he attributed this offense to
Piero himself and not to the citizens in general.

All the other Italian powers were now divided, some in
favor of the King of France, some against him; only the
Venetians decided to remain neutral and await quietly
the outcome of this affair. Either they were not sorry to
see Italy in turmoil, hoping to extend the Venetian do-
main through the long wars of others, or, being powerful
themselves, they did not fear they would be easy prey to
the victor, and regarded it as imprudent to join unnecessarily in the wars of other states. Ferdinand constantly
urged them to do so, and the King of France both this
year and the year before sent them ambassadors, who had
argued that there had never been anything but friendship
and good will between their states and affection and kind
offices on both sides on all occasions. The King, wishing
to increase still further this relationship, begged the most
wise senate to add their advice and support to his
expedition. They had replied briefly and prudently to this
message: the Most Christian King was so wise and had
the advantage of such grave and mature counsel that it

would be presumptuous on their part to advise him. They added that the Venetian senate would be delighted at any good fortune of his because of the friendship they had always had for the French crown. Therefore they much regretted their inability to translate their friendly feeling into action; but the Grand Turk kept them constantly in alarm, as he had the mind and the opportunity to attack them, and they were forced to guard at great expense all those numerous islands and shores which were near to him, and to abstain from getting involved in wars with other powers.

Chapter VII

[*The French King's preparations for the expedition against the Kingdom of Naples and Alfonso's preparations for defense. Open signs of enmity of Alfonso toward Lodovico Sforza. Alfonso's plans and projects for war. The Pope with Alfonso's help takes the fortress of Ostia held by the force of Cardinal della Rovere. Lodovico Sforza, assuring the Pope and Piero de' Medici of his desire for peace, makes them waver in their support for Alfonso. Agreements for mutual defense between the Pope and the King of Naples. The commissioning of Fabrizio and Prospero Colonna.*]

More important than the speeches of ambassadors and the replies they received were the preparations by land and sea which were being made everywhere. Charles had sent Pierre d'Urfé, his grand equerry, to Genoa, which was ruled by the Duke of Milan with the support of the Adorno faction and Giovan Luigi dal Fiesco, to prepare a powerful navy of great ships and narrow galleys. Other ships he had fitted out at Villefranche and Marseilles. It was therefore rumored at the French court that Charles intended to enter the Kingdom of Naples by sea as Jean, René d'Anjou's son, had done against Ferdinand. There were many in France who believed that owing to the King's lack of ability, the insignificant nature of those who were encouraging him and the lack of money, all these preparations would come to nothing. Nevertheless, because of the King's enthusiasm—he had recently on the advice of those closest to him assumed the title of King of Jerusalem and of the Two Sicilies (which was the title of the kings of Naples)—preparations for the war were being made with great energy, raising money, organizing troops and determining the final plans with Galeazzo da Sanseverino who held all the secrets and intentions of Lodovico Sforza locked in his bosom.

Alfonso, on the other hand, who had never ceased preparing by land and sea, thought it was no longer possible to allow himself to be deceived by the hopes held out to him by Lodovico, and that it would be better to frighten and harry him than to attempt to reassure and soothe him. So he ordered the Milanese envoy to leave Naples and recalled his own from Milan, took possession of the Duchy of Bari—which had been held by Lodovico for many years as a gift from Ferdinand—and sequestrated its revenues. Nor was he content with these open demonstrations of hostility (rather than insults): but he then made every effort to lure the city of Genoa away from the Duke of Milan. In the present situation this was a matter of the greatest importance, because if that city's allegiance changed, it would be very easy to turn the government of Milan against Lodovico, and the King of France would be denied the opportunity to harass the Kingdom of Naples by sea. Therefore he agreed secretly with Cardinal Paolo Fregoso, who had once been Doge of Genoa and had a following of many of the same family, and with Obietto dal Fiesco, both of them leaders of a considerable faction in that city and its neighboring coastlands, and with some of the Adorno family who for various reasons had chosen to leave Genoa; and he planned to reinstate them in the city with a powerful fleet. As he used to say, wars are won by anticipation and diversion. He likewise decided to go personally into Romagna with a strong army and thence into the territory of Parma. There raising his standard and proclaiming the name of Giovan Galeazzo he hoped that the people of the Duchy of Milan would rise against Lodovico.

Although these attempts might encounter difficulties, he regarded it as very valuable that the war should start in a place far away from his kingdom—and very important that the French should be overtaken by the winter in Lombardy. He was experienced only in the Italian wars in which the armies used to wait for the grass to grow to feed the horses, and so never entered on a campaign before the end of April; he therefore supposed that in the bad season the French would have to wait in a friendly state until spring. He hoped that this delay might give rise to some event which might save him. He also sent ambassadors to Constantinople to seek help in their common danger from Bajazet the Ottoman prince of the Turks, because it was said that Charles intended to invade Greece when he had conquered Naples. He knew Bajazet did not underestimate this threat, because the Turks remembered the expeditions made in the past by the French into Asia against the infidels, and were not a little afraid of their military strength.

While these matters were being arranged on both sides, the Pope sent his forces to Ostia under the command of Niccolò Orsini, Count of Pitigliano, with support from Alfonso by land and sea. The town was captured without difficulty, and they began to bombard the fortress with artillery when the governor, through Fabrizio Colonna as intermediary and with the consent of Giovanni della Rovere, Prefect of Rome and the brother of the Cardinal of San Piero in Vincoli, surrendered after a very few days. It was agreed that in exchange the Pope would not persecute with spiritual or temporal arms either the prefect or the cardinal, if they did not give him fresh cause. Fabrizio in whose hands the cardinal had left Grottaferrata was allowed to keep it on the same terms on payment of 10,000 ducats to the Pope.

Lodovico Sforza had been told by the cardinal on his way through Savona what Alfonso was plotting with the Genoese exiles on his advice and with his mediation, and Lodovico convinced Charles that this would be a serious obstacle to his own plans, persuading him to send 2,000 Swiss to Genoa, and to dispatch 300 lances immediately into Italy to serve under d'Aubigny, who had stopped at

Milan on his way back from Rome on the King's orders. These were to be ready to defend Lombardy and to advance if there were need or occasion for them to do so. With them there were to be 500 Italian men-at-arms recruited at the King's expense under Giovan Francesco da Sanseverino, Count of Gaiazzo, Galeotto Pico, Count of Mirandola, and Ridolfo da Gonzaga; and 500 more which the Duke of Milan was committed to give him. All the same, Lodovico with his usual cunning still went on assuring the Pope and Piero de' Medici of his desire for peace and quiet in Italy, offering various hopes that there would soon be clear proof of this. It is almost impossible that what is earnestly stated should not create some doubt even in minds determined to believe the opposite. Even if his promises were no longer believed, his affirmations somewhat slowed down his adversaries' preparations. The Pope and Piero would very much have liked to make the attempt on Genoa, but as this would be a direct attack on the state of Milan, the Pope, when asked by Alfonso for his galleys and for the papal troops to join his in Romagna, agreed that their forces should join for their common defense in Romagna but not advance any further. And he made difficulties over the galleys, saying that it was not yet the moment to drive Lodovico into such a desperate situation. The Florentines who were asked to allow the royal fleet shelter and provision at Leghorn, were undecided for the same reason. Having rejected the King of France's requests on account of their alliance with Ferdinand, they were unwilling, before they were compelled by necessity, to do more than they were obliged to by that pact.

When further delay was no longer possible, the fleet at last left Naples under the command of the admiral Don Federigo. Alfonso himself collected his army in the Abruzzi to enter Romagna, but before he went any further, he thought he ought to discuss with the Pope (who was of the same mind) everything they should do for their mutual safety. Thus on July 13th they met at Vicovaro, a possession of Virginio Orsino, where they stayed for three days and then left having reached full agreement. It was decided at this meeting on the Pope's advice

that the King himself should go no further, but that part
of his army—which the King said consisted of nearly 100
squadrons of soldiers of twenty men each, and more than
3,000 crossbowmen and light horse—should remain with
him on the borders of the Abruzzi near Celle and Tagliacozzo to defend the Church states and his own. Virginio
was to stay in the Roman region to counterbalance the
Colonna—out of fear of whom there should remain in
Rome 200 of the Pope's soldiers and part of the King's
light horse. Ferrando Duke of Calabria (this was the title
given to the eldest sons of the Kings of Naples) was to go
to Romagna with 70 squadrons, the rest of the light horse
and most of the papal troops, which were to be used only
defensively. The Duke who was a very promising young
man, was to have with him to guide his youthful inexperience, Giovaniacopo da Triulzi, governor of the royal
troops, and the Count of Pitigliano who had passed from
the Pope's service to that of the King—both captains of
great reputation and experience. Ferrando's presence
seemed very appropriate for an advance into Lombardy
because he was closely and doubly related to Giovan
Galeazzo, the husband of Isabella his sister and the son
of Galeazzo brother of Ippolita his mother. One of the
most important subjects discussed by the Pope and Alfonso was the problem of the Colonna, who it was clear
were planning some change. Prospero and Fabrizio had
been in the pay of the late King and had acquired lands
and honors from him; and after the King's death Prospero, despite many promises to Alfonso that he would
take service with him, had entered the joint service of
the Pope and the Duke of Milan through the agency of
Cardinal Ascanio; and he subsequently refused, when
asked by the Pope, to hold his commission only from him.
Fabrizio who had remained in the service of Alfonso,
seeing the Pope's and the King's' anger with Prospero, was
making difficulties about going with the Duke of Calabria
into Romagna if the situation of Prospero and the whole
Colonna family were not first settled and assured. This
was the excuse they offered for their difficulties; but in
secret they had taken service with the King of France.
They were inspired to do so by their close friendship with

Ascanio, who had left Rome a few days before out of distrust of the Pope, and taken refuge in their possessions; by hope of greater gain, and still more out of jealousy that Virginio Orsino should have the first place beside Alfonso and a greater share in his good fortune. To keep this secret until they thought it safe to declare themselves the King's captains, they pretended to wish to come to an agreement with the Pope and Alfonso, who were insisting that Prospero should leave the pay of the Duke of Milan and be commissioned on the same terms by them because otherwise they could not be sure of him. They continued negotiations, but so as not to come to a decision they kept on bringing up various difficulties over the conditions proposed. Over this matter there was a difference of opinion between the Pope and Alfonso. The former wanted to deprive them of the castles they held in the Roman territory and sought an opportunity to attack them. Alfonso had no other object than his own safety and saw in war only a last resort, though he did not dare to oppose the Pope's desires. Hence they decided to attack the Colonna, and they agreed on the necessary forces and strategy; but first they would wait and see if the affair could not be settled within the next few days.

Chapter VIII

[*Expedition of Alfonso's fleet to Genoa; attempts on the eastern seaboard and their failure. Alfonso's army sent to Romagna; their first difficulties. Piero de' Medici sends troops recruited by the Florentines to join the Aragonese army. Démarches of the Pope and Alfonso with the Venetian senate, the King of Spain and Bajazet. Fresh intrigues of Lodovico Sforza.*]

These and many other issues were being discussed in many quarters, but finally the Italian war was opened by Don Federigo[37] going to Genoa with a fleet beyond all doubt larger and better equipped than any seen in the Tyrrhenian sea for many years past. He had 35 narrow galleys, 18 ships and many other smaller vessels, much artillery and 3,000 soldiers for landing. Because of these preparations and because they had with them the exiles, they had left Naples with great hopes of victory; but they had left rather late, partly because of the difficulties which attend all great military movements, and partly because of the false hopes raised by Lodovico Sforza, and they had stopped in the ports of the Sienese to recruit as many as 4,000 soldiers; all of which made it difficult to achieve what a month earlier would have been easy. The enemy had had time to prepare; the Bailli of Dijon [Antoine de Baissey] had entered Genoa with 2,000 Swiss raised by the King of France, and many of the ships and galleys which were being armed in the port were ready. Likewise some of the ships fitted out at Marseilles had arrived; and Lodovico, sparing no expense, had sent Guasparri da San Severino—called Fracassa—and Antonio Maria his brother with many soldiers. He sought also to profit from the support of the Genoese themselves as well as from outside aid, and with gifts, provisions, money, promises and a variety of rewards he made sure of Giovan Luigi dal Fiesco, Obietto's brother, the Adorni, and many other nobles and commoners who were vital if that city were to be held firm in his cause. On the other hand he summoned to Milan from Genoa and the coastal regions, many of the followers of the exiles. To these arrangements, already powerful in themselves, not a little weight was added by the presence of Louis Duke of Orléans, who, at the very moment when the Aragonese navy appeared off Genoa, entered the city on behalf of the King of France, after discussions in Alessandria with Lodovico Sforza about their common interests. Lodovico had received him joyfully and with great honor but as an equal (so full are our mortal affairs of dark obscurities), not knowing that soon his life and his state would fall into that duke's power. These things caused the Aragonese, who had first planned to sail into Genoa—hoping for a rising of the exiles' supporters—to change their plans and attack along the coast. After some argument whether they should begin on the eastern or western seaboard, they followed Obietto's advice, who hoped much of the men of the eastern side, and made for Portovenere. Here they fought for several hours without result, as 400 soldiers had been sent in from Genoa and the morale of the inhabitants had been stiffened by Gianluigi dal Fiesco who had come to La Spezia. Seeing that there was no hope of taking the town, they retired to Leghorn to take on more provisions and troops. Hearing that the coastal towns were well defended, they felt they needed a larger force. While they were here Don Federigo heard that the French fleet was getting ready to sail out of Genoa, and as it was superior to his own in ships though inferior in galleys, he sent his ships back to Naples so as to be able to get away from the enemy faster if ships and galleys attacked him together—while still hoping to defeat them if for any reason the galleys became separated from the ships.

At this very time the Duke of Calabria was moving toward Romagna with the land forces, intending to go on into Lombardy as first planned. But to advance freely and without leaving an enemy behind him he had to win over the state of Bologna and the cities of Imola and Forlì, because Cesena, a city directly under the Pope, and Faenza, whose ruler was Astore de' Manfredi—a young boy in the pay and protection of the Florentines—were certain to give all facilities to the Aragonese troops of their own free will. Imola and Forlì were ruled, with the title of Vicar of the Church, by Ottaviano, son of Ieronimo da Riario, but under the tutelage and control of his mother Caterina Sforza. With her the Pope and Alfonso had negotiated several months before to commission Ottaviano in the joint cause on terms which would include his states. However, the matter had not been settled, partly because of the difficulties she raised to obtain better conditions and partly because the Florentines, persisting in their original decision not to go beyond their actual obligations with Alfonso against the King of France, could not make up their minds to join in this commission. Their agreement was necessary because the King and the Pope refused to bear the expense alone, and still more because Caterina refused to place these cities in jeopardy if the Florentines did not pledge themselves with the others to defend her son's states. These difficulties were removed at the meeting between Ferrando and Piero de' Medici at Borgo San Sepolcro while the former was leading his army into Romagna along the Marecchia valley road. In their first conference he offered Piero on behalf of his father Alfonso the use of that army and his own services for any purpose he chose in the affairs of Florence, Siena, and Faenza. This rekindled Piero's earlier enthusiasm, and when he got back to Florence he insisted—though the wiser citizens were against it—that they should agree to this commission because Ferrando had pressed him most urgently. When this had been done at the combined expense of the Pope, Alfonso, and the Florentines, they got the city of Bologna to join them a few days later, giving a similar commission to Giovanni Bentivoglio under whose authority and direction the city was governed. The Pope promised him, on the honor also of the King and Piero de' Medici, to make Antonio Galeazzo his son, a cardinal. He was at that time apostolic protonotary. These commissions increased Ferrando's reputation, but they would have increased it much more if with these advantages he had entered Romagna sooner. However they had been so slow in setting off from the kingdom, and Lodovico Sforza had been so energetic, that before Ferrando reached Cesena, Aubigny and the Count of Gaiazzo, Commander of the Sforza troops, had passed without hindrance through Bolognese territory with part of the army assigned to meet the Aragonese and had entered the country around Imola. So Ferrando's hopes of entering Lombardy were thwarted, and the war would have to stay in Romagna. There, while the other cities were on the side of Aragon, Ravenna and Cervia—cities subject to the Venetians— were neutral; and that little state of the Duke of Ferrara on the banks of the Po was ready with all supplies for the armies of the French and Sforza.

But the rashness of Piero de' Medici was not tempered either by the difficulties encountered in the Genoa expedition or by the obstacle which had arisen in Romagna. He had made a secret agreement with the Pope and Alfonso without the knowledge of the Republic—by which he was bound to declare open opposition to the King of France. He had not only consented to the Neapolitan fleet anchoring and provisioning in Leghorn harbor and allowed them to raise troops throughout Florentine territory, but being unable now to contain himself within any limits, he arranged that Annibale Bentivoglio, Giovanni's son, who was in the pay of Florence, should join with his men and those of Astore de' Manfredi the army of Ferrando as soon as he entered the region of Forlì. He had 1,000 foot soldiers and artillery sent to him as well. The Pope also showed a similar attitude. Besides providing arms, he had enjoined Charles in a letter not to enter Italy and to press his claims by legal means and not by force; and now not content with this he commanded him in another letter in the same sense under pain of excommunication. Through the bishop of Calahorra, who was papal nuncio in Venice where Alfonso's ambassadors were present for the same purpose together with those of the Florentines, though they made less explicit demands, he strongly urged the Venetian senate to send their armies against the King of France for the common good of all Italy; or they should at least inform Lodovico Sforza that they strongly objected to this turn of events. But the senate answered through the Doge that it was not the act of a wise ruler to invite war into his own domains in order to draw it away from other people; and they refused to do anything which might offend either party in word or deed. Because the King of Spain at the urgent request of Alfonso and the Pope promised to send his navy with a large force into Sicily to assist the Kingdom of Naples if it should be necessary—but regretted that he could not do so quickly because he was short of money—the Pope agreed that, in addition to certain sums sent by Alfonso, the King might use for this purpose the money raised in Spain with papal authority for a crusade, and which could not be used for anything but war against the enemies of the Christian faith. So far was it from Alfonso's mind to conquer these enemies that he sent Cammillo Pandone to the Grand Turk in addition to the other envoys he had sent earlier. With him, sent secretly by the Pope, went Giorgio Bucciardo, a Genoese, who had been sent there on previous occasions by Pope Innocent. These were received with great honors by Bajazet; and with their business rapidly concluded they returned with great promises of assistance. These, although confirmed shortly after by an ambássador sent by Bajazet to Naples, bore no fruit whatever, either because of the distances involved, or because mutual trust was difficult to achieve between Turks and Christians.

At this time, as their arms had been unsuccessful by land and sea, Alfonso and Piero de' Medici sought to deceive Lodovico Sforza with his own guile and cunning. But these efforts were no more successful than their armies. Many have thought that Lodovico, considering his own danger, did not wish the King of France to acquire the Kingdom of Naples, but planned—after having made himself Duke of Milan and let the French army into Tuscany—to act as intermediary for a peace treaty, by which Alfonso should hold his kingdom as a vassal of the French crown, pledging obedience to the King of France, while the Florentines might be deprived of the possessions they held in the Lunigiana, and the King should then return to France. By this means, with the Florentines humbled and the King of Naples diminished in power and authority, he as Duke of Milan would have done enough to ensure his own security without running the dangers which a French victory threatened. He may have hoped that Charles, particularly with the winter coming on, would meet some difficulties which would restrain the progress of his victory; and because of the natural impatience of the French, the King's lack of money and the objections to the expedition held by many of his people, it would be easy to find some way of reaching agreement. Whatever the truth of all this may be, it is certain that—although at the beginning Lodovico had worked hard to separate Piero de' Medici from the Aragonese—he later began in the greatest secrecy to encourage him to persevere in his course, promising that he would arrange either that the King of France should not invade or, if he did, would soon retreat before achieving anything on this side of the mountains. Through his envoy resident in Florence he continually pressed these arguments on Piero either because he really meant it, or because, being determined on Piero's downfall, he wished him to go so far against the King that no possibility of reconciliation might remain. Piero, therefore, decided with Alfonso's knowledge to inform the King of France of Lodovico's approaches. One day he called the Milanese ambassador to his own house pretending to be indisposed —having first hidden the French ambassador, who was then in Florence, where he could easily hear their conversation. Then Piero at length recalled the persuasions and promises of Lodovico and that on his advice he had resisted Charles' demands, complaining strongly that Lodovico should nonetheless be urging the French to invade; and concluding that as his actions did not match his words, he was compelled to decide to have no part in such a dangerous situation. The Milanese replied that Piero should not doubt Lodovico's good faith, if only because it was equally harmful to him if Charles should take Naples; and he urged him to continue in his policy, because if he did not it would mean reducing himself and all Italy to slavery. The French ambassador at once informed his king of this conversation, telling him that he was being betrayed by Lodovico. Nevertheless this ruse did not have the result King Alfonso and Piero hoped for: rather, revealed by the French themselves to Lodovico, it made his anger and hatred for Piero even greater and caused him to urge the King of France all the more insistently to waste no more time.

Chapter IX

[*Fearful portents and terror throughout Italy at the coming of the French. Sudden indecision of the King of France because of opposition at his court to the Italian expedition. The Cardinal of San Piero in Vincoli urges him on. The crossing of the Alps through Montgenèvre and entry of Charles VIII into Asti. His physical and moral portrait.*]

144

Now not only the preparations made by land and sea, but the heavens and mankind joined in proclaiming the future calamities of Italy. Those who profess to know the future either by science or by divine inspiration affirmed with one voice that greater and more frequent changes were at hand—events stranger and more horrible than had been seen in any part of the world for many centuries. Men were no less terrified by the widespread news that unnatural things in heaven and earth had appeared in various parts of Italy. One night in Puglia three suns stood in an overcast sky with horrible thunder and lightning. In the Arezzo district a vast number of armed men on enormous horses were seen passing through the air day after day with a hideous noise of drums and trumpets. In many places in Italy the sacred statues and images sweated visibly. Everywhere many monsters were born, both human and animal; and many other things outside the order of nature had happened in all kinds of places. All these filled the people of Italy with unspeakable fear, frightened as they were already by the rumors of the power of the French and the ferocity with which (as all the histories related) they had in the past overrun and despoiled the whole of Italy, sacked and put to fire and sword the city of Rome and conquered many provinces in Asia; indeed there was no part of the world that had not at some time felt the force of their arms. Men were only surprised that among so many portents there should not have been seen the comet which the ancients reputed a certain harbinger of the downfall of rulers and states.

The approach of realities daily increased belief in heavenly signs, predictions, prognostications and portents. For Charles, firm in his resolve, now came to Vienne in the Dauphiné. He could not be moved from his decision to invade Italy in person either by the entreaties of all his subjects or by lack of money, which was so scarce that he was only able to provide for his daily needs by pawning for a small sum certain jewels loaned to him by the Duke of Savoy, the Marchioness of Monferrat and other nobles of his court. The money he had earlier collected from the revenues of France, and that which

had been given him by Lodovico Sforza, he had spent
partly on the navy in which from the start great hopes of
victory were placed, and part he had handed out thought-
lessly to a variety of persons before he left Lyons. As at
that time princes were not so quick to extort money from
their peoples as—riding roughshod over respect for God
and men—they were later taught by avarice and excessive greed to do, it was not easy for him to accumulate
any more. On so weak a basis was it proposed to mount
so vast a war! For he was guided more by rashness and
impetuousness than by prudence and good counsel.

Yet as often happens when one begins to carry out
new, great and difficult enterprises, although the decision
has been made, all the reasons that can be adduced
against them come to mind; so when the King was about
to leave and in fact his troops were already on their way
toward the mountains, a grave murmur of complaint
arose throughout the court, some pointing out the difficulties of so large an expedition, others the danger of the
faithlessness of the Italians and especially of Lodovico
Sforza—recalling the warning that had come from Florence of his treachery (and as it happened, certain moneys
which were expected from him were slow in coming). So
the expedition was not only boldly opposed by those who
had always condemned it (as happens when events seem
to confirm one's opinion), but some of those who had
been its chief supporters—among them the bishop of
St. Malo—began to waver considerably. Finally when this
rumor reached the King's ears, it had such an effect
throughout the court and in his own mind and created
such a disinclination to go any further that he at once
ordered his troops to stop. As a result many nobles who
were already on their way, hearing the news that it had
been decided not to invade Italy, returned to the court.
And it is believed that this change of plan would have
been easily put into effect if the Cardinal of San Piero in
Vincoli—fatal instrument then and before and after of
the ills of Italy[38]—had not rekindled with all his authority and vehemence people's flagging enthusiasm and
keyed the King up to his original decision. He not only
reminded him of the reasons which had inspired him to

undertake so glorious an expedition, but showed him with grave arguments what infamy would be his throughout the world from the frivolous changing of so worthy a decision. Why then had he weakened the frontiers of his kingdom by returning the County of Artois? Why to the deep displeasure of nobles and commoners alike had he opened one of the gates of France to the King of Spain by giving him the County of Roussillon? Other kings might give away such things either to free themselves from urgent danger or to achieve some great gain. But what need, what danger had moved him? What reward did he expect, what fruit could result from it if it were not to have bought most dearly a greater humiliation? What accidents had arisen, what difficulties supervened, what dangers appeared since he had made known his intentions to all the world? Had not rather the hope of victory visibly grown? For the foundations on which the enemy had based all their hopes for defense had proved vain. The Aragonese navy, which had shamefully fled into the harbor of Leghorn after its unsuccessful attack on Portovenere, could do nothing further against Genoa, defended by so many troops and by a fleet greater than theirs; and the land army which had been halted in Romagna by the resistance of a small number of French troops did not dare to advance any further. What would they do when the news spread throughout Italy that the King had crossed the mountains with so great an army? What tumults would arise everywhere? What would be the Pope's terror when from his own palace he saw the Colonna troops at the gates of Rome? How terrified Piero de' Medici would be, finding his own family against him and the city faithful to the French and longing to regain the liberty he had oppressed! There was nothing that could hold back the King's advance to the borders of Naples; and when he got there he would find the same tumults and fears and everywhere retreat and rebellion. Was he afraid their money might run out? When they heard the clash of his arms and the terrible roar of his artillery, all the Italians would vie with one another to bring him money. If any resisted, however, the spoils, plunder and wealth of the conquered would support his

army. For in Italy, for many years used to the semblance
of war rather than to its realities, there was no strength
to restrain the fury of the French. What fears, therefore,
what confusion, dreams, vain shadows had entered his
mind? How had he lost his spirit so soon? Where was the
ferocity with which four days earlier he boasted that he
could conquer all Italy put together? He should consider
that his plans were no longer in his own hands. Things
had gone too far, with the handing over of territories,
the ambassadors he had heard, sent and expelled, the
expenses already laid out, the preparations made, the
declarations published everywhere, and his own advance
almost as far as the Alps. However dangerous the enterprise, he was obliged to go on with it; for there was now
no compromise between glory and infamy, triumph and
shame, between being either the greatest king in the
world or the most despised. And as his victory and
triumph were already prepared and manifest, what ought
he to do?

These things, which are the substance of what the
cardinal said—although conveyed according to his nature
with direct statements and impetuous and fiery gestures
rather than ornate words—so moved the King that without listening any longer except to those who urged him to
war, he left Vienne the same day accompanied by all the
nobles and captains of the Kingdom of France except the
Duke of Bourbon in whose hands he left the administration of the realm in his absence, and the admiral and a
few others delegated to govern and guard the most important provinces. He crossed into Italy over the pass of
Montgenèvre which is much easier than Mont Cenis, and
was the pass used by Hannibal the Carthaginian in ancient times though with incredible difficulty. The King
entered Asti on September 9, 1494, bringing with him
into Italy the seeds of innumerable disasters, terrible
events and change in almost everything. His invasion was
not only the origin of changes of government, subversion
of kingdoms, devastation of the countryside, slaughter of
cities, cruel murders, but also of new habits, new customs, new and bloody methods of warfare, diseases unknown until that day; and the instruments of peace and

harmony in Italy were thrown into such confusion that they have never since been able to be reconstituted, so that other foreign nations and barbarian armies have been able to devastate and trample wretchedly upon her. To make her unhappy fate worse, so that our humiliation should not be tempered by the qualities of the victor, the man whose coming caused so many ills, though amply endowed with material blessings, lacked practically all virtues of mind and body.

For it is true that Charles from boyhood was physically weak and unhealthy, small in stature, and extremely ugly in appearance except for the brightness and dignity of his eyes. His limbs were so proportioned that he seemed more like a monster than a man. Not only did he lack all knowledge of the arts, but he barely knew how to read and write. He was greedy to rule but quite incapable of it, because allowing himself to be continually influenced by his favorites, he retained neither majesty nor authority with them. Averse from all duties and tasks, he showed little prudence and judgment even in those he did attend to. If anything in him seemed at all praiseworthy, when looked at closely, it appeared further removed from virtue than from vice. He aspired to glory but out of impulse rather than wisdom; he was generous but without discretion or discrimination, often firm in his decisons but more often out of ill-founded obstinacy than true constancy; and what many called kindness in him was more deserving of the name of indifference and weakmindedness.

Chapter X

[*The Aragonese fleet again moves toward Genoa. Obietto dal Fiesco defeated at Rapallo. Don Federigo gives up the idea of any further major operation against the coastal towns.*]

The very day on which the King reached Asti fortune began to smile on him with a happy augury; for he received most welcome news from Genoa. Don Federigo, after retiring from Portovenere to the harbor of Leghorn where he provisioned his fleet and took on more troops, returned to the same coast and put ashore Obietto dal Fiesco with 3,000 soldiers. He occupied without difficulty the town of Rapallo twenty miles from Genoa, and began to lay waste the country around. This beginning was of no little importance, because on account of the strife between the factions every slightest movement was highly dangerous in the affairs of Genoa; and therefore it seemed essential to those within the city to put a stop to any further advance by the enemy. So leaving part of their forces to guard the city, there set out with the rest by land toward Rapallo the Sanseverino brothers and Giovanni Adorno, the brother of Agostino, the governor of Genoa, with the Italian foot soldiers; and by sea the Duke of Orléans with 1,000 Swiss aboard the fleet, consisting of 18 galleys, 6 galleons and 9 great ships. These forces were joined near Rapallo and launched a powerful attack on the enemy who had taken up positions at the bridge between the town of Rapallo and a narrow plain which stretches down to the sea. The Aragonese had on their side the advantage of the site as well as their own forces, for the places in that region are strong more from the roughness of the terrain than from fortifications. So the beginning of the attack was not successful for the enemy; and the Swiss, finding themselves in places where they could not deploy their ranks, were on the point of retreating. But from all parts great numbers of local inhabitants, followers of the Adorni, joined in, and they were most skilled in fighting among those rocks and steep hills. Moreover the Aragonese were at the same time bombarded on their flank by the guns of the French fleet, which had come as close inshore as possible, so that they began to have difficulty in repulsing the pressure of the enemy. They had already been thrown back from the bridge when news reached Obietto, whose partisans had not risen in his favor, that Gianluigi dal Fiesco was approaching with a large force. So fearing an attack from the rear they fled, and first among them Obietto, as exiles will, taking to the mountain paths; and between the fighting and the retreat more than a hundred of them were killed, which was quite a large number for the kind of warfare customary in Italy at that time. Also many prisoners were taken—among them Giulio Orsino who, in the King's pay, had followed the fleet with forty men-at-arms and some mounted crossbowmen, Fregosino, the son of Cardinal Fregoso, and Orlandino of the same family.

This victory finally settled the Genoa affair because Don Federigo, who, as soon as he had landed the soldiers, had put out to sea so as not to have to fight the enemy fleet in the Gulf of Rapallo, took his navy back again into the harbor at Leghorn, having given up hope of being able at that moment to do any more good. Although he recruited more soldiers there and had various plans to assault other towns on the coast, nevertheless, as courage and reputation are lost when enterprises start badly, he did not attempt anything else of importance. This gave Lodovico Sforza good reason to boast that he had tricked his enemies with his clever diplomacy—because the only thing that saved Genoa was the tardiness of their movements which had been brought about by his cunning and the vain hopes he had held out to them.

Chapter XI

[Charles VIII's army. The perfection of the French artillery. Other reasons which made the French army formidable. Differences between the Italian forces and Charles' army.]

Lodovico Sforza and his wife Beatrice had gone at once to Charles at Asti with the greatest pomp and a most noble company of many high-born and beautiful ladies of the Duchy of Milan, and with them Ercole Duke of Ferrara. There they discussed their affairs and decided the army should move as early as possible. So that this might be done the sooner, Lodovico, who greatly feared their having to spend the winter in the lands of the Duchy if they were caught by the bad weather, again lent money to the King who was in dire need of it. But he caught a disease which turned out to be smallpox and stayed in Asti about a month, distributing his army in the town and the surrounding country. This consisted (from what I can gather among a great variety of testimony to be the truest estimate) of about 1,600 men-at-arms counting the Swiss who had gone ahead with the Bailli de Dijon to Genoa and the force in Romagna under Aubigny, and in addition to the 200 gentlemen of the royal guard. Of these men-at-arms each had, according to the French usage, two bowmen, so there were six horses under each lancer (which is what their men-at-arms are called). Then there were 6,000 Swiss foot soldiers; 6,000 foot soldiers from his own kingdom—of which half came from Gascony, a province which in the opinion of the French is the best endowed with able infantrymen of any in France. To join up with this army there had been brought to Genoa by sea a great quantity of both siege and field artillery of a kind which had never been seen in Italy.

This pestilential armament—invented many years before in Germany—was first brought into Italy by the Venetians in the war which the Genoese had with them in about 1380. In this the Venetians, beaten on the sea and hard hit by the loss of Chioggia, would have accepted any conditions the victor liked to offer, if sober counsel had not been lacking on such an exceptional occasion. The name of the largest of these weapons was the bombard, which, after the invention had spread all over Italy, was used in sieges. Some were iron, some bronze, but they were all enormous; so that, because of the size of the machine, the lack of skill of the operators and the unsuitability of the apparatus, they were extremely slow and cumbersome to move. They were set up before towns with the same difficulties, and once set up there was so long an interval between shots that they used up a lot of time with relatively small effect compared with what came after. Hence the defenders of the besieged places had plenty of time to make repairs and fortifications inside. All the same the force of the explosion of the saltpeter with which the gunpowder is made, when it was lit, sent the cannon balls flying through the air with such a terrible noise and

astonishing violence that this engine, even before it attained its later perfection, made all the siege instruments used by the ancients with so much fame to Archi-
medes and the other inventors look ridiculous. But the
French made much more manageable pieces and only
out of bronze, which they called cannons, and used iron
balls where they used to be of stone and incomparably
larger and heavier; and they moved them on carts which
were drawn not by oxen as was the custom in Italy,
but by horses. The men and equipment assigned to this
work were so skillful that they could almost always keep
up with the rest of the army; and when brought up to
the walls they were set up with unbelievable rapidity.
With only the briefest interval between shots they fired
so rapidly and powerfully that they could do in a few
hours what in Italy used to take days. And they employed this diabolical rather than human instrument no
less in the field than at sieges, using the same cannon
and other smaller pieces—built and transported according to their size with the same skill and speed.

This artillery made Charles' army most formidable to
the whole of Italy; and it was formidable besides, not
for the number but the caliber of the troops. The men-
at-arms were nearly all from among the King's subjects,
and not common people but gentlemen, not just taken
on or laid off at the wish of the captains; and as the
companies were paid not by them but by the King's
ministers, they not only had their full numbers but were
well set up and well provided with horses and arms—
not being unable through poverty to equip themselves—
and all competed to serve best from the instinct of
honor which noble birth breeds in men's breasts as well
as from the hopes they had of rewards for courageous
deeds both inside and outside the service, which was arranged so that they could be promoted through various
ranks up to captain. The captains had the same incentives, being nearly all barons and lords or at least of
very noble birth, and nearly all subjects of the King of
France. When they had their full complement of lancers—for according to the custom of the kingdom no
one got more than 100 lancers to command—they had

153

no other ambition than to earn their King's praise; so that there did not exist among them either the instability of changing masters out of ambition or greed, or rivalries with other captains for command of more troops.

In the Italian armies everything was just the opposite, for many of the men-at-arms, peasants or common citizens, were subjects of other rulers and entirely dependent on the captains with whom they agreed to serve, and who were responsible for recruiting and paying them, so that neither by nature nor circumstances had they any special incentive to give good service. The captains who were very seldom subjects of those who employed them—and often had very different ambitions and objects—were full of jealousy and hatred for one another; and having no agreed term to their commission and being entirely masters of their companies, they did not keep the number of soldiers they had been paid for; and not satisfied with reasonable conditions they imposed excessive terms on their employers. Unreliable in any service, they often passed into other employment, driven either by ambition or greed or other interests to be not only unreliable but treacherous. Nor was there less difference between the Italian infantry and that of Charles: for the Italians did not fight in firm and orderly squadrons but scattered throughout the field, usually withdrawing to the shelter of banks and ditches. But the Swiss, a most warlike nation, who had revived their ancient fame for ferocity in many brilliant victories and long practice of war, fought in squares arranged with an exact number in each line; and never breaking from this order they faced the enemy like a wall, firm and almost invincible where they could fight in a place large enough to deploy their squadrons. And the French and Gascon infantry fought with the same discipline and method, though not with the same courage.

Chapter XII

[The Colonna occupy the fortress of Ostia and declare themselves openly for the King of France.

Lack of success of the Aragonese army in Romagna.]

While the King was held up in Asti by sickness, there arose a fresh disturbance in the country near Rome; for the Colonna, who in spite of Alfonso's having accepted all their excessive demands, had thrown off the mask and declared themselves for the King of France as soon as Aubigny had entered Romagna with the French troops, now occupied the fortress of Ostia through an understanding reached with some Spanish soldiers who were guarding it. This incident caused the Pope to protest to all the Christian princes against this injury done him by the French, and particularly to the King of Spain and the Venetian senate, from whom he sought help, though in vain, under the terms of the treaty they had concluded the year before. He then turned with determination to preparations for war, summoned Prospero and Fabrizio, whose houses in Rome he then had razed to the ground, and joining his troops with part of Alfonso's under Virginio on the Teverone near Tivoli, he sent them into the lands of the Colonna, whose forces were only 200 men-at-arms and 1,000 foot soldiers. Then, however, the Pope was afraid that the French fleet, which it was rumored was to leave Genoa and go to the relief of Ostia, might take shelter at Nettuno, a port in Colonna hands; so Alfonso collected at Terracina all the forces he and the Pope had in that area, and laid siege to the place, hoping to capture the town easily. But as the Colonna defended it boldly, and the company of Cammillo Vitelli from Città di Castello together with his brothers, who had newly entered the service of the King of France, had entered their territory without opposition, the Pope recalled to Rome part of his troops who were in Romagna with Ferrando.

The latter's affairs no longer went on with the good fortune which seemed to attend them at the beginning. When he got to Villafranca between Forlì and Faenza and then took the main road to Imola, the enemy army which was camped near Villafranca, being smaller in numbers, withdrew between the forest of Lugo and Co-

lombara near the Genivolo Stream, a site well fortified by nature, belonging to Ercole d'Este, in whose territory they were victualing. As Ferrando was not unable
to attack them without grave danger because of the
strength of their position, he left Imola and went to
camp at Toscanella near Castel San Piero in the territory of Bologna. As he wanted to fight, he tried, by giving
signs of moving toward Bologna, to force the enemy—if
they were not to allow him to proceed unimpeded—to
encamp in less well-fortified places. But after a few days
they moved toward Imola and stopped on the River
Santerno between Lugo and Santa Agata with the River
Po behind them and in a very well-defended spot. Ferrando camped the following day six miles from them
on the same river near Mordano and Bubano; and the
next day he led his army in battle order to within a mile
of them. He waited for several hours on the plain, which
would have been ideal for a battle because of its breadth,
but in vain; and as it was obviously too dangerous to attack them in their present encampment, he went to
lodge at Barbiano outside Cotignuola, not on the moun-
tainside as he had done until then, but on the enemy's
flank, still hoping to force them to come out of their
strong positions. Up to this time the affairs of the Duke
of Calabria appeared to have gone with greater success
because the enemy had clearly refused to fight, protecting themselves with the natural strength of their positions rather than with the valor of their arms; and in
some clashes between their light horse the Aragonese
had shown themselves slightly superior. But as the army
of the French and Sforza was continually reinforced by
the arrival of troops which had at first remained behind, the state of the war began to change. The Duke,
whose ardor was restrained by the advice of the captains who were with him, withdrew to Santa Agata, a
possession of the Duke of Ferrara, so as not to take
chances without advantage on his side. There, as he had
fewer foot soldiers and was in the midst of Ferrarese
territory, and that part of the papal troops recalled by
the Pope had already departed, he began to build fortifications. But a few days later, hearing that 200 lancers

and 1,000 Swiss foot soldiers, sent by the French King as soon as he had reached Asti, were expected in the enemy camp, he withdrew to the outskirts of Faenza to a place between the walls and a moat which is about a mile away from the city and surrounds it completely, making the position very strong. When he retreated, the enemy moved into the camp he had abandoned at Santa Agata. Both armies certainly showed courage when they saw that their adversary was weaker than they; but when things were about equal, each side avoided tempting fortune; because (and it very seldom happens that two hostile armies have the same idea) the French and the Sforza armies felt they achieved their purpose in leaving Lombardy if they prevented the Aragonese from advancing any further, while King Alfonso thought it no small gain if the enemy's advance was delayed until the winter, and had expressly told his son and commanded Gianiacopo da Trivulzi and the Count of Pitigliano not to gamble, unless they were obliged to, with the safety of the Kingdom of Naples, which would be lost if that army were destroyed.

Chapter XIII

[*Charles VIII visits Giovan Galeazzo Sforza lying ill in the castle of Pavia. Charles receives the news of Giovan Galeazzo's death at Piacenza. Lodovico Sforza assumes the titles and insignia of Duke of Milan. Rumors and suspicions at the death of Giovan Galeazzo. After further doubts the King of France decides to go on with the expedition.*]

But these remedies were not sufficient to save him, because Charles, not restrained by the weather or any other difficulty, moved forward with his army as soon as he had recovered from his illness. In the castle of Pavia gravely ill lay Giovan Galeazzo, Duke of Milan, his first cousin (the King and he were sons of two sisters, daughters of [Louis II] Duke of Savoy). The King kindly went to visit him when he was passing through that city and was lodged in the same castle. The conversation was general because of the presence of Lodovico, condoling with him on his illness and encouraging him to hope for an early recovery. However the King and all those present were greatly moved with compassion as they all felt sure that because of his uncle's treachery the young man's life would be very short. Their pity was greatly increased by the presence of his wife Isabella, who in her anxiety for the life of her husband and for their little son—and grieving too for the danger her father and the rest of her family were in—wretchedly threw herself at the feet of the King in the presence of everyone, begging him with infinite tears for mercy for her father and her family of Aragon. To this, though he showed pity for her tender years and beauty (as so great a movement could not be halted for so small a cause), he replied that as the enterprise had gone so far he had to go on with it.

From Pavia the King went to Piacenza. While staying there he received the news of Giovan Galeazzo's death, because of which Lodovico who had followed him, returned with the utmost speed to Milan. There it was proposed by the chief members of the Duke's council, whom he had bribed, that on account of the greatness of the state and the difficult times through which Italy was about to pass, it would be very harmful that Giovan Galeazzo's son, a boy of five, should succeed his father. They needed a Duke mature in years and experience. Therefore, dispensing with the provisions of the law, as the law itself permits, for the public good and necessity, Lodovico was compelled to accept the title of Duke in the general interest, though it was a heavy burden in times like these. Under this pretext—honesty being overridden by ambition—he made some pretense of resistance, and assumed the title and insignia of Duke of Milan the next morning after he had declared in secret that he received them as rightfully his by virtue of the investiture granted by the King of the Romans.

It was spread about that the death of Giovan Galeazzo had been caused by immoderate intercourse, but it was believed throughout Italy that he had died not from natural illness or from incontinence, but from poisoning. Theodore of Pavia, one of the royal doctors who was present when Charles visited him, stated that he had seen obvious signs of it. No one doubted that if it was poison, it had been given him by his uncle: because, not being satisfied to be absolute master of the Duchy of Milan, greedy with the appetite common to great men to make himself still greater with titles and honors, and above all convinced that the death of the legitimate prince was necessary for his own security and the succession of his own children, he wished to acquire for himself the powers and title of Duke; and this greed drove him to so wicked an act, though he was by nature gentle and hated bloodshed. Nearly everyone believed that this had been his intention from the moment he had begun to negotiate for the French to invade Italy—thinking it would be a most suitable occasion to put it into effect at a time when the King of France was present in the state with a large army. Thus no one would have the courage to react against his crime. Others thought it had been a sudden idea born of fear lest the King, with French impetuousness, might take hasty action to liberate Giovan Galeazzo from his position of subjection out of compassion for his youth and family feeling or because he thought it safer for himself for that state to be in the hands of his cousin rather than in Lodovico's —and there were plenty of important people around him who constantly sought to arouse his suspicions of Lodovico's treachery. But the fact that Lodovico had procured his investiture the previous year and had the imperial privileges urgently sent to him shortly before his nephew's death argues rather for a premeditated and completely determined plan than a sudden decision forced on him by present danger.

For some days Charles remained at Piacenza. He felt some inclination to return beyond the mountains because lack of money and the failure of anything new to materialize in his favor anywhere in Italy made him doubtful of the outcome. He also had his suspicions of the new Duke who, it was rumored, would not return; although when Lodovico left he had promised to do so.

It is not improbable that as in France the crime of poisoning—common in many parts of Italy—was almost unknown, Charles and all his court, besides distrusting Lodovico's good faith, also held him in horror. Indeed he may have felt it a grave offense to himself that Lodovico should have engineered his invasion of Italy in order to be able to carry out so abominable a crime with impunity. However, in the end he decided to go on, as Lodovico constantly begged him to do, promising to return to the King within a few days because it was quite contrary to his plan that the King should either remain in Lombardy or return hastily to France.

Chapter XIV

[Lorenzo and Giovanni de' Medici urge Charles VIII to come to Florence. Charles' anger against Piero de' Medici increases. The French army crosses the Apennines. Charles' Swiss troops take and sack Fivizzano. The fortresses of Sarzana and Sarzanella. Anger in Florence against Piero de' Medici. He hands over Florentine fortresses to Charles. The Aragonese army retreats from Romagna and the fleet from the port of Leghorn.]

Lorenzo and Giovanni de' Medici came to the King the same day he had left Piacenza. They had fled secretly from their country houses and begged the King to go to Florence, promising much from the friendly disposition of the Florentine people toward the house of France and no less from their hatred for Piero de' Medici. The King's anger against Piero had recently been given fresh stimulus. He had sent an ambassador from Asti to Florence to make all kinds of offers if they granted him free passage and abstained in the future from helping Alfonso, and to threaten them if they persevered in their original intentions. He had also instructed the ambassador, in order to frighten the Florentines, to return if they did not give him a definite answer immediately; and he had been told, as an excuse for delay, that as all the chief citizens in the government had gone to their country houses as the Florentines do during that season, they could not give him a definite answer so quickly. But they would soon send an ambassador themselves to inform the King of their decision.

In the royal council there had never been any question that the better way to proceed with the army was to take the road which leads straight to Naples through Tuscany and the lands of Rome, rather than the one which goes through Romagna and the Marches, across the River Tronto and into the Abruzzi. This was not because they were not confident of beating the Aragonese army which was barely holding its own against Aubigny, but because it seemed unworthy of so great a king and the glory of his arms that—the Pope and the Florentines having declared against him—he should give people cause to think that he was avoiding that road because he was not sure he could subdue them. Besides, it was thought dangerous to fight a war in the Kingdom of Naples leaving a hostile Tuscany and the Papal State in their rear. It was decided to cross the Apennines at Parma, as Lodovico Sforza—who was eager to capture Pisa—had suggested in Asti, rather than by the direct road through Bologna. The vanguard commanded by Gilbert de Montpensier, a Bourbon of the royal family, followed by the King and the rest of the army, went to Pontremoli a town belonging to the Duchy of Milan at the foot of the Apennines on the River Magra which divides the state of Genoa (called Liguria in antiquity) from Tuscany. From Pontremoli Montpensier entered Lunigiana, part of which was under Florentine rule, while some castles belonged to the Genoese and the remainder to the Marchesi Malespini, who each maintained their little states, some under the protection of the Duke of Milan, some of the Florentines and others of the Genoese. There they were met by the Swiss who had been defending Genoa and the artillery that had come by sea to Genoa and then to La Spezia. Moving up to Fivizzano, a castle of the Florentines to which they were led by Gabriello Malaspina, Marchese di Fosdinuovo, their protégé, they took it by storm and sacked it, massacring all the foreign soldiers who were in it as well as many of the civilians. This was unheard of and caused great terror in Italy which had been accustomed for a long time to seeing wars of great splendor, pomp and magnificence—almost like displays, rather than full of danger and bloodshed.

The Florentines put up their main resistance in Sarzana, a small town which they had heavily fortified, though they had not equipped it sufficiently to withstand so powerful an enemy because they had not put in an experienced captain or many soldiers—and these were already full of cowardice at the very news of the approach of the French army. Nevertheless it was not regarded as easy to capture—particularly the fortress; and Sarzanella was even stronger: a well-equipped fort built on the hill above Sarzana. Besides, the army could not remain long in the area because this small and sterile land, shut in between the sea and the mountain, could not support such a multitude. Victuals could only come from places far away and could not arrive in time to meet present needs. Hence it seemed that the King's progress might run into considerable difficulties because, though he could not be prevented from attacking Pisa, leaving behind him the town or the fortress of Sarzana and Sarzanella, or from entering some other part of Florentine territory through the country around Lucca (which had secretly decided to receive him at the instigation of the Duke of Milan), he was unwilling to make such a decision. He thought that if he did not take the first place that offered resistance, all the others would take courage to do likewise. But it was fated that either by good fortune or by order of some other higher power (if, that is, the errors and indiscretions of men deserve such excuses) an immediate solution to this dilemma should appear—for Piero de' Medici had no greater courage or constancy in adversity than he had moderation or prudence in prosperity.

The displeasure which the city of Florence felt from the start at the opposition offered to the King had continued to increase: not so much because the Florentine merchants had been recently banished from the entire

Kingdom of France, as from fear of the power of the French, which had grown tremendously since it was heard that their army had begun to cross the Apennines and later, when news came of their cruelty in taking Fivizzano. Everyone openly complained of the rashness of Piero de' Medici, who without any need and trusting in himself and in the advice of ministers reckless and arrogant in time of peace and useless in time of danger —rather than in those citizens who had been his father's friends and who had given him wise counsel—had senselessly provoked the armed might of a King of France, powerful himself and supported by the Duke of Milan, particularly since Piero knew nothing about war. There was Pisa, hostile and not fortified, with few soldiers and munitions, and the rest of Florentine territory likewise ill-prepared for defense against such an attack. As for the Aragonese—for whose sake they were exposed to such dangers—there was no one in sight but the Duke of Calabria, tied up in Romagna with his forces by the opposition of only a small part of the French army. In spite of this their country, abandoned by all, had earned the violent hatred and was certain prey to the man who had earnestly sought not to have to harm them. This feeling which was almost universal in the city, was fanned by many noble citizens who strongly disliked the present government and the fact that one family had usurped the power of the whole Republic. These, working on the fears of those who were already afraid and encouraging those who desired a change of government, had so roused the feelings of the people that it was beginning to be feared that there might be riots in the city. Men were further incensed by the arrogance and immoderate behavior of Piero, who in many ways had abandoned the civilized customs and the gentleness of his forebears. For this he had been disliked almost from boyhood by all the citizens; and it is well known that his father Lorenzo, observing his character, had often complained to his closest friends that his son's imprudence and arrogance would bring about the downfall of his family.

Piero, now terrified of the danger which he had

earlier rashly despised and lacking the help promised him by the Pope and Alfonso, who were preoccupied with the loss of Ostia, the siege of Nettuno and their fear of the French fleet, hastily decided to go and seek from his enemies the security which he no longer hoped for from his friends. He thought he was following his father's example, who in 1479 finding himself in grave danger through the war waged on the Florentines by Pope Sixtus and Ferdinand King of Naples went to see Ferdinand in Naples and brought back to Florence peace for his country and security for himself. But it is certainly very dangerous to imitate the example of others, if the same conditions do not apply not only in general but in every particular, if the matter is not managed with equal prudence and if in addition to everything else the same good fortune does not play its part. Leaving Florence with this intention he heard before he reached the King that the cavalry of Paolo Orsino and 300 foot soldiers sent by the Florentines to relieve Sarzana had been routed by some French cavalry which had pushed beyond the Magra. Most of them had been killed or taken prisoner. He awaited the royal safe-conduct at Pietrasanta. The bishop of St. Malo came with other nobles of the court to escort him safely. In their campment within the moat of Faenza, his enemies re- and his army caught up with the vanguard which was encamped before Sarzanella and was bombarding the fortress, though they had not made much progress and had little hope of taking it. When Piero was brought before the King and was received with a kindness more apparent than real, he softened his anger a good deal by agreeing to all his demands which were high and excessive: that the fortresses of Pietrasanta, Sarzana and Sarzanella—places which on that side were like keys to the Florentine dominion—and the fortresses of Pisa and Leghorn—which were most vital parts of their state —should be placed in the King's hands; and he gave an agreement in his own writing that he would give them all back as soon as he had conquered the Kingdom of Naples. Piero was to arrange for the Florentines to lend him 200,000 ducats and the King was to accept them as allies under his protection. The preparation of the documents of these agreements, which were simply promised verbally, was deferred until they were in Florence, through which the King intended to pass. But the handing over of the fortresses was not deferred because Piero immediately had those of Sarzana, Pietrasanta and Sarzanella handed over. And a few days later by his orders the same was done with those of Pisa and Leghorn. The French were astonished that Piero should have agreed so easily to matters of such importance, since the King would doubtless have settled for much less.

I feel I should not omit here Lodovico Sforza's witty reply to Piero de' Medici when he came up with the army the following day. Piero apologized for having missed Lodovico when he went to meet him to do him honor, and said that the reason was that Lodovico had missed his way. Whereupon Lodovico replied promptly: "It is true that one of us missed his way, but perhaps it was you"—as though to rebuke him for not having heeded his advice and so having fallen into such difficulties and dangers. However, later events showed that both of them had missed their way; but the one who did so with the greater misfortune and infamy was the one who from a position of greater eminence professed to be, in his wisdom, the guide of all the others.

Piero's decision not only made Tuscany safe for the King but freed him from all difficulty in Romagna where the Aragonese were already much weakened. It is difficult for one who can barely defend himself against dangers which threaten to provide against the dangers of others; and while Ferrando was safe in his strong encampment within the moat of Faenza, his enemies returned to the Province of Imola. After they had attacked the castle of Bubano with part of the army—though without success as it was so small that it required but few defenders and the country was so low lying that it was all flooded—they took the castle of Mordano by storm, though it was very strong and well-garrisoned. Such was the force of the artillery, such the ferocity of the French attack that, although many drowned crossing the moats full of water, those within were unable to resist; and such acts of cruelty were committed against them without regard to age or sex that the whole of Romagna was filled with horror. Because of this horrible event Caterina Sforza, despairing of any assistance, came to an agreement with the French to avoid the immediate danger and promised their army all facilities in the states ruled by her son. Whereupon Ferrando, not trusting the inhabitants of Faenza and considering it dangerous to stay on between Imola and Forlì —the more so when he heard of Piero de' Medici's visit to Sarzana—withdrew to the walls of Cesena. He showed such fear that to avoid passing near Forlì he led his army by a longer and more difficult route through the hills near Castrocaro, a Florentine castle. A few days later, when he heard of the agreement made by Piero de' Medici whereby the Florentine forces left his army, he set off on the way to Rome. At the same time Don Federigo left the port of Leghorn and retired with his fleet toward Naples, where, as his own affairs were progressing just as badly, Alfonso was beginning to need for his own defense those forces which he had sent so hopefully to attack the states of others. Since his siege of Nettuno had been unsuccessful, he had brought his army back to Terracina; and the French fleet, commanded by the Prince of Salerno and M. de Serenon [Louis de Villeneuve], had appeared off Ostia; but they declared that they had no intention of attacking the states of the Church and they did not put men ashore or show any sign of hostility to the Pope—though a few days before the King had refused to hear Francesco Piccolomini, Cardinal of Siena, whom the Pope had sent to him as legate.

Chapter XV

[*The anger of the Florentines increases against Piero de' Medici because of his agreement with the King. Lodovico Sforza obtains the investiture of Genoa. Piero de' Medici is prevented from entering the Palazzo della Signoria. Rising of the*

*people and Piero's flight. The former power of
the Medici in Florence. The Pisans regain their
liberty with the consent of Charles VIII. Contrary
advice to the Pisans from the Cardinal of San
Piero in Vincoli.*]

When the news reached Florence of the agreement
made by Piero de' Medici—with such loss to their states
and such severe and shameful damage to the Republic
—violent indignation was felt throughout the city. What
enraged the people besides these losses was the fact that
Piero had done something his forefathers had never
done; he had given away, without the agreement of
the citizens or decree of the government, a large part of
Florentine territory. For this reason criticism of him was
most bitter; everywhere citizens could be heard inciting
each other to regain their freedom; those who supported
Piero did not dare to oppose this movement either with
words or deeds. Though they had no means of defending Pisa and Leghorn and did not think that they could
persuade the King not to take over the fortresses, yet in
order to distinguish the policy of the Republic from
that of Piero—so that at least what belonged to the
Republic should not be accepted as belonging to a private person—they at once sent many ambassadors to
the King from among those who were dissatisfied with
Piero's power. At this Piero, realizing that it was the beginning of a change of government and wishing to see
to his own interests before some greater disorder should
arise, left the King with the excuse that he was going
to attend to the carrying out of the promises he had
made. Then Charles also left Sarzana to go to Pisa
and Lodovico Sforza returned to Milan, having succeeded, for the payment of a certain sum of money, in
getting the investiture of Genoa—which the King had
granted a few years earlier to Giovan Galeazzo and his
heirs—transferred to himself and his descendants. But
he felt annoyed with Charles because he had refused
to leave in his care, as he said he had promised, Pietrasanta and Sarzana, which Lodovico claimed had been
unjustly taken from the Genoese by the Florentines a

very few years before; and he wanted them as a stepping stone in his ambitious greed for Pisa.

When Piero de' Medici returned to Florence, he found the greater part of the magistrates turned against him and his most valuable friends uncertain because he had done everything so imprudently and against their advice. He found the people so turbulent that when he tried the next day, November 9th, to enter the Palazzo della Signoria, the highest office of the Republic, he was prevented by some armed officials guarding the door—the chief of whom was Jacopo de' Nerli, a rich young nobleman. When this was known in the city, the people immediately rose and took up arms. Their agitation was all the greater because Paolo Orsino with his soldiers recalled by Piero was approaching. Piero had already gone home and his courage and counsel was failing him when he heard that the Signoria had declared him a rebel. He fled from Florence with all speed followed by Cardinal Giovanni and Giuliano, his brothers on whom the same penalties as rebels were imposed; and they went to Bologna. There Giovanni Bentivoglio, requiring in others that strength of mind which he in his later adversities failed to show, sarcastically rebuked Piero at their first meeting for having, not only to his own detriment but to that of all oppressors of their countries' freedom, abandoned his high position in so cowardly a way and without the loss of a single man. Thus through a young man's temerity the Medici family fell for the time being from that power which they had held continuously in Florence for sixty years virtually as private citizens in name and appearance. It began with Cosimo his great-grandfather, a citizen of rare wisdom and vast wealth and famous on that account throughout Europe; but much more because with splendid liberality and a truly regal spirit, thinking more of the perpetuation of his name than the good of his heirs, he spent more than 400,000 ducats in building monasteries, churches and other fine buildings not only at home but in many parts of the world. Lorenzo, Cosimo's grandson, a man of great brilliance and excellent counsel, no less generous than his grandfather, and

holding more absolute authority in the government of
the Republic, though far less rich and enjoying a shorter
life, was greatly admired throughout Italy and by many
foreign princes. And after his death his reputation became a memory of great renown, for it seemed that with
his life the peace and happiness of Italy had come to an
end.

The very day the government changed in Florence
Charles was in Pisa. The Pisans appealed to him with
a public demonstration to restore their freedom, complaining strongly of the harm they said the Florentines
had done to them. Some of his people who were present
assured him that it was a just demand because the
Florentines ruled them harshly. The King, without considering what this request implied and that it was contrary to the agreement made at Sarzana, at once agreed.
At this reply the people of Pisa took up arms, pulled
down the Florentine insignia in all the public places,
and with great enthusiasm proclaimed their regained
freedom. Nevertheless the King, contradicting himself
and not knowing what he was conceding, wanted the
Florentine officials to stay on and govern as usual, but
on the other hand he left the old citadel in the possession
of the Pisans, keeping for himself the new one which
was of much greater importance. The truth appeared
in these affairs of Pisa and Florence of the popular
proverb that men, when their misfortunes draw near,
first lose all prudence, with which they might have prevented the things that were destined to happen: for the
Florentines, who never trusted the Pisans at any time,
failed, when so serious a war was imminent, to order
to Florence the principal citizens of Pisa as they used to
do in large numbers to make sure of them at the slightest
approach of danger. Nor did Piero de' Medici, threatened
with such dangers, fill the palace and the piazza with
foreign troops, as had often been done before for much
slighter cause. Similar measures would have placed a
serious obstacle in the way of these changes. But as for
Pisa, there is no doubt that the Pisans, who naturally
hated the Florentines, were encouraged in their action
by the authority of Lodovico Sforza who had earlier had

secret talks to this effect with certain Pisans exiled for private crimes. And that very day Galeazzo da San Severino, whom he had left with the King, roused the people to this revolt—through which Lodovico hoped he would soon obtain control of Pisa for himself. He did not know that this was soon to be the origin of all his troubles. But it is likewise known that the night before a few Pisans told the Cardinal of San Piero in Vincoli what they meant to do, and that he, who up to that time had perhaps never been a source of peaceful advice, urged them with grave words to consider not only the appearances and beginnings of things but also what their results might be in course of time.

Freedom was a precious and desirable thing and worth facing any danger for, if there was the slightest hope of being able to maintain it. But Pisa, an impoverished and depopulated city, was not able to defend herself against the might of the Florentines; and it was a mistaken idea to think that the authority of the King of France would preserve them; because even if Florentine money no longer weighed with him, as very probably it might—especially considering the agreements reached at Sarzana—the French would not stay in Italy forever, as one could easily foresee the future from the example of what had happened in the past. It was very imprudent to put oneself in permanent danger on a basis that was impermanent, and for uncertain hopes to undertake a certain war with enemies so much more powerful than they, in which they could not hope for outside help because it depended on the disposition of others—and, what is more, on very varied circumstances. And even if they got such help, the calamities of war would not be averted but would be all the greater; for they would be simultaneously attacked by enemy forces and preyed upon by those of their friends. The dangers and calamities would be all the harder to bear when they realized that they were not fighting for their own freedom but for foreign domination, exchanging one servitude for another. For no prince would be willing to get involved, unless it were to dominate them. For the expense and difficulties of this war could only be sustained with great hardships because of the wealth and proximity of the Florentines, who would never cease to harass them as long as they had life to do so.

Chapter XVI

[*Charles VIII marches on Florence and stops at Signa with hostile intentions. Precautions taken by the Florentines and secret preparations for defense. Charles enters Florence. His excessive demands and the irritation of the Florentines. Piero de' Medici, sent for by Charles, takes counsel with the Venetians who urge him not to leave Venice. Angry words of Pier Capponi to Charles: the pacts concluded between him and the Florentines.*]

Next Charles stopped at Signa—a place seven miles from Florence—to wait until the tumult of the Florentine people was somewhat abated before he entered the city. The Florentines had not laid down the arms they had taken up on the day of Piero de' Medici's expulsion. Charles also wished to give Aubigny time to arrive. So as to make his entry into Florence more terrifying he had sent for him, with orders to leave behind his artillery at Castrocaro and pay off the 500 Italian soldiers, who were in Romagna with him; and also the men-at-arms of the Duke of Milan, so that of all Sforza's troops he was followed only by the Count of Gaiazzo with 300 light horse. There were many signs that the King's intention was to induce the Florentines to give him absolute dominion over the city out of terror of his army. He was unable to conceal this even from the ambassadors who went to Signa on several occasions to discuss the manner of his entry into Florence and to arrange the details of the agreement which was being negotiated. There is no doubt that the King, because of the opposition he had met, had conceived great anger and hatred for the Florentines. And though it was clear that it had not been the fault of the Republic and though the city had very carefully explained its position, he was not

171

satisfied. It was believed he was influenced by many of his people who either thought that this opportunity to capture Florence should not be lost or, out of greed, did not wish to miss this chance of sacking so rich a city. It was loudly rumored throughout the whole army that Florence should be burned as an example to all others— as she had been the first in Italy who had had the presumption to oppose the power of France. There were also some leading members of his council who advised Charles to restore Piero de' Medici—especially Philippe de Bresse, the brother of the Duke of Savoy, who was inspired by private friendships and promises. Thus, against the advice of the bishop of St. Malo—either because the counsels of the former prevailed or because he hoped that fear of Piero would make the Florentines readier to obey him or so that he could more easily make up his mind which course he would prefer when the moment came—he wrote a letter to Piero, and also had Philippe de Bresse write to him. The letters urged Piero to come to Florence, saying that because of the friendship between their fathers and the good will shown by him in the handing over of the fortresses the king had decided to restore him to his former greatness. These letters did not find him, as the King thought, in Bologna because Piero, moved by the harsh words of Giovanni Bentivoglio and fearing persecution by the Duke of Milan and perhaps by the King of France, had gone to Venice in his misfortune. The letters were sent on to him there by his brother the cardinal who had stayed behind in Bologna.

In Florence there were grave doubts of the King's intentions; but as they did not see with what forces or hopes they could resist him, they had decided the least dangerous course was to receive him in the city, hoping to be able to win him over somehow. Yet in order to be ready against any emergency they had arranged for many citizens to take secretly into their homes men from the Florentine dominion and ordered that the commanders in the pay of the Republic find some pretext to enter Florence with many of their troops. At the same time every man in the city and the places around should be ready to take up arms at the sound of the great bell of the palace.

Then the King entered the city with his army. All was arranged with the utmost care and splendor both by the court and the city. With great pomp and show he rode in as a conqueror—he and his horse fully armed and lance on hip. Discussions for the treaty began at once, but met with serious difficulties. Besides the excessive favor of some of his people for Piero de' Medici and the intolerable demands for money, Charles openly claimed to rule Florence. He said that because he had entered the city armed in that way, he had lawfully taken it according to the military laws of France. Although in the end he abandoned that demand, he wished to leave in Florence certain "long-robed" ambassadors (as the French call doctors and persons who wear gowns) with so much authority that according to French laws he would have been able to claim that considerable jurisdiction had been vested in him in perpetuity. The Florentines on the other hand were absolutely determined to preserve their freedom in spite of any danger. Hence, as they negotiated from such opposite points of view, feelings constantly ran high on both sides. However neither side was anxious to settle their differences by force of arms, because the Florentines—long devoted to mercantile pursuits and not to military exercises— were very much afraid at having within their walls so powerful a king and so great an army full of unknown and ferocious people, while the French were nervous because the population was so numerous and had shown in the days when the government was changed, unexpected signs of boldness; and it was rumored that at the ringing of the great bell a countless multitude of men would rush in from all the surrounding country. Amid this mutual fear false rumors often arose; both sides would hastily take up arms but neither would attack or provoke the other.

The King's reliance on Piero de' Medici turned out to be useless: Piero, torn between the hopes thus offered him and the fear of being handed over to his enemies, asked the advice of the Venetian senate about the King's letters. Certainly nothing is more necessary when making difficult decisions than asking advice; on the other hand nothing is more dangerous. No doubt wise men are less in need of advice than fools; nevertheless the wise derive much more profit from taking it. Who is so universally wise that he can always know and judge everything on his own, and in conflicting arguments can always see the better cause? But what certainty has the man who seeks advice of being faithfully advised? The one who gives the advice, if he is not particularly fond of or faithful to the one who asks, is not only moved by considerable interest but for any small convenience of his own, for any slight satisfaction, will often give such advice as will bring about the result most profitable or pleasing to himself. As the one who asks advice is usually unaware of these purposes, he does not realize—if he is not very prudent—the unreliability of the advice. This is what happened to Piero de' Medici. The Venetians, thinking that his going would make it easier for Charles to do as he wished with Florence—which would be contrary to their own interests, and therefore advising themselves rather than Piero—urged him most strongly not to place himself in the power of the King who felt he had been offended by him. To encourage Piero further to follow their advice they offered to take up his cause and to lend him, when times were favorable, every assistance to re-establish him in his country. Not content with this and to make sure that he did not then leave Venice, they placed secret guards on him—if, that is, what was later rumored was true.

Meantime in Florence tempers were running high on both sides and almost on the verge of open conflict. The King refused to withdraw from his latest demands and the Florentines refused to contract to give excessive sums of money to the King, or allow him any jurisdiction or overlordship in their state. These difficulties, practically inextricable except by force of arms, were solved by the courage of Piero Capponi, one of four citizens chosen to negotiate with the King. He was a man of great intelligence and spirit, greatly respected in Florence for these qualities—and because he was born of an honored family and descended from men who had been powerful in the Republic. One day he and his companions were in the presence of the King; one of the royal secretaries was reading the immoderate terms which were the King's final demands. Capponi with an impetuous gesture seized the document from the secretary's hands and tore it up before the eyes of the King, adding in an angry voice: "As such improper things are being asked, you shall blow your trumpets and we shall ring our bells"—meaning that their differences should be decided by force of arms. And with this he at once left the room followed by his companions. It is certain that the words of this citizen—who was already known to Charles and all his court because a few months earlier he had been in France as ambassador of the Florentines—alarmed them all so much, as they did not believe his boldness was unfounded that they called him back and gave up the demands to which he refused to consent. The King and the Florentines then agreed on these terms: all past injuries would be forgiven, and the city of Florence would be friend and ally under the perpetual protection of the crown of France; the city of Pisa and the town of Leghorn with all their fortresses would remain in the King's hands for his security, and he undertook to restore them without any payment to the Florentines as soon as he had concluded the Naples expedition—which would be either when he had taken the city of Naples or settled the affair with a peace or a truce for two years, or when for any reason the King himself left Italy. The officers in charge of the fortresses were to take an oath at once to restore the castles in the above-named cases. In the meanwhile the sovereignty, jurisdiction, government, and income of these lands were to belong to the Florentines as usual. The same should be done with Pietrasanta, Sarzana, and Sarzanella, but as the Genoese claimed these places, the King would be allowed to try to end their differences either by negotiating agreement or by legal inquiry; however, if he could not do so within the above-mentioned time, he would hand them back to the Florentines. The King was to leave two ambassadors in Florence, and nothing relating to the expedition would be discussed except in their presence; and during the same period the Florentines could not choose a captain-general of .their forces without their participation. All the other lands taken from the Florentines or which had revolted against them, were to be returned at once; and the Florentines might retake them by force if the inhabitants refused to have them back. They were to give the King as a subsidy for his expedition 50,000 ducats within 15 days, 40,000 the following March and 30,000 in June. The Pisans were to be pardoned for their rebellion and other crimes committed since. Piero de' Medici and his brothers were to be freed from banishment and confiscation of their goods; but Piero was not to come nearer than 100 miles to the borders of Florentine territory (which was done to prevent him from living in Rome); and his brothers were not to come within 100 miles of the city of Florence. These were the principal articles of the treaty between the King and the Florentines. Besides being stipulated legally, it was published with great ceremony in the cathedral during the celebration of the divine office. There the King himself, at whose request this was done, and the magistrates of the city swore to observe the treaty with solemn oaths on the high altar in the presence of the court and the Florentine people. Two days later Charles left Florence where he had spent ten days and went to Siena. This city, allied with the King of Naples and the Florentines, had followed their lead until Piero de' Medici's going to Sarzana forced them to look to their own safety.

Chapter XVII

[*From Siena, with its free government but disturbed by factions, Charles VIII goes toward Rome. Fears of the Venetian senate and the Duke of Milan aroused by Charles' success. The Pope hesitates while the French army nears Rome. Secret*

The city of Siena, well-populated and with very fertile lands, had for a long time past been the most powerful place in Tuscany after Florence. She ruled herself, but in such a way that she knew liberty in name rather than in fact. Divided by many factions or parties of citizens, which they called "orders," she was ruled by whatever party happened according to the fortune of the times and the favor of foreign powers to be the most powerful. At this time the order of the Monte de' Nove was in the ascendancy. The King remained a few days in Siena and left a garrison there because he distrusted the city which had been inclined since ancient times to favor the Empire. He then went on toward Rome. Every day he grew more arrogant because his success was greater than he had ever hoped for; and as the weather was unusually favorable for the season, he decided to press on in his good fortune, menacing not only his overt enemies but also his allies and those who had never provoked him in any way. Both the Venetian senate and the Duke of Milan, frightened by the King's success and afraid— especially as he had kept the Florentine fortresses and left a garrison in Siena—that his ambitions were not confined to the conquest of Naples, began to try to make a new alliance against the common danger. They would have arranged it sooner if Rome had put up the resistance many hoped for.

The intention of the Duke of Calabria, who had been joined near Rome by the papal troops and Virginio Orsino with the rest of the Aragonese army, was to stop at Viterbo to prevent Charles from going any further. The place was very suitable: it was surrounded by the lands of the Church and was near the states of the Orsini. But all the country around Rome was already in tumult because of the raids the Colonna were making beyond the Tiber, and because supplies, which were usually brought to Rome by sea, were being interfered with from Ostia; and so he did not dare to stop there.

177

He had doubts besides of the Pope's intentions, because ever since he heard of Piero de' Medici's change of policy, he had begun to listen to the demands of the French, which Cardinal Ascanio had gone to discuss with him in Rome. The Cardinal of Valencia had first gone to Marino—a place belonging to the Colonna—for his own safety. And although Ascanio left again without a definite reply—because in Alexander's mind suspicion of Charles' intentions contended with fear of his forces —when Charles left Florence he again took up the discussions for an agreement. The Pope sent to him the bishops of Concordia and Terni and Maestro Graziano his confessor with a view to settling his affairs as well as those of King Alfonso. But Charles' intention was quite different: he was determined to come to an agreement only with the Pope; and so he sent to him M. de la Trémouille and Ganay, president of the Parliament of Paris; Cardinal Ascanio and Prospero Colonna also went there for the same purpose. Hardly had they arrived than Alexander changed his mind and suddenly brought the Duke of Calabria with all his army into Rome, arrested Ascanio and Prospero and had them shut up in the Mole d'Adriano, which used to be called the Castello di Crescenzio, and is now known as the Castello Sant' Angelo. He demanded the return of Ostia from them. In this tumult the French ambassadors were taken prisoner by the Aragonese troops, but the Pope set them free at once. A few days later he also freed Ascanio and Prospero though obliging them to leave Rome immediately. Later he sent to the King who had stopped at Nepi, Cardinal Federigo da San Severino to begin to negotiate for settlement of his own affairs. At the same time the Pope was very undecided, because now he thought to stay and defend Rome; and so he allowed Ferrando and the captains to see to the strengthening of the weaker points of the city. Then again, thinking it would be difficult to hold out because the supply route by sea was cut by those holding Ostia and the city was full of unreliable strangers and divided by factions, he was inclined to leave Rome, and so he made all the cardinals in the College promise in writing that they would follow him. At other times, fearing the difficulties and dangers inherent in either of these plans, he thought of reaching an agreement instead.

While he hesitated amid these doubts, the French overran all the country on this side of the Tiber, occupying now one place now another as they encountered no resistance anywhere, met no one who did not give way before their advance, each following the example of the others—even those who had the strongest reasons to oppose them. Even Virginio Orsino, bound with so many ties of faith, obligation, and honor to the house of Aragon, captain-general of the royal army, grand constable of the Kingdom of Naples and closely related to Alfonso (because Gian Giordano, his son, was married to a natural daughter of the late King Ferdinand, and he had received from them lands and favors), did not oppose Charles. Forgetting all these things and forgetting too that the calamities of the house of Aragon had all started with his affairs, he agreed—to the astonishment of the French who were unused to these subtle distinctions of the Italian captains—that, while he remained in the pay of the King of Naples, his sons would serve with the King of France. He also undertook to give them in the state he held in the territory of the Church, accommodation, free passage and victuals, and to place Campagnano and certain other places in the hands of the Cardinal of Gurk, who promised to return them as soon as the French army had left Roman territory. The Count of Pitigliano and the other members of the Orsini family also made similar agreements. When this was concluded Charles went from Nepi to Bracciano, Virginio's principal possession, and sent to Ostia Louis, M. de Ligny, and Yves d'Alègre with 500 lancers and 2,000 Swiss —so that when they crossed the Tiber and met up with the Colonna forces which were overrunning everything, they would try to enter Rome. The Colonna hoped to succeed in this through the Romans belonging to their faction, though the times were bad and the difficulties had increased.

Civitavecchia, Corneto, and finally nearly all the territory of Rome had been brought into alliance with the

French. The whole court and the entire population of Rome were in great tumult and terror and ardently desired a peaceful agreement. The Pope, now in a most dangerous situation and seeing the basis of his defense continually weakening, was held back only by the recollection that he had been one of the first to urge the King to attempt the Naples expedition. And then, without any reason, he had obstinately resisted him with his authority, counsel and arms. Hence the Pope had good reason to wonder whether the King's good faith to him might not be of the same kind as that which he had shown the King. His fear was increased when he saw the highly influential Cardinal of San Piero in Vincoli at the King's side with many other cardinals who were his enemies. He was afraid lest the King might be thinking, as was already being rumored, of reforming the affairs of the Church on the advice of these cardinals. His fear was further inspired by the title of Most Christian borne by the kings of France, by the long-standing reputation for religious fervor of that nation and by an exaggerated respect for people as yet known only by name. It was an unspeakably terrible thought to him, remembering by what infamous means he had risen to the papacy and how he had continued to administer it with customs and methods entirely appropriate to that wicked beginning. This fear was allayed by the King's diligence and promises—for, desiring above all else to speed his journey to Naples and so neglecting nothing which would remove the obstacle of the Pope, he again sent ambassadors to him: the Seneschal of Beauedire, the Marshal de Gié, and President de Ganay. These ambassadors tried to persuade him that it was not the King's intention to interfere in things which concerned papal authority, nor to ask him for more than was necessary to his safety in passing through his territory; and they urged him to allow the King to enter Rome. They said that he greatly desired this permission, not because he was unable to force an entry, but so as not to be obliged to fail in that respect in which his forefathers had always held the Roman pontiffs. As soon as the King had entered Rome their differences would be transformed into the sincerest good

will and concord. It seemed a very hard condition to the
Pope to have to give up the help of his allies, place himself entirely in the power of the enemy and receive
him in Rome before the relations between them were
settled. In the end, feeling that this was the lesser of
his dangers, he agreed to these demands and had the
Duke of Calabria depart from Rome with his army,
first having obtained from Charles a safe-conduct for
him to pass safely through the whole territory of Rome.
But Ferrando bravely refused this and left Rome by
the Porta di San Sebastiano on the last day of 1494 at
the very hour when the King was entering with the
French army by the Porta di Santa Maria del Popolo—
again armed and lance on hip as he had entered Florence. At the same time the Pope, full of unspeakable
dread and anxiety, had retired into the Castel Sant'
Angelo, accompanied only by the cardinals Batista Orsini and Ulivieri Caraffa, a Neapolitan.

Vincoli, Ascanio, the cardinals Colonna and Savelli, and
many others constantly pressed the King to remove from
the See a pope full of such great vices and abominations
and to elect another, maintaining that it was no less
glorious to his name to free the Holy Church from the
tyranny of a wicked pope than it had been for Pepin and
Charlemagne, his predecessors, to free popes of saintly
life from the persecution of those by whom they were
unjustly oppressed. They reminded Charles that this decision was no less necessary for his own safety than
desirable for his renown. How could he trust Alexander's
promises, a man treacherous by nature, insatiably greedy,
shameless in all his actions, and as experience had
shown, full of violent hatred for the name of France—
especially now that Alexander was reconciled not of his
own accord but compelled by necessity and fear? As
a result of their persuasions, and because the Pope refused in the treaty they were negotiating to hand over
to Charles Castel Sant' Angelo as a guarantee of his
promises, the artillery was twice brought out of the
palace of San Marco where Charles lodged, to be set
up around the castle. However the King was not disposed
by nature to offend the Pope; and in his closest counsel

181

there prevailed those whose good will Alexander had
bought with gifts and promises. So finally they reached
agreement: there was to be perpetual friendship between
the Pope and the King and alliance for their common defense. The King should be given for his security, to keep
until he had conquered the Kingdom of Naples, the forts
of Civitavecchia, Terracina and Spoleto—though the
latter was never handed over. The Pope was not to regard himself as injured or offended in any way by the
cardinal bishop, and (according to the ancient rite) he
had taken the King's part. The Pope gave Charles the
investiture of the Kingdom of Naples and also handed
over Bajazet's brother Gemin, who after the death of
Mahomet their father, had been persecuted by Bajazet
(according to the savage custom of the Ottomans who
establish their succession to the throne by shedding the
blood of their brothers and all their nearest kinsfolk)
and had taken refuge in Rhodes. After being taken from
there to France he had finally been delivered into the
hands of Pope Innocent. Bajazet, making use of the
avarice of the Vicars of Christ as a means for maintaining in peace an empire inimical to the Christian faith,
each year paid the Popes 40,000 ducats—ostensibly as
expenses incurred for keeping and feeding Gemin, so
that they would not be in a hurry to let him go or to
hand him over to other princes who were his enemies.
Charles insisted on having him assist in his expedition
against the Turks. Puffed up with the vain flatteries of
his advisers he intended to begin this expedition as soon
as he had conquered the Aragonese. And as the last
40,000 ducats had been taken at Sinigallia by the Prefect of Rome, the Pope was to leave him the task of
restitution and punishment. In addition the Cardinal of
Valencia was to follow the King for three months as
apostolic legate—but in reality, as assurance for his
father's promises. When this agreement had been reached
the Pope returned to the Papal Palace in the Vatican.
Then with the pomp and ceremony usual in welcoming
great kings, he received Charles in the Church of St.
Peter. The latter, after having (according to ancient
usage) knelt and kissed his feet, was then allowed to kiss

his cheek; and on another day he took part in the Pontifical Mass, sitting immediately next to the first cardinal bishop and (according to the ancient rite) he gave the Pope water for his hands as he celebrated Mass. The Pope had a painting made of these ceremonies in a loggia of Castel Sant' Angelo, so that their memory might be preserved for posterity. Further, at the King's request, the bishop of St. Malo and the bishop of Le Mans of the house of Luxemburg were made cardinals; and Alexander omitted nothing to show that he was faithfully and sincerely reconciled with him.

Chapter XVIII

[The people of the Kingdom of Naples favor the French. Alfonso of Aragon abdicates in favor of his son Ferdinand and flees to Mazari in Sicily. Ferocity of the French at the Monte di San Giovanni.]

Charles remained in Rome about a month, though he constantly sent forces to the borders of the Kingdom of Naples where everything was already in such disorder that Aquila and almost the whole of the Abruzzi had raised his standard before the King left Rome. Fabrizio Colonna had occupied the country districts around Albi and Tagliacozzo and the rest of the kingdom was hardly less in tumult. As soon as Ferrando left Rome, the fruits of the people's hatred for Alfonso became apparent. They also remembered the many cruelties of Ferdinand his father. Denouncing vehemently the wickedness of the government in the past and the cruelty and arrogance of Alfonso, they openly showed their welcome for the arrival of the French: so much so that the ancient remains of the Angevin faction, in comparison with the other causes, made very little difference, even though they were backed by the memory and following of the many barons who had been driven out and imprisoned at various times by Ferdinand—a thing in itself of great moment and a powerful instrument of change. So power-

ful, even without these stimuli, was the feeling against
Alfonso throughout the kingdom. When he heard of his
son's departure from Rome Alfonso was so afraid that—
forgetting his great fame and glory which he had won
in long experience in many wars in Italy and despairing
of being able to resist this fatal storm—he decided to
abandon his kingdom and give up his royal title and
authority to Ferrando. He hoped perhaps that with his
departure the intense hatred would disappear and that
by making king a young man of great promise who had
never offended anyone and was universally popular, he
would perhaps diminish his subjects' desire for the
French. This decision might have been effective if taken
earlier; but put off to a time when things were not only
in violent commotion but had already begun to go down-
hill, it was powerless to prevent his ruin. It is also said
(if one may give any credence to such things) that Ferdinand's ghost appeared three times on different nights
to Jacopo, principal court surgeon. First with gentle
words and later with threats the ghost ordered him to
tell Alfonso in his name that he should not hope to
resist the King of France because it was destined that
his line, afflicted by many tribulations and finally deprived of this fine kingdom, should die out. The cause
of this (he said) lay in their many crimes—especially
in the one he had committed in the Church of San
Lionardo in Chiaia near Naples on Alfonso's advice when
he returned from Pozzuolo. As he gave no details, people thought that Alfonso had persuaded him to murder
many barons who had been in prison for many years.
Whatever the truth of this may be, it is certain that Alfonso, tortured by his own conscience, found no peace
by day or night, seeing in his sleep the spirits of those
dead noblemen and the people rising in tumult to obtain his execution. He told only the Queen, his stepmother, what he had decided, refusing her requests to
inform either his brother or his son; and without waiting
two or three days longer to complete the single year of
his reign, he left with four light galleys laden with all
kinds of valuables. In his departure he showed as much
terror as though he were already surrounded by the

French: he turned around in alarm at every sound as though fearing that the heavens and the elements were conspiring against him. He fled to Mazari, a place in Sicily which had once been given to him by Ferdinand King of Spain.

Charles had news of his flight at the very hour he left Rome. When he reached Velletri, the Cardinal of Valencia secretly escaped from him. Though his father complained bitterly of his son's action, offering any security the King liked in exchange, it was believed that it had been done by his order, as he wished it to be in his power to observe or not the agreements made with the King. From Velletri the vanguard went to Montefortino, a place in the lands of the Church ruled by Jacopo Conte, a Roman baron. He had first been in Charles' pay; but then his hatred for the Colonna got the better of his own honor and he had been commissioned by Alfonso. His castle was bombarded by the artillery and though a very strong site, it was taken by the French in a few hours. All those within were killed, except three of his sons and a few others, who had fled into the fort and gave themselves up when they saw the artillery trained on it. The army then moved to Monte di San Giovanni, which belonged to the Marquis of Pescara, standing on the borders of the kingdom in the same stretch of country. This was a strong position, well-supplied and manned. There were 300 infantry from outside and 500 of the inhabitants ready to face any danger, so that it was thought it would take a good many days to capture. But the French bombarded it for a few hours and then assaulted it with such ferocity—in the presence of the King who had come there from Veroli—that overcoming all difficulties they took it by storm that very same day. There, because of their natural fury and in order to discourage other places from resisting by this example, they slaughtered great numbers. After having committed every other possible kind of barbarous atrocity, they set the buildings on fire. This manner of warfare, unknown in Italy for several centuries, filled the whole kingdom with terror; because in victories, however achieved, the cruelty of the victors usually did not go beyond disarming the defeated soldiers and setting them free, sacking towns taken by force and taking prisoner the inhabitants until they paid a ransom, but always sparing the lives of those who had not been killed in the heat of battle.

Chapter XIX

[*The Aragonese forces retreat to Capua. Gianiacopo da Trivulzio in Ferrando's absence agrees on terms of surrender with Charles VIII. Ferrando's words to the Neapolitans. Virginio Orsino and the Count of Pitigliano taken prisoner by the French. Charles enters Naples.*]

This was the sum of the opposition and difficulty which the King of France encountered in the conquest of so noble and splendid a realm, in defense of which neither virtue, courage nor good sense was shown—nor desire for honor nor strength nor constancy. The Duke of Calabria, who after he left Rome had retreated to the frontiers of his kingdom, had been recalled to Naples after his father had fled. There he assumed the royal title and authority with solemn ceremony but without the customary pomp and joyful celebrations. He then collected his army, in which were 50 horse squadrons and 6,000 foot soldiers, all chosen troops led by the most respected captains in Italy, and took up position at San Germano to prevent the enemy advancing farther. The position was very favorable: bounded on one side by high steep mountains and on the other by marshy country full of water; and before it was the River Garigliano (which the ancients called Liri), though it is not so deep at that point that it cannot sometimes be forded. As the way through is so narrow, it is rightly said that San Germano is one of the keys of the gates to the Kingdom of Naples. He also sent troops up the nearby mountain to hold the pass of Cancelle. However, his army had begun to become frightened at the very name of the French and no longer showed any energy whatever; while his captains, partly thinking of saving themselves and their states—as though they did not believe the kingdom could be defended—and partly desiring a change, began to waver no less in their faith than in their courage. It was also feared that with the whole country in great upheaval some dangerous revolt might arise behind their lines. So cowardice prevailed over good counsel. And when they heard that the Marshal de Gié was approaching with 300 lancers and part of the infantry after taking Monte di San Giovanni, they shamefully withdrew from San Germano and retired to Capua. They were so full of fear that they abandoned eight pieces of heavy artillery along the road. The new King hoped to defend this city, relying on the affection of the Capuans for the house of Aragon and the strength of the place with the Volturno before it, very deep at this point. He hoped at the same time to hold Naples and Gaeta without dispersing his forces elsewhere. The French followed closely behind him, but scattered and in disorderly array, advancing more like travelers than men at war, each of them going where he pleased after booty, without order, without standards, without commanders; some of them more often than not lodging at night in the places' which the Aragonese had left that same morning.

However, no better luck or courage was evident at Capua, for after Ferrando had billeted his army there—now much diminished in numbers since the retreat from San Germano—he learned in letters from the Queen that because of the loss of San Germano there had arisen such a tumult in Naples that if he did not come there would be a revolt. He went off to Naples with a few men to avert that danger by his presence, promising to return to Capua the following day. But Gianiacopo da Trivulzio, to whom he committed the care of that city, had already secretly asked the King of France for a herald so that he could go to meet him safely. When the herald arrived, Trivulzio went with a few Capuan nobles to Calvi which the King had entered the same day—though many others, who wished to keep faith with Ferrando, opposed his going with scornful words. At

Calvi he was at once brought into the King's presence, armed just as he was. He spoke in the name of the Capuans and the soldiers: seeing that Ferrando lacked the strength to defend himself, though they had served him faithfully while there had been any hope at all, they now decided to follow the King's fortunes if they were taken on with reasonable conditions; and he added that he was sure he could bring Ferrando himself to meet the King—as long as he was willing to acknowledge him in the proper way. The King replied to all this with gracious words accepting the offers of the Capuans and the soldiers and also welcoming a visit from Ferrando provided he understood that he was not to retain even the smallest part of the Kingdom of Naples, but would receive lands and honors in France. It is difficult to say what induced Gianiacopo da Trivulzio to such treachery, as he was a brave commander who professed to be a man of honor. He swore that he had gone at Ferrando's wish to try to settle his affairs with the King of France; and when there was no hope of that—and it was clear that the Kingdom of Naples could no longer be defended—he had thought it not only permissible but laudable to provide at the same time for the safety of the Capuans and the troops. But people on the whole thought differently. It was believed that he had been inspired by a desire for the victory of the King of France, hoping that when he had occupied the Kingdom of Naples, he would turn his attention to the Duchy of Milan. Trivulzio came from a very noble family of Milan and because he felt that he was not appreciated by Lodovico Sforza in proportion to his virtues and deserts —either because of the excessive favor accorded to the Sanseverini or for some other reason—he had completely turned against him. For this reason it was suspected by many that he had earlier, in Romagna, urged Ferrando to act more cautiously than the occasion sometimes required.

However, in Capua, even before Trivulzio's return, everything had changed. Ferrando's quarters and horses had been looted, the men-at-arms had begun to disperse in various directions and Virginio and the Count

of Pitigliano with their companies had retreated to
Nola, a town which had been given to the Count by the
Aragonese, having first written to ask Charles for a safe
conduct for themselves and their troops. Ferrando returned at the time he had said, having calmed the agitation of the Neapolitans with his promise to defend
Capua, but not knowing what had happened in his absence. He was only two miles away when, hearing of his
return, the whole populace rose up in arms refusing to
receive him. Some of the nobles were sent to meet him
to warn him not to come any nearer because the town—
seeing itself abandoned by him, his commander Trivulzio
gone over to the King of France, his quarters and horses
looted by his own soldiers, Virginio and the Count of
Pitigliano departed and nearly all the army broken up—
had been obliged for its own safety to surrender to the
conqueror. So Ferrando, after begging even with tears
to be let in, went back to Naples quite sure that the
whole kingdom would follow the example of Capua. The
town of Aversa lying between Capua and Naples was
the first; and it at once sent ambassadors to surrender
to Charles. And as the Neapolitans were openly negotiating for the same, the unhappy King decided no longer
to resist this sudden turn of fortune. He called into the
main square of Castelnuovo, the royal residence, many
of the nobles and the populace and spoke to them as
follows:

"I can call to witness God and all those who have
known my thoughts in the past, that the main reason
why I ever wished to come to the throne was so as to be
able to show the whole world that the harsh government
of my father and grandfather was hateful to me—and to
regain by good deeds the love which they had lost
through their harshness. The ill luck of our House has
prevented me from gathering the fruit which is far more
honorable than the fact of being king, because to become
king often depends on mere chance, but to be a king
whose only desire is the welfare and happiness of his
people depends only on oneself and one's own virtue.

"Our affairs have been reduced to a sorry state. We
might sooner complain of having lost the kingdom

through the faithlessness and cowardice of our captains and armies, than the enemy might boast of having taken it by their own skill and courage. Nevertheless we should not be entirely without hope if we held out just a little longer, because the King of Spain and all the princes of Italy are preparing powerful assistance. Their eyes have been opened to the fact that the conflagration consuming our kingdom will inevitably spread to theirs if they do not take precautions against it.

"I at least would not lack the courage to end at one and the same time my reign and my life with the glory worthy of a young king, descended from so long a line of great kings, and worthy of the hopes you have had of me up to now. But as these things cannot be attempted without placing our common fatherland in gravest danger, I am content rather to yield to fortune, to hide my courage, than by endeavoring not to lose my kingdom to be the cause of results opposite to the ambition which made me wish to be king. I advise and urge you to send someone to negotiate with the King of France. And so that you may do so without stain on your honor, I freely absolve you from the homage and oath you gave me a few days ago; and I counsel you to try to soften the natural arrogance of the French by showing obedience and readiness in receiving him. If their barbarous behavior makes you hate their rule and desire my return, I shall be where I can assist your wishes and ready always to risk my life for you in any danger. But if you like their rule, this city and this kingdom shall never be troubled by me.

"My misfortunes will be consoled by your well-being, and it will be a much greater consolation if I know you remember that either as crown prince or as king I never harmed anyone; that no hint of greed or cruelty was ever seen in me; that not my own faults but those of my forefathers have harmed me; that it is my intention never to be the cause of anyone's suffering in this kingdom either by attempting to keep or to regain it; that it grieves me more to lose the opportunity to make up for the mistakes of my father and grandfather than to lose the royal title and authority. Although an exile deprived

of my native land and my kingdom, I shall think myself
not entirely unfortunate if any memory of these things
remains with you and the conviction that I would have
been a king more like Alfonso my great-grandfather,
than Ferdinand and this last Alfonso."

It was impossible for them to hear these words without
great compassion; and certainly many were moved to
tears. But the name of the last two kings was so abhorred
among all the people and almost all the aristocracy, and
so strong their desire for the French, that the riots were
not halted in any way. As soon as Ferrando had withdrawn into the castle, the mob began to loot his stables
which were in the square. As he could not endure such
an indignity, he bravely ran out to stop it, accompanied
by a few followers; and such was the power of the royal
name in the rebellious city that they all stopped the attack and left the stables. When he returned to the castle
and was having the ships in the port burned and sunk,
as it was the only way to deprive the enemy of their use,
he began to suspect that the 500 German soldiers guarding the castle were planning to take him prisoner. So he
quickly decided to give them everything that was in the
castle; and while they were sharing out the spoils, he
left by the sally port and embarked in the light galleys
which were waiting for him in the port. Before he left
he freed from imprisonment all the barons who had survived the cruelty of his father and his grandfather with
the exception of the Prince of Rossano and the Count of
Popoli. With him went Don Federigo and the old queen,
his grandfather's widow, and his daughter Giovanna.
And together with a few followers he sailed to the island
of Ischia—called Enaria by the ancients—which is thirty
miles from Naples. And while Naples was still in sight
he frequently repeated in a loud voice the verse of the
psalm of the prophet, which says that the labors of those
are vain who guard the city which is not guarded by
God. Henceforth meeting nothing but difficulties, he had
to prove his courage in Ischia and experience the ingratitude and faithlessness that is shown to those who
are struck by misfortune. For the warden of the castle
would allow him to enter with one companion only; and

as soon as the King was within, he threw himself on the warden with such violence that between this ferocity and the memory of the royal authority he so frightened the others that the warden and the fort at once surrendered to him.

When Ferrando left Naples everyone surrendered everywhere—as before a violent torrent—merely to the reputation of the conquerors and with such cowardice that 200 horse of Ligny's company went to Nola, where Virginio and the Count of Pitigliano had gone with 400 men-at-arms, and captured them all without opposition. They surrendered without a blow, partly out of belief in the safe-conduct which their agents assured them had been granted by the King and partly out of the same fear which influenced all the rest. Then they were taken prisoner to the fortress of Mandracone and all their troops were stripped.

Meantime the Neapolitan ambassadors sent to surrender the city, met Charles at Aversa. With great generosity he gave them many privileges and exemptions and entered Naples the following day, February 21st. He was greeted with indescribable joy and acclamation by all the population regardless of sex, age, condition, quality, or faction, as though he were the father and founder of the city—and not least by those who either themselves or their ancestors had been given rank or fortune by the Aragonese. Amid these rejoicings he went to the cathedral and thence, as Castelnuovo was held by the enemy, to lodge in Castelcapuano which was formerly the residence of the French kings. He had—with a marvelous run of unparalleled good fortune—done even better than Julius Caesar, and conquered even before he had seen; and with such ease that during this expedition he never needed to pitch a tent or break a lance; and so many of his preparations were superfluous that the navy, prepared at enormous expense, struck by storms and carried to Corsica, was so long in reaching the shores of the kingdom that the King was by then already in Naples. Thus through internal dissensions which blinded the wisdom for which our princes were celebrated, a famous and powerful part of Italy was lost to Italian rule and fell into the hands of foreigners with humiliation and ridicule of the Italian armies and grave danger and shame to all. For old Ferdinand, although born in Spain, had lived in Italy continuously from his earliest youth as the King's son and then as King, and had ruled over no other state; and for this reason he and his sons and grandsons, all born and brought up in Naples, were deservedly regarded as Italians.

BOOK II

Chapter I

[*The Pisans seek help from Siena, Lucca, Venice, and Lodovico Sforza against Florence. He aspires to rule Pisa. Burgundio Lolo, a Pisan, denounces to Charles in Rome the misrule of the Florentines in his city. Francesco Soderini replies for the Florentines. Underhand behavior of Charles toward the Florentines. The Duke of Milan gives help to Pisa.*]

While these things were being done in Rome and the Kingdom of Naples, in another part of Italy a small fire was growing which was destined to turn into a vast conflagration to the detriment of many, but principally of the man who had kindled and fed it with his excessive greed for power. The King of France had agreed in Florence that if he held Pisa until Naples were taken then the revenues and jurisdiction would belong to the Florentines, but when he left the city, he had not made any arrangement or provision for carrying out that promise. So the Pisans, who were favored by the commissioner and the soldiers left by the King to guard the town and were determined not to go back to being ruled by the Florentines, had ejected or imprisoned the officials and all the Florentines who had stayed behind, sequestrated their property and all their possessions, and thus completely confirmed their rebellion with words and deeds. In order to further the rebellion, they sent ambassadors not only to the King (after he left Florence) to urge their cause, but, as soon as they had rebelled, to Siena and Lucca to secure outside help. These cities, also enemies of Florence, were delighted to hear of the Pisan rebellion, and so they both gave Pisa a certain sum of money, and Siena immediately sent some cavalry. The Pisans also sent ambassadors to Venice to sound the senate. Though they were received kindly, they did not bring back any hopes.

However, the Pisans' main expectations lay with the Duke of Milan, because they were sure that he would be willing to support them since he had been the chief cause of their rebellion. Although he spoke quite differently to the Florentines, the Duke secretly encouraged the Pisans with offers and he secretly persuaded the Genoese to provide the Pisans with arms and munitions and to send a commissioner to Pisa with 300 foot soldiers. The Genoese—angry at the Florentines for their acquisition of Pisa, for their purchase of the port of Leghorn when Tommaso Fregoso was doge, and, lately, for the Florentine seizure of Pietrasanta and Sarzana— were ready to comply with the Duke. In fact they had already occupied most of the lands which the Florentines held in Lunigiana and were already interfering in the affairs of Pietrasanta under the guise of a royal letter obtained for the restitution of certain confiscated properties. When the Florentines complained of these matters to the Duke, he replied that his treaty with the Genoese did not give him power to stop them, and while he tried to satisfy the Florentines with words and lull them with various hopes, he secretly acted in just the opposite way throughout. He hoped that if Pisa were not regained by the Florentines he could easily bring it under his own rule, which he ardently desired because of the nature of the city and its strategic position. This was not a new desire. It had taken root when, just after the death of his brother Galeazzo he was driven from Milan by the distrustful Madonna Bona, mother and guardian of the young Duke, and was forced to spend many months in Pisa. Besides, he remembered that Pisa had been ruled by Giovan Galeazzo Visconti, first Duke of Milan, before it fell into the hands of the Florentines, and he thought it to his honor to regain what had been owned by his forefathers. He also believed this fact might give some legal color to his claim on Pisa, as if Giovan Galeazzo had had no right to leave Pisa by will to his natural son Gabrielmaria instead of to his successors as Duke of Milan, since he had captured the city with the arms and the money of the Duchy of Milan.

The Pisans, not satisfied with having removed the city from Florentine jurisdiction, proceeded to occupy the places in the country district around. Almost all of these, following the lead of the city as country districts nearly always do, accepted their commissioners in the early days of the rebellion. At first the Florentines did not put up any opposition, as they were busy with more serious matters until they had arrived at an agreement with the King, and they expected after his departure that he would see to it, being bound by so solemn and public an oath. Then, since he put off doing anything about it, they sent troops and recovered, part by force and part by treaty, everything that had been occupied—except Cascina, Buti and Vicopisano, where the Pisans, who were not strong enough to hold the whole area, had concentrated their forces.

Charles was secretly pleased at this action of the Pisans, whose cause many of his people openly supported, some out of sympathy in the belief created in the court that the Pisans had been harshly ruled, others out of opposition to the Cardinal of St. Malo who showed himself favorable to the Florentines. This was the case particularly with the Seneschal de Beaucaire, because he had been bribed by the Pisans—but most of all because he was jealous of the cardinal's increased authority and had begun to disagree with him out of the same ambition which had earlier led him to support the cardinal in order to defeat the others. These, without regard for what was appropriate to the honor and good faith of a great king, urged on him that it would be more

to his advantage to hold out on the Florentines and keep
Pisa as it was—at least until he had taken the Kingdom of Naples. Their arguments prevailed with him and
so he tried to nourish both sides with varied hopes; and
while in Rome he brought in the Florentine ambassadors
to hear in his presence the complaints of the Pisans.

For them spoke Burgundio Lolo, a citizen of Pisa and
consistorial advocate at the court of Rome. He complained bitterly that the Pisans had been held for eighty
years in such wicked and dreadful servitude that the city
which had once extended its dominion through many
glorious victories as far as the Orient, and had been one
of the most powerful and noble cities of all Italy, had
been brought to the depths of desolation by the cruelty
and avarice of the Florentines. Pisa was almost empty of
inhabitants because most of her citizens, unable to bear
so harsh a yoke, had left of their own accord. They had
been well-advised—as the miseries of those who had remained out of love for their country had shown—for
they had been stripped of nearly all their substance by
the fierce exactions of the state and the insolent greed
of private Florentines. Now they had no means of supporting themselves: for with unheard of wickedness and
injustice they were forbidden to engage in commerce or
exercise any arts except the mechanical ones, and were
not eligible for any position in offices and administration
in the Florentine dominion, even for those usually open
to foreigners. The Florentines were also deliberately endangering their health and their very lives: in order to
get rid of the last relics of the Pisans they had stopped
maintenance of the ditches and dikes of the country
around Pisa, which had always been preserved by the
ancient Pisans with the utmost care, because otherwise
they would inevitably be exposed to serious disease every
year owing to the low-lying nature of the land and its
extreme liability to flooding. Because of this there were
everywhere falling into ruin the churches and palaces
and countless noble public and private buildings raised
with inestimable magnificence and beauty by their forefathers. It was no disgrace to great cities if after many
centuries they at last fell into servitude, because

it was inevitable that everything in the world should be subject to decay; but the memory of their greatness and noble past should engender in the minds of their conquerors compassion rather than harsh and bitter feelings —especially as all should consider that some day they might, indeed must, endure the same fate which is destined to overtake all empires and cities. The Pisans now had nothing left to tempt the insatiable greed and impiousness of the Florentines. It was impossible for them to bear such misery any longer; and so they had all agreed to abandon their home, to abandon life itself rather than return under the iniquitous, impious rule of the Florentines. He begged the King with tears (which he could imagine as the tears of all the Pisan people prostrated in wretchedness at his feet) to remember with what pity and justice he had restored to the Pisans their unjustly usurped liberty; as a constant and magnanimous prince he should uphold the benefits he had conferred on them, choosing rather to keep the name of father and liberator of that city, than to plunge them again into such hateful servitude and so become the agent of the rapacity and inhumanity of the Florentines.

Francesco Soderini, bishop of Volterra (and later cardinal), one of the Florentine ambassadors, replied to these accusations with no less vehemence, showing his republic's claim to be entirely just because they had bought Pisa from its legitimate overlord, Gabrielmaria Visconti, in 1404. No sooner had they taken possession than the Pisans had violently ejected them. And so they had had to retake the city in a long war whose outcome had been no less happy than its cause had been just and the Florentines' mercy no less remarkable than their victory; for when they could have left the Pisans to die of hunger, they had, in order to revive their spirits which had fallen to the lowest ebb, brought in with their army a greater quantity of food than of weapons. At no time in history had Pisa been powerful on land; in fact it had never been able to conquer Lucca which was so near, let alone anything else, and had always been enclosed in narrow territorial limits. Her maritime power had been short-lived because, by a just judgment of God provoked by their many iniquities and wicked dealings and by the long internal quarrels and discords among themselves, she had lost all greatness in wealth and population many years before she was sold to the Florentines, and had become so feeble that Iacopo d'Appiano, a low-born notary from the country around Pisa, had been able to make himself master of the city. After he had ruled for many years he left it to his heirs. The Florentines were only interested in holding Pisa because of its important position and outlet to the sea; for the revenues derived from the city were of slight consideration, as the exactions were so light that they barely sufficed to cover the necessary expenditure; and most of these were taken from foreign merchants for the use of the port of Leghorn. As far as trade, professions, and appointments were concerned, the Pisans were governed by exactly the same laws as other cities subject to the Florentines. These others admitted that they were governed with gentle moderation and had no desire to change masters; they had not that arrogance and obstinacy natural to the Pisans or their perfidy, which was proverbial throughout Tuscany. If when the Florentines took Pisa many of its inhabitants at once left of their own free will, it was simply due to their pride which would not allow them to adapt their outlook to their true strength and to fate. It was not due to any fault of the Florentines who had ruled them with justice and mercy and treated them in such a way that Pisa had not diminished in wealth or population. In fact they had recovered the port of Leghorn from the Genoese at great expense, without which that city had lacked all advantage and profit. They had also instituted a university for all branches of knowledge. In this and many other ways—including continual care of the ditches—they had always sought to increase the population. The truth of these matters was so apparent that it could not be obscured by false lamentations and calumnies. It was reasonable for everyone to desire to improve their lot; but it was also a duty to bear with patience what fortune might bring. Otherwise all governments and states would fall, if all subjects were allowed to acquire their liberty. The Florentines felt it to be unnecessary to labor to persuade Charles, the Most Christian King of France, where his duty lay; because being a most wise and just king, they were sure he would not allow himself to be moved by such empty complaints and calumnies, and would remember of his own accord what he had promised before his army was received in Pisa, and what he had sworn so solemnly in Florence—considering also that the greater and more powerful a king may be, the more glorious it is for him to use his power to maintain justice and good faith.

It was quite clear that Charles listened more kindly to the Pisans; and that in their interests he wished the complaints on both sides to be suspended while the war with Naples was on—or desired the Florentines to agree to his holding the whole of the country district, saying that when he had taken Naples he would at once carry out what he had promised in Florence. The Florentines firmly rejected this, regarding all his statements as suspect; and persistently they demanded that he should maintain his promises. To make a show of satisfying them—but really to obtain before the due time the 70,000 ducats they had promised him—he sent the Cardinal of St. Malo to Florence on his departure from Rome, pretending to the Florentines that he was sending him to settle their demands. But secretly he gave him orders that he should feed them with hopes until they gave him the money and should in the end leave matters where they stood. Although the Florentines strongly suspected the fraud, they paid him the 40,000 ducats which were nearly due. When the cardinal got them he went to Pisa, promising to restore the Florentines to the possession of the city. Then he went back without having done anything. He made the excuse that he had found the Pisans so obstinate that his authority had been unable to move them, and he had been unable to force them because he had no orders from the King to do so—and he as a priest could not make any decision which might result in the spilling of Christian blood. Nevertheless he put more guards in the new citadel and would have done likewise with the old one if the Pisans had allowed him. They were growing daily in strength and courage because the Duke of Milan, thinking there ought to be a larger garrison and an experienced commander in Pisa, had sent Lucio Malvezzo with fresh troops, though he did this as usual under cover of the Genoese. He lost no opportunity to stir up trouble for the Florentines so that they would be hindered in attacking the Pisans; and he commissioned Iacopo d'Appiano, lord of Piombino, and Giovanni Savelli jointly with the Sienese, to give them courage to hold on to Montepulciano. This town had recently gone over from the Florentines to the Sienese and had been accepted by them without regard for their alliance with Florence.

Chapter II

[*Paolantonio Soderini's speech on the internal government of Florence. Guidantonio Vespucci's speech on the same subject. Authority of Girolamo Savonarola in Florence. Organization of the Republic.*]

The Florentines at this time were no less anxious about internal affairs, because in order to reorganize the government of the republic immediately after the King's departure, they had called a "parliament," which according to their ancient customs is a gathering of all the citizens in the square before the palace to consider in open discussion the proposals put forward by the highest authority; and they had set up a kind of constitution which under the name of a popular government in many ways tended more toward the power of a few than the participation of all. This was unwelcome to many who had hoped for greater latitude; and as the private ambitions of some of the principal citizens tended to the same effect, it was necessary to reconsider the form of the government. While it was being discussed one day among the principal magistrates and leading citizens, Paolantonio Soderini, a wise and much respected citizen, is said to have spoken as follows:

"It would certainly be very easy, most worthy citizens,

200

to show that although those who have written of civic matters have praised popular government less than government by a prince or by the optimates; nevertheless because the desire for liberty is of very long standing and, as it were, native to this city and the conditions of its citizens appropriate to political equality—a very necessary basis for popular government—it should undoubtedly be preferred by us to any other. But such a dispute would be superfluous because in all the recent discussions and with universal agreement it has always been decided that the city should be governed in the name and with the consent of the people. The difference of opinion arises, however, because in the parliament's constitution some wished to see something like the form of government with which the city was ruled before its liberty was suppressed by the Medici family; others, of whom I confess I am one, believing that that system had in many respects the name rather than the substance of popular government and alarmed by the disasters which often arose from such governments, desire a more perfect form—one whereby the harmony and safety of the people might be assured, which is something neither reason nor past experience leads one to hope for in this city, except under a government entirely dependent on the power of the people, but properly organized.

"This has two principal foundations. The first is that all magistrates and offices—both in the city and in the dominion abroad—should be distributed from time to time by a general council of all those who are qualified under our laws to take part in government; and without the approval of this council new laws cannot be passed. In this way as the distribution of positions and authority will not be in the hands of private citizens or of any particular group or clique, no one will be excluded from them either by the prejudice or the whim of others. They will be allotted according to the virtues and merits of men. So everyone will have to strive by virtue and good behavior, by furthering the public and private interests, to open the way to honors for himself. Everybody will have to abstain from vice, from harming others, and from all things abhorrent to well-constituted cities. And it will not be in the power of one or a few to introduce a new government through the authority of an office or by passing new laws, as this can only be changed by the wish of the general council. The other main basis is that the important decisions—that is those regarding peace and war, the examination of new laws, and generally all the things needful to the administration of such a city and state—should be dealt with by magistrates specially appointed for this task, and by a more select council of experienced and prudent citizens deputed by the popular council. For, as it does not fall within everyone's powers to understand these matters, they must be dealt with by those who know about them; and as speed and secrecy are often necessary, they cannot be discussed or decided by the multitude. Nor is it necessary for the preservation of freedom that such matters should be dealt with by a large number of people, because freedom is safe as long as the distribution of offices and the voting of new laws depend on universal consent. When these two points are provided for, a truly popular government is organized, the freedom of the city is well-founded and the good and durable form of the republic is established.

"It is desirable to put off to a later time many other things, which tend to make the government of which we speak more perfect, so as not to confuse men's minds at the beginning. They are suspicious because they remember the tyranny of the past; and as they are not used to considering the idea of free government, they cannot fully know what organization is needful for the preservation of liberty. Those are things which, being of less substance, can be safely put off to a more convenient time and a better occasion. The citizens will love this form of republic more every day, and as they become through experience more and more aware of the truth, they will want the government to be constantly improved and brought to complete perfection. In the meantime it will stand firm on the two bases we spoke of. How easy these are to establish and how fruitful they are can not only be proved by many arguments, but also appears most clearly by example. Although the government of the

Venetians is in the hands of the nobles, these nobles are none other than private citizens, and are so numerous and of such varied condition and quality that one cannot deny that it bears much resemblance to a popular government, and that it could be imitated by us in many ways; for it is principally founded on the two bases on which that republic has preserved for many centuries its unity and civic harmony together with its liberty, and has risen to such glory and greatness. The unity of the Venetians has not been caused, as many believe, by the situation of the city—for on that site there could be, and have occasionally been, discord and sedition—but by the fact of the form of government being so well-constituted and well-proportioned to itself that it inevitably produces such admirable and valuable results. Nor should we be influenced less by our own examples than by foreign ones, considering them, however, from the opposite point of view; for the fact that our city has never had a form of government like that has been the reason why our affairs have always been subject to such frequent changes—now oppressed by the violence of tyrannies, now torn by the ambitious and greedy factions of the few, now a prey to the unbridled license of the mob. And whereas cities were built for the peaceful and happy life of their inhabitants, the fruits of our system, our happiness and our repose, have been the confiscation of our goods, exile and decapitation of our unhappy citizens. The government brought in by the parliament is no different from those we have had before in this city, which gave rise to discord and disaster, and after endless public and private vicissitudes finally gave birth to tyrannies; for these were the sole causes why our ancestors' freedom was oppressed by the Duke of Athens[39] and in later times by Cosimo de' Medici. Nor should we be surprised; because when the appointment of magistrates and the passing of laws do not daily require the consent of all, but depend on the judgment of a small number, then the citizens are no longer intent on the public good but on private interest and gain, and sects and factions arise which entail the division of the entire city and are the plague and certain death of all republics and empires.

"How much more prudent it is therefore to avoid the forms of government which by the light of reason and our own example we know to be pernicious, and to turn instead to those which by reason and the example of others we may know to be healthy and successful! Truth obliges me to say this: that in our city always, a government organized in such a way that a few citizens have excessive authority will be the government of a few tyrants; and they will be all the more damaging than a single tyrant in that evil is greater and more harmful when it is multiplied; and apart from anything else, because of the difference of opinions and the differing ambitions and desires of men, one cannot hope they would agree for long. Discord, pernicious at all times, would be more so now when you have just sent into exile a most powerful citizen, when you have been deprived of so large a part of your dominion, and while all Italy, with foreign armies at her very heart, is in the gravest danger.

"Rarely if ever has it been absolutely in the power of the whole city to organize itself according to its own wishes. As God in His goodness has now given you that power, do not, by inflicting grievous harm on yourselves and obscuring forever the fame of Florentine wisdom, lose the chance of founding a free government, and one so well-ordered that not only will it make you happy while it lasts, but also give you promise of enjoyment in perpetuity; and so bequeath to your children and your heirs a treasure and happiness such as neither we nor our ancestors have ever possessed or known."

These were the words of Paolantonio. Opposing him, Guidantonio Vespucci, a famous lawyer and a man of remarkable intelligence and skill, spoke as follows:

"If, most worthy citizens, a government organized in the manner proposed by Paolantonio Soderini produced the desired results as easily as they are described, it would certainly be perverse of anyone to wish for any other form of government for our country. It would be a wicked citizen who did not passionately love a form of republic in which the virtues, merits and abilities of men were recognized and honored above all else. But I do not understand how one can hope that a system placed entirely in the hands of the people can be full of such benefits. For I know that reason teaches, experience shows and the authority of wise men confirms that in so great a multitude there is not to be found such prudence, such experience and such discipline as to lead us to expect that the wise will be preferred to the ignorant, the good to the bad, and the experienced to those who have never handled any affairs whatever. For as one cannot hope for sound judgments from an unlearned and inexperienced judge, so from a people full of confusion and ignorance one cannot expect—except by chance— a prudent or reasonable election or decision.

"Are we to believe that an inexpert, untrained multitude made up of such a variety of minds, conditions and customs, and entirely absorbed in their own personal affairs, can distinguish and understand what in public government wise men, thinking of nothing else, find it difficult to understand? Quite apart from the fact that each person's self-conceit will lead them all to desire honors—and it will not be enough for men in the popular government to enjoy the honest fruits of liberty—they will all aspire to the highest posts and to take part in the decisions on the most difficult and important matters. In us less than in any other city there rules the modesty of giving way to the man who knows best or has most merit. But if we persuade ourselves that we must by right all be equal in all things, the proper positions of virtue and ability will be confused when it rests with the judgment of the multitude. And this greed spreading to the majority will ensure that the most powerful will be those who know and deserve least; for as they are more numerous, they will have more power in a state organized in such a way that opinions are merely numbered and not weighed. So what certainty will you have that, satisfied with the forms you introduce at present, they will not soon destroy those prudently devised systems and replace them with new inventions and imprudent laws which wise men will not be able to resist? These things are always a danger in such a government, but will be much more so now, because it is natural for men when they depart from one extreme in which they have been held by force, to rush headlong to the opposite extreme without stopping at the middle course. Thus those who are freed from a tyranny, if they are not restrained, plunge into unbridled license, which can also justly be described as a tyranny, because a people resembles a tyrant when it gives to those who do not deserve and takes from those who do, and when it confuses degrees and distinctions between persons; and perhaps their tyranny is the more pestilent insofar as ignorance is more dangerous, having no weight nor measure nor law, than wickedness, which has at least some rule, some restraint, some limitation.

"The example of the Venetians should not influence you; for with them the situation of their city is of some importance and their ancient form of government counts a good deal. And things are so arranged that the important decisions are in the power of a few rather than of many; and they are not perhaps by nature as lively as we are, and so much more easily calmed and satisfied. Nor does the Venetian government only depend on the two factors which have been mentioned, for its perfection and stability are much affected by the presence of a doge appointed for life, and many other arrangements which would meet with strong opposition if anyone tried to introduce them into our country, because our city is not being founded today nor is this the first time it is being given a constitution. Therefore, where long-standing customs are often against the public good and men suspect that under the guise of preserving liberty there may be an attempt to create a new tyranny, sound advice is not likely easily to do them good—just as in an infected body full of corrupt humors medicines are not as useful as in a clean one.

"For these reasons and by the very nature of human affairs which commonly tend toward decay, it is to be feared that what is imperfectly organized now at the beginning will in the process of time be completely disorganized, rather than hoped that either by time or by later opportunities it will be brought to perfection. But have we not our own examples without looking for those of others?

206

For never when the people have been in absolute control of this city has she not been full of dissension and totally disrupted, and in the end soon had to have a change of government. And if we do wish to seek out the examples of others, why should we not remember that the absolutely popular government of Rome gave rise to so many disorders that, if it had not been for their military skill and ability, the republic's life would have been short? Why do we not remember that Athens, a most flourishing and powerful city, lost its empire and then fell into slavery under its own citizens and foreigners for no other reason than that they would decide important issues with the deliberations of the multitude? But I do not see why one should say that in the system introduced by the parliament freedom is not entirely to be found, because everything is referred to the discretion of the magistrates who are not permanent but regularly change, and are not elected by only a few. On the contrary, once approved by the majority they have, according to the ancient custom of the city, to be drawn by lot. How can they then be distributed by cliques or at the whim of individual citizens? We will certainly be better assured that the most important affairs will be examined and directed by the men who are wisest, most experienced and most serious, who will manage them with far more order, secrecy and judgment than the people would do— for they are incapable in affairs, and sometimes when it is least necessary, extremely extravagant in spending; and at others in matters of greatest need so avaricious that often to make some miserable saving they run into heavy expenditure and danger.

"As Paolantonio has said, the ills of Italy are an important factor—and particularly those of our own country; but how unwise it would be, when the most experienced and expert doctors are needed, to depend on those who have least experience and skill. Finally you must consider that you will keep your people in greater peacefulness, and more easily lead them to decisions profitable to themselves and the universal good, by giving them a moderate share and authority in government; because if one depends absolutely on their judgment for

everything, the danger is that they will become arrogant
and too difficult and resistant for the counsels of your
wise and loyal citizens."

In the councils, in which relatively few citizens took
part, this opinion tending to a more restricted form of
government would have been more influential—if in the
deliberations of men there had not intervened divine
authority speaking through Girolamo Savonarola of Ferrara, a friar of the Preachers' Order. This man had for
some years publicly preached the word of God in Florence, and combining with remarkable learning a great
reputation for saintliness, he had attained fame and
following as a prophet with most of the population. For
at the time when there was no sign of anything in Italy
but the most perfect peace, he had in his sermons repeatedly foretold the coming of foreign armies to Italy,
saying that men would be so terrified that neither walls
nor armies would offer them resistance. He stated that he
did not predict this and many other things which he continually foretold, through human reasoning or knowledge
of books, but from divine revelation. And he had also
hinted at the changes which would take place in the
government of Florence; and now, publicly deploring the
forms debated in the parliament, he affirmed that it was
God's will that an absolutely popular government should
be set up, and in such a way that it should not be in
the power of a few citizens to affect the security or the
liberty of the rest. In consequence, with the respect accorded to his name combined with the wishes of many, it
was impossible for those who felt differently to resist this
powerful tendency. And so, after the subject had been
thoroughly discussed in many meetings, it was finally
decided to have a council of all the citizens, without the
participation, as rumor had it in many parts of Italy,
of the dregs of the people, but consisting only of those
who according to the ancient laws of the city were qualified to take part in government. In this council they were
to deal only with the election of the magistrates for the
city and the territory outside and to approve provisions of
money and all the laws which had first been passed by
the magistrates and other smaller councils. And so as to

remove the causes of civil strife, and to give everyone greater reassurance, it was forbidden by public decree, following in this the example of the Athenians, to proceed against anyone for crimes and misdemeanors against the state committed in the past. On this basis they might perhaps have created a stable and well-regulated government, if they had at the same time introduced all those provisions which then came into the minds of prudent men; but as nothing could be decided without the consent of the many—who, mindful of past events were full of suspicion—it was resolved that for the time being they should set up the great council as the basis for the new liberty, putting off everything else until a favorable time when the requirements of the state should be discovered by experience by those who were incapable of discerning them by reason and judgment.

Chapter III

[*Charles VIII captures Castelnuovo, Castel dell' Uovo and the fortress of Gaeta. Before the surrender of Castel dell' Uovo he sends for Don Federigo and proposes giving lands in France to Ferrando. Federigo's reply. Ferrando goes to Sicily from Ischia to which he had escaped. Death of Gemin the Grand Turk's brother who had been handed over to Charles by Alexander VI.*]

This was the state of affairs in Tuscany. In the meantime the King of France, having taken Naples, was seeking to complete his victory in two ways: first by capturing Castelnuovo and Castel dell' Uovo, the two fortresses of Naples which were still being held for Ferdinand, as he had taken almost without difficulty the tower of San Vincenzio, built to guard the port; and second by reducing the whole kingdom to his obedience. In both of these fortune continued to show him the same favor. Castelnuovo, the King's palace standing on the shore, put up a slight defense and then through the baseness and greed of the 500 Germans guarding it, surrendered on condition that they should leave with a safe-conduct and with all the property they themselves could carry. There was a great quantity of victuals in the castle, which Charles, without thought of the consequences, gave to some of his people. Castel dell' Uovo is built in the sea on a rock formerly connected to the land but cut off from it in ancient times by Lucullus and is now joined to the shore near Naples by a narrow bridge. The castle was continually bombarded by the French artillery which could only damage the walls but not the foundation of the rock; yet they agreed after a few days to surrender if they were not relieved within a week. The barons and representatives of the towns were making several days' journeys to meet the commanders and men-at-arms sent out into different parts of the kingdom. They vied with one another to be the first to welcome them with so much good will or fear that the wardens of the fortresses nearly all surrendered without a struggle; and the castle of Gaeta which was well provisioned, on being slightly attacked, surrendered unconditionally. So in a very few days with incredible ease all the kingdom fell into Charles' hands except the island of Ischia and the forts of Brindisi and Galipoli in Puglia; and in Calabria the fortress of Reggio, a city set on the farthest point of Italy opposite Sicily—the city itself being held for Charles—also Turpia and Mantia, which had at first raised the French standard, but refusing to be ruled by anyone but the King himself, who had given them to some of his people, they changed their minds and went back to their former masters. The city of Brindisi did the same shortly afterward. Charles had not sent troops there; and in fact out of indifference he had not only not satisfied their representatives, sent to Naples to capitulate, but had barely listened to them. So that those who were for Ferrando in the fortresses were able to bring the city back to its Aragonese loyalty of its own accord. Following this example, the city of Otranto which had acclaimed the French, changed its mind when no one went there to accept it.

All the lords and barons of the realm went to pay homage to the new king with the exception of Alfonso

d'Avalos, Marquis of Pescara, who had been left by
Ferrando in Castelnuovo. When he realized the Germans
meant to surrender, he had followed his king—and two
or three others besides who had fled to Sicily because
Charles had given their states to others. Charles wished
to establish this great acquisition by means of an agreed
settlement, and before he took Castel dell' Uovo he sent
for Don Federigo under a pledge of safe-conduct. Because
he had lived some years at the court of Charles' father
and had ties of marriage with the King, Don Federigo
was popular with all the French nobles. Through him
Charles offered to give Ferrando great lands and revenues in France if he would surrender the remains of
his kingdom, and to compensate Don Federigo hand-
somely for all his possessions there. But as Don Federigo
knew his nephew was determined not to accept any
settlement if he could not keep Calabria, he replied with
grave words that as God, fate, and the will of all men
had concurred in giving him the Kingdom of Naples,
Ferrando did not wish to resist this disposition of fate.
He thought it no shame to yield to so great a king and
desired no less than the others to be bound in obedience
and loyalty to him: as long as he were allowed to keep
some part of the realm—meaning Calabria—where he
might remain not as king but as one of his barons and
revere the clemency and magnanimity of the King of
France. In his service he hoped he might sometime have
the opportunity to show that courage which ill fortune
had prevented him from exercising in his own defense.
This course could not but add to Charles' greater glory
and resemble the actions of kings memorable in antiquity who with similar deeds had made their names
immortal and attained divine honors among their peoples. And it would be a course no less safe than glorious;
for, with Ferrando as his vassal, the whole kingdom
would be firmly in his hands and he would not have
to fear a change of fortune which so often smirched
with some unexpected reverse the glory that had been
won, whenever victory was not followed with moderation
and prudence.

But as Charles felt that giving away any part of the kingdom to his rival would place all the rest in obvious danger, Don Federigo left him in disagreement. And Ferrando, after the surrender of the castles, went off with the poorly armed fourteen light galleys with which he had left Naples and sailed to Sicily to be ready for any opportunity. He left to guard the rock of Ischia Inigo d'Avalos, the brother of Alfonso—both men of great courage and outstanding loyalty to their king. In order to deprive the enemy of this foothold, which was very convenient for causing trouble in the kingdom, Charles sent the navy there which had finally arrived in the port of Naples. Finding the town abandoned they did not attack the fort, feeling it too strong for them to take. So the King decided to have more ships brought from Provence and Genoa to take Ischia and make safe the seas which were occasionally raided by Ferrando's ships. However, neither diligence nor counsel was equal to the opportunity; for everything was done slowly and with great negligence and confusion. The French had become more arrogant than usual as a result of their good fortune and left important matters to chance, while they thought of nothing but feasting and pleasure. Those who were in greatest favor with the King sought privately to get as much profit as they could from the victory without any regard for the dignity or interests of their master.

At that time Gemin the Ottoman died in Naples to the great disappointment of Charles, who regarded him as an important factor in the war he intended to wage against the Turkish Empire. It was firmly believed that he had died of poison which the Pope had given him at a certain moment, either because he had been forced to hand him over against his will—and having thus lost the 40,000 ducats that his brother Bajazet paid him every year, he made sure by way of consolation that those who had taken him should derive no benefit—or because he was jealous of Charles' glory. Perhaps he also feared that if Charles was successful against the infidels, he might then turn his thoughts to the reform of Church affairs, as he was constantly being urged to do so by many, though for reasons of private interest. The Church had completely abandoned its ancient customs, which caused the authority of the Christian religion to diminish daily. Everyone felt sure that it would decline still further during his papacy. Acquired by evil arts, it was probably never in the memory of man administered with worse. Some even believed, because the wicked nature of the Pope made any iniquity credible in him, that Bajazet—when he heard the King of France was preparing to enter Italy—had bribed the Pope through Giorgio Bocciardo to murder Gemin. However, his death did not deter Charles from continuing to think about his war against the Turks, though he acted more on impulse than on wisdom and good counsel. He sent into Greece the Archbishop of Durazzo, an Albanian, because he gave him hopes of being able to raise some revolt in that province through the agency of certain exiles. But new events forced him to think about other things.

Chapter IV

[*Fears and worries of Lodovico Sforza and the Venetians over the political situation in Italy. Concern of the Pope and Maximilian. Alliance between the Pope, the King of the Romans, the King of Spain, the Venetians and the Duke of Milan. Charles VIII still fails to keep faith in his pact with the Florentines. Beginning of dissatisfaction among the peoples of the Kingdom of Naples against the French.*]

I said above that his desire to usurp the Duchy of Milan and his fear of the Aragonese and Piero de' Medici led Lodovico Sforza to urge the King of France to invade Italy. When it was done and he had thereby satisfied his ambition, and when the Aragonese were in such difficulties that they could hardly ensure their own safety, he began to realize a second danger far greater and more real than the first; that is, the subjection imminent for himself and all other Italians if the Kingdom of Naples were added to the power of the King of France. For this reason he had hoped that Charles might encounter greater difficulties in Florentine territory; but when he saw that Charles had won the Republic to his side with the greatest ease, and with the same ease had overcome the opposition of the Pope, and was entering the Kingdom of Naples without any hindrance whatever, his own danger seemed to increase daily as the course of the French victory became easier and more successful. The same fear began to worry the Venetian senate which, having persevered in its original decision to remain neutral, had so circumspectly abstained not only from action but from all demonstrations which might show that it leaned to one side or the other that, having elected Antonio Loredan and Domenico Trivisano as ambassadors only when they heard the King had crossed the mountains, they delayed so long in sending them that the King reached Florence before them. Then seeing the swiftness of Charles' good fortune and that the King shot through Italy like a thunderbolt without meeting any resistance, they began to regard the disasters of others as dangers to themselves. They began to fear that their own ruin might follow that of others: particularly when Charles had occupied Pisa and other fortresses of the Florentines, left a garrison in Siena and subsequently had done the same in the states of the Church—which seemed to show that he was thinking of something more than just the Kingdom of Naples. Therefore they were very ready to listen to the proposals of Lodovico Sforza, who, as soon as the Florentines had given way to Charles, had begun to urge them to join him in providing against their common dangers. It is believed that if Charles had met any difficulty either in the territory of Rome or when he entered the Kingdom of Naples, they would have jointly taken up arms against him. But his rapid victory forestalled all the measures they were discussing to prevent it. Charles was already suspicious of Lodovico's movements; he had commissioned Gianiacopo da Trivulzio after the taking of Naples, with 100 lances and a good salary, and had won over with many promises Cardinal Fregoso and Obietto dal Fiesco; the latter as powerful instruments in the affairs of Genoa, and the former as head of the Guelph party in Milan and strongly opposed to Lodovico. At the same time he refused to give Lodovico the Principality of Taranto, saying he was under no obligation to do so until he had conquered the whole kingdom. All these things were extremely galling to Lodovico and he gave orders to retain twelve galleys which were being fitted at Genoa for the King—and forbade any of his ships to be fitted there. The King complained that this was the reason he had not again sought with greater forces to capture Ischia.

Therefore suspicion and anger grew on both sides; and as the rapid conquest of Naples had shown the Venetian senate and the Duke of Milan how great and close the danger was, they were forced to put their plans into action without delay. They were encouraged to do so by the powerful support they received, for the Pope was no less anxious to do the same, being extremely frightened of the French. So was Maximilian, who, because of the many causes of enmity with the crown of France and the serious offenses Charles had committed against him, was always more displeased than anyone at the success of the French. But those on whom Lodovico and the Venetian senate placed most reliance were Ferdinand and Isabella, King and Queen of Spain. Not long before they had undertaken not to hinder Charles in taking Naples—simply in order to get Roussillon back from him; but they had astutely left a loophole in this so that they could do just the opposite; for (if what they said was true) there was a clause in the agreement for the restitution which said that they should not be bound by anything which might harm the interests of the Church. By this exception they inferred that if the Pope in the interests of his vassal asked them to help the Kingdom of Naples, they might do so without failing in their oath and promises. They also added that by the same agreement they might not oppose Charles if it were shown that the kingdom legally belonged to him. But whatever the truth of this may be, it is certain that as soon as they had their lands restored, they not only began to give the Aragonese hopes of assistance and secretly to urge

215

the Pope not to abandon their cause, but having at first encouraged the King with mild words (out of regard for his honor and zeal for religion) to turn his arms against the infidel rather than against Christians they subsequently continued their pleas to this end in much stronger terms and in more suspect words the further he proceeded with his expedition.

To give their words more weight and to fill the Pope and the Aragonese with greater hopes while on the other hand letting it be understood that they were only interested in defending Sicily—they prepared to send a fleet there, which arrived after the fall of Naples—though there was typically more show than substance, because it had on board only 800 light cavalry and 1,000 Spanish infantry. They had gone on with these dissimulations until Ostia was taken by the Colonna faction and the King of France's threats against the Pope gave them a better chance to declare openly what they had in mind. They seized this opportunity eagerly, and had their ambassador Antonio Fonsecca protest openly to the King while he was in Florence, that in accordance with their duty as Christian princes they would come to the defense of the Pope and the Kingdom of Naples, vassal of the Roman Church. They had already begun to negotiate with the Venetians and the Duke of Milan when they heard of the flight of the Aragonese. They begged them urgently to combine with them against the French for their common defense. Finally in April in the city of Venice, where the ambassadors of all these states were present, an alliance[40] was signed between the Pope, the King of the Romans, the King of Spain, the Venetians and the Duke of Milan. According to the published terms of the treaty it was simply for mutual defense, and was open to anyone wishing to join on appropriate conditions. But as they all felt that it was essential to ensure that the King of France did not keep Naples, it was agreed in the secret clauses that the Spanish troops which had gone to Sicily should help Ferdinand of Aragon to recover his kingdom (he was planning to invade Calabria with great hopes of popular support); that the Venetians would simultaneously attack the seaboard towns with their navy; that the Duke of Milan would try to prevent help coming from France by taking the town of Asti where the Duke of Orléans had remained with a small force; that the Kings of Spain and of the Romans would be given a certain sum of money by the other allies so that each could invade French territory with a powerful army.

Besides all this the allies wanted the whole of Italy to be joined in the same purpose. And so they pressed the Florentines and the Duke of Ferrara to enter the same alliance. The Duke refused when he was asked before the publication of the treaty to take arms against the King; yet on the other hand, with typical Italian caution, he agreed to his eldest son Don Alfonso being commissioned by the Duke of Milan with 150 men-at-arms and with the title of lieutenant of his forces. The case of the Florentines was different. They were invited to join with great offers, and had good reason to abandon the King's cause; because, when the treaty was published, Lodovico Sforza offered them on behalf of all the allies, if they joined, all their forces to resist the King if on his way back from Naples he tried to attack them, and to help them as soon as they could to regain Pisa and Leghorn. On the other hand the King, scorning the promises he had made in Florence, had neither immediately given them back the possession of their lands nor restored the fortresses after taking Naples. He preferred to his own good faith and the oath he had sworn the advice of those who, favoring the Pisan cause, persuaded him that the Florentines would unite with the other Italians as soon as they were back in Pisa. The Cardinal of St. Malo put up feeble opposition to this view, although he had been bribed heavily not to quarrel with the other nobles at court on account of the Pisans. Not only in this but in many other ways the King had shown that he did not set much store either by his own word or by the value which the Florentine alliance could have for him at such a time. So when their spokesmen complained to him about the rebellion of Montepulciano and insisted that he should, according to his obligation, force the Sienese to give it back, he replied almost in mockery:

"Can I help it if your subjects rebel because they have been ill treated?" However, the Florentines did not allow themselves to be carried away by anger against their own interests and decided not to listen to the requests of the league. They tried to avoid provoking an attack on themselves by the French armies when the King returned, because they had better hopes of the return of their possessions from those who in fact held them; and also because they had little faith in the allies' promises, knowing themselves to be hated by the Venetians because of their opposition at various times to their ambitions; and it was quite evident that Lodovico Sforza had designs on Pisa for himself.

At this time the reputation of the French had already begun to diminish rapidly in the Kingdom of Naples because, absorbed by their pleasures and proceeding without system, they had not bothered to drive the Aragonese out of the few places still held for them—as they would easily have done if they had followed up their good fortune. Their popularity was even more diminished because, though the King had shown himself very liberal and kind to the people, granting throughout the kingdom privileges and exemptions that amounted in a year to more than 200,000 ducats, other matters had not been handled with due order and prudence. Charles disliked business and listening to people's complaints and requests; and he left all the weight of affairs to his counsellors, who partly out of inability and partly out of avarice made a muddle of everything. The nobility was not won over by kindness or by gifts; it was extremely difficult to enter the chamber or have audience of the King; no distinction of persons was made; people's merits were not recognized at all or only by chance; reassurance was not given to those who were natural enemies of the Aragonese; all kinds of difficulties and delays held up the return of the possessions and goods of the Angevin faction and of the other barons ejected by Ferdinand; grace and favor were for those who bought them with gifts and special means; from many, things were taken without reason, and to many, other things were given without cause; almost all the offices and the possessions of many were distributed among the French, who also received nearly all the crown lands (those, that is, which are directly ruled by the King)—which was all the more displeasing to the subjects in that they were accustomed to the prudent and orderly government of the Aragonese kings and had hoped so much more from the new king. In addition there was the natural arrogance of the French, fed by the ease of their victory which had given them such a high opinion of themselves that they despised all Italians. Also there was their insolence and high-handedness in billeting, no less in Naples than in the other parts of the realm where the men-at-arms were distributed. The French behaved so badly everywhere that the burning desire people had felt for their coming had already turned into burning hatred. On the other hand, the hatred for the Aragonese had given place to compassion for Ferrando, as they remembered the expectations they had always had of his virtues and recalled the day when with such kindness and constancy he had spoken to the Neapolitans before his departure. As a result that city and almost the whole kingdom were waiting for a chance to recall the Aragonese—no less passionately than a few months before they had desired their downfall. Even the loathed name of Alfonso began to be popular; and they described as just severity what they used to call cruelty when he managed the internal affairs of the kingdom in his father's day. They called truthful sincerity of mind what for years they had regarded as pride and arrogance. Such is the nature of people, inclined to hope more than they should and to endure less than they must, and always to dislike the present state of affairs. And this is especially true of the people of the Kingdom of Naples, who are famous among all the peoples of Italy for instability and eagerness for change.

Chapter V

Decisions of Charles VIII as a result of the league of the Italian states. Before leaving Naples he

*distributes offices and responsibilities. King and
court strongly wish to return to France. Negotiations between Charles and the Pope over the investiture of the Kingdom of Naples. After assum-
ing the title and royal insignia Charles leaves
Naples. The Orsini ask in vain to be granted
their freedom. The Pope, to avoid meeting
Charles, goes to Orvieto and thence to Perugia.
New attempts by the Florentines to get back their
fortresses. Charles takes Siena under his protection, but only for a short time.]*

Even before the new league was formed, the King
had almost made up his mind to return to France. He
was moved more by a frivolous impulse and the strong
wishes of all the court than by considerations of prudence; because in the kingdom there remained countless
important affairs of princes and states to be settled.
The victory had not been complete, as the whole of the
realm had not been conquered. But when he heard that
a league of so many princes had been formed against
him, he was very agitated and discussed with his advisers what should be done in this situation; and they all
said—which was quite true—that it was many years
since so powerful an alliance had been formed among
Christian peoples. On their advice it was decided that
their departure should be hastened, fearing that the
longer they stayed the greater the difficulties would become, for it would give the league time to make greater
preparations (it was already rumored that a large force
of Germans would enter Italy, and there was already
much talk of the Emperor himself). The King was to
arrange for fresh troops to come to Asti from France
to hold the town and to force the Duke of Milan to con-
centrate on defending his own possessions, and also to
be ready to move farther up if the King thought it necessary.

At the same council meeting it was decided to make
every effort and generous offers to separate the Pope
from the other members of the league, and to persuade
him to confer on Charles the investiture of the King-

dom of Naples. Although in Rome he had agreed to confer it without reserves, he had until now refused to do so even with a declaration that such concession was made without prejudice to the rights of others. Amid such serious decisions and important preoccupations the affairs of Pisa were not forgotten. The King, who wished for many reasons to keep it in his power—fearing lest the citadel might be taken from him by the Pisans with the help of the league—sent there by sea 600 French infantry together with the Pisan ambssadors to his court. When these troops reached Pisa, they were seized with the same urge as the other forces left behind in the city; and inspired by the desire for loot they went with the Pisan armies, from whom they received money, to besiege the castle of Librafatta. The Pisans under Lucio Malvezzo had camped there a few days earlier, taking courage from the fact that the Florentines had sent part of their forces toward Montepulciano; and then hearing that the enemy was approaching, they had moved off before dawn. Now returning with this French garrison they captured the castle in a few days. The Florentine army which was coming to the rescue was prevented by the floods from crossing the River Serchio and had not dared to take the road leading alongside Lucca because of the attitude of the Luccan people, who were strongly in favor of the freedom of the Pisans. After taking Librafatta, which the French kept for themselves, they and the Pisans overran the whole of the country around Pisa as open enemies of Florence. When the Florentines complained of this, Charles merely replied that when he returned to Tuscany he would fulfill his promises. He urged them to suffer this brief delay with patience.

But the decision to leave was not as easy for Charles as the desire to do so was strong. His army was not large enough to divide into two, so as to escort him safely to Asti against the opposition of the league, while leaving enough to defend Naples adequately against the attacks which threatened. In these difficulties he was forced—so that the kingdom would not be stripped of defenders —to cut down the forces needed for his own safety and at the same time—so as not to expose himself to obvious

221

danger—he could not leave behind the powerful garrison that was really needed. So he decided to leave half the Swiss and part of the French infantry, 800 French lances and about 500 Italian men-at-arms commissioned at his expense partly under the Prefect of Rome and partly under Prospero and Fabrizio Colonna and Antonello Savelli. All these were commanders who had been favored by him in the distribution he made of almost all the lands and states of the Kingdom—especially the Colonna, because he had given to Fabrizio the country districts of Albi and Tagliacozzo formerly held by Virginio Orsini; and to Prospero the Duchy of Traietto and the town of Fondi with its many castles, which belonged to the Gaeta family, and Montefortino together with other neighboring places taken from the Conti family. Charles thought that in any emergency these forces could be joined by those of the barons who were obliged in the interest of their own safety to desire his rule, and particularly the Prince of Salerno whom he had restored to the office of Admiral, and the Prince of Bisignano.

As lieutenant general of the whole kingdom he appointed Gilbert de Montpensier, a commander more respected for his high position and royal blood than for his own ability. In addition he deputed various commanders in many parts of the realm, to all of whom he had given lands and revenues. The principal of these were Aubigny as governor of Calabria, appointed Grand Constable; in Gaeta, Senechal de Beaucaire, whom he had made Grand Chamberlain; and in Abruzzi, Graziano di Guerra, a brave and highly reputed captain. He promised them he would send money and early relief; but meanwhile he left no other provision than the assignment of the funds produced from day to day by the revenues of the kingdom. The kingdom was already wavering, and in many places the Aragonese cause was reviving. At the very time when Charles intended to leave Naples, Ferrando had landed in Calabria with the Spanish force sent with the fleet to Sicily. They were joined at once by many of the inhabitants and the city of Reggio surrendered immediately—its fortress always having been held in Ferrando's name. At the same moment the

Venetian navy appeared off the coast of Puglia, under the command of Antonio Grimano, a man of great authority in the republic. But neither this nor any other portents of future change put off or in any way delayed the decision to depart; because apart from force of circumstances the anxiety of the King and all the court to return to France was quite incredible—as though they believed that the chance which had enabled them to achieve such a victory would suffice to preserve it. At this time Ferrando held Ischia and the Lipari islands, part of the Kingdom of Naples though so near to Sicily, and Reggio which he had recently retaken; also in Calabria Terranuova and its fortress together with a few other forts and places around; Brindisi, where Don Federigo had taken refuge, Galipoli, Mantia, and Turpia.

But before the King left, various things were discussed with the Pope not without hope of agreement. On this account the Cardinal of San Dionigi went from the Pope to the King and then returned to Rome, while the King sent to the Pope Monsignor Franzi. The King desired above all the investiture of the Kingdom of Naples and hoped that the Pope, if he would not be his ally, at least would not join his enemies and would be willing to receive him in Rome as a friend. Although the Pope listened to all this from the first, he did not trust Charles. As he did not wish to abandon the league or allow him the investiture, thinking it would not ensure a true reconciliation, he raised various difficulties with regard to his other requests. As for the investiture, although the King agreed to accept it without prejudice to the rights of others, he replied that he wished it first to be shown to whom it legally belonged. On the other hand, anxious to prevent by force of arms the King's entry into Rome, he asked the Venetian senate and the Duke of Milan to send help. They sent him 1,000 light horse and 2,000 foot soldiers, and promised to send 1,000 men-at-arms. He hoped to be able to hold out with these and his own forces. But he later thought it was too dangerous to send their troops so far away from their own states, considering also that their army was not yet organized, since part of the troops were occupied with the question of

223

Asti. They also remembered the Pope's treachery when
he had called Ferrando with his army into Rome and
then sent him away again. So they changed their minds
and began to urge him to move to a safe place rather
than expose himself to grave danger in trying to defend
Rome. For even if the King entered Rome, he would depart at once without leaving any forces behind. These
factors increased the King's hopes of reaching a settlement with the Pope.

The King therefore left Naples on May 20th; but as
he had not yet taken the royal title and insignia with
the usual ceremonies, a few days before his departure
he solemnly received the royal insignia and the honors
and oaths which were usually given to new kings in the
cathedral with great pomp and celebrations according to
the custom of the kings of Naples. Giovanni Ioviano
Pontano delivered an oration in the name of the people.
This was a discredit to his reputation, which was distinguished for the excellence of his learning, his character and his part in civil affairs—for he had been secretary to the Aragonese kings for a long time and very
influential with them, and had also been tutor in Latin
and Greek to Alfonso. It therefore seemed that either out
of concern for the forms of oratory or to ingratiate himself with the French he went too far in the vituperation
of the kings by whom he had been so greatly favored.
So difficult is it sometimes to observe oneself that moderation and those precepts with which, full of erudition
and writing of moral virtue, he created for himself a
marvelous reputation for the universality of his genius
in every branch of learning and gave instruction to all
men. With Charles went 800 French lances and 200
gentlemen of his guard, Trivulzio with 100 lances, 3,000
Swiss foot soldiers, 1,000 French and 1,000 Gascons.
Cammillo Vitelli and his brothers with 250 men-at-arms
were ordered to join him in Tuscany, while the navy
was to return to Leghorn.

The King was followed by Virginio Orsino and the
Count of Pitigliano without any guard but on their oath
not to leave without permission. When they complained

that they had been unjustly taken prisoner, their case
had first been referred to the royal council, before which
they claimed that when they had surrendered, their safe
conduct had not only been confirmed to their envoys
by word of mouth by the King himself, but had even
been set down in writing and signed by his own hand.
So that when they heard from their representatives that
they were merely waiting for the secretaries to prepare
the documents, they had on this assurance raised the
King's standard when the first herald arrived in Nola and
handed over the keys to the first captain who came with
only a few cavalry, though they had more than 400
men-at-arms with them and could easily have resisted.
Virginio and the Count recalled the ancient loyalty of
the Orsini who had always supported the Guelph faction;
and that they and all their forefathers and their descendants forever would have engraved on their hearts the
name and arms of the crown of France. This was the
reason why they had been so prompt in welcoming the
King in their states around Rome. Therefore it was not
right or fair or in accordance with the King's assurance
or with their own actions that they should be held prisoner. But Ligny, whose troops had taken Nola, replied
no less promptly that the safe-conduct, although agreed
and signed by the King, was not regarded as absolutely
in force until it was confirmed by the royal seal and the
signatures of the secretaries, and then delivered to the
addressees. This was the ancient custom of all the courts
in all concessions and patents, so that some control
might be exercised over what the prince might say without due consideration either because of the multiplicity
of his cares and duties or because he was not fully informed of the circumstances. It was not their trust in
the King's undertaking which had induced the Orsini to
surrender to so small a force, but fear and necessity;
because they had no possibility either of defense or of
flight, as all the country around was already occupied
by the conquerors. It was not true what they said about
their merits, and even if other people said so, they ought
for their own honor to deny them, because it was quite
obvious to everyone that they had opened their territory

to the King not of their own free will but to avert danger, abandoning in adversity the Aragonese from whom in times of prosperity they had received great benefits. Therefore, as they were in enemy pay and most hostile to the French cause, and had not received in proper form any assurance of their safety, they had been made prisoner by the just laws of warfare. These things were said against the Orsini. And as they were supported by the power of Ligny and the authority of the Colonna, who were openly hostile because of their ancient feuds and opposing factions, no ruling had ever been made by the court; but it had been decided that they should follow the King, although given some hopes of being freed when he got to Asti.

The Pope, though the league had urged him to leave, still thought that he might be reconciled with Charles and went on negotiating with him. However in the end his mistrust won the day. Though he had given the King some hopes that he would wait for him in Rome, two days before Charles entered the city he went to Orvieto accompanied by the College of Cardinals, 200 men-at-arms, 1,000 light cavalry, and 3,000 foot soldiers. He felt that Castel Sant' Angelo was adequately garrisoned; and the Cardinal of Santa Anastasia stayed behind as his legate in Rome to receive and honor the King. Charles entered from Trastevere to avoid Castel Sant' Angelo and went to lodge in the *borgo,* refusing the lodgings offered him on behalf of the Pope in the Vatican palace. From Orvieto the Pope went on to Perugia where he heard that the King was approaching Viterbo. He had again given him some hope of a meeting somewhere between Viterbo and Orvieto and his intention was, if Charles came that way, to go on to Ancona so as to be able to flee by sea to some place of absolute safety. However the King, though he was very angry with the Pope, released the fortresses of Civitavecchia and Terracina, keeping Ostia, which on his departure from Italy he left in the hands of the Cardinal of San Piero in Vincoli, bishop of Ostia. He also passed through the lands of the Church as though they were friendly territory—except that the vanguard, when the people of Toscanella refused to billet them, entered the town by force and put it to the sack, killing many.

After that the King remained six days in Siena for no good reason whatever. He did not consider, although he was pressingly reminded of it by the Cardinal of San Piero in Vincoli and by Trivulzio, how dangerous it was to allow the enemy so much time to prepare and unite their forces. Yet he did not compensate for the loss of time by the usefulness of his decisions; for in Siena they discussed the restitution of the Florentine fortresses which had been absolutely promised by the King when he left Naples, and then several times confirmed on the way. On this account the Florentines—besides being ready to pay him the remaining 30,000 ducats of the money agreed in Florence—offered to lend him 70,000 and to send with him as far as Asti Francesco Secco, their captain, with 300 men-at-arms and 2,000 foot soldiers. The King's need for money, the advantage of augmenting his army and concern for the royal good faith and sworn oath led almost all the members of the council to strongly advise the return of the fortresses, keeping back Pietrasanta and Sarzana as a means of more easily influencing the Genoese in his favor. But it was fated that there should remain alight in Italy the material for further calamities. Ligny, young and inexperienced, but whose mother had been a sister of the King's mother and was a great favorite of his, moved either by caprice or by anger that the Florentines should have taken the side of the Cardinal of St. Malo, prevented this decision from being made, offering no other grounds than compassion for the Pisans and despising the proffered assistance of the Florentines; because, he said, the French army was able to beat all the Italians put together. Ligny was supported by M. de Piennes because he hoped that the King would give him the dominion of Pisa and Leghorn.

In Siena they also discussed the government of that city. Many of the people and magistrates, in order to weaken the power of the Monte de'nove, were urging the introduction of a new form of government and the re-

227

placement of the guard of the Monte on the city hall by a guard of French troops under Ligny. Although this suggestion was rejected in the royal council as too temporary and inappropriate to the present time, Ligny, who was vainly planning to make himself master of the city, got Charles to take Siena under his protection under the terms of an agreement by which he undertook to defend all their territory except for Montepulciano, where he said he did not wish to interfere either on the side of the Florentines or of the Sienese. Though there was no mention of this in the treaty the commune of Siena elected Ligny as its captain with Charles' consent, promising him 20,000 ducats a year with the obligation to keep a lieutenant there with 300 foot soldiers to guard the town. He left some troops of the French army. The vanity of these decisions was soon apparent, for not long after the Monte de'nove reasserted its customary authority by force, drove the guard out of Siena, and dismissed M. de Lille whom Charles had left there as ambassador.

Chapter VI

[*The preparations of the league against the French. Messages and threats from Lodovico Sforza to the Duke of Orléans who prepares Asti against attack. The Duke of Orléans occupies Novara, but fails to take Vigevano.*]

The affairs of Lombardy were already in turmoil because the Venetians and Lodovico Sforza were making great preparations to prevent Charles from returning to France—or at least to assure the safety of the Duchy of Milan, through which he had to pass for a long distance. Sforza had just recently received from the Emperor with great solemnity the privileges of the investiture of the Duchy, and publicly paid homage and sworn an oath of loyalty before the ambassadors who had brought them. He and the Venetians had reorganized their armies, and jointly or separately raised again a large force of men-at-arms. After various difficulties they

228

got Giovanni Bentivoglio to accept their pay and join the league with the city of Bologna. At Genoa for the defense of the city Lodovico armed ten galleys at his own expense and four great ships jointly with the Pope and the Venetians. In the meantime, to carry out his obligations under the terms of the league to capture Asti, he had sent to Germany to raise 2,000 foot soldiers and put Galeazzo da San Severino in charge of the expedition with 700 men-at-arms and 3,000 foot soldiers. He was so sure of victory that, being very insolent by nature in times of good fortune, and wishing to insult the Duke of Orléans, he sent to warn him not to usurp any longer the title of Duke of Milan, which his father Charles had assumed at the death of Filippo Maria Visconti; not to allow more French troops to enter Italy and to send back across the Alps those who were in Asti; and to attest to his compliance with these terms, he asked him to hand over Asti to Galeazzo da San Severino, whom the King could trust no less than him, having admitted him the year before in France into the Order and Brotherhood of St. Michael. Furthermore, with the same boastfulness he exaggerated the strength of his forces, the preparations made by the league to oppose the King in Italy and the armaments being made ready by the King of the Romans and the King of Spain to make war on him beyond the Alps. Orléans, however, was not very impressed by such vain threats. As soon as he heard of the first moves to form the league, he attended to the fortifying of Asti and urgently requested fresh forces from France. These began to come across the mountains with great speed, as they had been sent for by the King as reinforcements for himself. So Orléans, not fearing the enemy, led his troops out and captured the town and fortress of Gualfinara in the Marquisate of Saluzzo, the property of Antonio Maria da San Severino. As a result Galeazzo, who had taken a few small castles, retreated to Anon with his army, a place near Asti in the Duchy of Milan, without hope of attacking or fear of being attacked. But Lodovico was by nature very inclined to involve himself suddenly in enterprises requiring great expenditures, and on the other hand very averse, even in the greatest need, to spending—and this was the cause of his placing his state in the gravest danger. Because payments were not forthcoming, very few German soldiers had arrived, and for the same reason the forces with Galeazzo diminished daily. At the same time reinforcements continually arrived from France, entering Italy with great speed because they had been summoned for the relief of the King in person; and the Duke of Orléans already had 300 lances, 3,000 Swiss infantry and 3,000 Gascons. Although he had express orders from Charles that he should avoid any sorties and be ready to come and meet him when he was called for, nevertheless, as it is difficult to resist one's own interests, he decided to take the opportunity to occupy the town of Novara, which two Opizini Caza, noblemen of Novara, one nicknamed "Black" and the other "White," offered to place in his power. They hated the Duke of Milan because with false calumnies and unjust legal rulings he had usurped from them and many other people of Novara certain waterways and lands. Having come to an agreement with them, Orléans, accompanied by Lodovico, Marquis of Saluzzo, crossed the River Po by night at Ponte Stura which belonged to the Marquis of Monferrato. He was received by the conspirators in Novara together with his troops without encountering any resistance. From there he sent on part of his force to Vigevano, and it is believed that if he had gone on rapidly with the whole army toward Milan, a great uprising might have occurred; for after hearing the news of the loss of Novara, the Milanese were keyed up to a change in government. Lodovico, no less timid in adversity than arrogant in prosperity (as insolence is always combined with timidity), showed his cowardice with futile tears, while the troops left behind with Galeazzo, on whom alone his defense depended, were nowhere to be seen.

But as commanders do not always know the circumstances and troubles of their enemies, splendid chances are often missed in war; and it did not seem possible that so sudden a change of fortune could overtake so powerful a prince. Orléans, in order to consolidate his taking of Novara, stopped to capture the fortress, which agreed to surrender on the fifth day if it were not relieved the following day. In this interval of time San Severino was able to reach Vigevano with his troops and the Duke to increase his army and win over the population by removing by public announcement many taxes he had earlier imposed. Nevertheless Orléans came up to the walls of Vigevano and offered battle to the enemy, who were so terrified that they were inclined to abandon Vigevano and cross the Ticino by a bridge of boats they had constructed. As they refused to fight, Orléans then retreated to Trecate; after which Lodovico Sforza's position began to improve. Cavalry and infantry continued to flock into his army because the Venetians, happy to allow him to carry most of the burden of opposing Charles, agreed to his recalling part of the forces he had sent to Parma, and in addition sent him 400 *stradiotti*.[41] Thus Orléans was prevented from advancing further; and when he sent 500 horse cavalry on another expedition to Vigevano, the enemy cavalry came out to attack them. Orléans' troops suffered heavy losses. Then San Severino, whose forces were now superior, went to offer battle at Trecate; and massing his entire army, which besides Italian soldiers now contained 1,000 horse cavalry and 2,000 German foot soldiers, he finally camped about a mile from Novara where Orléans had retreated with all his troops.

Chapter VII

[*At Poggibonsi Savonarola vainly urges Charles VIII to restore the Florentines' possessions. Contradictory promises of the King to the Pisans and the Florentines. Charles sends part of his troops against Genoa. Sack of Pontremoli.*]

The news of the rebellion of Novara inspired Charles, who was at Siena, to hasten his movements. So to avoid any incident which might delay him, having heard that the Florentines—warned by past dangers and suspicious because he had with him Piero de' Medici—were filling the city with arms and men as a safeguard, though pre-

231

paring to receive him with great honors, he went to Pisa through Florentine territory, leaving the city of Florence on his right. He was met at Poggibonsi by Girolamo Savonarola who, calling on God's name and authority in his speeches as he usually did, strongly urged him to restore their possessions to the Florentines. He added grave threats to his persuasions, saying that if Charles did not observe what he had so solemnly sworn with his hand on the Bible and as it were in the divine presence, he would soon be punished severely by God. The King, according to his shifting nature, gave different answers here and the next day at Castelfiorentino. Now he promised to restore their property when he reached Pisa, and now he stated contrary to his sworn word that he had promised the Pisans to preserve their freedom before taking the oath in Florence; but at the same time he still gave the Florentine spokesmen hopes that he would carry out the restitution when he arrived in Pisa.

There the subject was again considered in the royal council. As every day more was heard of the preparations of the league and the massing of their forces near Parma, they were beginning to weigh the difficulties of passing through Lombardy, and many members of the council were in favor of having the money and assistance offered by the Florentines. But such a decision was opposed by the same people who had been against it in Siena, saying that even if they had some trouble or difficulty in getting through Lombardy because of enemy opposition, it was still better to keep that city in their own hands to be able to retire to it if necessary, than to let the Florentines have it. When they got their lands back they would be no more reliable than any other Italians. And, besides, for the defense of the Kingdom of Naples it was a great advantage to hold the port of Leghorn, because when the King had succeeded, as they hoped, in taking Genoa, he would be in control of almost all the coast from the port of Marseilles to that of Naples. Certainly these arguments had some influence on the King, who was little able to choose the right course himself. But much more influential were the prayers and tears of the Pisan people. With their women and children they came and fell at the

King's feet, and urged their cause on all and sundry in the court and even among the soldiery, lamenting with great weeping and miserable cries the disasters that awaited them, the insatiable hatred of the Florentines, the final desolation of their country, whose only cause of complaint would be that the King had given them their freedom and promised to maintain it. And as they believed the word of the Most Christian King to be firm and constant, this had given them courage to provoke still further the enmity of the Florentines. With these tears and outcries they moved even the private soldiers, even the archers of the army and also many of the Swiss, and they went in large numbers with great disorder to the King. With Salazart, one of the King's pensioners as their spokesman, they begged him passionately for his own honor, for the glory of the crown of France, for the satisfaction of so many of his servants ready to lay down their lives for him at a moment's notice, and more able counsellors than those who were corrupted by Florentine money, not to take from the Pisans the blessing he himself had conferred upon them. They said that if he were considering this infamous act because he needed money, he should sooner take their chains and silver and keep back the pay and pensions they received from him. This strong feeling among the soldiers went so far that a simple archer dared to threaten the Cardinal of St. Malo; and some others spoke haughty words to the Marshal de Gié and President de Ganay, who were known to favor the restitution. The King, confused by such contrary advice, left the matter open. He was so far from making any definite decision that at this very moment he again promised the Pisans that he would never put them back in the power of the Florentines; and he told the Florentine ambassadors who were waiting at Lucca that what he did not do now for good reasons he would do immediately on reaching Asti, and so the Republic should not fail to send him ambassadors there.

He left Pisa, changing the warden of the castle and leaving the necessary guard in the citadel and doing the same in the fortresses of the other places. Being seized of his own ambition by an inordinate greed to take Genoa and urged on by the cardinals San Piero in Vincoli and Fregoso, and by Obietto del Fiesco and other exiles who gave him hopes of an easy revolution there, he sent with them on the expedition from Sarzana, against the advice of all his council who criticized this weakening of the forces of the army, M. Philippe with 120 lances and 500 foot soldiers who had recently arrived by sea from France. He also gave orders that the men-at-arms of the Vitelli, who had been left behind and so were not in time to join them, should follow, and that certain other exiles with men provided by the Duke of Savoy should enter the western Riviera; while the navy, which was reduced to seven galleys, two galleons and two small galleys, with Miolans in command should go in support of the land forces. In the meantime the vanguard led by the Marshal de Gié had reached Pontremoli. The town paid off 300 outside troops who were guarding it and surrendered at once on the advice of Trivulzio, on the understanding that no harm would come to persons or property. But the commander's word was worthless, because the Swiss broke in violently and sacked and burned the place, cruelly massacring all the inhabitants, in order to revenge the fact that when the army passed through Lunigiana before, about forty Swiss had been killed in a chance brawl with the men of Pontremoli.

Chapter VIII

[*The French army face to face with that of the league at Fornovo. Doubts and disagreements in the army of the league. Uncertainties in Charles' army.*]

At this time the army of the league was urgently being organized in the territory of Parma. There were 2,500 men-at-arms, 8,000 infantry and more than 2,000 light horse, most of them from Albania and the Greek provinces around there. These were brought into Italy by the Venetians, and keeping the name they bear at home, they are called *stradiotti*. The principal force of this army was the Venetian troops; because those of the Duke of Milan, who had directed nearly all his men to Novara, did not amount to a quarter of the entire army. The Venetian troops, among whom there were many famous *condottieri,* were commanded by Francesco Gonzaga, Marquis of Mantua, with the title of governor-general—a very young man who bore a reputation greater than his years, being thought courageous and eager for glory. With him as commissioners were two of the chief members of the senate, Luca Pisano and Marchionne Trivisano. The Count of Gaiazzo commanded the Sforza troops with the same title of governor. He was greatly trusted by the Duke; but lacking the glory in arms of his father Roberto da San Severino, he had acquired the reputation of being a cautious rather than a bold captain. With him as commissioner was Francesco Bernardino Visconti, leader of the Ghibelline party in Milan and therefore the enemy of Gianiacopo da Trivulzio. When it was discussed among these captains and other principal officers of the army whether to go and lodge at Fornovo, a village of a few houses at the foot of the mountains, it was decided instead, because of the narrowness of the place and perhaps also (as they said) to allow the enemy to come down into the plain, to stop at the abbey of Ghiaruola three miles from Fornovo. This enabled the French vanguard to lodge at Fornovo, having crossed the mountain long before the rest of the army, which was delayed by the heavy artillery they were dragging with immense difficulty over that steep part of the Apennines.

This difficulty would have been much greater if the Swiss, eager to wipe out their offense to the King's honor in the sack of Pontremoli, had not made tremendous efforts to bring the guns through. When the vanguard reached Fornovo, the Marshal de Gié sent a herald to the Italian camp to request free passage for the army in the name of the King, who wished without harming anyone and paying fair prices for victuals to pass that way to return to France. At the same time he sent out a few of his cavalry to gain information about the enemy and the terrain; but they were put to flight by some *stradiotti* sent out to meet them by Francesco Gonzaga. On this occasion, if the Italians had advanced as far as the French camp, it is thought that they would easily have defeated the vanguard; and once that was done the royal army would have been unable to proceed. The opportunity was still there the next day, though the Marshal had realized the danger and moved his men to higher ground. But the Italian captains did not dare to go and attack him— frightened by the strength of his position and by the belief that the vanguard was greater than it was, and the rest of the army probably nearer at hand. It is true that at this moment all the Venetian forces had not yet been brought together. They had been so slow in collecting at the camp at Ghiaruola that it is clear that if Charles had not delayed so long on the road—at Siena and Pisa and many other places where he stopped needlessly—he would have got through without any resistance or hindrance whatever. Joining up at last with the vanguard, he camped at Fornovo the next day with his entire army.

The princes of the league had never believed that the King with an army so much smaller than theirs would dare to cross the Apennines by the direct route. They had therefore convinced themselves from the start that he would leave the greater part of his army in Pisa and go to France with the remainder in his fleet. Then when they heard that he was following the land route, they thought that in order to avoid their army he would aim to cross the mountain by the road through Valditaro and Monte Centocroce—a very steep and difficult mountain— and then to Tortona, hoping to be met by the Duke of Orléans in the vicinity of Alessandria. But when it appeared certain that he was on his way to Fornovo, the Italian army which earlier had been full of courage inspired by their numerous commanders and the rumor that the enemy were few in number, now lost some of its spirit. They thought of the valor of the French lances, the courage of the Swiss to whom the Italian infantry was regarded as vastly inferior, the skillful handling of their artillery and, what greatly impresses men when they have thought just the opposite, the unexpected boldness of the French in approaching them with an army so much smaller.

For these reasons even the commanders' morale was lowered and they discussed what reply should be given to the herald sent by the Marshal. On the one hand it seemed very dangerous to place the whole of Italy at the risk of fortune, and on the other it appeared that Italian arms would be shamed if they showed no courage to oppose the French army, which was so much smaller in numbers and dared to pass beneath their very eyes. As the opinions of the captains in this discussion were very different, they decided after much wrangling to notify Milan of the King's request and to do what the Duke and the allied ambassadors agreed should be done.

When they took counsel the Duke and the Venetian ambassador, who were nearest the danger, were of the same opinion: the enemy, if he really wanted to return home, should not be hindered, but rather (as the proverb goes) they should build him a bridge of silver. Otherwise there was the danger that fear changed into despair (as could be shown by many examples) might force a way through, with much bloodshed of those who imprudently opposed them. But the King of Spain's orator, wishing them to try their luck without danger to his own sovereign, argued insistently, almost in protest, that they should not be allowed to pass and that the opportunity should not be missed of defeating this army; for if it remained intact the affairs of Italy would still be in the same danger as before—indeed in worse danger because, as the King held Asti and Novara, and controlled the whole of Piedmont, and as he had behind him the rich and powerful Kingdom of France, with the Swiss nearby and ready to enter his pay in any numbers he liked, he would attack Italy with greater ferocity if his reputation and courage were now increased by the league's army— so much larger than his own—allowing him to pass in so cowardly a fashion. The Spanish monarchs, he went on, would practically be forced to reconsider the position in the knowledge that the Italians either would not or were afraid to fight the French. However the counsels of caution prevailed, and they decided to write to Venice where the same opinion was prevalent.

But these discussions were now useless because the captains of the army, after writing to Milan, thought it unlikely that the answer would arrive in time; and reflecting how dishonored Italian arms would be if they let the French pass freely, they sent back the herald without a definite answer and decided to attack the enemy when they moved. The Venetian commissioners agreed with this decision, though Trivisano did so more readily than his colleague. The French meanwhile advanced full of arrogance and daring, as though, having so far met no opposition in Italy, they thought the enemy army would not fight; and if they did, they would easily be put to flight—so little account did they take of the Italian forces. But when they began to come down the mountain, they found the army encamped with an infinite number of tents and pavilions, and in so vast an encampment that according to the Italian practice they could all form into battle order inside it; and seeing the enemy so numerous and thinking that if they had not intended to fight they would not have come so close, their arrogance began to cool, and they would have been glad to hear that the Italians would be satisfied simply to let them pass. The more so since Charles had written to the Duke of Orléans to move up to meet him at Piacenza on July 3rd with as many men as possible. He had received an answer saying that they would not fail to be there at the appointed time; but later he heard from the Duke that the Sforza army facing his, with 900 men-at-arms, 1,200 light horse and 5,000 foot soldiers, was so powerful that he could not advance without obvious danger—especially as he was obliged to leave part of his force guarding Asti and Novara. Therefore the King, forced to reconsider the position, instructed Philippe d'Argenton to send a herald to the Venetian commissioners with a letter saying he wished to speak to them for their mutual advantage. Argenton had recently been the King's ambassador to the Venetian senate, and when he left he had offered Pisano and Trivisano, who had already been appointed commissioners, to work to persuade the King toward peace. They now agreed to meet him the following morning at a suitable place between the two armies. However, Charles, either because he lacked supplies in his present camp or for some other reason, changed his mind and decided not to wait there for the result of these discussions.

Chapter IX

[The positions of the two armies. The battle of Fornovo; the danger run by the King of France. The Venetians as well as the French claim victory. Refutation of the rumors concerning the behavior of Lodovico Sforza. Charles reaches Asti without loss although closely pursued by enemy troops. Failure of the French attempt on Genoa.]

The positions of the two armies were a little less than three miles apart, lying along the right bank of the River Taro—a torrent rather than a river—which rises in the Apennines, and after running through a little valley bounded by two hills, flows across the wide plain of Lombardy to the River Po. On the right of these two hills, running down to the banks of the river, the army of the league was encamped. It had stopped, on the advice of its captains, on this side rather than on the left bank where the enemy's road would be, so as to prevent them from going toward Parma. Because of the quarrels between its factions the Duke of Milan was not really sure of this city, particularly since the King had got the Florentines to lend him as far as Asti their *condottiere* Francesco Secco, whose daughter was married to one of the Torelli, a powerful noble family in the territory of Parma. The allied camp was fortified with ditches and earthworks, and had plenty of artillery. The French, if they wished to reach Asti and cross the Taro near Fornovo, would have to pass this position with only the river between them.

The French army spent a very troubled night because the Italians kept sending their *stradiotti* right up to their tents so that there were frequent calls to arms in their camp, which was in turmoil at every noise; then came a sudden and very heavy rainfall with fearful peals of thunder and terrible flashes of lightning—which seemed

an augury of some dreadful disaster. This frightened the
French much more than the Italian army, not only because, being surrounded by mountains and the enemy and
in a place where if any disaster occurred they had no
hope of escape, they were in a much more difficult position and had just cause to be more afraid; but also
because it seemed more likely that the threats of heaven,
which usually show themselves only for some great occasion, must point rather to the camp which held a king of
such power and dignity.

The next morning, July 6th, the French army began to
cross the river at dawn. Most of the artillery went first,
followed by the vanguard. The King had included in this
force, thinking that it would have to bear the brunt of the
enemy's attack, 300 French lances, Gianiacopo da Trivulzio with his 100 lances, and 3,000 Swiss who were the
mainstay and hope of the army. And with them on foot
Englebert, brother of the Duke of Cleves, and the Bailli of
Dijon who had enlisted them; and to these the King added
300 archers on foot and some mounted crossbowmen
from his own guard and nearly all the remaining infantry
he had with him. Behind the vanguard came the main
force with the King himself in its midst, fully armed and
mounted on a mettlesome charger; and beside him to
command this part of the army with his authority and
advice M. de Trémouille, a very famous captain in the
Kingdom of France. Behind them followed the rearguard
led by the Comte de Foix, and finally the transport
wagons. Nevertheless, not being averse to reaching an
agreement, the King asked Argenton to go and negotiate
with the Venetians at the very moment when his army
began to move. But at the time of this move the Italian
army was already up in arms and its captains had decided to fight and the time was too short and the armies
too near to allow room or opportunity for talking. The
light cavalry were already skirmishing on all sides, the
artillery firing everywhere with terrible effect and the
Italians had already come out of their camp and were
deploying their squadrons ready for battle on the bank of
the river. The French did not, however, halt their advance. Part of them were on the riverbed, and part,

because they could not deploy their ranks on the narrow plain, on the lower slopes of the hill; and when the vanguard was right in front of the enemy camp, the Marquis of Mantua crossed the river behind the French rearguard with a squadron of 600 picked men-at-arms, a large force of *stradiotti* and 5,000 infantry, leaving on the farther bank Antonio da Montefeltro, the natural son of the late Federigo Duke of Urbino, with a large squadron ready to cross when called to reinforce the first assault. He had also arranged that when they had begun to fight, another section of the light cavalry should strike at the enemy's flank and that the rest of the *stradiotti,* crossing the river at Fornovo, should attack the French transport wagons. These had been left without guards—exposed to anyone wishing to plunder them—either through lack of troops or (as it was rumored) on the advice of Trivulzio.

The Count of Gaiazzo with 2,000 foot soldiers and 400 men-at-arms, among them the company of Don Alfonso d'Este, which had come into camp without him at his father's request, crossed the Taro at another place to attack the French vanguard, leaving Annibale Bentivoglio on the farther shore with 200 men-at-arms to assist when called for. There remained two large companies of men-at-arms and 1,000 foot soldiers to guard the camp, because the Venetian commissioners wished to retain some safe protection for themselves against all eventualities. When the King saw so great a force attacking his rearguard contrary to his captains' expectations, he turned his back on the vanguard and began to lead his main force to support the rearguard, moving so rapidly himself with one squadron before the others that when the attack began he was among the first of his men in the front line. Some have recorded that the forces of the Marquis did not cross the river without some disorder because of the height of the banks and the obstacles provided by the trees, roots and branches which commonly cover the banks of torrents. Others add that his foot soldiers, because of these difficulties and of the waters swollen by the night's rain, were delayed in reaching the battle and did not all cross, not a few remaining on the other side of the river. Whatever the reason, it is certain that the

241

Marquis' attack was very fierce and furious, and was met with like ferocity and courage. The squadrons entered the battle from all sides in a mêlée and not according to the custom of the wars of Italy, which was to fight, one squadron against another, and to replace this with another when the first was worsted or began to fall back, and not to make up one large squadron from several small ones except as a last resort. As a result the battles, in which very few men were ever killed, usually lasted nearly all day and were often brought to an end by nightfall without certain victory on either side.

When the lances were broken, many men-at-arms and horses fell to the ground in the encounter, and then they all began to wield with like ferocity maces, short swords and other small arms, the horses fighting with kicks, bites and blows no less than the men. Certainly at the beginning the Italians showed splendid courage thanks largely to the fighting spirit of the Marquis who, followed by a brave company of young noblemen and *lancie spezzate* (these are picked soldiers maintained outside the ordinary companies), and promptly affronting all dangers, did not lack any quality proper to a very valiant captain. The French bravely withstood this ferocious onslaught; but being hard pressed by a much superior force, they were already almost visibly beginning to fall back, thereby endangering the King. In fact a few steps away from him the bastard Bourbon was taken prisoner though fighting fiercely. At this the Marquis hoped to have the same success with the King himself, who had rashly moved himself into a position of great danger without the guard and precautions suitable to so great a prince. The Marquis made great efforts to get near Charles with a large number of his troops. The King with few of his men about him, showed great courage and defended himself nobly against the Marquis' attack more by the ferocity of his charger than the help of his soldiers. In such danger he did not lack those thoughts which fear usually brings to mind in difficult situations.

He saw himself almost abandoned by his men and turned to heaven for help and vowed to St. Denis and St. Martin—reputed to be the special protectors of the

Kingdom of France—that if he got through safely with his army into Piedmont, he would go as soon as he returned to France to visit with rich gifts the churches dedicated to their names, one near Paris, the other at Tours, and that every year he would bear witness with solemn feasts and offerings to the grace he had received through them. When he had made these vows his strength renewed and he began to fight more vigorously than seemed possible for a man of his strength and physique. But the King's danger had so roused those who were not far away that they all hastened to protect his royal person and they held back the Italians. At this moment his company, which had been left behind, came up; and one squadron fiercely attacked the enemy on the flank, which curbed their impetus a good deal. Then Ridolfo da Gonzaga, the uncle of the Marquis of Mantua, a commander of great experience—while urging on his men and reforming them wherever their ranks were beginning to break and moving here and there doing the work of an excellent captain—chanced to raise his visor and was wounded in the face by a Frenchman's sword and fell from his horse. His own men were unable to help him in the great confusion and tumult and the press of ferocious horses, and indeed with other men and horses falling on top of him he was rather suffocated in the crush than killed by enemy arms. It was certainly an end unworthy of him because in the discussions the day before and that same morning he had thought it imprudent to risk so much unnecessarily. He had advised, against his nephew's wishes, that they should avoid a battle.

As the battle swayed one way and the other and neither the Italians nor the French appeared to gain any advantage, it was more doubtful than ever who would be the victor. So as fear and hope ran equal on both sides, they fought with unbelievable ardor, every man feeling that victory lay in his right hand and in his valor. The courage of the French was stimulated by the presence and the danger of their King—for the King's majesty is venerated among that nation by ancient custom no less than the name of God—and by the fact that they were in a position where only victory could save them. The Italians were encouraged by the greed for plunder, the ferocity and example of the Marquis, their success in the early part of the fight and the great number of their army, so that they could expect help from many on their own side. The French could have no such hopes because their forces were either all engaged in the fighting or expected at any moment to be attacked by the enemy. But in all human actions (as everyone knows) the power of fortune is enormous—greater in military affairs than in any others; but immeasurable, immense, infinite in deeds of arms, where an order misunderstood, a maneuver badly executed, a rash move, a vain cry even from a simple soldier, often brings victory to those who seemed vanquished; where innumerable incidents arise unexpectedly which cannot possibly be foreseen or controlled by the commander's skill. So in this indecisive state of the battle, fortune, not forgetting its usual power, did what neither men's courage nor force of arms had succeeded in doing.

The *stradiotti*, who had been sent to attack the wagons of the French, had begun to plunder them unopposed and were busy leading mules, horses and other equipment over to the other bank, when not only the other part of the *stradiotti* which was supposed to attack the French flank, but also those who had already entered the battle, saw their companions returning to camp laden with spoils. Fired with greed for gain, they turned to rob the wagons. Cavalry and infantry followed their example and abandoned the battle in large numbers for the same purpose. Therefore, as the Italians not only lacked their planned reinforcements but the number of combatants was diminishing through such disorder; and as Antonio da Montefeltro made no move because it was Ridolfo da Gonzaga's job to call him at the right moment—and Ridolfo was dead so no one called him—the French began to gain so much ground that the only thing still supporting the Italians, who were now visibly failing, was the courage of the Marquis. Fighting most bravely he still held the enemy attack, inspiring his men with his example and shouts of encouragement to prefer death to dishonor. But it was no longer possible for a

few to resist many. The fight was thickening around
them on all sides, many were dead and many wounded
particularly in the Marquis' own company, and they
were all forced to flee across the river. Because of the
rains that had fallen that night, and which continued
to fall with much hail and thunder while they were
fighting, the river had risen so high that it was very
hard to cross. The French pursued them vigorously to the
river, concentrating with great fury on killing those who
fled, without taking any prisoners or stopping for plunder or gain. Frequent cries were heard in the field:
"Comrades, remember Guinegate." Guinegate is a place
in Picardy near Thérouanne, where in the last years of
the reign of Louis XI the French army, which had almost
achieved victory in a battle against Maximilian, King of
the Romans, fell into disorder when it started to plunder, and was put to flight.

But at the very moment when this part of the army
was fighting with such courage and ferocity, the French
vanguard, against which the Count of Gaiazzo sent part
of his cavalry, moved into battle with such frightening
violence, that the Italians, especially when they saw that
they were not being followed by their own troops, fell into disarray almost of their own accord. And when some of
their number had been killed—among them Giovanni
Piccinino and Galeazzo da Coreggio—they returned in
flight to the main squadron. The Marshal de Gié, however, seeing that besides the Count's squadron there was
on the farther shore of the river another column of men-
at-arms in battle order, would not allow his troops to
pursue them. This was a decision which many, when it
was later discussed, judged prudent; while many others
who considered the effect more than the cause, regarded
it as more cowardly than circumspect. For there is no
doubt that if they had pursued them, the Count and his
column would have turned tail, filling with such fear all
the other troops on the other side of the river that it
would have been virtually impossible to prevent them
from running away. The Marquis of Mantua, fleeing
from the other part of the army, crossed the river with
part of his troops in as good order as he could manage

245

and found these forces in such agitation that they were all thinking of saving themselves and their goods. The main road from Piacenza to Parma was already full of men, horses and wagons retreating toward Parma. His presence and authority put a stop in part to this tumult because he re-formed them and put some order into things. But the arrival of the Count of Pitigliano did much more; for amid all the confusion on both sides he had seized the opportunity to flee to the Italian camp, where he revived and strengthened their spirits by insistently assuring them that the enemy was in much greater alarm and confusion. Indeed it was almost universally claimed that if it had not been for his words, either then or the following night the whole army would have fled in terror.

The Italians had now retreated to their camp except for those who, driven by the confusion and tumult (as always happens in such circumstances) and frightened by the high waters of the river, had run away in different directions—many of them being found and slaughtered by the French scattered over the countryside. The King then went with his troops to join the vanguard which had not moved from its position, and there took counsel with his captains whether they should cross the river at once to attack the enemy in their camp. He was advised by Trivulzio and Cammillo Vitelli (whose company had been sent after the forces going on the Genoa campaign, while he had followed the King with a few cavalry to be present at the battle) to attack. Francesco Secco urged this course most strongly of all, pointing out that the road which could be seen in the distance was full of men and horses—which showed that either they were fleeing toward Parma or, having begun to flee, were now returning to their camp. Nevertheless it was not easy to cross the river. The troops who had either been fighting or had stood to arms in the field were so weary that on the advice of the French captains they decided to camp. They went to camp in the village of Medesano on the hill not much more than a mile from the place where they had fought. There they camped without any plan or order and with no little discomfort because many of their wagons had been looted by the enemy.

This was the battle fought between the Italians and the French on the River Taro, memorable because it was the first for a very long time which had been fought with killing and bloodshed in Italy. Before this very few men died in any armed encounter. But in this, though on the French side less than 200 men were killed, the Italians lost more than 300 men-at-arms and as many as 3,000 others, among them Rinuccio da Farnese, the Venetians' *condottiere,* and many noble gentlemen; and Bernardino dal Montone was left for dead, struck down by a blow from a mace—also a *condottiere* of the Venetians, but famous more for the renown of Braccio dal Montone, his grandfather, one of the foremost champions of Italian arms, than for his own success or valor. Such a great slaughter was all the more astonishing to the Italians because the battle lasted no more than an hour and the fighting everywhere was man to man with very little artillery used. Both sides tried to claim the victory and honor of the day. The Italians because their camp and wagons were saved (whereas the French had lost a great deal of theirs, including some of the King's own tents); and they also boasted that they would have beaten the enemy if part of their troops which should have entered the battle had not turned to looting. The French did not deny the truth of this. The Venetians tried hard to attribute the victory to themselves: by official decree, throughout their territory and particularly in Venice itself, there were bonfires and other demonstrations of joy. Private individuals in later years followed this public example no less readily, because on the tomb of Marchionne Trivisano in the Church of the Minor Friars were inscribed the following words: On the River Taro he fought King Charles of France and won. However public opinion adjudged that it was a French victory, because of the great difference in the number of those killed, because they drove the enemy across the river and because they were free to continue their advance, which had been the matter of dispute over which they had fought.

The following day the King remained in the same camp. That day there was some parley with the enemy through Argenton, a truce being declared until that night. On the one hand the King sought free passage because he knew that many Italian troops had not fought. He saw that they still remained in their camp and thought a journey of so many days through the Duchy of Milan too dangerous with the enemy at his back. On the other hand he could not make up his mind what to do because he was in the habit of scorning better advice and pursuing his own weak counsel in reaching decisions. There was similar uncertainty in the minds of the Italians, who though they were very much afraid at first, had gained such confidence that on the evening after the battle they discussed a proposal urged on them by the Count of Pitigliano for a night attack on the French camp, which was lodged in great discomfort and had no defenses at all. However, as many were against it, this suggestion was set aside as being too dangerous.

A rumor then spread through Italy that Lodovico Sforza's men, on a secret order from him, had been unwilling to fight because with so powerful a Venetian army on his territory he was no less afraid of their victory than of a French one. He desired the French to be neither victorious nor vánquished and wanted to keep his own forces intact to be safer himself in any eventuality. This was said to have been the reason the Italian army had not achieved victory. This belief was encouraged by the Marquis of Mantua and the other Venetian commanders to improve their own reputation, and was readily accepted by all those who wished to see the glory of Italian arms increase. But I heard a very reliable person who was at that time in such a position in Milan that he had full information of the matter, absolutely refute this rumor because, as Lodovico had sent nearly all his forces to the siege of Novara, he did not have enough troops on the Taro to make much difference in the battle. The confederate army would have achieved that victory if it had not been hampered more by the disorders among its troops than by not having more of them—particularly since many of the Venetian soldiers did not enter the

battle. Even if the Count of Gaiazzo sent only one part
of his force against the enemy, and that with little enthusiasm, this may have been because the French vanguard was so strong that he realized it would be dangerous to risk it; and normally it would be more surprising
to see him commit brave actions than safe ones. Nevertheless the Sforza troops were not entirely useless because, though they did not fight, they prevented the
French vanguard from rescuing the King when he was
bearing all the brunt of the battle with a much smaller
and weaker part of his army. And this view, if I am
not mistaken, is supported as much by reason as by
authority; for is it not likely that if Lodovico Sforza had
such an intention, he would rather have ordered his
captains to speak against opposing the passage of the
French? If the King had been victorious, his own troops
would have been no safer than the rest, being so near
the enemy although they had not entered the battle.
And from what reasoning, what consideration, what experience, could he be sure that in any battle fortunes
would be so equal that the King of France would be
neither victor nor vanquished? Nor would they have
fought at all against the advice of his captains, because
the Venetian forces, which had been sent into that state
solely for its defense and protection, would not have
gone against the will of his captains.

Charles moved off with his army the following day before dawn, without sound of trumpets—to hide his departure as much as possible. And for that day he was
not followed by the allied army, which was prevented,
had they wished to do so, by the waters of the river
which had risen so high during the night because of a
new rainfall, that it could not be forded for most of the
day. Only at sundown the Count of Gaiazzo with 200
light cavalry crossed over, not without danger from the
force of the waters. Following with them in the tracks
of the French, who were traveling along the direct road
to Piacenza, he was able, especially on the following
day, to cause them much inconvenience and delay. However, though very tired, the French went on their way
without any trouble and without losing a single man.

Victuals were to be had in abundance from the country around, partly because the inhabitants were afraid of being plundered, partly through Trivulzio, who rode ahead for that purpose with the light cavalry and persuaded people with threats or with his own authority—which was very great everywhere in that state and particularly among the Guelphs.

The army of the league moved on the day after the French left and was not at all disposed, especially the Venetian commissioners, to tempt fortune again. They never drew near enough to the French to cause them the slightest trouble. On the contrary, on the second day when they were camped on the River Trebbia a little beyond Piacenza, and 200 lances, the Swiss and almost all the artillery had stopped between the river and the city as a more convenient encampment, during the night the river rose so high with the heavy rain that in spite of all their efforts neither horse nor foot could cross until the day was far advanced, and then only with difficulty although the water had begun to go down. And still they were not attacked either by the enemy army which was far away, or by the Count of Gaiazzo who had entered Piacenza for fear there might be some uprising there. His suspicions were not unfounded because it is believed that if Charles had followed Trivulzio's advice and raised a standard in the name of Francesco, Giovan Galeazzo's little son, there might easily have been a revolution in the Duchy, so well loved was the name of their rightful lord, so hated that of the usurper and so powerful the following and friendships of Trivulzio. But the King, intent only on pressing forward, listened to no counsel and pursued his course with all speed; after the first few days he was even short of victuals because as he went farther he found the places better guarded, as Lodovico Sforza had spread out—partly in Tortona under Guasparri da San Severino, nicknamed Fracassa, and partly in Alessandria—many cavalry and 1,200 German infantry who had been detached from the siege of Novara. The French too had been harassed from the rear—ever since they crossed the Trebbia—by the Count of Gaiazzo who had augmented his force of light horse with 500 German infantry who had been guarding Piacenza. He had not been able to secure the rest of the light horse and the 400 men-at-arms he had asked for because the Venetian commissioners, warned by the danger experienced on the Taro, would not allow it. Yet the French, who on reaching Alessandria had taken the upper road near the mountains, where the River Tanaro is shallower, proceeded to the walls of Asti in eight marches without loss of men or any other casualty. When the King entered the town he had the troops camp outside, with the object of increasing his forces and remaining in Italy until he had relieved Novara. The forces of the league which had followed him to Tortona, gave up hope of harming him further, and went off to join the Sforza troops around Novara. This place was already short of supplies because the Duke of Orléans and his officers had made no effort to provide them, as they could very easily have done since the surrounding country was very fertile. In fact, not realizing their danger until the possibility of a remedy was out of reach, they had used up those they had without stint.

At almost the same moment the cardinals and captains returned to Charles from their unsuccessful attempt on Genoa. When the navy had taken the town of La Spezia on their first arrival, they went on to Rapallo, occupying it without difficulty. But a fleet came out from Genoa consisting of eight light galleys, one galleon and two Biscay barques, and by night put ashore 700 soldiers, who without the least difficulty took the town of Rapallo and the French garrison which was inside. Then moving up to the French fleet which had anchored in the bay, they captured and burnt all the ships and took the captain prisoner after a long battle. With this victory those same places where the Aragonese had been defeated the year before were made even more famous. Nor was this French defeat remedied by the land forces; for, having gone by the eastern shore as far as the Val di Bisagna and the outskirts of Genoa, they found themselves disappointed in their hopes of a rising in Genoa; and when they heard of the loss of the navy, they went off practically in flight through the mountains by a very

251

rough and difficult route into the Valle di Pozzeveri, which is on the other side of the city. From there, though their numbers were much increased by peasants and troops sent to support them by the Duke of Savoy, they continued with the same speed into Piedmont. There is no doubt that if those within had not refrained from coming out for fear that the Fregoso party might cause an uprising, they would have completely defeated them and put them to flight. But because of this reversal the Vitelli cavalry which had reached Chiavari, when they heard what had happened to those they were going to meet, returned in haste and not without peril to Sarzana. Apart from La Spezia, the other towns on the Riviera which had been occupied by the exiles recalled the Genoese at once, as did the town of Ventimiglia on the western Riviera, which at the same time had been occupied by Pol Battista Fregoso and some other exiles.

Chapter X

[*Fighting between the French and Spanish-Aragonese in the Kingdom of Naples. Return of Ferrando of Aragon to Naples. Some towns rebel against the French. The Venetians occupy some parts of Puglia. Castelnuovo surrenders to Ferrando. Agreement to surrender Castel dell' Uovo. Death of Alfonso of Aragon.*]

At this time there was no less trouble and change in the Kingdom of Naples than in Lombardy, though with more varied results. After he had taken Reggio, Ferrando was endeavoring to retake the surrounding area. He had with him about 6,000 men, between volunteers from the area and from Sicily and the Spanish cavalry and infantry led by Gonzalo Hernandez of the house of Aguilar, a Cordoban and a man of great valor with long experience in the wars of Granada. When he first came into Italy, Spanish boastfulness nicknamed him the "Grand Captain," indicating by this title his supreme authority over them; but he later earned by his brilliant victories the perpetuation and confirmation of this name, to signify his great ability and excellence in military discipline. Aubigny, with the French men-at-arms who had stayed to guard Calabria and with cavalry and infantry contributed by local nobles who supported the King of France, went to meet them near Seminara, a place near the sea. When they met in battle, the ability of regular seasoned soldiers overcame the inexperience of raw troops —as not only the Italians and Sicilians hastily recruited by Ferrando, but even the Spaniards were new men with little experience of war. Nevertheless for some time there was fierce fighting, because the courage and authority of the captains, who failed in no part of their duty, sustained those who were inferior in every way. Particularly Ferrando, fighting as his valor demanded; and when his horse had been killed under him, he would surely have been killed or captured if Giovanni di Capua —brother of the Duke of Termini, who had been his page since his boyhood—had not dismounted and given him his horse, thus exposing his own life with a memorable example of loyalty and love to save that of his king—for he was immediately killed.

Gonzalo fled across the mountains to Reggio; Ferrando to Palma which is on the coast near Seminara, where he embarked and returned with his fleet to Messina. His will and desire to try his fortune again were increased by these reverses because he knew how greatly the whole city of Naples wished for his return, and he had also received secret messages from many leading nobles and commoners. Therefore, fearing that delay and news of his defeat in Calabria might cause this favor to cool, he collected, besides the galleys he had brought from Ischia and the four with which his father Alfonso had left Naples, the ships of the fleet from Spain and as many as he could from the cities and barons of Sicily. He then set out from Messina, undeterred by the shortage of men to arm them, like one who, lacking the resources proper to such an enterprise, was forced to rely as much on show as on substance. He left Sicily with 60 great ships and 20 other smaller ones, and with him Ricaiensio the Catalan, commander of the Spanish fleet, a man of great

ability and experience in naval affairs—but with so few
fighting men that the majority were simply the men
needed to work the ships. So his force was small, though
his favor and support with the people were great. When
he reached the shore at Salerno, the town, the Malfi coast,
and la Cava immediately raised his standard. He beat
to and fro off Naples for two days in the hope that a revolt would occur in the city—in vain because the French,
promptly taking arms and placing a strong guard in strategic places, repressed the rebellion which already threatened; and they would have solved all their troubles if
they had boldly followed the advice of a few among
them who, guessing that the Aragonese ships were poorly provided with troops, urged Montpensier to fill the
French fleet, which was in port, with soldiers and fighting men and attack the enemy. But on the third day
Ferrando gave up hope of an uprising in the city and
put out to sea for Ischia. Then the conspirators in Naples,
thinking that their conspiracy was practically uncovered
—Ferrando's cause had become their own—got together
and decided to make a virtue of necessity, and secretly
sent a ship to ask him to return. They requested him to
help and encourage those who wanted to rise in his favor
by landing all or part of his forces. So he again returned
to the neighborhood of Naples on the day after the battle
on the River Taro, and came in with his fleet to disem-
bark his troops at Maddalena, a place a mile away from
Naples where the Sebeto flows into the sea—a small
stream rather than a river, which would be completely
unknown if it had not been mentioned by the Neapolitan poets. When Montpensier saw this, no less prompt
in acting boldly when caution was needed than he had
been cautious the day before when boldness was called
for, he marched out of the city with almost all his troops
to stop him from landing. As a result the Neapolitans
had an opportunity such as they would not have dared
to hope for. They rose at once in arms, the signal for the
rising being given first by ringing the bells at the Carmel-
ite church near the city walls, followed then by all the
other churches. They manned the gates and began openly shouting the name of Ferrando. This sudden revolt so

frightened the French that, feeling it was not safe to be between the city in rebellion and the enemy forces, and fearing they would not be able to return to the city by the road from which they had come, they decided to skirt the walls of the city (a long, hilly and difficult road) and to enter Naples by the gate near Castelnuovo.

In the meantime Ferrando had entered Naples and had been mounted on horses with some of his men by the Neapolitans. He rode through the city amid indescribably joyful scenes. The crowds received him with great shouts of enthusiasm, while the women continually showered flowers and perfumes on him from their windows: indeed, some of the most noble ladies ran into the streets to embrace him and wipe the sweat from his brow.

In spite of all this revelry the necessary preparations for defense were not neglected. The Marquis of Pescara with the troops which had entered with Ferrando, and the young men of Naples set about blocking and fortifying the entrance to the streets by which the French could attack the town from Castelnuovo. When the French reached the castle square, they made every effort to re-enter the town itself; but being fired upon with crossbows and small artillery and finding adequate defenses at the entrance to every street, they withdrew at nightfall into the castle, leaving their horses behind on the square—little less than 2,000 of them—because there was no room for them in the castle and no means of feeding them. Yves d'Alègre a highly reputed captain, Antonello Prince of Salerno and many other French and Italian nobles shut themselves in the castle with Montpensier; and though for some days they made frequent skirmishes in the square and around the port and bombarded the city with artillery, they were always thrown back by the enemy and lost hope of retaking the city. The example of Naples was at once followed by Capua, Aversa, the fort of Mondragone and many other places; and the larger part of the Kingdom began to think of change. Among these the people of Gaeta took up arms with greater courage than strength because some of Ferrando's galleys had appeared off the port; but they were

overcome by the French garrison with great loss of life—
and in the heat of victory all the town was sacked. At
the same time the Venetian fleet put in at Monopoli, a
town in Puglia, landed the *stradiotti* and many soldiers,
and attacked the place by land and sea. In the fighting
Pietro Bembo, master of a Venetian galley, was killed
by a cannon shot of the defenders. Finally the town was
taken by storm and the castle handed over by the French
warden out of fear. Later Pulignano was taken over by
treaty.

But Ferrando was determined to take Castelnuovo and
Castel dell' Uovo, hoping that they might soon be starved
into surrender because their provisions were small in re-
lation to the number of men within. He kept continuous
guard on all the places around the castle and sought to
increase their difficulties still more. As the French fleet
of five ships, four light galleys, one galliot and one galleon could not safely remain in the port, they had withdrawn to a place between Torre di San Vincenzio, Castel
dell' Uovo and Pizzifalcone which were loyal to the
French. They also held the area behind Castelnuovo
where the royal gardens were, and as far as Cappella; and
having fortified the monastery of La Croce, they ranged
as far as Pié di Grotta and San Martino. Ferrando, having
captured and taken their horses to a safe place, moved
secretly toward Incoronata and occupied the Monte di
Sant' Ermo and after that the hill of Pizzifalcone—the
fortress on the top being held by the French. In order to
prevent the fortress from being relieved—because if they
could take it they could bombard the enemy fleet from
above—Ferrando's troops attacked the monastery of la
Croce; but being heavily bombarded, they lost hope of
taking it by force, and decided to try and take it by
treachery, which turned out to be fatal for its origina-
tor. For when a Moor who was within falsely promised
the Marquis of Pescara, who had once been his master,
to let him in, and so lured him one night up a wooden
ladder leaning against the monastery wall to talk to
him and establish the time and means by which they
should enter that same night, he was betrayed and

killed by the arrow of a crossbow which pierced his throat.

Prospero and later Fabrizio Colonna changed sides with no small benefit to Ferrando. Although still bound by their commission with the King of France, they passed into Ferrando's service almost as soon as he had recaptured Naples, excusing their behavior by saying that they had not received their promised pay at the right time, and that Virginio Orsino and the Count of Pitigliano had been highly favored by the King without regard for their merits. These arguments seemed to many people of little weight in comparison with the benefits the King had bestowed on them. Yet who knows if those very things which might have been expected to hold their loyalty, were not in fact the cause of their doing the opposite. For the greater the rewards they had received, the greater perhaps their anxiety to hold on to them when they saw the French cause beginning to weaken.

With the castle surrounded in this way and the sea blockaded by Ferrando's ships, the scarcity of provisions grew worse and worse and the French were sustained only by the hope of being relieved by sea from France. As soon as he reached Asti, Charles had sent off Perron de Baschi, and had a fleet dispatched from Villefranche near Nice with 2,000 Swiss and Gascons and supplies, under the command of M. d'Arban, a warlike man though with no experience of the sea. This fleet reached the island of Ponza and sighting Ferrando's navy in the vicinity, which consisted of 30 sail and two Genoese great ships, it fled at once. It was pursued as far as the island of Elba and lost on the way a Biscayan round ship. The fleet took refuge in the port of Leghorn in such a state of alarm that the captain was unable to prevent most of the infantry from disembarking and going off to Pisa against his orders. With the withdrawal of this fleet Montpensier and the others, compelled by lack of food supplies, agreed to give Ferrando the castle in which they had been besieged for three months and to leave for Provence if they were not relieved within thirty days—on condition that no harm was done to the

257

persons and property of all those within. As guarantees
of this agreement they handed over Yves d'Alègre and
three others to Ferrando. But they could not in so short
a time expect any help except from their forces already
in the kingdom. Therefore M. de Persi, one of the royal
commanders, with the Swiss and part of the French
lances, set off toward Naples, accompanied by the Prince
of Bisignano and many other barons. Hearing of their
coming, Ferrando sent the Count of Matalona to meet
them at Eboli with an army for the most part hastily
gathered from among friends and supporters. They met
the enemy at Lake Pizzolo near Eboli, and though they
were much superior in number, they ran away without
fighting as soon as they came near; and in their flight
Venanzio, son of Giulio da Varano, lord of Camerino, was
taken prisoner. But as the French did not pursue them
any distance, they retreated to Nola with few casualties,
and then to Naples.

The victors continued their march to relieve the castles,
with a reputation so enhanced by their victory that
Ferrando was tempted to abandon Naples again. But
taking heart again with the encouragement of the Neapolitans, moved as much by their own fears arising out of
the rebellion as by their love for Ferrando, he stopped at
Cappella; and to prevent the enemy reaching the castle
he finished a great trench which he had already started
between the Monte di Sant' Ermo and Castel dell' Uovo
and set artillery and infantry on all the hills as far as
Cappella and beyond. So that although the French, who
had come by the Salerno road to Nocera through la Cava
and the hill of Pié di Grotta, got to Chiaia near Naples,
nevertheless they were unable to go any farther or move
up to Cappella—as everywhere was well guarded and Ferrando made a brave show and gave them a great deal
of trouble with his artillery, especially the guns stationed on the hill of Pizzifalcone which overlooks Castel
dell' Uovo (and is where Lucullus held his famous
luxurious parties)— Nor could they stay where they
were because nature, which is abundant in all other
amenities along that coast, has denied it a supply of
fresh water; and so they had to withdraw sooner than

they would otherwise have done, leaving behind two or three pieces of artillery and part of the supplies brought to relieve the castle.

They went off toward Nola. In order to bar their road Ferrando left a force blockading the castle and took up a position with his troops in the Plain of Palma near Sarni. But Montpensier who, with the departure of the French had now lost all hope of relief, left 300 men in Castelnuovo, a number proportionate as much to the remaining supplies as to the needs of defense, and a garrison in Castel dell' Uovo. He then embarked at night with 2,500 soldiers in the ships of his fleet and sailed to Salerno. Ferrando was extremely indignant at this, saying he had no right during the period agreed for the surrender to leave Castelnuovo with his troops without handing over the castle and also Castel dell' Uovo. So he was minded to revenge himself with the blood of the hostages for this offense and for Montpensier's failure to surrender the castles at the agreed time. But after about a month those who remained in Castelnuovo, no longer able to hold out, surrendered on condition that the hostages would be released. Almost simultaneously the defenders of Castel dell' Uovo agreed for the same reason to surrender the first day of the coming Lent if they had not been relieved before then.

About this time Alfonso of Aragon died at Messina. During his reign the glory and fortune for which he had become famous everywhere while he was Duke of Calabria had changed into infamy and misfortune. It is said that shortly before his death he had begged his son to allow him to return to Naples, where the hatred once felt for him had almost turned into good will. As in human nature the desire for power is generally stronger than filial respect, Ferrando is supposed to have replied no less sharply than cleverly that he should wait until the kingdom had been sufficiently consolidated for him not to have to flee again. And so as to support his position by a stronger link with the King of Spain, he married, with the Pope's dispensation, his aunt Giovanna, daughter of his grandfather Ferdinand and Giovanna, the King of Spain's sister.

Chapter XI

[*Venetian and Sforza troops besiege Novara. Charles VIII recruits more Swiss. Fears and precautions of the league because of the Duchess of Savoy's support for Charles. The Pope's warning to Charles and his ironical reply. Pact between Charles and the Florentines.*]

While, as we have said, the siege was going on with varying success around the castles of Naples, the siege of Novara was becoming more and more critical. The Duke of Milan had a powerful army there, and the Venetians had come to his assistance so readily that one could hardly remember a time when they had spent so freely on any campaign. Thus in a very short time there were in the camp of the league 3,000 men-at-arms, 3,000 light horse, 1,000 German cavalry and 5,000 Italian infantry. But the army's main strength was in 10,000 *landsknechte* (as they commonly call the German infantry), largely recruited by the Duke of Milan to face up to the Swiss: for the very name of the Swiss was too much for the Italian infantry, which had greatly diminished in reputation and courage since the arrival of the French. The Germans were commanded by many brave captains. The one with the highest repute was Giorgio di Pietrapanta, a native of Austria, who a few years before in the service of Maximilian King of the Romans had won great renown when he took St. Omer in Picardy from the King of France. The Venetian senate not only hastened to send many troops to the siege, but to give their forces greater courage they had promoted the Marquis of Mantua from governor to captain-general in recognition of the valor he had shown in the battle on the Taro; and they had also set a very welcome and praiseworthy example by increasing the commissions of those who had fought bravely, as well as giving pensions and rewards to sons of many men who had fallen in the battle and dowries to the daughters. This extremely powerful army was being

used in the siege because the league had decided—
largely at Lodovico Sforza's desire—not to risk battle with
the King of France unless forced to do so; but by digging
themselves in around Novara in suitable positions, to
prevent supplies from reaching the defenders, hoping
that as there was only a small quantity within and they
needed a great deal, they would not be able to hold out
for very long. In addition to the population of the town
and the peasants who had taken refuge there, the Duke
of Orléans had more than 7,000 picked troops between
French and Swiss. Therefore Galeazzo da San Severino
with the ducal army, giving up any thought of storming
the town since it had so large a force of defenders, was
camped at Mugne, a place on the main road very convenient for stopping provisions coming from Vercelli. The
Marquis of Mantua with the Venetian troops had on his
first arrival taken by force some of the surrounding area
and a few days afterward the castle of Brione which
was of some importance. He then fortified Camariano
and Bolgari between Novara and Vercelli. To cut off supplies more effectively they had distributed the army in
many places around Novara and fortified all their camps.

On the other hand the King of France had moved from
Asti to Turin to be nearer Novara; and though he often
went as far as Chieri for love of a lady living there, his
preparations for war did not cease for that, continually
expediting troops from France with the object of putting
2,000 French lances in the field. They were also pressing
with equal urgency for 10,000 Swiss whom the Bailli of
Dijon had been sent to recruit. As soon as they arrived,
they planned to make every effort to relieve Novara, but
without them they did not dare to attempt anything important. The Kingdom of France, though at that time
very well provided with cavalry and a great quantity of
artillery and great skill in handling it, was extremely
weak in infantry of its own. This was because arms and
the military profession were reserved to the nobility; and
thus the ancient warlike spirit of the nation had disap-
peared among the plebs and the common people, long unused to war and entirely given up to the arts and occupa-
tions of peace. Many of their kings, fearing the strength

of the people after the lessons of various conspiracies and rebellions which had occurred in that kingdom, had deliberately disarmed them and divorced them from military pursuits.

So the French no longer had confidence in their own infantry and were timid in going to war if there were no company of Swiss in their army. That nation which had been ferocious and warlike from times immemorial, had greatly increased its reputation about twenty years earlier. Then they had been attacked with a most powerful army by Charles Duke of Burgundy, who for his power and aggressiveness was greatly feared by the Kingdom of France and all his neighbors. Yet the Swiss in a few months had defeated him three times; and in the last battle he had been killed either while fighting or while fleeing (because the manner of his death was uncertain). Therefore for their bravery and because the French had no rivalry or quarrel with them or any cause to suspect them (as they did the Germans), they recruited no other foreign infantry except Swiss and used them in all their important wars. On this occasion they employed them all the more readily because they knew that the relief of Novara, surrounded by such a great army and against so many German infantry who fought with the same discipline as the Swiss, was a difficult and dangerous enterprise.

The town of Vercelli, lying between Turin and Novara, was once a part of the Duchy of Milan but had been ceded by Filippo Maria Visconti during the long wars he had with the Venetians and the Florentines to Amideo Duke of Savoy in order to persuade him to leave their alliance. Neither side had yet entered Vercelli because the Duchess, mother and guardian of the young Duke of Savoy, and entirely French in her sympathies, had not been willing to come out on the King's side until his position was stronger. Meantime she gave the Duke of Milan kind words and hopes. But when the King and his reinforced army went to Turin, a city of the same duchy, she allowed some of his troops to enter Vercelli. This improved his chances of relieving Novara when all his reinforcements had arrived, as Vercelli was very

conveniently placed; and the allies began to entertain
serious doubts. So in order to decide more thoroughly
what to do in these difficult circumstances, Lodovico
Sforza went to the army with his wife Beatrice, who
was his constant companion in serious affairs no less
than in his pleasures. In his presence, and, it was said,
largely on his advice, it was unanimously decided by
the captains after much argument that for the greater
safety of all, the Venetian army should join up with
Sforza's at Mugne, leaving sufficient garrison in all the
places around Novara to maintain the siege. Bolgari was
to be abandoned because, as it was only three miles from
Vercelli, it would be necessary if the French went in
force to take it, either shamefully to lose it or else go and
rescue it with the whole army contrary to the decisions
they had already made. The garrison at Camariano—
three miles from the camp at Mugne—was to be increased, and the whole camp itself was to be fortified
with ditches and banks and a large quantity of artillery.
All other decisions were to be taken from day to day according to the enemy's movements. In the meantime the
country should be laid waste and all the trees cut down
up to the walls of Novara, so as to present an obstacle
both to the troops and the pillaging sorties of the cavalry,
of which there were a great number in the city.

When these things had been decided and a general
review held of the whole army, Lodovico Sforza returned
to Milan in order to attend more promptly to any arrangements which might become necessary from day to
day. To assist the temporal forces with spiritual arms
and authority, he and the Venetians got the Pope to send
to Charles one of his bedels to command him to leave
Italy with all his army within ten days and to remove
his troops from the Kingdom of Naples within a further
brief period. Otherwise he should appear personally
before the Pope at Rome under threat of those spiritual
punishments which the Church may inflict. This was a
course previously adopted by earlier Popes, for we read
that with similar arms Adrian I compelled Desiderio
King of the Lombards, who was on his way to attack
Rome with a powerful army, to withdraw to Pavia from

Terni, which he had already reached. But as the reverence and majesty which the holiness of their lives inspired in men's hearts were now lacking, it was absurd
to hope for the same results from habits and examples
which were so different. Therefore, Charles, mocking the
vanity of this command, replied that, as the Pope had
not been willing to wait for him in Rome on his return
from Naples when he desired devoutly to kiss his feet,
he was astonished that he should now so urgently request his presence. However, he was busy reopening the
way to Rome in order to obey him, and begged the Pope
to wait for him there so that he should not have gone
to so much trouble in vain.

At this time Charles concluded new treaties with the
Florentine ambassadors in Turin. This was not done without considerable opposition from those who on other occasions had taken the same attitude. Their hand was
strengthened by the fact that when the Florentines had
recovered the other castles in the hills around Pisa which
they had lost during Charles' return, they had besieged
Ponte di Sacco and taken it by capitulation with a guarantee of the safety of the soldiers within; and then, contrary to this assurance, when they came out, nearly all
the Gascon infantry and the Pisans were slaughtered
and the dead mutilated. However this occurred against
the orders of the Florentine commissioners who with
great difficulty saved some of them, and was the work
of some soldiers who had been treated very harshly when
they were prisoners of the French army; nevertheless at
the King's court it was interpreted by their enemies as
a clear sign of deep hostility to the French and so made
an agreement all the more difficult. However in the end
it was concluded, all other considerations being overridden not by the memory of their promises and solemn
oath but by the urgent need to obtain money and send
relief to the Kingdom of Naples.

It was therefore agreed as follows: that without any
delay all the fortresses and possessions in Charles' hands
should be returned to the Florentines on condition that
within the next two years, if the King so desired and
in return for appropriate compensation, they would give

up Pietrasanta and Sarzana to the Genoese—if the latter became subjects of the King. In expectation of such restitution the Florentine ambassadors were to pay at once the 30,000 ducats agreed in Florence, but receiving jewels in pawn as security for their money in case their territories were not restored for some reason or other. When the restitution had been made, they would lend the King under the guarantee of the generals of France (this is the title of the four ministers who receive the revenues of the whole kingdom) 70,000 ducats, paying them on his behalf to the forces in the Kingdom of Naples, including a sum to the Colonna if they had not gone over to Ferrando. The King had already had some news of the agreement made by Prospero, but as yet he had no certainty of it. Further, if there was no war in Tuscany, they would send to Naples in support of the French army, 250 men-at-arms; and if they did have war in Tuscany but it was only the one over Montepulciano, they were to send this force to accompany the troops of the Vitelli, who were in Pisan territory, as far as Naples, but would not have to keep them there later than October. The Pisans would be pardoned for all offenses committed; arrangements made for the restitution of property seized, and certain provisions made for the exercise of the arts and professions. Six of the principal citizens of Florence chosen by the King would be handed over as hostages to remain a certain time at his court to ensure the execution of these terms. When this agreement was concluded and the jewels pledged against payment of the 30,000 ducats, which were sent off at once to pay for the recruitment of Swiss troops, royal commands and letters were dispatched to the wardens of the castles to restore them immediately to the Florentines.

Chapter XII

[*Difficult position of the French in Novara. Secret negotiations for agreement between the King of France and the Duke of Milan. Peace proposals*

made by the King of France and discussed in the
royal council. Charles VIII makes peace with the
Duke of Milan and returns to France.]

However, conditions in Novara daily became harder
and more difficult, though the courage of the soldiers
was great; and even greater in view of their rebellion
was the determination of the people of Novara to defend
themselves. Their supplies were now so low that the people were beginning to suffer greatly from lack of food.
Although Orléans, when he saw himself in such difficulties, had banished all those who were of no use, this
was not enough. In fact many of the French and Swiss
soldiers, little able to bear this deprivation, began to fall
ill. Orléans, himself suffering from quartan fever, begged
Charles with frequent envoys and letters not to delay in
sending relief; though as they had not yet collected sufficient troops, it could not be in time to meet his urgent
need. Nevertheless the French tried several times to send
supplies into Novara by night with a strong escort of
horse and infantry, but each time they were discovered
by the enemy and compelled to retreat—sometimes with
great losses to those escorting them. In order to cut off
their supplies from all sides, the Marquis of Mantua attacked the monastery of St. Francesco near the walls of
Novara; and capturing it, he put in a guard of 200 men-
at-arms and 3,000 German infantry. This made the
army's work much easier, as the road along which their
own supplies had to come was made safe, and the road
was barred to the gate facing the Monte di Biandrana,
which was the easiest way into Novara. Furthermore on
the following day he took the bastion the French had
built on the edge of the Borgo di San Nazaro, and the
next night captured the Borgo itself and the other bastion near the gate.

On this occasion the Count of Pitigliano—who had
been commissioned by the Venetians with the title of
governor—was wounded in the stomach by an arquebus
and lay in great danger of his life. Because of these suc-
cesses the Duke of Orléans feared that he could not defend the other suburbs which he had fortified when he

withdrew into Novara. He therefore set fire to them and the following night withdrew all his troops to defend the city alone, comforting himself in the extremity of hunger with his increasing hopes of relief. For the Swiss had now begun to arrive; and the French army, crossing the River Sesia, had gone to camp a mile outside Vercelli. And having put a guard in Bolgari, it was waiting for the rest of the Swiss to arrive, in the belief that when they did, they would immediately go to the relief of Novara. This would be a very difficult task because the Italian armies were encamped in a strong place with powerful defensive weapons and the road from Vercelli to Novara was full of water and arduous because of the very broad, deep ditches all over the countryside. Between Bolgari, guarded by the French and the Italian camp, was Camariano, defended by them. Because of these difficulties the King and the others showed little enthusiasm. Nevertheless, if the whole Swiss force had arrived earlier, they would have risked a battle, the outcome of which could only have been very doubtful for both sides. Therefore, as everyone realized the dangers, secret negotiations for peace were continually going on between the King of France and the Duke of Milan. These did not seem very hopeful because of their strong mutual distrust and because both, to bolster up their reputation, pretended not to wish to reach agreement.

Chance, however, opened a more rapid road to this important end. For, as the Marchioness of Monferrato had died at that very time, and discussions were going on as to who should have charge of her small son, both the Marquis of Saluzzo and Constantine, the dead Marchioness' brother (one of the former rulers of Macedonia, occupied many years before by Mahomet the Ottoman), sought to become his governor. The King was anxious to ensure the peace of that state and sent Argenton to Casale Cervagio to settle the matter according to the wishes of the inhabitants. A master of the household of the Marquis of Mantua had also gone there to offer condolences for the death of the Marchioness. Thereupon between these two there arose some discussion of the benefits which peace would bring to both sides. This conversation progressed so far that Argenton, at his suggestion, wrote on the subject to the Venetian commissioners repeating the points he had begun to discuss with them on the Taro. They showed interest and passed on the information to the captains of the Duke of Milan; and finally all in agreement sent to ask the King, who had come to Vercelli, to send some of his people to parley at some convenient spot with their own representatives. When the King agreed, they met the following day between Bolgari and Camariano: for the Venetians the Marquis of Mantua and Bernardo Contarino, commissioner of the *stradiotti;* for the Duke of Milan Francesco Bernardino Visconti; and for the King of France the Cardinal of St. Malo, the Prince of Orange, who had recently entered the country and with the King's commission had charge of the whole army, Marshal de Gié, Piennes, and Argenton. These met several times and on different days some of them went to and fro between the armies, until the main difficulties were reduced to those concerned with Novara. For the King, though he did not object to surrendering the town, made difficulties about the manner of doing so. To save his own honor he insisted that in the name of the King of the Romans, immediate overlord of the Duchy of Milan, the town should be given into the hands of one of the German captains in the Italian camp. But the allies insisted that it should be freely surrendered.

As this and other difficulties which arose could not be resolved as quickly as those who were in Novara needed—reduced as they were to such extremity that nearly 2,000 of Orléans' men had died through starvation and the diseases consequent on famine—a week's truce was arranged enabling Orléans and the Marquis of Saluzzo to go to Vercelli with a small company with the promise that they would all return to the town if peace were not made. To ensure the Duke's safety—as he had to pass through the enemy army—the Marquis of Mantua went to a tower near Bolgari, in the hands of the Comte de Foix. The troops remaining in Novara would not have let the Duke go if he had not given them his word that within three days either he would return or

they would be able to leave the town through his efforts
—and if they had not received from Marshal de Gié,
who had gone to Novara to escort him, one of his
nephews as hostage. Not only had all their food been
eaten, but even all the garbage, which the men had not
refrained from consuming in their terrible need. But
when the Duke of Orléans reached the place where the
King was, the truce was prolonged for a few days, and
it was agreed that all his troops should march out of
Novara leaving the town in the hands of the inhabitants,
under oath not to hand it over to either side without
the consent of both parties, and that 30 soldiers should
hold the fortress for Orléans, with food sent in daily from
the Italian camp. So all the troops left Novara, escorted
to safety by the Marquis of Mantua and Galeazzo da San
Severino. However, they were so weakened and con-
sumed by famine that many died when they reached
Vercelli, and the others could not be used again in this
war.

During these very days the Bailli of Dijon arrived
with the rest of the Swiss. Although he had asked for
only 10,000, he had not been able to prevent an almost
universal flocking to his standard, lured by the fame of
the King of France's wealth, so that they numbered
nearly 20,000. Half joined up with the camp near Vercelli and the other half stopped ten miles away. It was
not thought quite safe to have so large a number of the
same nation all together in one army. If they had arrived a few days earlier, it might easily have broken off
the negotiations for agreement because the King's army
had, besides, 8,000 French infantry, 2,000 Swiss who
had been at Naples, and the companies of 1,800 lances.
But as the negotiations were so far advanced and Novara had already been evacuated, they were not broken
off; though the Duke of Orléans did all he could to urge
against it, and many others supported him.

Therefore the envoys were every day in the Italian
camp for discussions with the Duke of Milan, who had
recently returned in order to deal personally with a matter of such importance—though always in the presence
of the ambassadors of the allies. The envoys returned

at last to the King with the final terms of agreement. There would be perpetual peace and friendship between the King of France and the Duke of Milan without the Duke's renouncing his other alliances. The King consented that the inhabitants would restore Novara to the Duke, and the French would hand over the fortress, while La Spezia and the other places occupied by either side would be returned. The King was to be allowed to fit out at Genoa, his feudal state, as many vessels as he wished, and use all the resources of that city except in favor of the enemies of that state; and the Genoese were to give certain hostages as guarantee of this. The Duke of Milan was to make them replace the ships lost at Rapallo and hand over the twelve galleys detained at Genoa, and immediately fit out for the King at their own expense two great Genoese galleons, which together with four others fitted out at his own expense he planned to send to the relief of the Kingdom of Naples; and the following year Genoa was to give him three more ships in the same way. The troops which the King sent overland to the relief of Naples were to have free passage from the Duke; but no more than 200 lances at a time were to pass through his territory. If the King were to return in person for this campaign, the Duke was to follow him with a certain number of men. The Venetians were to be allowed two months to join this pact and when they did so, they would withdraw their fleet from the Kingdom of Naples and give no aid to Ferrando. If they did not comply with this, the Duke would be obliged to assist the King if he made war against them, and the Duke and he could keep any Venetian territory taken in these operations. The Duke was to pay by the end of the following March 50,000 ducats to Orléans for his expenses of Novara. Of the moneys lent to the King when he had entered Italy, the Duke would write off 80,000 ducats and the rest was to be paid, but at a later date. Trivulzio was to have the sentence of banishment passed on him by the Duke lifted and his possessions restored; and the bastard of Bourbon captured in the Taro battle and Miolans who had been taken at Rapallo and all the other prisoners were to be freed. The Duke would recall from Pisa, Fracassa, whom he had recently sent there, and all his own troops as well as the Genoese; and he would not stop the Florentines from retaking their territories. Within a month he would place the little fort at Genoa in the hands of the Duke of Ferrara, who had arrived at the Italian camp on a summons by both parties for this purpose. He was to hold the fort two years at their common expense, undertaking on oath to return it even within that time to the King of France, if the Duke of Milan did not fulfill his obligations. The latter, as soon as peace was concluded, would at once give hostages to the King as security that he would hand over the fort at the agreed time.

These conditions were reported to the King by his envoys who had negotiated them, and he set them before the council. Here there was much difference of opinion, and M. de Trémouille spoke as follows:

"If by the present discussion, magnanimous King, we were only trying to bring fresh glory to the crown of France by acts of valor, I might be slower to urge that your royal person should be exposed to fresh dangers— though your own example should advise you the opposite, since moved only by the desire for glory you determined last year against the advice and pleas of nearly all your kingdom to enter Italy to conquer the Kingdom of Naples. There the success of your expedition was crowned with such fame and honor that clearly we are not only discussing today whether to refuse the opportunity to acquire fresh honor and glory, but whether to decide to despise and lose that honor and glory which you have achieved at such great expense and danger, and convert honor gained into utter ignominy, with you yourself reversing and condemning your own decisions. For Your Majesty could have stayed in France without any blame whatever, and a decision which all will now attribute to great timidity and cowardice would then have been ascribed only to carelessness or youth's love of pleasure.

"Your Majesty could, on reaching Asti, have returned to France with much less shame, showing that the affairs of Novara were of no interest to you; but now, having stopped here with the army has made plain your intention of relieving the siege of Novara; and as you have sent to France for so many noblemen and recruited so many Swiss at crushing expense, who may doubt that if you do not save Novara, you and your kingdom's glory will not be changed into eternal infamy? But there are more powerful (if in the magnanimous breasts of kings any impulse can be greater or more passionate than the desire for fame and glory) or at least more urgent reasons. For if we withdraw to France, agreeing to the loss of Novara, it involves no less than the loss of all the Kingdom of Naples, the destruction of so many captains, so many French noblemen, who stayed behind trusting in you and your promise to send them help before long, to defend that kingdom. They will despair of succor when they learn that you, standing on the frontiers of Italy with so great an army and such great forces, are giving way to the enemy. The events of war depend, as everyone knows, to a large extent on reputation. When that declines, with it the soldiers' courage dwindles, the trust of nations weakens, the revenues set aside to support the war vanish; on the other hand the courage of the enemy grows, the waverers turn against us, and all difficulties are infinitely increased. Therefore, learning this unhappy news, our army will lose its vigor, and the strength and reputation of the enemy will increase; so what doubt can there be that we shall soon hear of the rebellion of the entire Kingdom of Naples and of the defeat of our army, and that the expedition begun and executed with such glory will have borne no other fruit than inestimable harm and infamy? For anyone who believes that this peace is being concluded in good faith shows that he is taking little account of the present state of affairs and that he has little understanding of the character of those with whom we are dealing. It is easy to understand that as soon as we have turned our backs on Italy, none of the terms now agreed on will be honored; and that instead of giving us their promised assistance, help will be sent to Ferrando, and those very troops who will boast of having made us flee in cowardly fashion from Italy will go to Naples to enrich themselves with the spoils of our army.

"I could bear such ignominy more easily if there were any likely reason to doubt of our victory. But how can anyone doubt our success when he considers the greatness of our army and the advantages we have from the surrounding country, and remembers that, weary with our long journey, short of food, very few in number and surrounded by hostile country, we fought so fiercely against a vast army on the River Taro? The river ran fast that day more with the blood of the enemy than with its own waters. We opened the way at sword point, and for a week rode victoriously through the Duchy of Milan, though it was all hostile country. Here we have twice as much cavalry again, and twice as many infantry as we had then; and instead of the 3,000 Swiss we now have 22,000. The enemy, though increased by the German infantry, are not increased anything like as much as we are. Their cavalry has remained the same, and so have their captains; and having once been beaten with so much loss by us, they will be terrified to fight us again.

"Are the fruits of victory likely to be so small that we should despise them? Are they not rather such that we should seek them through any danger? For we are not only fighting to preserve the great glory we have won, to maintain the Kingdom of Naples, the safety of so many of your captains and so many nobles, but the dominion of all Italy will be at issue in the battle. If we are victorious here, all Italy will be the spoils of our victory. For what other troops, what other armies, can the enemy draw on? In their camp are all the arms and all the captains which they have been able to put together. Every ditch we cross, every barrier we break through puts in our possession these great things: the dominion and riches of all Italy, and the ability to avenge so many injuries. If these two incentives which usually spur on pusillanimous and cowardly men do not move our warlike and fierce nation, we shall certainly be able to say that courage rather than opportunity has failed us. This has given us the chance to win in so small

273

a field, in so short a time, such great and worthy prizes that we could not ourselves have wished for greater or worthier ones."

The Prince of Orange then spoke thus in opposition:

"If our affairs, Most Christian King, were not so pressed by time, and allowed us to accompany force with prudence and industry, and did not compel us, if we wish to continue the war, to proceed rashly and against all the precepts of the art of war, I should also be one to advise refusing the agreement; because in truth we have many reasons for not accepting it, as one cannot deny that to go on with the war would be very honorable and very useful for our situation in Naples. But the straits to which Novara and the fort are reduced, where there are not even supplies for one day, force us, if we wish to relieve it, to attack the enemy immediately. And even if we let Novara go and thought of transferring the war to some other part of the state of Milan, the winter season which is approaching, making it very difficult to fight in these low-lying places full of water; the character of our army, which by the nature and number of the Swiss, if it is not used soon, could be more dangerous to us than to the enemy; the serious lack of money which makes it impossible for us to maintain ourselves here for any length of time—will all compel us, even if we do not accept the agreement, to seek an early end to the war. And this can only be done by going immediately to fight the enemy. This would be so dangerous a step because of their situation and the condition of the country, that it cannot be denied that to proceed thus would be the height of temerity and imprudence.

"Their camp is so strong by nature and art—as they have had ample time to fortify it—the places around which they have garrisoned are so well situated for their defense and so well provided, the country is so difficult to ride over because of the deep ditches and the water obstacles, that whoever tries to attack them directly and not approach them gradually with ease and advantage and (as they say) gaining ground and strategic positions bit by bit, is merely taking risks with the prospect of great and almost inevitable dangers. For by what argument, what reasons of war, what example of excellent commanders, should one rashly assault so great an army in so strong a position with such abundant artillery? If one wants to proceed otherwise than by chance, one must try to dislodge them from their position of strength by taking some position superior to theirs or by cutting off their supplies. I do not see how any of these things can be hoped for without proceeding carefully and with plenty of time; and we all know how long we can afford to wait. Apart from that, our cavalry is not as numerous or as strong as many perhaps believe; for as everyone knows, many of them are sick, many others have gone back to France with or without leave, and most of the remainder are worn out by long soldiering and more anxious to go away than to fight. The great number of the Swiss which is the principal sinew of our army, is perhaps as much to our disadvantage as a small number would be useless. For who, knowing the nature and habits of that nation and how difficult they are to control when there are so many together, can assure us that they may not start some dangerous revolt particularly if the fighting should drag on? And if it did, there might arise a thousand occasions to anger them over questions of pay for which they are insatiably greedy, and other incidents. So we are never sure whether their assistance is to be medicine or poison; and in this uncertainty how can we come to our decisions? How can we make up our minds to some great and brave resolve?

"No one doubts that it would be more honorable and better for the defense of the Kingdom of Naples to have victory than to have the treaty. But in all human actions and particularly in wars one must often adapt one's decisions to necessity and not—out of desire to obtain what is too difficult and almost impossible—expose everything one has to obvious danger. It is no less the duty of a brave captain to act wisely than to act courageously. The Novara enterprise was not specially Your Majesty's own, and it pertains only indirectly to you, as you are not pretending to the Duchy of Milan. Nor did you leave Naples in order to stop and make war in Piedmont

275

but to return to France to supply yourself afresh with men and money so as to be able to help the Kingdom of Naples more effectively. In the meantime Naples will defend itself with the help of the navy sent from Nice, with the Vitelli troops and the assistance and money supplied by the Florentines; and will easily be able to await the powerful provisions which you will make on your return to France. I am not one to say for sure that the Duke of Milan will observe this treaty; but with hostages given by him and the Genoese and the castle handed over according to the terms of the agreement, you will have some pledge and some surety. It would not be very surprising if he desired peace so as to avoid always being the first to be attacked by you. Of their very nature, leagues in which many participate have not such strength or harmony that one may not hope that one or other of them will cool off or break away from the others. If we can make any small rift in them, if we can see any slight gap, then our victory is easy and certain.

"In conclusion I urge you, Most Christian King, to make the agreement, not because it is in itself useful or laudable, but because it is the duty of wise princes in difficult and troublesome decisions to approve as easy and desirable what is necessary or what is less full of difficulty and displeasure than any other."

The Duke of Orléans took up the words of the Prince of Orange so sharply that both rushed impetuously from heated words to insults; and Orléans gave him the lie before the whole council. Yet there was a great desire for peace among most of them and among almost all the army; because they all—and the King no less than the others—longed to return to France. Thus it prevented them from realizing the danger of the Kingdom of Naples or the ignominy of letting Novara go under their very eyes and leaving Italy under conditions so iniquitous because there was no certainty that they would be honored. The decision to make peace was urged so strongly by the Prince of Orange that many suspected that at the desire of the King of the Romans to whom he was very devoted, he sought the interests of the Duke of Milan more than those of the King of France. His influence with Charles was considerable, partly for his ability and intelligence, partly because princes readily regard as wiser those counsels which accord best with their own desires.

Peace was therefore made. And as soon as the Duke of Milan had sworn to observe it, the King, intent on returning to France, went off to Turin. He hastened to leave Vercelli also because the Swiss who were in his camp were threatening to detain either the King or the principal men at his court in order to make sure of having their pay for three whole months—as they said had always been done by Louis XI—though they had not been promised it and had not been that long in Charles' service. Although he escaped this danger by a sudden departure, they took as prisoner the Bailli of Dijon and the other officers who had enlisted them; and in the end it was necessary to meet their demand with promises and hostages.

From Turin the King, wishing to establish more firmly the peace they had made, sent Marshal de Gié, President de Ganay and Argenton to the Duke of Milan to persuade him to a meeting, which he indicated he was willing to do but feared he might be betrayed. Either because of this suspicion or perhaps intentionally raising difficulties so as not to offend his allies, or out of ambition to appear at the meeting as an equal of the King of France, he proposed that the meeting should take place on some river over which a bridge should be built either of boats or some other material with a strong wooden partition between them. In this manner the kings of France and England had once met, and other great princes of the West. This was rejected by the King as unworthy of himself; and having received the hostages, he sent Perron de Baschi to Genoa to receive the promised galleons and to fit out four others at his own expense to relieve the Neapolitan castles. It was now known that the castles had not received the help of the fleet sent from Nice and had therefore agreed to surrender if they were not relieved within thirty days. They planned to embark 3,000 Swiss in these ships and join up with the fleet which had retired to Leghorn—and with some other ships which were expected from Provence. Without the

Genoese great ships there would not have been enough for this expedition of relief, as the port of Naples was already full of a great fleet. For besides the vessels brought in by Ferrando, the Venetians had sent twenty galleys and four ships from the fleet which had taken Monopoli. The King also sent Argenton to Venice to ask them to join the peace treaty. Then he and all the court took the road to France with such speed and longing to get there quickly that he would not even stop in Italy a few days to wait for the Genoese to send him the promised hostages—as they would no doubt have done if he had waited. Thus at the end of October 1495 he returned across the mountains more like a man defeated than a conqueror, in spite of the battles he had won. He left in Asti—which he pretended to have bought from the Duke of Orléans—Gianiacopo da Trivulzio as governor with 500 French lances, nearly all of whom followed after him of their own accord a few days later. He had left nothing behind to assist the Kingdom of Naples except the order for the ships being armed in Genoa and in Provence, and the assignment for this purpose of the help and money promised him by the Florentines.

Chapter XIII

[*Appearance of the sickness which the French call "Neapolitan" and the Italians call "French." Its place of origin and its diffusion.*]

After our account of other matters, it does not seem unworthy to report that at this period—when it was Italy's fate that all her ills should originate with the French invasion or should at least be attributed to them —the disease which the French called "the Neapolitan sickness" and the Italians commonly called *buboes* or "French sickness," made its first appearance.

The French caught this disease in Naples, and they spread it all over Italy on their way home to France. It was either quite new or until this time entirely unknown in our hemisphere except in its most remote parts and was for many years so horrible that it deserves to be mentioned as a grave disaster. It showed itself either in hideous boils which often became incurable sores, or with intense pains in the joints and nerves all over the body. The doctors, who knew nothing about the disease, did not employ suitable remedies but quite often wrong ones which made the symptoms much worse. Many people of every age and sex died from it, and many others were hideously deformed and became helpless and subject to almost continual agonies of pain. Indeed most of those who appeared to have recovered in a short time fell again into the same misery. However, after many years the influence of the stars which had made the disease so virulent was mitigated or the appropriate cures for it became known through long experience, and it became much less malignant.

It had of its own accord also produced several types different from the first form of the disease. This was a calamity of which the men of our age might the more reasonably complain if it had fallen upon them without any fault of their own: for it is agreed by all those who have closely observed the characteristics of the disease, that it never, or hardly ever, occurs save by contagion in coitus. Yet one should rightly remove this smirch from the French name, because it was later seen that the disease had been brought from Spain to Naples and was not characteristic of that nation but brought in from those islands which, as we shall narrate at some more appropriate moment, began to be known to our hemisphere during those years through the voyages of a Genoese, Christopher Columbus.[42] In those islands, however, this malady finds a prompt remedy through the benevolence of nature; for they cure it easily, simply by drinking the juice of a tree distinguished for its many remarkable properties.

BOOK III

Chapter I

[*General praise of the Venetian senate and the Duke of Milan for having freed Italy from the French. Lodovico Sforza keeps faith over only a few of the peace conditions. He has the Florentine ambassador robbed of the documents concerning their treaty concluded with Charles VIII. Ambitions of Sforza and the Venetians to take Pisa. Restitution of the town and forts of Leghorn to the Florentines. In spite of the royal letters Entragues does not hand over Pisa to the Florentines and prevents them from capturing it.*]

The somewhat inglorious return home of the King of France—though it resulted more from imprudence or lack of design than from weakness or fear—left men with no small hope that Italy,· which had been struck by so severe a misfortune, might soon be completely freed from the insolent rule of the French. And so praises were voiced everywhere for the Venetian senate and the Duke of Milan, who, taking arms with wise and courageous decision, had prevented so noble a part of the world from falling under the domination of the foreigner. And if these powers had not been blinded by private greed and had not destroyed the common weal with shame and harm also to themselves, there is no doubt that Italy, restored to its pristine glory by their counsels and resources, would have been safe for many years from the attacks of foreign nations. But ambition, which would not allow them to remain content within their due bounds, was the reason Italy was soon involved in new disorders, and the reason she did not enjoy the fruits of the victory which was later gained over the French army, remaining behind in the Kingdom of Naples. The King's carelessness and imprudence enabled them to win that victory with ease; as the relief measures he had ordered when he had left Italy failed. For neither the preparation of the fleet nor the assistance promised by the Florentines came to anything.

Lodovico Sforza had not entered the peace with Charles in sincere good faith because, remembering (as is natural in the offender) the injuries he had done the King, he believed that he could no longer rely on his good faith; but the desire to regain Novara and free his own state from war had led him to promise what he had no intention of observing. There was no doubt either that the Venetian senate had agreed to the peace concluded with such dissimulation, wishing to put an end without loss of honor to the enormous expense which was being borne by the Republic on account of Novara. Nevertheless Lodovico, so as not to abandon the terms of the treaty, quite brazenly but with some semblance of excuse, carried out what he could not deny lay in his ability to do: he gave the hostages; had the prisoners freed, paying their ransom himself; handed back the ships captured at Rapallo; removed Fracassa from Pisa, as he could not hide the fact that he was in his pay; and, within the month agreed in the treaty, handed the little fort of Genoa over to the Duke of Ferrara who went in person to receive it. On the other hand, however, he left Luzio Malvezzo in Pisa with a considerable force, ostensibly in the pay of the Genoese. He allowed two galleons to go to Naples which had been fitted at Genoa for Ferrando—with the excuse that because he had commissioned them before peace was concluded, the Genoese could not agree to keep them back. He secretly prevented the Genoese from giving their hostages; and, what was more important for the loss of the castles of Naples, after the King had finished fitting out the four ships, and after he had arranged for the other two as he had undertaken to do, Lodovico persuaded the Genoese to refuse to have the King's soldiers on board, pretending to be afraid, unless they first received adequate guarantee from the King that he would not appropriate them or try by their means to change the government of Genoa.

When the King complained through his envoys of these cavillings, Lodovico replied that he had promised the ships but had given no understanding about their being filled with French troops. And he said that his power over Genoa was not absolute but limited by such conditions that he could not compel them to do everything he wanted—and especially things which they maintained were a danger to their own city and state. To corroborate further these excuses he got the Pope to command the Genoese and himself under threat of excommunication not to allow the King of France to remove ships of any kind from Genoa. Hence that relief which was awaited with great anxiety by the French in the Kingdom of Naples, was rendered vain. The money and help promised by the Florentines turned out to be equally useless. For after the agreement reached at Turin, Guidantonio Vespucci, one of the envoys sent to conclude it, left at once with all the documents and was traveling without concern through the Duchy of Milan because the Florentine Republic had not declared itself anyone's enemy, when he was arrested by the Duke's orders at Alessandria, transferred to Milan, and all his papers taken from him. When Lodovico heard of the terms of the treaty and the promises of the Florentines, he and the Venetians decided it would be a mistake to leave the Pisans to perish. They, as soon as the King left Pisa, had recommended their cause to Venice and Milan through new ambassadors. Both acted with the consent of the Pope and the envoys of the other allies—under pretext of stopping the money and troops that the Florentines were to send to the Kingdom of Naples as soon as they had regained Pisa and their other territories. And also because they were allies of the King of France, the Florentines, becoming more powerful on regaining that city and freeing themselves from this hindrance, might do harm to the safety of Italy in many ways.

Yet they were chiefly inspired by their greed to be masters of Pisa. Lodovico had long before planned to seize it; and now the Venetians also turned their ambitions in this direction. Since the old alliance of the other powers had collapsed and some of those who used to oppose it had been weakened, they now had hopes of making themselves masters of Italy. For this purpose the possession of Pisa seemed most useful: so as to be able through the convenience of her port (which it was felt the Florentines could not keep for long if they did not retake Pisa itself) to extend their power over the seas farther south, and with the city to have a foothold of no small importance in Tuscany. Yet the assistance of the Duke of Milan had been more prompt. While engaging at the same time in various discussions with the Florentines, he had ordered Fracassa to go to Pisa under the pretext of some private affairs (as he had property in the surrounding country) and directed the Genoese to send in troops again. In the meantime the Venetians were busy encouraging the Pisans with promises of aid, and for this purpose they had sent a secretary to Genoa to recruit soldiers and to urge the Genoese not to abandon the Pisans. But they were slow in sending the troops to Pisa because, while the citadel was held for the King, and particularly while the King was still in Italy, they did not think it wise to build a great deal on this affair.

On the other hand the Florentines, when they learned of the new agreements made by their envoys with the King at Turin, had increased their army so as to be able to force the Pisans to admit them as soon as the royal orders arrived. While these were delayed because of the arrest of their ambassador, they took the castle of Palaia and laid siege to Vico Pisano. The siege was unsuccessful however, partly because the captains, either through bad planning or because they felt they had not enough troops to set their camp on the side facing Pisa —especially as the Pisans had built a bastion there on a height quite near the town—encamped instead on the lower side toward Bientina, a position not very suitable for attacking Vico, which also left open the road from Pisa and Cascina to the besieged castle; and partly because Pagolo Vitelli with his own and his brother's company received 3,000 ducats from the Pisans and entered

the city to defend it, saying he had letters from the
King and orders from the General of Languedoc, brother
of the Cardinal of St. Malo, who was ill and had stayed
behind in Pietrasanta, to defend Pisa and the country
around until he received orders to the contrary. It was
certainly a remarkable thing that at the same time the
Pisans should be defended by the troops of the King of
France and likewise helped by those of the Duke of Milan,
as well as fed with hopes by the Venetians, though both
the senate and the Duke were in open war with the King.
With the help of Vitelli's troops Vicopisano was easily defended and much damage was done to the Florentine
camp, which was in so open a position that it was heavily
bombarded by the artillery brought into Vico by the
Pisans. So that, having remained there for some time,
the captains were dishonorably forced to move off. However the royal letters arrived which had been dispatched
by different routes in duplicate copies, and the town,
the port and fortresses of Leghorn were immediately
handed over to the Florentines by Saliente, lieutenant
of M. de Beaumont, whom the King had appointed to
guard them; and M. de Lille, who had been appointed
commissioner to receive from the Florentines the ratifica-
tion of the agreement made in Turin and to see the
restitution effected, began to discuss with Balzac d'Entragues, warden of the citadel of Pisa and the forts of
Pietrasanta and Motrone, to agree on the day and manner of handing them over.

However, Entragues began to raise various difficulties.
Either he was influenced by the same sentiments which
all the French felt in Pisa or by secret orders from Ligny
in whose name and under whose orders he had been
given this command when the King left Pisa, or else
he was moved by his love for a daughter of Luca del
Lante, a citizen of Pisa. For one cannot say that he was
only inspired by greed for money, which he could have
hoped to receive more of from the Florentines. He gave
interpretations outside their real meaning to the royal
patents and affirmed that he had had orders from the
first not to hand over without a secret countersign from

Ligny. When they had argued these points for several days, the Florentines were obliged to make new approaches to the King who was still at Vercelli, requesting him to deal with this confusion which had arisen with such offense to his dignity and purpose. The King was very annoyed by the disobedience of Entragues and angrily commanded Ligny to compel him to obey. He intended to send a man of authority with this order and new patents, and also with persuasive letters from the Duke of Orléans whose subject Entragues was. But the obstinacy of Ligny and his favors were more effective than the King's weak resolve, and the dispatch was put off for a few days; and in the end it was sent not with a person of authority but with a private gentleman, Lanciaimpugno. Cammillo Vitelli went with him to lead his troops —which had joined up with the Florentine army as soon as the royal letters arrived—into the Kingdom of Naples with part of the money Florence was to provide. This dispatch bore no more fruit than the first one had done, though the warden (Entragues) had already received 2,000 ducats from the Florentines to maintain the troops guarding the citadel until the King's answer arrived, and Cammillo had been paid 3,000 ducats because otherwise he would not allow the royal letters to be presented. The warden, who it was believed had received contrary orders secretly from Ligny, after wavering for many days, decided that, as there were 1,000 foreign troops in Pisa besides the men of the town and surrounding country, the Florentines would not be strong enough to take the Borgo San Marco near the Florentine gate next to the citadel —before which, with Entragues' consent, they had earlier built a large bastion. And so to achieve his purpose without losing all possible excuses with the King, he informed the Florentine commissioners that they should present themselves with their army at the Florentine gate, which they could not do without capturing the Borgo. For, if the Pisans were not willing to let them in, he would compel them to abandon the gate, as it was covered by the artillery of the citadel and so could not be defended against the will of those within. However, with great show and the whole army full of courage and boldness,

the Florentines went there from their camp at San Ri-
medio, a place near the Borgo, and attacked the bastion
from three sides with such vigor—having been informed
beforehand by Pagolo Vitelli about its construction and
defenses—that they soon put to flight those defending it.
And pursuing the defenders in a mêlée into the Borgo
by a drawbridge connecting it with the bastion, they
killed and made prisoner many of them. There is no doubt
that in the same advance and without help from the
citadel they would have taken Pisa through the gate
which some of their men-at-arms had already penetrated;
for the fleeing Pisans offered no resistance. But the ward-
en, seeing things turning out the reverse of what he had
intended, began to fire his artillery at the Florentines.
The commissioners and captains were taken aback at
this unexpected occurrence, as many soldiers were
wounded or killed by the guns—among them Pagolo
Vitelli, wounded in the leg. So despairing of taking Pisa
that day against the opposition from the citadel, they
sounded the retreat and withdrew their troops. The
Borgo remained in their hands, though within a few days
they were obliged to give it up as they were continually
bombarded by the artillery of the citadel which did great
damage. They withdrew toward Cascina to await the
King's action against such flagrant disobedience of his
own men.

Chapter II

[*The powers of the league make difficulties for the
Florentines. Struggle of factions in Perugia and
Umbria. Vain attempts by Piero de' Medici to ob-
tain sufficient backing to enter Florence. Virginio
Orsino passes into the pay of the King of France.*]

While such action was being awaited, there was no
lack of new and dangerous troubles for the Florentines
in other directions, largely created by the powers of the
league. These, in order to prevent the retaking of Pisa

and to force them to break off their alliance with the
King of France, urged Piero de' Medici to try to re-enter
Florence with the assistance of Virginio Orsino, who had
fled from the French camp the day of the battle on the
Taro and returned to Bracciano. Both men were easily
persuaded to this course because, whatever the outcome
of this attempt, it suited Virginio to be able to gather
together at other people's expense his former soldiers
and partisans and rebuild his reputation as a commander; while Piero, as is the wont of exiles, entertained various hopes because of his friends in Florence, where he
knew many of the nobles disliked the popular government, and because of the many adherents and followers
that the long-standing eminence of his family ensured
him throughout Florentine territory. It was believed that
this plan originated in Milan because, on escaping from
the French, Virginio had gone at once to visit the Duke;
but the affair was settled in Rome where it was discussed
for several days with the Pope by the Venetian ambassador and Cardinal Ascanio who was acting on behalf of
his brother Lodovico. The hopes of this enterprise were
founded on the fact that, besides the troops which Virginio could get together from his old soldiers, and with
10,000 ducats that Piero had collected of his own and
from friends, Giovanni Bentivoglio, who was in the pay
of the Venetians and the Duke of Milan, was to start
hostilities at the same time from the frontiers of Bologna;
and Caterina Sforza, whose sons were in the service of
the Duke of Milan, was to attack from the towns of Imola
and Forlì on the Florentine borders. Also they had some
reason to rely on the Sienese because of their inveterate
hatred of the Florentines and their strong desire to keep
Montepulciano—which they were not certain of being
able to hold unaided.

A few months earlier, with their own troops and those
of the Lord of Piombino and Giovanni Savello, employed
jointly by them and the Duke of Milan, the Sienese
had tried to capture the road through the Chiana
swamp which on that side for some distance formed
the boundary between them and the Florentines; to that
effect they had begun to work on a bastion by the

Ponte a Valiano in order to attack a tower of the Florentines built at the edge of the bridge on the Montepulciano side. But this attempt had the opposite result from the one they intended, as the Florentines, alarmed by the danger of losing the bridge, which would deprive them of the means of attacking Montepulciano and enable the enemy to enter the territories of Cortona and Arezzo and other places of their dominion on the other side of the Chiana, sent strong reinforcements and assaulted the bastion begun by the Sienese; and to secure the road completely for themselves they built near the bridge— on the other side of the Chiana—a bastion capable of holding many troops. By means of this they were able to make excursions as far as the gates of Montepulciano and harry all the territory held by the Sienese in that direction. Furthermore, shortly after the King of France had marched through, they had defeated the Sienese army near Montepulciano and had taken prisoner Giovanni Savelli, their captain. Virginio and Piero de' Medici also hoped to be welcomed and assisted by the Perugians. The Baglioni, who virtually dominated that town by force of arms and the following of their partisans, were connected with Virginio, as they all belonged to the Guelph faction; and with Lorenzo, Piero's father, and with Piero himself while he remained in Florence, they had had the closest ties of friendship and always received support against their enemies. Also, being subjects of the Church, though more in appearance than in fact, it was believed that in an affair like this, which did not closely touch their state, they would be amenable to the wishes of the Pope—especially when supported by the authority of the Venetians and the Duke of Milan.

Virginio and Piero therefore left Rome with these hopes, believing that the Florentines would find it hard to resist them, being divided amongst themselves and attacked by all their neighbors in the name of the league. After stopping for a few days between Terni and Todi and neighboring places, where Virginio extracted money and soldiers from the Guelphs for his campaign to put down the Ghibelline faction, they laid siege to Gualdo on behalf of the Perugians. This was a place which once belonged to the commune of Foligno, but was sold by the Pope for 6,000 ducats to the Perugians, who were inspired less by the desire to own the place than by the quarrels of rival parties, because of which at that time the neighboring towns were in great tumult. A few days earlier the Oddi, exiles from Perugia and heads of the party opposing the Baglioni, assisted by men of Foligno, Assisi, and other places which supported the Ghibelline cause, had entered Corciano—a stronghold five miles from Perugia—with 300 horse and 500 foot soldiers. With feelings running high throughout the country because of this incident, because Spoleto, Camerino, and other Guelph towns were supporters of the Baglioni, the Oddi secretly entered Perugia one night a few days later and so terrified the Baglioni that they lost hope of defending themselves and began to flee. Nevertheless the Oddi lost, through an unexpected minor event, a victory which the enemy was powerless to wrest from them. For they had reached without hindrance one of the entrances to the main square, and one of them, who had brought an axe for the purpose, wanted to cut a chain which was put across the street as is done in factious cities; but he was prevented from swinging his arms by the press of his own men around him; so he shouted loudly: "Back! back!"—so that they should give him room to do his work. This cry, taken up and repeated by those behind and understood by the rest as a warning to flee, put them all to flight, no one knowing who was pursuing them or why they fled, though no obstacle or resistance had been met. From this disorder their adversaries took courage; and banding together again they killed many in flight and captured Troilo Savelli who had been sent to help the Oddi by Cardinal Savelli, who favored the same party. They pursued them as far as Corciano and recaptured it in their headlong advance; and not satisfied by the death of those killed in flight, they hanged many others in Perugia with the cruelty partisans habitually use to one another.

From these disturbances there arose much bloodshed in the neighboring towns between the parties, always

289

quick to rise in troubled times, either through desire to kill their enemies or out of fear of being forestalled by them. So the Perugians, angry with the people of Foligno, had gone to attack Gualdo; but having fought in vain, and fearing that they could not take it with their own forces, they accepted the help of Virginio who offered it so as to attract soldiers more readily with the sound of war and hope of booty. Nevertheless, when both he and Piero de' Medici urged the Perugians to assist their cause openly, or at least to give them some field pieces and a base for their troops at Castiglione del Lago, which borders on the territory of Cortona, and food for their army, they would agree to none of these requests—though pressed to do so by Cardinal Ascanio in the name of the Duke of Milan and commanded by the Pope with strongly worded and threatening letters. This was because after the occupation of Corciano they had been assisted with a certain sum of money by the Florentines, who had also given Guido and Ridolfo, heads of the Baglioni family, an annual stipend, and engaged Giampagolo, son of Ridolfo, in their pay; so they had become allies. Besides, the Perugians were against an alliance with the Pope; for they feared that he favored their enemies, or that taking advantage of their divisions he sought to place the city again entirely under the sway of the Church.

At this time Paolo Orsini, who with sixty men-at-arms from Virginio's old company had been at Montepulciano for a long time, had gone to Castello della Pieve and on Piero de' Medici's orders was engaged in secret negotiations with people in Cortona—with the intention of putting them into effect as soon as Virginio's troops arrived, though these were not in number and quality such as they had originally planned. During this delay, the betrayal came to light through some man of low degree who had been banished; and thus part of their support fell through and other greater difficulties began to arise. For the Florentines, quick to meet these dangers, leaving 300 men-at-arms and 2,000 infantry in the Pisan area, sent to camp near Cortona 200 men-at-arms and 1,000 foot soldiers under their captain Count Rinuccio da Marciano. Also, to prevent the Sienese forces from joining up with

Virginio as they had agreed, they had sent to Poggio Imperiale on the borders of Sienese territory 300 men-at-arms and 1,500 foot soldiers under the command of Guidubaldo da Montefeltro Duke of Urbino, whom they had recently taken into their service; and to these forces they added many Sienese exiles so as to keep that city in a state of greater alarm. But Virginio, after various attacks on Gualdo, where his natural son Carlo was wounded by a shot from an arquebus, secretly accepted money from the people of Foligno (so it was believed) and raised the siege without any reference to the interests of the Perugians. He moved camp to Tavernelle and then to Panicale in the territory of Perugia, again pressing them to declare against the Florentines. The Perugians not only refused this demand but, because of their dissatisfaction over the Gualdo affair, practically forced him with threats to leave their territory. So Piero and he first went with 400 horse cavalry to Orsaia a village near Cortona, hoping for some revolt in the town which had refused to admit the Florentine troops so as not to suffer harm from the soldiers. Then seeing everything quiet there, they crossed the Chiana with 300 men-at-arms and 3,000 foot soldiers, most of them undisciplined troops as they had been recruited at little expense. They moved into Sienese territory near Montepulciano between Chianciano, Torrita, and Asinalunga, where they remained for many days without any action apart from some looting and forays, because the Florentine troops had crossed the Chiana at Ponte a Valiano and now faced them on the Monte a Sansovino and other surrounding places. Nor was anything being done from Bologna as they had been given to understand—because Bentivoglio was determined not to get involved to promote the interests of others in a war with a powerful neighboring republic; and though he allowed all sorts of representations to be made to him by Giuliano de' Medici, who had come to Bologna to try to raise the friends they usually had in the hills near the city, he refused to begin operations in spite of pressure from the league, putting things off and making various excuses.

Yet among the members of the league there was not

absolute unanimity, because the Duke of Milan was glad
for the Florentines to have troubles which would weaken
their efforts at Pisa; but he would not have been pleased
for Piero de' Medici, whom he had so gravely offended, to
return to Florence, although Piero had sent his brother
the cardinal to Milan to show that in the future he intended to rely entirely on the Duke's authority. The
Venetians did not wish to embark on this war alone; and
besides, they and the Duke were concentrating on their
preparations for driving the French out of Naples. Hence
Piero and Virginio not only lost the hope they had had,
but also money needed to support their troops; and with
a good many fewer horse and foot soldiers they withdrew
to Bagno a Rapolano in the territory of Chiusi—a town
subject to the Sienese. There, a few days later, destiny led
Virginio on his course in the shape of Cammillo Vitelli
and M. de Gemel, who came from the King of France to
engage him in the King's service and send him to the
Kingdom of Naples, where, learning of the defection of
the Colonna, the King wished to use him. He accepted
this proposal in spite of the opposition of many of his
followers who begged him either to join the league which
was pressing him to do so, or return to the service of the
Aragonese. Perhaps he hoped thereby to regain the country districts of Albi and Tagliacozzo more easily; or
remembering what had happened in the loss of the kingdom and seeing the influence of his enemies the Colonna
was very great with Ferrando, he doubted that he would
ever be able to return to his former position of trust and
importance with that King. Or possibly, as he said himself, he was dissatisfied with the princes of the league
because they had failed to carry out the promises they
had made to him in support of Piero de' Medici. He was
therefore commissioned with 600 men-at-arms for himself
and the other members of the Orsini family—but with
the obligation to send his son Carlo to France as security
for the King (this is the reward of those who have already rendered their loyalty suspect). Having received
his money, he made ready to accompany the Vitelli to
Naples.

Chapter III

[Further events in the struggle between the French and the Aragonese in the Kingdom of Naples. The fortunes of the French decline in Calabria. Charles VIII spends his time at Lyons in diversions. He rejects proposals advanced by the Venetians to settle the affairs of the Kingdom of Naples.]

In the Kingdom of Naples both before and after the loss of the castles there had been and continued to be fighting in various places with various results. At first Ferrando had made a stand in the Plain of Sarni, and the French, withdrawing from Piè di Grotta, had stopped at Nocera four miles away from the enemy. Here, as both armies were nearly equal in strength, they spent their time in useless skirmishing, doing nothing important or significant, except that, having been admitted into the castle of Gifone near San Severino by a treacherous agreement, about 700 horse and foot soldiers belonging to Ferrando were nearly all either killed or taken prisoner. But as the Pope's troops arrived in support of Ferrando, the French, now outnumbered, moved off from Nocera; and the town with its fortress was taken by Ferrando with much slaughter of the followers of the French. In the meantime Montpensier had supplied the troops which had left Castelnuovo with him with horses and other necessities of war; and having reorganized them, he joined up with the others and came to Ariano, a place well provided with victuals. Ferrando, on the other hand, being less powerful than the enemy, stopped at Montefoscoli to temporize without trying his luck in battle until he had more help from the league.

Montpensier took the town and then the fortress of San Severino and would doubtless have made greater progress if he had not been prevented by difficulties over money. As none had been sent him from France and he was unable to obtain any from the Kingdom of Naples, he could not pay his soldiers; and with the army dissatisfied

on this account—especially the Swiss—he did not achieve
what his strength would otherwise have permitted him to
do. Nearly three months were spent by both armies in
these operations. During this time Don Federigo, and with
him Don Cesare d'Aragona, was fighting in Puglia with
local support against the barons and people who favored
the French cause. In the Abruzzi Graziano di Guerra,
harassed by the Count of Popoli and other barons supporting Ferrando, defended himself with great courage.
The Prefect of Rome, who had a command of 200 men-at-
arms from the King, harassed the places around Montecassino and the surrounding country from his own estates.

Events in Calabria were, however, of greater impor-
tance, for there the fortunes of the French had somewhat
declined, as Aubigny was wasted by a long illness which
interrupted his victorious progress. Although nearly all
Calabria and the Principality were loyal to the King of
France, Gonzalo, having again collected together the
Spanish troops and the local inhabitants friendly to the
Aragonese, who had increased in number after the taking
of Naples, had captured a few towns and was keeping
Ferrando's name alive in that province. The French were
having the same difficulties through lack of money as
they were with the army. Nevertheless, when the town of
Cosenza rebelled against them they recaptured and
sacked it. Yet no help came from France in these ex-
tremities and dangers, because the King had stopped at
Lyons and was entirely given up to jousting, tournaments,
and pleasures, having forgotten all about war. He constantly said he intended to deal with the affairs of Italy,
but his actions showed no sign of it. Argenton reported
from Venice that the senate had replied that they had no
quarrel with the King and had taken arms after the
occupation of Novara simply for the defense of their ally,
the Duke of Milan. Hence they thought it superfluous to
reconfirm their ancient friendship with a new peace
treaty. On the other hand they had offered through a
third party to persuade Ferrando to give the King a sum
of money immediately and pay him a tribute of 50,000
ducats a year, leaving Taranto in his hands for a certain

length of time as security. But the King refused to listen to all this, as though he had effective relief ready to hand. And yet, besides his difficulties in Italy, he was not without troubles on the frontiers of France; for Ferdinand King of Spain had come in person to Perpignan, and had his forces make forays into Languedoc, laying waste and looting and giving every sign of further trouble. Also the Dauphin of France, the King's only son, had recently died. All these were things which should have made him more inclined to an agreement—if he had the capacity to make up his mind between peace and war.

Chapter IV

[*The King of France orders the warden of the fortress of Pisa to obey his commands with regard to the restitution of the fort. The warden hands over the fortress to the Pisans. They demolish it and turn to the King of the Romans and various other Italian states for help. The Pisans place themselves under the protection of the Venetians. The senate receives them under its protection. The wisdom and cleverness of Lodovico Sforza praised in Milan. Through his efforts the forts of Sarzana and Sarzanella are handed over to the Genoese and not to the Florentines.*]

At the close of this year the affair of the citadel of Pisa was brought to an end. For the King, hearing of the obstinacy of the warden, had finally sent to Pisa with forceful and threatening orders addressed to him and all the French in the town, M. Gemel, and shortly after Bono, the warden's brother-in-law; so that a person he could trust would assure him that he could atone for his former errors by present obedience and point out the punishments he would incur if he persevered in his disobedience. The King hoped in this way to make him better disposed to carrying out his orders. Even so the warden persisted in the same obstinacy, paying no heed to Gemel's words. The latter remained only a few days, as he had been ordered by the King to accompany Cammillo Vitelli to Virginio. Nor did the arrival of Bono—who was long delayed as he was detained at Sarzana on the orders of the Duke of Milan—move the warden from his resolve. On the contrary, he won Bono over to his own view and made an agreement with the Pisans, in which Luzio Malvezzi acted on behalf of the Duke. By this agreement he handed over the citadel to the Pisans on January 1, 1496, and received from them 12,000 ducats for himself and 8,000 to distribute to the soldiers of the garrison. Since the Pisans had no means of paying all this themselves, they had 4,000 from the Venetians, 4,000 from the Genoese and 4,000 from the Duke of Milan. At the same time the Duke with his usual cunning, though inspiring little confidence, pretended to be endeavoring to establish firm friendship and understanding with the Florentines, and had already agreed on conditions with their envoys. It did not seem at all possible that either Ligny or Entragues or anyone else could have disobeyed in this way without the complicity of the King, particularly as it was to his own considerable disadvantage since the city of Pisa—though Entragues had stipulated that it should remain subject to the French crown—clearly remained attached to the league; and as a result of its not being handed back to the Florentines the French in the Kingdom of Naples were deprived of the very necessary assistance in men and money promised in the treaty of Turin. All the same, the Florentines, carefully observing the course of all these events, though very distrustful at first, were finally convinced that it had all been done against the King's wishes. This might seem incredible to anyone who did not know his character, the qualities of his mind and manners and the weak authority he had over his own people—and how much can be dared against a prince who has become contemptible.

The Pisans entered the citadel and immediately demolished it to its very foundations. Realizing their inability to defend themselves alone, they sent ambassadors simultaneously to the Pope, the King of the Romans, the Venetians, the Duke of Milan, the Genoese, the Sienese and the Luccans, begging all for help—especially from the Venetians and the Duke of Milan. To the latter they were at first disposed to transfer the rule of their city, feeling themselves obliged to make their first object not the preservation of liberty but to avoid the necessity of falling again into the power of the Florentines. They had more hopes of the Duke than of anyone else because it was he who had originally incited them to rebellion, because his territory was near and because, while the other members of the league had given them only encouragement, he had sent them prompt assistance. But the Duke, though longing to accept, hesitated to do so for fear of angering the other confederates in whose council the affairs of Pisa were now being discussed as a common concern. He urged them to put the matter off and then he proposed that the offer should be made under cover of the name of the Sanseverini so that he could later reveal it as made in fact to him, when he thought it appropriate to do so. And then when the King of France had left Italy and he felt less need for his allies, he decided to accept. But by this time the Pisans' enthusiasm for this plan had begun to cool because of their great hopes of receiving help from the Venetian senate. Others had also shown them that it was easier to preserve themselves with the help of many than by limiting themselves to just one; and they conceived greater hopes of maintaining freedom in this manner. These considerations were strengthened after they had obtained the citadel and they endeavored to win support from everyone. This object was favored by the attitude of the states of Italy.

The Genoese hated the Florentines; the Sienese and the Luccans hated and feared them, and were therefore ready to give permanent help. To do so more systematically they negotiated an agreement to this effect with fixed obligations. The Venetians and the Duke of Milan were greedy to have the city for themselves and not disposed to see it return under Florentine rule. Their cause was furthered with the Pope and the envoys of the King of Spain by the desire on the part of these princes to see a reduction in the power of the Florentines, who were for them too closely allied with the French. Therefore everyone gave the Pisans a friendly hearing: from the Emperor they

received confirmation of their liberty by diploma; and
from Venice and Milan they brought back a repetition of
their earlier common promises to maintain their freedom
and to help them get free from the French. The Pope in
the name and with the agreement of all the allies urged
the Pisans in a letter to maintain their liberty, promising
that they would receive powerful support from them all.
However, the effective assistance came from the Venetians
and the Duke of Milan, the latter increasing his forces in
Pisa and the former sending in a good number of troops.
If both had continued in this way the Pisans would have
had no need to side with one rather than the other, and
their concord might have been more easily preserved. But
before long the Duke, who always hated spending money
and was naturally inclined to proceed by stealth and
cunning—and moreover felt that for the time being he
would not be able to take over the rule of Pisa—began to
reduce his assistance to the Pisans and thus gave them
occasion to turn more to the Venetians who abundantly
supplied their needs. In consequence, only a few months
after the French had left the citadel, the Venetian senate,
urgently besought by the Pisans, decided to take the city
under its protection. Lodovico Sforza seemed to encourage
them in this plan rather than object to it; but they said
nothing to the other allies, though from the beginning
they had urged them to send troops to Pisa. Subsequently
these others claimed they had been released from their
promise to help the Pisans, since without their consent
they had made private arrangements with the Venetians.

It is absolutely certain that neither the desire to preserve for others the freedom which they love so much in
their own country nor considerations of mutual defense,
as they claimed with high-sounding words then and later,
but simply greed to acquire the dominion of Pisa led the
Venetians to this decision. They were sure of fulfilling
their desire promptly and with the agreement of the
Pisans themselves, who would gladly choose to be under
Venetian rule in order to be safe from Florentine servitude forever. Nevertheless this matter was several times
debated at length in the senate, where the almost unanimous desire to accept was checked by the authority of

a few older senators of greater reputation who strongly opposed it. They said that to assume responsibility for the defense of Pisa was a matter full of difficulties because that city was a long way from the Venetian borders by land and much farther by sea and they could only reach it through other people's territory and ports or by a long sea voyage around Italy through both the seas which surround her. Thus Pisa could not be defended from the continual attacks of the Florentines without very heavy expense. It was true that the acquisition of the city would be very useful to the Venetian empire, but one should consider first the difficulty of keeping it and still more the state of the times and the possible results of such a decision. As the whole of Italy naturally distrusted their power, such an increase would certainly displease all the other states; and this might easily give rise to greater dangers than some might think. Those who believed the other powers would idly permit the great advantage of the rule of Pisa to pass to the Venetian empire, which already seemed a threat to all Italians, were very much deceived. Though the rest of Italy might not be as powerful as they had been to prevent this themselves, they had a better chance of opposing Venice with foreign aid, now that the foreigner had been shown the way to invade Italy, and there was no doubt that they would have prompt recourse to such assistance both out of fear and hatred, for it is a common human failing to prefer serving foreigners to yielding to one's own people.

How could one believe that the Duke of Milan, who was so easily swayed by greed and hope or by fear—and was moved now by anger and jealousy that the Venetians should have the prey which he had prepared for himself with such cunning—would not rather again disturb the peace of Italy than allow Pisa to be occupied by them? Although he appeared to think otherwise from his words and advice, it was easy to see that this was not his sincere opinion but a trap, and his statements a pretense. It would be prudent to support Pisa jointly with him, if only to prevent the Pisans from giving themselves into his power; but to make their cause one's own and draw down upon oneself so much envy and responsibility was

not a wise decision. They should consider how contrary
this step would be to their labors for many months past
and with which they were still concerned; for the only
thing which had moved the senate to take up arms with
so much expense and danger was the desire to make
themselves and all Italy safe from the barbarians. This
operation had been begun with glorious success; and yet
the King of France had only just withdrawn beyond the
mountains, while the greater part of the Kingdom of
Naples was still being held for him by a powerful army;
so how imprudent and infamous it would be to sow the
seeds of further discord when the time had come to
establish firmly the freedom and safety of Italy! Such
troubles might well enable the King of France to return
or give the Emperor cause to enter Italy, for it was well
known that such was his dearest wish on account of his
claims against their state. The Venetian Republic was not
in a situation where it was forced to adopt dangerous
counsels or be over hasty in seizing opportunities before
they were ripe. Indeed no state in Italy could better afford
to wait for the right moment and for opportunities to
ripen. Hasty and dangerous decisions were appropriate to
those in difficult or unpropitious situations, or those who
feared that time might be too short for the fulfillment of
ambition and greed to make their name famous. They
were not suitable for the Republic which in a position of
power, dignity and authority was feared and envied by all
the rest of Italy, and which by comparison with kings
and other princes was almost immortal and everlasting
under the unchanging name of the Venetian senate, and
so had no reason to prematurely hasten its decisions. It
was more suitable to the wisdom and gravity of the senate
to consider, as befitted truly wise men, the dangers
hidden beneath these hopes and desires and the ends of
things rather than their beginnings. They should accordingly reject rash counsel and refrain in the affairs of
Pisa, as in others which might present themselves, from
alarming and irritating other people—at least until Italy
was freer from dangers and fear of attack by foreign
powers. Their first aim must be not to give cause for the
return of the foreigners; as experience had shown within

a very few months that when Italy was not oppressed by foreign nations, she nearly always followed the lead of the Venetian senate; but when there were barbarians in Italy, instead of being feared and followed by the others, Venice was forced along with the rest to fear the foreign armies.

These and similar arguments were overwhelmed by the ambition of the majority and even more by the persuasions of Agostino Barbarigo, doge of the city, whose authority had become so great that it surpassed the respect accorded to former doges and deserved to be called power rather than authority. Besides having held his position with success for so many years, and possessing many excellent gifts and graces, he had cunningly contrived a following of senators who took his advice more as a political party than as individuals acting with senatorial gravity and integrity, and gladly opposed those who had a reputation for wisdom because of their long experience and their having reached the highest offices in the Republic. Barbarigo was extremely anxious to leave behind him a great reputation for increasing the territory of the empire. His appetite for glory had not been satisfied with the addition of the island of Cyprus to the Venetian empire during his rule when the line of Lusignan kings died out. He was therefore eager to grasp any opportunity for the aggrandizement of the state. Hence he opposed those who advised otherwise in the Pisan affair and pointed out with strong arguments how useful and opportune it would be for the senate to acquire Pisa and how important to repress by this means the ambition of the Florentines. It was their doing that on the death of Filippo Maria Visconti the Venetians had lost their chance to seize the Duchy of Milan; and by their readiness with money they had done them more harm than any other major power in the war with Ferrara and other enterprises. He reminded them how seldom such great opportunities arose, how shameful it was to lose them and what sharp remorse was suffered by those who failed to embrace them.

The state of Italy was not such that the other powers

could oppose them alone, and it was still less to be feared
that they might out of fear or anger turn to the King of
France. The Duke of Milan, who had so greatly offended
the King, would never dare to trust him; nor was the Pope
likely to have such an idea; nor would the King of Naples,
even if he regained his kingdom, be able to tolerate the
name of the French. Their entry into Pisa, although
unwelcome to others, was not so rash an action nor the
danger so imminent that it might cause the other powers
to rush into those remedies which are used only in the
last resort. For in slowly developing diseases there is no
haste in using dangerous medicines, as men think that
there will be plenty of time for them in due course. If in
the present weakness and disunity of the other states of
Italy they refused this opportunity out of timidity, they
might wait in vain to do it more safely when the other
powers had regained their former strength and felt secure
from foreign dangers. To counteract their fears, it should
be remembered that all worldly actions were subject to
many dangers, but wise men knew that the worst did not
always happen because either by accident or good fortune
many dangers vanish of their own accord, while many
others disappear through the exercise of prudence and
care. Hence timidity should not be confused with prudence as many men affirm who are unaware of the propri-
ety of terms and the reality of things; and one should not
regard as wise those who consider as certain all doubtful
dangers, and' so fearing them all, argue as though they
were all sure to happen. Indeed one should not call prudent or wise those who fear unduly for the future. That
name and praise was much more suitable to courageous
men, because knowing and taking into account all dangers—and in this unlike the rash who neither know nor
consider them—they observe how often by chance or by
ability men free themselves from many difficulties. Therefore in their decisions they are counseled no less by hope
than by cowardice, they do not regard as certain what is
uncertain, and they do not reject as easily as the other
sort of men opportunities that are both useful and honorable. And so, bearing in mind the weakness and disunity

of the rest of Italy, the great power and fortune of the Venetian Republic, the magnanimity and glorious examples of their forefathers, they should frankly accept the protectorate of the Pisans, through which they would eventually gain power over that city, which was undoubtedly one of the most useful steps by which to rise to the domination of all Italy.

The senate therefore received the Pisans under its protection by public decree, expressly undertaking to defend their freedom. This decision was not at first given due weight by the Duke of Milan because as it did not prevent him from keeping his troops there, he was pleased to have someone to share the expense; and as he intended out of avarice to reduce the number of his soldiers in Pisa, he thought it to his benefit that Pisa was a cause of heavy expenditure both to the Venetians and the Florentines. Further he was convinced that the Pisans, because of the power and nearness to them of his state, and the memory of what he had done toward their liberation, were so devoted to him that they would always prefer him to all others. These mistaken plans and hopes were supported by the belief in which he encouraged himself— forgetting the variations in human affairs—that he had fortune virtually at his feet, stating openly that he was fortune's favorite child: so vain had he become in prosperity and puffed up with pride that by his doing and his advice the King of France had entered Italy, claiming that it was he who had deprived Piero de' Medici, disobedient to his wishes, of his power in Florence, he who had brought about the rebellion of the Pisans from the Florentines and he who had caused his enemies the Aragonese to be driven out of the Kingdom of Naples. Then, he said, he had changed his mind and by his advice and authority had arisen the league of so many powers against Charles, the return of Ferrando to the Kingdom of Naples, and the King of France's departure on terms unworthy of his greatness. He even claimed that his intrigues or authority had been more powerful with the captain of the citadel of Pisa than the wishes and orders of his own king. Measuring the future by these rules and judging the prudence and the intelligence of all the others to be far inferior to his own, he expected always to be able to direct the affairs of Italy to suit himself and to circumvent everyone else by his cleverness. As this vain belief was not kept hidden either in words or actions by himself or by his people, but rather taking pleasure that it should be accepted and proclaimed by all, Milan resounded day and night with acclamations; and everyone celebrated in verse in Latin and the vulgar tongue and with public orations and encomiums, the wonderful wisdom of Lodovico Sforza on which peace or war in Italy depended. They praised to the skies his name and his nickname "the Moor"; this had been given him in youth because of his dark complexion and because of the reputation for cunning he had already begun to acquire; and he was proud to keep it as long as his rule endured.

The influence of the Moor was no less in the other Florentine fortresses than it had been in Pisa, so that his enemies as well as his friends in Italy seemed to be under his control. The King had been seriously annoyed when he heard the strong complaints made by the Florentine ambassadors. And so that they might at least have back the other fortresses, he had sent his chamberlain Robert de Veste with fresh orders and letters from Ligny. Yet, as his authority was no greater over others than it was over himself, Ligny's boldness was such, telling many people that he did not proceed thus without the King's authority, that on his instructions, added to the unwillingness of the wardens of the castles, the royal commands were treated with scant respect. Hence the bastard of Bienne, who held Sarzana in Ligny's name and under his command, after he had got the Florentine troops and commissioners to come there to receive the fort, handed it over to the Genoese for 25,000 ducats. The warden of Sarzanella did likewise, having been paid a certain sum of money; and the Moor was the instigator and intermediary of this action. And he too, though he did it in the name of the Genoese, sent Fracassa with 100 cavalry and 400 infantry against the Florentines and prevented them from regaining all the other places they had lost in

Lunigiana, of which they had recovered a part with the help of the troops sent to take over Sarzana. Shortly afterward Entragues, who still held the forts of Pietrasanta and Motrone, and into whose hands Librafatta had also fallen, kept this last place for a few months and then handed it over to the Pisans, selling the others for 26,000 ducats to the Luccans, exactly as the Duke of Milan ordered. He had at first wanted the Genoese to have them, but later changed his mind and chose to bribe the Luccans with them so that they might have reason to help the Pisans more readily and to bind them more firmly to him by this benefaction.

When these things were reported in France, the King became angry with Ligny and had Entragues banished from the kingdom, but when Bono returned, having taken some of the Pisans' money and negotiated the sale of Sarzana in Genoa, his excuses were accepted; and an ambassador from Pisa was graciously received who had been sent with him to convey their wish to be faithful subjects of the crown of France and swear an oath of loyalty. However, soon afterward he was dismissed, and his commission was declared null and void. Ligny received no other punishment than that, as a sign of exclusion from royal favor, he lost the privilege he had had of sleeping in the King's chamber; but this was soon restored to him. Entragues alone remained in disfavor, though not for long. The settlement of these matters was assisted as well by the King's nature and other influences and favors as by the belief (which was not unfounded) that the Florentines could not afford to abandon him; for the ambitions of the Venetians and the Duke of Milan were quite evident, and it was felt that they would certainly not have allowed the Florentines to regain Pisa even if they had agreed to join the league for the defense of Italy. They sought to draw them into the league with alarms and threats; though for the time being they attempted nothing against them, being satisfied with the troops they had put into Pisa to keep the city alive and not to allow it to completely lose the country district around.

Chapter V

[*Ferrando of Aragon threatened by the arrival of fresh enemy forces. Assistance given by the Venetians and other allies to Ferrando. Further incidents in the fighting. The balance of opposing forces.*]

The danger to the Kingdom of Naples distracted them from any other preoccupation. Virginio had collected a large force at Bagno a Rapolano and then around Perugia, where he remained some days and was on his way with other members of the Orsini family toward the Abruzzi, while Cammillo and Pagolo Vitelli were moving in the same direction with their company. When the castle of Montelione refused the latter food rations, they put it to the sack; and the other Church territories through which their road lay, were so frightened by this that, regardless of the Pope's solemn orders to the contrary, they allowed them lodging and provisions everywhere. Because of this, and still more because it was being said that fresh help was arriving from France by sea, it seemed as though the French in the Kingdom of Naples were about to receive strong reinforcements; and as Ferrando, who had no money and was in serious difficulties, could not withstand such an attack without more help, he was obliged to consider new strategies for his defense.

At the beginning the other powers had not included Ferrando in their league, and though the King of Spain had urged them to admit him after he had retaken Naples, the Venetians had refused to have him, thinking that his difficulties might offer the means for the acquisition they already had in mind of part of his kingdom. So Ferrando, deprived of any other hope as he did not expect further assistance from Spain—and the other members of the league did not want the expense—came to an agreement with the Venetians. By this, which was guaranteed for both sides by the Pope and the ambassadors of the King of Spain in the name of their king, the Venetians were to send into the kingdom in aid of Ferrando, the Marquis of Mantua, their captain, with 700 men-at-arms, 500 light horse and 3,000 foot soldiers, and were to maintain their fleet that was already there, with the understanding that they could recall these forces whenever they were needed for their own defense; and they were to lend him 15,000 ducats for his immediate needs. To guarantee their expenses Ferrando was to hand over to them Otranto, Brindisi, and Trani, and allow them to keep Monopoli and Pulignano which they already held, on condition that they should be handed back when they had been reimbursed. But the expenses they claimed either for the war or garrisons or building of defenses, were not to exceed 200,000 ducats. These ports, being on the Adriatic, were very useful to Venice and increased her power substantially. This now began to be extended all over Italy, as there was no one to oppose it; and after the Pisan protectorate was accepted, no one listened any more to the counsels of those who would have preferred the sails to be more cautiously unfurled to such favorable winds of fortune. For, besides their dealings in Naples and Tuscany, they had recently commissioned Astore Lord of Faenza in their service and accepted the protectorate of his state, which was well calculated to alarm the Florentines, the city of Bologna, and all the rest of Romagna. In addition to the aid arranged separately by the Venetians, other assistance came from the allies. The Pope, the Venetians, and the Duke of Milan sent to Ferrando's relief some other men-at-arms whom they recruited jointly. The Duke, however, who had not entirely abandoned his pretense of not going against the Vercelli treaty, although it was at his suggestion that most of these things were done, refused to have his name used in the commissioning of troops or other apparent ways, and had agreed to pay secretly 10,000 ducats a month for the defense of Naples.

The march of the Orsini and the Vitelli put an end to trouble in the Abruzzi, where there was open rebellion against the French. Teramo and Civita di Chieti had already rebelled, and it was feared that Aquila, the chief

city of that region, might do the same. They made sure
of this city for the French, recovered Teramo by agreement and sacked Giulianuova, so that almost all the
Abruzzi supported the French cause, and Ferrando's affairs in consequence seemed clearly to be declining
throughout the kingdom. Calabria was almost entirely
held by Aubigny, although his long illness which had
kept him in Ghiarace allowed Gonzalo to carry on the
war in the province with his Spanish troops and those
of a few nobles of the region. Gaeta with many places
around was in the hands of the French. The Prefect of
Rome with his own company and the forces of his state
had recovered the castles of Montecassino and was harassing Terra di Lavoro on that side. Montpensier, though
lack of money greatly impeded the use of his troops,
compelled Ferrando to shut himself up in his stronghold, likewise hampered by lack of money and many
other essentials but relying entirely on his hopes of
Venetian aid. This could not arrive as soon as it was required, as the agreement had only recently been made.
Montpensier attempted to occupy Benevento by secret arrangement, but Ferrando got wind of this and promptly
occupied it with his troops.

The French moved up to Benevento, taking Fenezano,
Apice, and many other places around and made camp at
the Ponte a Finocchio. As they lacked provisions in that
area and as the time was approaching for the tax on
sheep in Puglia to be collected—which was one of the
most important revenues of the Kingdom of Naples,
amounting to 80,000 ducats a year and all collected in
the space of one month—Montpensier, to deprive the
enemy of this resource and still more to meet the urgent
needs of his own men, moved off toward Puglia, part of
which was held by him and part by the enemy. Ferrando
was close behind him, eager rather to hold up the enemy's
progress by some stratagem than to fight, until his reinforcements arrived. At that moment a French fleet
reached Gaeta consisting of fifteen great ships and seven
smaller ones, which had taken on board at Savona 800
German foot soldiers raised in the territory of the Duke
of Guelders, and those Swiss and Gascons whom the

King had first commanded should be embarked in the
ships to be commissioned at Genoa. Ferrando's fleet,
which was off Gaeta to prevent supplies reaching it, had
given way to the French ships, as they were ill provided
with the things they needed owing to lack of money.
Having thus safely entered the port, the soldiers disem-
barked and took Itri and other nearby places, and having
obtained much booty throughout the area, they hoped to
capture Sessa with the help of Giovambatista Caracciolo,
who promised to let them secretly into the town. However, Don Federigo, who had moved to Taranto with his
troops and had then been sent by Ferrando to govern
Naples, heard of this plan, entered the town by surprise
and took prisoner the bishop and some others who were
party to the betrayal.

However, in Puglia where the main struggle was now
being carried on, the fortunes of war varied. Both armies
had taken up quarters in the towns and villages because
of the inclement weather; neither of them occupied one
place alone but several, as they were not large enough
to accommodate them. They spent their time making
raids and cavalry sorties to plunder cattle, using speed
and cunning rather than skill in arms. Ferrando had
stopped at Foggia with part of his troops and left the
others, some at Troia and some at Nocera. There he
heard that between San Severo, where Virginio Orsino
was lodged with 300 men-at-arms, and Porcina where
Mariano Savelli was with 100 men-at-arms there had
been collected a vast quantity of sheep and cattle. He
therefore advanced with 600 men-at-arms, 800 light
horse and 1,500 foot soldiers, and reaching San Severo
at dawn he stopped there with the men-at-arms to counter Virginio if he made a move. He also sent off the light
horse which spread out over the countryside and captured some 60,000 head of stock. When Mariano Savelli
came out from Porcina to attack them, they forced him
to retire with the loss of 30 men-at-arms. This loss and
humiliation caused Montpensier to collect all his troops
and march toward Foggia to regain his lost honor and
booty. On the way he met something he had not bar-
gained for: between Nocera and Troia he encountered

800 German foot soldiers recruited by Ferrando and recently arrived by sea. They had left Troia where they were based, and were going on their own initiative, rather than by order of the King and against the advice of Fabrizio Colonna who was also based at Troia, to join up with Ferrando at Foggia. They could not retreat or fight their way out and would not surrender, and so were all killed fighting, inflicting some losses on the French. Montpensier then advanced to Foggia and drew up his army in battle order. But Ferrando only sent out his light cavalry, so the French went into camp at the wood of Incoronata. They stayed there for two days suffering from a scarcity of supplies, and regained most of the stock which had been plundered. They then returned to Foggia. And having spent the night before the town, they went back to San Severo without part of the booty they had regained because on the way it was taken from them again by Ferrando's light horse. In this way the cattle were split up, and neither side gained much from the collection of the tax.

A few days later the French, driven out by the shortage of provisions, went on to Campobasso which was in French hands; from there they captured Coglionessa, otherwise called Grigonisa, a nearby town, where the Swiss against their officers' orders behaved with such cruelty that, although the whole region was terrified, it turned many people against them. In the meantime Ferrando, while trying to defend his possessions as best he could and waiting for the arrival of the Marquis of Mantua, was reorganizing his forces with the help of 16,000 ducats sent him by the Pope and what money he had been able to collect himself. During this time the Swiss and the other troops which had come by sea to Gaeta, joined up with Montpensier. The Marquis of Mantua entered the kingdom and came to Capua via San Germano, taking many places on the way, some by agreement and others by force, though they were of small importance. At the beginning of June he joined up with the King at Nocera, where Don Cesare d'Aragona brought the troops which had been around Taranto. Thus nearly all the troops of the French and of Ferrando were collected in nearby positions. The French had superiority in infantry and the Italians in cavalry; and so the outcome appeared very doubtful. One could not guess which side would emerge victorious.

Chapter VI

[*Charles VIII turns his attentions again to Italy and is encouraged from various quarters. Deliberations in the royal council and preparations for a fresh expedition to Italy. Lodovico Sforza's fears and political actions. Delays imposed on the expedition by the Cardinal of St. Malo. Meager assistance sent by Charles to Italy.*]

While all was thus in suspense, the King of France was taking steps to send relief to his people. When he heard of the loss of the Neapolitan castles and learned that his troops lacked the promised Florentine money and reinforcements because their fortresses had not been returned to them, he was roused from the indifference which seemed to possess him on his return to France and again began to turn his mind to Italian affairs. To be clear of all obstacles and to be able to rely more confidently once more on divine assistance by showing his gratitude for help received in the dangers he had been through, he went in haste to Tours and then to Paris to fulfill the vows he had made on the day of the battle of Fornovo to St. Martin and St. Denis. Returning with equal speed to Lyons, he became daily more enthusiastic about an Italian expedition. He was himself very much in favor of such a plan, as he considered it to his great glory to have acquired such a kingdom and to be the first French king after so many centuries to have revived in person the memory of French prowess and victories in Italy. He believed that the difficulties he had encountered on his return from Naples had arisen more from his own lack of organization than from the strength and courage of the Italians, who in matters of war were now esteemed at naught by the French. He was further

311

encouraged by the Florentine envoys, by the Cardinal of
San Piero in Vincoli and Gianiacopo Trivulzio, who
had returned to the court for this purpose. Vitellozzo and
Carlo Orsino likewise encouraged him; and later the
Conte di Montorio, who was sent for this purpose by the
barons who followed the French cause in the Kingdom
of Naples; and finally the Seneschal of Beaucaire went
to France from Gaeta and showed that there were good
hopes of victory if help were sent without delay, but
otherwise the French could not go on much longer in
that kingdom without support. Besides all these, some of
the great nobles of the court who had formerly been
against the Italian expedition now supported it because
of the dishonor to the French crown if the kingdom acquired were allowed to be lost; and much more because
of the harm to France that so large a number of her
nobles should be lost in the Kingdom of Naples. These
ideas were not impeded by the movements of the King
of Spain around Perpignan; for they were demonstrations
more formidable in name than in fact, and the forces
of that King were better able to defend his own kingdom than to attack others. It was therefore regarded as a
sufficient precaution to have sent to Narbonne and other
places on the frontiers of Spain a large force of men-
at-arms and a good number of Swiss.

The King called together in council all the nobles and
people of importance at his court and it was decided that
Trivulzio should return to Asti as rapidly as possible
with the title of royal lieutenant and with him 800
lances, 2,000 Swiss and 2,000 Gascons; the Duke of
Orléans was to follow him shortly after with more troops;
and finally the King himself would cross the Alps with
all the other necessary forces and equipment. No one
doubted that if he entered Italy in great strength, the
states of the Duke of Savoy and the Marquesses of Monferrato and Saluzzo would join his cause and would be
very useful for making war on the Duke of Milan. Furthermore, apart from the canton of Berne which had
undertaken not to fight the Duke of Milan, all the Swiss
cantons would enter French pay with the greatest alacrity. These deliberations proceeded with all the more

agreement because of the King's enthusiasm. Before they went into council he had begged the Duke of Bourbon to make the point very strongly that they must wage war with really powerful resources; and then in the council he hotly contradicted the admiral who with a few supporters had attempted, not so much by direct opposition but by suggesting many obstacles, to dampen the enthusiasm of the others.

The King stated categorically that it was not in his power to do otherwise, as the will of God forced him to return to Italy in person. At the same council it was decided that 30 ships, among them a huge galleon called the Normande and another great galleon belonging to the Knights of St. John would sail down the Atlantic coast and into the ports of Provence, where 30 light galleys and galleons would be fitted out; and in this great fleet would be sent to the Kingdom of Naples vast reinforcements of men, supplies, munitions and money. But, without waiting for this fleet to be ready, some ships would be sent at once with men and supplies. Besides all this, Rigault, the master of the King's household, was to go to Milan because the Duke, although he had not given the two galleons nor allowed the King to fit out ships at Genoa, and had only returned the ships taken at Rapallo but not the 12 galleys held in the port of Genoa, had tried to excuse himself with the disobedience of the Genoese and had continuously kept his representatives with the King for various negotiations.

Recently he had sent Antonio Maria Palavicino, stating that he was prepared to observe the terms of the treaty he had made and asking for longer time in which to pay the Duke of Orléans the 50,000 ducats promised in that agreement. From these subterfuges he derived little profit, as the King understood him too well, both from his other actions and because letters and instructions of his had been intercepted which revealed that he was constantly pressing the King of the Romans and the King of Spain to wage war against France. Nevertheless, in the hope that fear might persuade him to change his mind, Rigault was instructed not to stress the

313

Duke's failure to observe the treaty, but let him know
that he might efface the memory of his failure by beginning to honor his promises, handing over the galleys,
supplying the galleons and allowing the King's ships to
fit at Genoa. He should also tell him of the King's decision to invade, which would be to his great detriment
if, while he had the chance, he did not return to that
friendship which the King was sure he had imprudently
rejected more from groundless suspicions than any other
cause.

When the news of the French preparations reached
Italy, it caused great perturbation among the allies, particularly Lodovico Sforza, as he was the most exposed
to enemy attack. He was in a state of great anxiety, especially when he heard that after Rigault's departure
from the court the King had dismissed all his agents
with very brusque words and gestures. Because of this,
turning over in his mind the gravity of the danger, and
thinking that all the troubles of war were going to return to his territory, the Duke might easily have acceded
to the King's requests if he had not been held back by
the fear, knowing how much he had offended him and
how much distrust these injuries had provoked on both
sides, that it was easier to come to agreement about
their differences than to find a means of guarantee for
both of them. For neither was willing to trust the other
where the other refused to trust him, when it came to
subtracting from the one what had been agreed as assurance for the other. So with necessity obliging him
to adopt the course he least liked, Sforza tried at least
to put off the dangers as long as possible and continued
the same subterfuges with Rigault that he had used up
to now. He earnestly stated that he would make the
Genoese obey as soon as the King provided in the city
of Avignon adequate security for the return of the ships;
and both parties should promise, giving hostages as
guarantee, not to attempt anything to the detriment of
the other. These negotiations went on for several days
and ended much as the others had done because of the
many arguments and difficulties raised.

Lodovico however did not spend this time in vain. For during the negotiations he sent men to the King of the Romans to persuade him to enter Italy with his help and that of the Venetians. To Venice he sent ambassadors to ask them to agree to share this expense for defense against the common danger, and to send to Alessandria the aid needed to stand up to the French. The Venetians agreed to do this most promptly. But they did not show the same accommodating spirit with regard to the entry of the King of the Romans, who was hardly a friend of the Republic because of their possessions on the mainland which belonged to the Empire and the House of Austria. Nor were they pleased that an army which would be entirely controlled by Lodovico should be brought into Italy at their joint expense. Nevertheless Lodovico went on pressing his plan because, in addition to his other reasons, he distrusted the Venetian forces alone in the state of Milan. The senate, knowing that he was seriously alarmed, feared that he might suddenly be reconciled with the King of France, and so finally gave its consent and sent ambassadors to the Emperor for this purpose. The Venetians and the Duke were also afraid that the Florentines might mount an attack on the Genoese Riviera once the King had crossed the mountains; and therefore they asked Giovanni Bentivoglio to attack the Florentines from the Bolognese border with 300 men-at-arms with which the league had commissioned him. They promised that the Florentines would be simultaneously harassed by the Sienese and by their own troops in Pisa and they offered to guarantee his possession of Pistoia if he succeeded in taking the town. Although Bentivoglio gave them some hopes, he had no intention of doing so. And being much afraid of the coming of the French, he sent secretly to the King to apologize for what he had done in the past, saying it had been forced on him by the situation of the city of Bologna, offering allegiance, and promising to refrain from troubling the Florentines out of respect for him.

But the King's desire, however ardent, was not sufficient to put into effect what had been decided, though his own honor and the dangers in the Kingdom of

315

Naples demanded the promptest action. The Cardinal of
St. Malo in whose hands lay all the actions of government as well as the control of financial affairs, though
he did not openly dissent, so delayed all the preparations by putting off the necessary payments that nothing
was done. He did this either because it seemed to him
the best means of perpetuating his own importance not
to allow any expenditure which was not immediately
necessary or was not for the pleasures of the King, and
so not to have to raise daily problems of materials and
money; or, as many thought, he had been bribed with
gifts and promises—and had secret intelligence either
with the Pope or with the Duke of Milan. The King's
commands and persuasions had no effect, though sometimes full of anger and harsh words, because, understanding the King's character, St. Malo satisfied him
with promises that were the opposite of his actions. When
the carrying out of the plans had thus begun to be delayed by his tactics, they were almost completely upset
by an unexpected event.

At the end of May when everybody thought he would
soon be moving into Italy, the King decided to go to
Paris, saying that according to the custom of the ancient kings he wanted to take leave of St. Denis with
the usual ceremonies before his departure from France,
and also from St. Martin as he passed through Tours. He
also said that he had decided to go into Italy well provided with money so as not to find himself in the same
difficulties as the year before. And so he must persuade
the other cities of France to furnish him with money after
the example of the city of Paris, which he would not induce to oblige him without going there in person. While
he was up there he could hurry on the men-at-arms who
were coming from Normandy and Picardy. He said that
he would send ahead the Duke of Orléans and be back
in Lyons within a month. However it was believed that
the real and principal reason was that he had fallen in
love with someone in the service of the Queen who had
recently moved to Tours with her court. Neither the advice of his own people nor the urgent prayers and almost

tears of the Italians could dissuade him from this decision. They explained to him how harmful it was to lose the right moment for the war, particularly when his people in Naples were in such straits, and how disastrous the news which would fly all over Italy that he had gone farther away when he ought to have been drawing nearer. The fame of enterprises varied with every small event, every slightest rumor, and it was very difficult to regain reputation once it had begun to decline, even though afterward much greater feats were performed than men had formerly expected. However, he paid no attention to these warnings; and after spending another month at Lyons, he set out for Paris without dispatching the Duke of Orléans, but simply sending Trivulzio to Asti with only a few troops, not so much to prepare for war as to confirm the loyalty of M. Philippe who had lately succeeded to the Duchy of Savoy through the death of his little nephew, the Duke.

Before the King's departure nothing was done for the affairs of the Kingdom of Naples beyond the sending of six vessels to Gaeta with provisions, giving hope that the great fleet would soon follow. He also provided through merchants in Florence—though the assistance came rather late—40,000 ducats to be paid to Montpensier; because the Swiss and Germans had protested that if they were not paid before the end of June, they would go over to the enemy. The Duke of Orléans, the Cardinal of St. Malo and all the council remained in Lyons with orders to hurry on with preparations. Slow as the cardinal had been when the King was there, he was much slower in his absence.

Chapter VII

[*Further incidents in the war in the Kingdom of Naples. French fortunes again in decline. Victory of Gonzalo in Calabria. Surrender of Atella. Further progress of the Aragonese. Death of Ferrando and succession of Federigo. Further delays to the French expedition into Italy.*]

Affairs in the Kingdom of Naples could not, however, wait for these slow remedies. The war had reached a point, with both armies facing one another and innumerable difficulties arising on either side, where it must be ended without further delay. After he had joined up with the Venetian forces, Ferrando had taken Castelfranco. There he was joined by Giovanni Sforza, Lord of Pesaro, and Giovanni da Gonzaga, brother of the Marquis of Mantua, both captains of the league, with 200 men-at-arms; so that he had in all 1,200 men-at-arms, 1,500 light horse and 4,000 infantry. Meantime the French had camped at Circello, ten miles from Benevento. Ferrando moved up to a position four miles from them and besieged Frangete di Monteforte; but as the place was well defended they did not take it at the first assault. The French left Circello to relieve Frangete, but they arrived too late, as the German troops defending it had already surrendered unconditionally out of fear of a second attack. Though this seemed a loss to the French, it could have been turned into victory if they had not wasted their opportunity either through imprudence or ill luck. For, as almost everyone agrees, they might easily have defeated the enemy army that day because most of them were busy sacking Frangete and paid no heed to the commands of their officers who, realizing that only a valley separated their camp from the French, energetically strove to get their men together.

Montpensier saw this great opportunity and so did Virginio Orsino: one commanded, the other implored with tears, crying that victory was assured, that they should cross the valley at once while the Italian camp was full of confusion and disorder and while the soldiers, intent on plunder and on bearing away their booty, paid no heed to their captains' orders. But Percy, one of the chief officers of the army after Montpensier, either out of youthful folly or, as more people believed, out of jealousy for Montpensier's reputation, pointed out the disadvantages of crossing the valley and climbing the hillside practically under the enemy's feet while they were in so strong a position. He openly dissuaded the soldiers from fighting and prevented the carrying out of

this excellent plan. It is also believed that at his instigation the Swiss and Germans rioted, demanding money.
Hence Montpensier was forced to withdraw near Circello, where the following day a battle was fought in which
Cammillo Vitelli, while brilliantly carrying out his task
as a soldier and captain beneath the walls, was struck
on the head by a rock and killed. Because of this
tragedy the French withdrew to Arriano without taking
Circello, though the captains were still prepared to try
their fortune in battle if they had the opportunity. The
Aragonese army felt quite differently—especially the
Venetian commissioners. They knew that the enemy was
beginning to run short of supplies and money and realized that relief from France was being long delayed;
and so they hoped that their troubles and disadvantages
would increase daily and that in other parts of the kingdom the French would run into more serious difficulties.
In the Abruzzi where Annibale the natural son of the
Lord of Camerino had recently gone to serve Ferrando
as a volunteer with 400 horse troops raised at his own
expense, he had defeated the Marquis of Bitonto, and
was awaiting the arrival of the Duke of Urbino with 300
men-at-arms, recently commissioned by the league. The
Duke, attracted by the league's good fortune and better
conditions, had given up his commission with the Florentines which had still more than a year to run. He gave
as his excuse that as he was a feudatory of the Church
he could not disobey the commands of the Pope. When
Graziano di Guerra was on his way to oppose the Duke,
he was attacked in the plain of Sermona by the Conte
di Celano and the Conte di Popoli with 300 horse troops
and 3,000 local foot soldiers whom he put to flight.

Yet with the lost opportunity for victory at Frangete
the fortunes of the French had clearly begun to decline.
Innumerable difficulties arose at one and the same time:
extreme lack of funds, shortage of provisions, antago-
nism from the people, disagreements between the officers,
disobedience among the troops and the departure of
many from the camp—part of necessity and part of their
own desire, for they had had little opportunity to collect
any money in the kingdom and none whatever had come

to them from France, as the provision of 40,000 ducats sent to Florence had come too late. For this reason and because they were surrounded by places sustained by the nearness of the enemy, they were not able to make the necessary arrangements for supplies. The army was disorganized as the soldiers' morale was low and the Germans and Swiss riotously demanded their pay every day. All decisions were rendered more difficult by Percy's constant opposition to Montpensier. Necessity compelled the Prince of Bisignano to leave with his troops to go and protect his own state for fear of Gonzalo's men; and many native troops deserted daily. For besides never receiving any pay, they were always ill treated by the French and the Swiss in the division of spoils and the distribution of rations. Owing to these difficulties and particularly the lack of food, the French army was forced to retreat bit by bit from one place to another, which greatly lowered its reputation with the local population. Although the enemy followed them all the time, it was not that they hoped for an opportunity to fight, as Montpensier and Virginio would have liked—for they always camped in strong places where their supplies could not be cut off, so as not to be forced to fight. While on his way to join them with his company of 100 men-at-arms, Filippo Rosso, one of the Venetian captains, was defeated by the troops of the Prefect of Rome. Finally, when the French were camped below Montecalvoli and Casalarbore near Arriano, Ferrando drew close to them —only a bowshot away, but still camped in a strong position—and reduced the enemy almost to starvation, depriving them at the same time of water supplies.

They decided therefore to move into Puglia where they hoped to get sufficient supplies. But they feared, with the enemy so near, such difficulties as may easily accompany armies in retreat and quietly broke camp early in the night and marched twenty-five miles before stopping. Ferrando followed them in the morning but, afraid he could not catch up, he camped outside Gesualdo, which had already withstood for fourteen months a siege by a most celebrated captain, and took the town in a single day. This misled the French, because, as they had decided to stop at Venosa, a place in a strong position and well supplied with provisions, their belief that Ferrando would not take Gesualdo so quickly caused them to waste time at Atella which they had taken and sacked.

They were caught here by Ferrando who had hastened on after taking Gesualdo; and though they defeated a part of his troops which had run ahead of the main army, they could not reach Venosa eight miles away and stayed on at Atella, intending to wait and see if assistance came from any quarter and hoping to get plenty of supplies, being near Venosa and many other places loyal to the French. Ferrando camped there at once with the intention of cutting off their supplies because he saw a chance of victory without danger or bloodshed; he devoted his efforts to preparing many trenches and capturing places nearby. But the difficulties of the French made his task even easier. The German soldiers had only had two months' pay since they left home, and when all the time limits were passed without result, they deserted to Ferrando's army. He therefore had greater means of harassing the enemy and spreading out his forces, so that it was even harder to bring in supplies from Venosa and other places around. In Atella there was not enough food to keep the French for many days, as there was only a small quantity of grain; and as the Aragonese had destroyed a mill on the river running by the walls, they were also short of flour. Their present difficulties were not lightened by any hope for the future, as there was no sign of help from any quarter.

The final ruin of their cause was the disaster which overtook them in Calabria. Because of Aubigny's long illness which had caused many of his men to go off to join Montpensier's army, Gonzalo had taken many towns in that province and had finally stopped at Castrovillole with the Spanish troops and many local soldiers. There he heard that the Count of Meleto and Alberigo da San Severino and many other barons with a force almost equal to his own were at Laino, and as their numbers were continually increasing, they planned, when their army was stronger, to come and attack him. He decided to surprise them, hoping they would be off their guard because they were sure of being in a strong position, as the castle of Laino stands on the River Sapri which forms the boundary between Calabria and the Principality, and the town is on the far side of the river. Encamped here they were protected by the castle from anyone coming to attack by the direct road; while between Laino and Castrovillole were Murano and various other places belonging to the Prince of Bisignano, which were on their side. Gonzalo, however, with a different plan, left Castrovillole with all his troops shortly before nightfall, and leaving the direct road, took the long way around through it was much farther and more difficult as they had to cross some mountains. When he reached the river, he sent the infantry toward the bridge between the castle of Laino and the town, which because of their feeling of security was not well guarded. Gonzalo himself with the cavalry forded the river two miles upstream, reached the town before daylight and, catching the enemy without lookouts and guards, he defeated them in an instant, capturing eleven barons and nearly all the troops, because as they fled toward the castle they met the infantry which had already occupied the bridge. From this honorable achievement which was the first of Gonzalo's victories in the Kingdom of Naples, he went with 6,000 men to join the siege around Atella, having first recaptured some other parts of Calabria and strengthened his forces. A few days before there had arrived at Atella 100 men-at-arms of the Duke of Candia, an officer of the league, though he himself had remained with the rest of his company around Rome.

With the arrival of Gonzalo the siege was intensified, Atella being surrounded on three sides. On one were the Aragonese, on another the Venetians and on the third the Spanish; so that supplies were prevented from arriving, particularly as the Venetians' *stradiotti* ranged the country and captured many of the French bringing in provisions from Venosa. Those within the town could no longer go out to forage except at odd times and with a large escort. And in the end they were entirely prevented from doing so because when Paolo Vitelli went out at midday with 100 men-at-arms he fell into an

ambush laid by the Marquis of Mantua and lost some
of them. Thus having lost all their facilities, they were
in the end reduced to such straits that even with an escort they could not water their horses at the river; and
within the encampment there was not enough water for
the men. So overcome by all these difficulties and devoid
of all hope, when they had withstood the siege 32 days
they were forced to surrender; and after asking for a
safe-conduct they sent Percy, Bartolomeo d'Alviano, and
one of the Swiss captains to parley with Ferrando. These
conditions were then agreed: a truce was to be observed
for 30 days, during which time none of the besieged
were to leave Atella; they would receive rations daily
from the Aragonese. Montpensier was to be allowed to
inform his King of the agreement and if he received no
relief within 30 days he would abandon Atella and all
other places he held in the Kingdom of Naples with all
the artillery he had in them; the persons and possessions
of the soldiers to go free and all of them should be permitted to return to France by land or sea. The Orsini
and other Italian officers could go anywhere they liked
outside the kingdom. The barons and others who had
followed the cause of the King of France would be freed
of all penalty and restored to the possessions they held
at the beginning of the war, provided they went over
to Ferrando within 15 days.

When the term was up, Montpensier with all the
French and many Swiss and the Orsini were escorted
to Castello a Mare di Stabbia. There was some dispute as
to whether Montpensier, as the King's lieutenant general
and senior officer of all, was obliged to have returned, as
Ferrando insisted, everything which was held in the
name of the King of France in the Kingdom of Naples.
Montpensier claimed that he was obliged to give only
what was actually in his power to restore, and that his
authority did not extend over the captains and wardens
of castles in Calabria, the Abruzzi, Gaeta, and many other
places and fortresses, who had received them in charge
from the King and not from himself. After they had disputed over this for some days, they were escorted to
Baia where Ferrando pretended that he meant to let

them go. He kept them there so long, spread out between Baia and Pozzuolo, under the pretext that the ships in which they were to embark were not yet ready, that because of the bad air and many hardships they began to fall ill. Montpensier himself died along with so many of his 5,000 men that barely 500 returned safely to France. Virginio and Paolo Orsini, at the request of the Pope who planned to seize that family's estates, were shut up in Castello dell' Uovo, and their troops led by Giangiordano, Virginio's son, and Bartolomeo d'Alviano were, by the Pope's orders, plundered and stripped in the Abruzzi by the Duke of Urbino. Giangiordano and Alviano, who had earlier come back to Naples on Ferrando's orders, leaving their troops on the way, were thrown into prison. However, Alviano was able to escape either through his own cunning or with the secret consent of Ferrando, who had once been very fond of him.

After the victory at Atella, Ferrando divided the army into several parts to recapture the rest of the kingdom. He sent Don Federigo and Prospero Colonna to besiege Gaeta and Fabrizio Colonna to the Abruzzi where Aquila had already gone over to the Aragonese. He himself captured the fort of San Severino and had the warden and his son beheaded as an example to terrify the rest. Then he went on to besiege Salerno. There the Prince of Bisignano came to parley with him and reached an agreement on behalf of himself, the Prince of Salerno, the Count of Capaccio, and some other barons, that they might continue to hold their estates; but Ferrando, for his security, would hold the fortresses for a certain period. After this agreement was made they went to Naples. Not much opposition was put up in the Abruzzi, as Graziano di Guerra who was there with 800 cavalry was unable to defend himself and withdrew to Gaeta. Gonzalo went back to Calabria which was largely held for the French. Although Aubigny made some show of resistance, he retired in the end to Groppoli; and after losing Manfredonia and Cosenza, which was sacked by the French on leaving, all hope was gone and he agreed to leave all Calabria and was allowed to return by land to France. There is no doubt that many of these events re-

sulted from the negligence and imprudence of the
French: Manfredonia, though a strong town in a rich
area where it was easy to get plenty of supplies, and
though governed on the King's behalf by Gabriello da
Montefalcone whom he regarded as a brave man, was
starved into surrender after a brief siege. Others who
could have defended themselves surrendered out of cowardice or unwillingness to bear the hardships of a siege.
Some wardens whose castles had been well supplied had
sold their provisions early so that when the enemy appeared they had to surrender at once. As a result the
French lost in the Kingdom of Naples the reputation
gained for them by the courage of the man who, left by
Jean d'Anjou to guard Castello dell' Uovo, held it for
many years after Ferrando's victory, until having used
up all his provisions he was forced to surrender.

Practically the only places still to be recaptured in the
whole realm were Taranto and Gaeta and some places
held by Carlo de Sanguine, and the Monte di Sant' Angelo from which Don Giuliano of Lorraine harassed the
surrounding villages with great success. Ferrando at the
height of his glory and with hopes of rivaling the greatness of his forefathers, had gone to Somma, a place at
the foot of Mt. Vesuvius, where his wife the Queen was.
And there, either because of his recent exertions or some
new disease, he fell so gravely ill that he was taken to
Naples with little hope of recovery, and died there within
a few days, less than a year after the death of Alfonso
his father. He left behind him, not only throughout his
own kingdom, but in the whole of Italy, the highest respect for his courage and ability, because of the victory
he had won, the nobility of his mind and the royal
virtues which shone out in him. He died childless and
was succeeded by his uncle Don Federigo, the fifth king
that realm had known in three years. Don Federigo came
at once from the siege of Gaeta and the old queen his
stepmother handed over Castelnuovo to him, though
many suspected that she might wish to keep it for her
brother Ferdinand King of Spain. At this time Federigo
received the good will not only of the people of Naples

but also of the Princes of Salerno and Bisignano and the Count of Capaccio, who were the first to proclaim him in Naples; and when he landed they were the first to go to meet him and hail him as king. They liked him much better than the dead king because of his gentle nature and because they had begun to fear that Ferrando intended, once firmly established, to punish all those who in any way had shown themselves supporters of the French. To win them over completely Federigo freely restored all their fortresses.

Yet all these shameful disasters did not rouse the King of France or hasten his preparations. He could not drag himself away from his pleasures and delayed four months before returning to Lyons. Although during this time he frequently urged those who had stayed behind in Lyons to press on with the preparations by land and sea, and although the Duke of Orléans had made ready to leave, owing to the usual tactics of the Cardinal of St. Malo the army was late in being paid and was moving slowly toward Italy. The fleet which was to be collected at Marseilles was being organized in so leisurely a fashion that the league had time to send first to Villefranche, a large port near Nice and then as far as the Ile Pomègues off Marseilles, a fleet got together at joint expense at Genoa to prevent French ships leaving for Naples. It was believed that in addition to the delays caused primarily by the Cardinal of St. Malo, there must be some other hidden factor nourished with diligence and cunning in the King's mind by those who for a variety of reasons sought to dissuade him from an Italian expedition. It was suspected that he himself might be jealous of the aggrandizement of the Duke of Orléans who stood to gain the Duchy of Milan in the event of victory; and furthermore he felt it was not safe to leave France without first making some agreement with the King and Queen of Spain, who had shown some desire to be reconciled with him and had sent ambassadors to propose a truce and other means of concord. Many also advised him to wait until the Queen gave birth as she was soon to do, for it was not prudent, they said, or fitting to the love he should bear his people to expose himself to such grave dangers without first having a son to succeed him. This argument became all the more powerful when the Queen was brought to bed of a son who died within a few days. Thus partly by the King's carelessness and lack of judgment and partly by the difficulties cunningly interposed by others, his preparations were so long delayed that his army was destroyed and the Kingdom of Naples entirely lost. And the same thing would have happened to his allies in Italy if they had not themselves constantly defended their own interests.

Chapter VIII

[*Lodovico Sforza's conversations and agreement with Maximilian. Maximilian in Italy. The loyalty of the Florentines to the French and Savonarola's political advice. Death of Piero Capponi. More help from the Venetians to Pisa, and the Pisans' diminished faith in Lodovico Sforza.*]

We said above that, fearing the preparations of the French, negotiations had been begun—more to please Lodovico Sforza than the Venetians—to have Maximilian enter Italy. While these fears lasted it was agreed that the Venetians and Lodovico would give him 20,000 ducats a month for three months to bring with him a certain number of cavalry and infantry. When this pact was made, Lodovico, accompanied by the envoys of the league, went to Manzo—a place beyond the Alps on the frontiers of Germany—to have talks with the Emperor. When they had talked there at length, Lodovico returned the same day to Bormio, on this side of the Alps, a town belonging to the Duchy of Milan. The following day Maximilian, with the pretext that he was out hunting, also went to Bornio. In these two days of discussion Maximilian agreed on the time and manner of his invasion, and then returned to Germany to hasten his preparations. However, in the meantime French preparations seemed to have slackened off and Maximilian's invasion appeared no longer necessary; so Lodovico planned to use for his own ambitions what he had first arranged for his own security. He went on urging him to come, and as the Venetians would not agree to join in promising Maximilian 30,000 ducats which he was demanding in addition to the first 60,000 he had been promised, he undertook to satisfy this demand himself; and in the end Maximilian did enter Italy just before the death of Ferrando. He heard this news when quite near Milan and had some idea of favoring the succession to the Kingdom of Naples of his son-in-law Juan, the only son of the King of Spain. But when Lodovico persuaded him that this would be unwelcome to the whole of Italy and would split the allies and in consequence further the designs of the King of France, he not only gave up this project but wrote letters in support of the succession of Federigo.

He entered Italy with very few troops and said he would soon bring in all those he had contracted for. He stopped at Vigevano and there in the presence of Lodovico and the Cardinal of Santa Croce, who had been sent to him as the Pope's legate, and the other envoys of the league, it was decided that he would go into Piedmont to take Asti and cut off from the King of France the Duke of Savoy and the Marquis of Monferrato. He requested the latter to meet him at some place in Piedmont, as they were dependent states of the Empire; but as his forces were negligible and the authority of the imperial name was not supported by effective power, neither of them would agree to meet him and there was little hope of his attempt on Asti being successful. He also demanded that the Duke of Ferrara, who held the cities of Modena and Reggio as vassal of the Empire, should come and meet him, offering as security the word of his son-in-law Lodovico. But the Duke refused to go, saying it would be dishonorable, as he still held the castle of Genoa as a pledge. Lodovico, therefore, still greedy for Pisa and displeased that the city he wanted so badly had fallen into the hands of the Venetians to the peril of all Italy, wished above all to prevent this happening. He urged Maximilian to go there, and believed by a process of false argument that the Florentines, powerless to resist him and the forces of the league, would be obliged to give up their alliance with the French and would not be able to refuse to allow Maximilian to arbitrate in their differences with the Pisans, if not by negotiating agreement, at least by giving a legal decision; and he thought that Pisa and all its country districts would be placed in the Emperor's hands. Lodovico hoped by his own authority to get the Pisans to agree to this proposal, and that the Venetians, if all the other allies agreed, would not object to a solution which in itself appeared reasonable and to everyone's benefit. As Pisa had formerly belonged to the Empire, it seemed that only Maximilian should decide on the rights of those claiming it; and once Pisa was placed in Maximilian's hands, Lodovico hoped through his money and influence with Maximilian that he would easily get it from him.

This plan, which was put forward in the council under the pretext that, as the fear of war with the French had now lessened, Maximilian's expedition should be used to persuade the Florentines to join the other confederates against the King of France, appealed to Maximilian who was displeased that his coming to Italy should be quite without result; and as he always needed money because of his vast ambitions and also because of his lack of organization and excessive prodigality, he hoped that Pisa might be the means of acquiring a great quantity either from the Florentines or from others. It was likewise approved by the other allies as a very useful plan for the safety of Italy. Even the Venetian envoy did not oppose it, because though the senate could see very well where Lodovico's plans were tending, they felt sure they would easily be able to block them, and hoped that if Maximilian went there he might acquire the port of Leghorn for the Pisans, which would probably deprive the Florentines of all hope of ever regaining Pisa.

Earlier the allies had often pressed the Florentines to join them. And during the period when they were most afraid of the French invasion they had held out hopes of undertaking to secure the return of Pisa to their rule. But as the Florentines distrusted the acquisitiveness of the Venetians and Lodovico, and would not lightly decide to give up their alliance with the King of France, they had not listened very willingly to these offers. Further they hoped by the King's return to regain Pietrasanta and Sarzana which they could not hope to obtain from the allies. Moreover they believed his victory would bring them not only Pisa but nearly all the rest of Tuscany, though this belief was based more on a sense of their own desires and what they had suffered on the King's account than on appreciation of his nature or habits.

They were encouraged in these hopes by Girolamo Savonarola who constantly predicted great good fortune and increase of power which would come to the Republic after many tribulations, together with great disasters to the court of Rome and the other rulers of Italy. Though many opposed him, the majority of the people believed devoutly in him; and many of the principal citizens supported him, some out of piety, some from ambition and others out of fear. Thus, as the Florentines were inclined to continue in alliance with the King of France, it did not seem unreasonable for the allies to try to force them to do what they would not do willingly. It was thought a simple matter, as the Florentines were hated by all their neighbors and they could not expect any help from the King of France, for as he had abandoned his own people in Naples it was likely he would forget the welfare of foreigners. Moreover the heavy expenses they had incurred during the last three years together with the fall in their revenues had so exhausted them that it was believed they could not stand up to prolonged hardships.

In this year too the Florentines had carried on their war with the Pisans. There had been various incidents notable more for the military skill shown by both sides in many operations and for the determination with which things were done, than for the size of the armies or the importance of the places for which they fought, which were insignificant castles of little importance in themselves. The Florentine army had taken the castle of

Buti shortly after the citadel was handed over to the Pisans and before they received Venetian aid. They had then besieged Calci and before they took it, to make sure of their supplies, they started to build a bastion on the Monte della Dolorosa, but their troops on guard there were attacked and beaten by the Pisans through their own negligence. A short while after Francesco Secco was stationed at Buti with a large body of horse troops to protect the supply line to Ercole Bentivoglio—who with the Florentine infantry was surrounding the small fortress on the Monte della Verrucola—when he was suddenly attacked by troops sent out from Pisa. And being in a position where it was difficult to use the horses, he lost a good number of them. Because of these events the Pisans seemed to be more successful, and they had hopes of even better things as Venetian aid had already begun to reach them. When Ercole Bentivoglio, who was stationed in the castle of Bientina, heard that Giampaolo Manfrone, a captain of the Venetians, had reached Vico Pisano two miles from Bientina with the first detachment of their troops, he pretended to be alarmed, making sorties into the country and withdrawing into the castle when the Venetians appeared. Then when he saw that Manfrone had become over bold and incautious, he one day cunningly led him into an ambush where he defeated·him with the loss of most of his infantry and cavalry and pursued him as far as the walls of Vico Pisano. However, that victory was not unmixed, for as they withdrew, Francesco Secco, who had joined Ercole that morning, was killed by a shot from an arquebus. Then the rest of the Venetian troops arrived with 800 *stradiotti* and Giustiniano Morosino as commissioner.

As the Pisans were then more numerous, Ercole Bentivoglio, who knew the country extremely well and did not want to endanger himself or abandon the area entirely, took up a very strong position between the castle of Pontadera and the River Era; and from this well chosen situation he was able to curtail the enemy's effectiveness a good deal. In all this time they only took the castle of Buti, which surrendered unconditionally; and they spent their time raiding the countryside with their *stradiotti*, 300 of which had ridden into Val d'Era and been routed by troops sent after them by Ercole Bentivoglio. At the same time the Florentines were attacked by the Sienese, who taking advantage of their difficulties in the Pisan area and urged on by the league, sent the Lord of Piombino and Giovanni Savello to besiege the bastion at Ponte a Valiano. However, when they heard help was coming under Renuccio da Marciano, they withdrew in disorder leaving behind part of their artillery. Thus things were made safe on that side and the Florentines sent Renuccio with his troops toward Pisa; so that, with the forces about equal on both sides, the fighting centered on the hill castles. As these were on the side of the Pisans, events went rather against the Florentines. The Pisans, who had entered the castle of Ponte di Sacco by secret negotiation, stripped a company of men-at-arms and took Lodovico da Marciano prisoner—though from fear of the Florentine troops in the vicinity they at once abandoned the place. The better to hold the hills, which were of the greatest importance for the supplies to Pisa, and because they cut off Florentine trade through the port of Leghorn, they fortified most of these castles. One of them, Soiano, became famous for an untoward incident which took place there.

The Florentines went to besiege it, expecting to capture it the same day. To this end they had destroyed all the crossings of the River Cascina and had drawn up their men in battle order on the bank to prevent the enemy relieving the place. Then while Piero Capponi the Florentine commissioner was attending to setting the artillery in position, he was shot in the head by one of the arquebuses in the castle and instantly killed. This was an end unworthy of a man of his quality, because of the insignificance of the place and the small importance of the enterprise. Therefore the siege was raised without further action—particularly as the Florentines were at this time obliged to send troops into Lunigiana to relieve the fort of Verrucola, which was attacked by the Malaspini with the assistance of the Genoese. They easily drove them off.

For some months the Pisan forces had been strong, because in addition to the men of the city and the surrounding country who had grown warlike from long habit, the Venetians and the Duke of Milan had large numbers of cavalry and infantry there; though the Venetians had by far the most. Then the Duke's men began to diminish because they had not received all their pay; and so the Venetians sent another 100 men-at-arms and six light galleys with supplies of corn, avoiding no expense necessary for the defense of the city and likely to win them the friendship of the Pisans. These were daily weaned away from their affection for the Duke of Milan, displeased both with his thrift in spending money to help them and with his changeable attitude: for sometimes he showed himself keenly interested in their affairs and sometimes he acted coldly toward them. Distrusting his intentions, they went so far as to attribute to him the fact that Bentivoglio had not moved against the Florentines as the league had requested—particularly as they knew he had failed to provide most of his share of the payments to him, either out of avarice or because he wished the Florentines to be harassed but not completely crushed. By these actions he had himself brought about in the affairs of Pisa conditions quite opposite to his own intentions and to the aims which had caused him to propose in the council of the league that Maximilian should go to Pisa.

Chapter IX

[*Maximilian asks the Florentines to refer their quarrel with Pisa to him. The Venetians send fresh troops to Pisa. The Florentines reply to Maximilian. The Florentine envoys talk with the Duke of Milan.*]

When this had been decided, Maximilian sent two ambassadors to Florence to inform them that he had judged it necessary, for the powerful expedition he was planning against the infidel, to enter Italy to pacify and settle her affairs. On this account he sought a declaration from the Florentines that they stood with the other allies for the defense of Italy; and if they disagreed with this, they were to make clear their position. He wished for the same reason and because it concerned his imperial authority, to be apprised of their differences with the Pisans. He therefore desired that until he had heard both sides state their cause, all hostilities should cease. The Pisans, he was sure, would agree to this, as he had already sent them the same orders. He stated in friendly terms that he was ready to administer justice impartially. To this communication the Florentines replied, with words of respectful approval for his proposal and showing that they had the greatest faith in his kindness, that they would soon be sending ambassadors to him to explain their position in detail.

Now, however, the Venetians, to prevent Maximilian or the Duke of Milan from occupying Pisa, sent their captain Annibale Bentivoglio and 150 men-at-arms there with the Pisans' consent, and soon after some more *stradiotti* and 1,000 foot soldiers. They told the Duke they had sent them because their Republic which loved free cities, wanted to help the Pisans recover their country districts; and indeed with the help of these troops the Pisans were finally able to regain almost all the hill castles. Because of this assistance and the prompt satisfaction of all their requests which were many, now for troops, now for money and now for food and munitions, the Pisans had drawn so close to the Venetians that they had transferred to them all the friendship and confidence they used to have for the Duke of Milan. They desired above all things that the senate go on protecting them. Nevertheless they welcomed the coming of Maximilian, hoping, with the troops who were in Pisa and those Maximilian would bring with him, that they might easily acquire Leghorn.

On the other hand the Florentines who, besides their other troubles were at that time suffering from a serious shortage of supplies, were very much afraid at finding themselves alone in resisting the power of so many princes. They had no one to help them in Italy and let-

ters from their envoys in France informed them that they
could expect no assistance from the King whom they
had most strongly urged to help them—at least with a
certain sum of money. The only threat which vanished
was that of Piero de' Medici, as the league decided not
to use his name and influence in this enterprise, experience having shown that under that threat the Florentines closed their ranks for the preservation of their freedom. Lodovico Sforza, pretending to be eager for their
well-being and displeased at the increased power of the
Venetians, ceaselessly urged them to rely on Maximilian,
pointing out the many dangers and disasters. He said
there was no other way of getting the Venetians out of
Pisa: for when they were out, the Florentines would at
once have Pisa restored to them, and this was essential
for the peace of Italy and for this reason was desired
by the King of Spain and all the other allies. However
the Florentines were not moved by these empty and in-
sidious flatteries nor alarmed by their many difficulties
and dangers. They decided to make no declaration to
Maximilian and not to submit their claims to his judgment unless Pisa were first restored to their possession.
They had no confidence in his intentions or in his
authority, as it was well known that, having neither
troops nor money of his own, he did just what the Duke
of Milan wanted; and there appeared to be no inclination or need on the part of the Venetians to leave Pisa.
Therefore they courageously proceeded to provision and
fortify Leghorn as far as they could, and gather together all their forces in the territory around Pisa. Yet
in order not to seem unwilling for an agreement, and
in an effort to conciliate Maximilian, they sent him ambassadors on his arrival in Genoa to reply to the communication made by his envoys in Florence.

They were instructed to persuade him that no declaration on their part was necessary, because owing to their
reverence for his name he could expect from the Republic whatever he desired. They were to remind him that
nothing could be more essential to his most pious proposal to pacify Italy than the immediate restitution of
Pisa to the Florentines, as this was the root cause of all

their actions which he and the league objected to, and because Pisa was the reason why others aspired to the domination of Italy and so tried to keep the country in perpetual turmoil. These words were aimed at the Venetians though they were not named directly. It was not, they said, in accord with his justice that those who had been violently despoiled should, contrary to the disposition of imperial law, be obliged to state their case until their possessions were restored to them. Finally they said that if he began in this way, the Florentine Republic would have no further cause to desire anything but peace with everyone and would make any declaration which he considered appropriate; and trusting completely in his justice they would promptly refer to him the recognition of their claims.

This answer did not satisfy Maximilian who desired before all else that they should join the league; and though he gave them his word that Pisa would be restored within a reasonable time, they had no other reply from him after much discussion, except that when he was about to sail he told them on the pier at Genoa that they would learn his intentions from the papal legate in Genoa. The legate in turn referred them to the Duke who had returned to Milan from Tortona where he had accompanied Maximilian; and so the ambassadors went there. They had already requested an audience when instructions reached them from Florence, where the progress of their mission had become known, to return home at once without seeking any further reply. Therefore, when they came into the Duke's presence at the appointed hour, they changed their request for a reply into a statement that, as they were on their way home to Florence, they had not failed to make a detour to pay their respects before leaving his state, as befitted the friendship between him and their Republic.

The Duke, who supposed that they were going to ask him for a reply, had summoned all the envoys of the league and all his own council, in order to show off (as he often did) his eloquence and guile and take pleasure in other people's discomfit. However, taken aback, amazed by their statement and unable to hide his displeasure, he asked them what reply they had received from Maximilian. They answered that according to the laws of their Republic they might not discuss their mission with any other prince than the one to whom they were sent as ambassadors: to which he replied with some loss of composure: "So if we give you the answer we know Maximilian referred you to us for, will you refuse to hear it?" They said that they were not forbidden to listen and could not prevent others from speaking. He rejoined: "We shall be pleased to give you the reply, but this cannot be done unless you explain to us what you explained to him." The envoys said that they could not do that for the reasons already stated, and that it would be superfluous in any case, as Maximilian must have communicated their proposal to those whom he had commissioned to reply in his name. Then Sforza, unable to conceal his irritation in word or gesture, dismissed the envoys and all those he had called together, having been made to look ridiculous when he had wished the ridicule to fall on others.

Chapter X

[*Successful landing of grain at Leghorn for the Florentines. Failure of Maximilian's attempt to seize Leghorn. Maximilian with great loss of imperial prestige abandons Tuscany and Italy and returns to Germany. Lodovico Sforza withdraws his troops from Pisa.*]

Meanwhile Maximilian had left the port of Genoa with six galleys that the Venetians kept off Pisa and with a large number of Genoese ships carrying plenty of artillery but few fighting men, as there were only 1,000 German infantry on board. He sailed as far as La Spezia and then went on to Pisa by land. There he picked up 500 horse troops and another 1,000 German infantry who had traveled by land, and he decided to go with these troops and those of the Duke of Milan and part of the Venetian force to lay siege to Leghorn and attack

337

it by land and sea, while the other Venetian troops were to go to Ponte di Sacco so that the Florentine army, which was not very strong, could neither attack the Pisans nor bring help to Leghorn. But no attack alarmed the Florentines less than an attempt on Leghorn, which was well supplied with troops and artillery and where they were expecting help to arrive from Provence any day. Not long before, to strengthen their own forces with the reputation which French arms enjoyed at that time in Italy, they had commissioned, with the agreement of the King of France, M. d'Albigion, one of his captains, with 100 lances and 1,000 Swiss and Gascon infantry; and they were to come by sea to Leghorn in certain ships which the Florentines had ordered to be loaded with grain to relieve the scarcity which afflicted the whole Florentine dominion. This provision had been made with other thoughts and aims in mind than that of defending themselves against Maximilian, and though it encountered many difficulties—because Albigion refused to embark when brought to the ships with his company and only 600 of the infantry went on board—they were so favored by fortune that no better or more opportune provision could have been desired.

The very day that a Pisan commissioner appeared at Leghorn—sent ahead by Maximilian with many foot soldiers and horse troops to make bridges and level the roads for the army which was to follow—the fleet from Provence of five ships and several galleons, accompanied by a great Norman ship which the King was sending to refurnish Gaeta with supplies and men, was sighted off Leghorn. It enjoyed such favorable winds that Maximilian's fleet was unable to attack them and was forced by the weather to go out beyond Meloria (a famous reef, because it was near there that the Pisan forces were completely routed by the Genoese in a naval encounter). So the French ships were able to enter port unharmed, except that one galleon laden with grain, which had become separated from the rest of the fleet, was taken by the enemy. This timely relief gave great encouragement to those who were in Leghorn, and also to the Florentines who felt that its having arrived so opportunely was a sign that where human assistance failed them, God would come to their aid—which was what Savonarola had often said in his sermons to the people in those days when others were sorely afraid.

However, the King of the Romans still went on with his siege of Leghorn. He sent by land 500 men-at-arms and 1,000 light horse and 4,000 foot soldiers, while he came with the galleys up to the mouth of the Stagno which is between Pisa and Leghorn. He assigned the attack on one side to the Count of Gaiazzo, who had been sent with him by the Duke of Milan, and took up his own position on the other, although it was difficult to settle in on the first day because of the artillery fire from Leghorn. He then began to attack Magnano with his cannon, wishing to take the port first, and brought up his troops before dawn from Fontana. Magnano had been fortified by those within; and when they saw the siege laid on that side, they dismantled the Palazzotto and the tower by the sea, believing it to be indefensible and liable to lead to the loss of the new tower. At the same time, in order to be able to bombard from the sea, Maximilian had his fleet brought up to the port, as the French ships, although begged to stay, had returned to Provence after disembarking their troops and unloading part of the grain, and the Norman ship had gone on to Gaeta. The siege of Magnano, undertaken in order to be able to attack Leghorn by sea, was not successful. Leghorn was fortified in such a way that the artillery could make little impression on it, and those within often came out to skirmish. However it was fated that the hopes first raised by the favorable winds would also be fulfilled by the winds. A great storm blew up and threw the fleet into such confusion that the Grimaldi ship in which Maximilian had traveled was battered for a long time by the gales and wrecked in front of the new fort at Leghorn with all the men and guns on board; two Venetian galleys were also wrecked on the point near San Jacopo. The other ships were widely dispersed and suffered so much damage that they were rendered useless for the present campaign. Because of this misfortune those inside Leghorn were able to recapture the galleon which had earlier fallen into the hands of the enemy.

After the wrecking of the fleet Maximilian returned to Pisa, and there, after much discussion, all agreed that they could not now take Leghorn. It was decided to raise the siege and wage the war elsewhere. So Maximilian went to Vico Pisano and had a bridge built over the Arno between Cascina and Vico and another over the Cilecchio. Then just when they thought he would cross, he suddenly departed and returned overland to Milan without having made any progress in Tuscany except the sacking by 400 of his cavalry of Borgheri, an insignificant castle in the Pisan Maremma. His excuse for this sudden departure was that his difficulties were constantly increasing, that his frequent demands for money were not met, that the Venetian commissioners would not allow most of their troops out of Pisa any more because they distrusted him, and that the Venetians had not paid him the whole of their share of the 60,000 ducats. So, though praising the Duke of Milan, he made serious complaints against the Venetians.

At Pavia where he moved to, there were new consultations; and though he let it be known that he wished to return to Germany, he agreed to stay in Italy all winter with 1,000 horse troops and 2,000 foot soldiers on condition he were paid 20,000 Rhenish florins a month. While waiting for an answer from Venice, he went to Lomellina when he was expected in Milan—it was his fate, as later events showed, never to enter this city. Then he changed his mind and returned from Lomellina to Cusago six miles from Milan; and then unexpectedly to Como without the knowledge of the Duke and the ambassadors who were in Milan. There he heard while dining that the papal legate, to whom he had sent word not to follow him, had just arrived. He rose from table and went to embark with such haste that the legate was able only to speak a few words with him at the boat. He told him he was obliged to go to Germany but would soon be back. However, when he reached Bellagio on Lake Como, he heard that the Venetians had agreed to the arrangements made at Pavia, and he again held out hopes that he would return to Milan; but a very few days later, behaving with his characteristic instability, he went off to Germany, leaving behind part of his cavalry and infantry. He had succeeded, with little glory to imperial prestige, in displaying his weakness to all Italy where emperors in arms had not been seen for a very long time.

Because of his departure Lodovico Sforza, now despairing of ever taking Pisa for himself or wresting it from the Venetians—short of some unforeseen event—removed all his troops from that city. He was partly consoled for his disappointment by the fact that only the Venetians were now embroiled in the war with the Florentines; and he believed that in time the exhaustion of both sides might offer him some opportunity. At the departure of his force the Florentines became more powerful in the country districts than the enemy, and captured all the hill castles; and so the Venetians, obliged to make further provision in order to impede their progress, raised their existing force in Pisa to a total of 400 men-at-arms, 700 light horse and more than 2,000 foot soldiers.

Chapter XI

[*Taranto surrenders to the Venetians. The King of France plans to seize Genoa. The Pope declares the Orsini lands confiscated. War with the Orsini and the treaty ending it. Taking of Ostia. Gonzalo received in triumph in Rome and by the Pope.*]

In the meantime almost all the remains of the war with the French in the Kingdom of Naples had been cleared up. The city of Taranto with its fortresses, worn out by famine, surrendered to the Venetians who had besieged it with their fleet. They held the city for some days, giving rise to suspicion that they wanted to keep it for themselves, and finally restored it to Federigo when pressed to do so by the Pope and the King of some difficulties which had arisen over the delivery of Spain It was learned at Gaeta that the Norman ship had been engaged by some Genoese ships above Porto Ercole; and then continuing on her way, had been wrecked in a storm at sea. So the French in that city, which was again being besieged by the new King, though it was rumored that they had supplies to last them for some months, decided that in the end their King would not be in any more hurry to rescue them than he had been to rescue many of his nobles and the towns held in his name. They agreed therefore with Federigo through Aubigny—who had not yet left Naples because of the forts in Calabria—to abandon the town and fortress of Gaeta on condition they were allowed to return safely to France by sea with all their baggage.

As a result of this agreement the King of France was relieved of the necessity of rescuing the kingdom. On the other hand, stung by his losses and by humiliation, he decided to attack Genoa, founding his hopes on the party of Batistino Fregoso, formerly doge of that city, and on the following of the Cardinal of San Piero in Vincoli in his native Savona and other places on the coast. It also seemed a favorable moment as Gianluigi dal Fiesco and the Adorni were then at odds with one another and all the Genoese were dissatisfied with the Duke of Milan because he was responsible for the Luccans being preferred to them in the sale of Pietrasanta; and because, having later promised that they should have it back, and having used the authority of the Venetians to pacify them, he had vainly gone on feeding them for months and months. Fear that the King might intervene in Genoa forced Lodovico, who was almost estranged from the Venetians over Pisa, to renew their alliance and send to Genoa the German horse and foot soldiers which Maximilian had left behind in Italy. Indeed if this emergency had not arisen, no arrangements whatever would have been made for these troops.

While these affairs were going forward, the Pope believed he had a good opportunity to occupy the states of the Orsini while the heads of the family were being held at Naples; and in the consistory he declared Virginio and the others to be rebels and confiscated their states for having taken service with the King of France against his orders. Having done this, he attacked their lands at the beginning of 1497 and ordered the Colonna to do likewise where their states bordered on those of the Orsini. This action was supported by Cardinal Ascanio because of his old friendship with the Colonna and quarrels with the Orsini, and was agreed to by the Duke of Milan. But it did not please the Venetians who wished to gain the friendship of the Orsini; yet, as they had no excuse for preventing the Pope from pursuing his course —and it would be a mistake to make an enemy of him at this moment—they agreed that the Duke of Urbino, the allies' commander, should join up with the forces of the Church, which had the Duke of Gandia as captain-general and as papal legate the Cardinal di Luna, who came from Pavia and was entirely dependent on Ascanio. King Federigo also sent Fabrizio Colonna to help him. This army forced the surrender of Campagnano and Anguillara and many other castles, and laid siege to Trivignano, which defended itself bravely for a few days before surrendering unconditionally. During this time Bartolomeo d'Alviano came out from Bracciano and defeated, eight miles from Rome, 400 horse troops escorting artillery to the Pope's army. Another day, having ridden as far as Croce a Montemari, he nearly captured the Cardinal of Valencia, who had come out from Rome to hunt, and fled to safety. After taking Trivignano the army moved on to Isola, which they obtained by treaty after bombarding part of the fortress. Finally all the fighting was concentrated around Bracciano, which held all the Orsini hopes of defense—as the place was already strong and had been well prepared and supplied, and the borgo fortified with a bastion built in front of it; while inside there were plenty of defenders under the leadership of Alviano. He was young but of ferocious character and incredible swiftness, experienced in arms and full of the promise which was fully borne out in his later actions. The Pope was increasing his army all the time and had recently added 800 German infantry from the fighting in the Kingdom of Naples. The battle went on for many days with great determination on both sides. Those outside had positioned artillery all around, while those within repaired their defenses with great energy and courage. However, after a few days they were forced to abandon the borgo. Once that was taken, the papal forces launched a violent attack on the town; but though they managed to plant their standards on the walls, they were forced to retire with heavy losses; and in this battle Antonio Savelli was wounded. The defenders showed the same courage in another attack, again repulsing the enemy with even greater losses—more than 200 being killed or wounded. Alviano earned great praise, as the glory of this defense was largely attributed to him. Within he was swift to deal with all necessities, and without he kept the enemy army in almost continual alarm day and night. His reputation was further increased when, having ordered a body of light horse to ride out from Cervetri, which was held for the Orsini, and up to the besiegers' camp, he took advantage of this disturbance to make a sortie and put to flight the troops guarding the artillery, of which he brought a few small pieces into Bracciano. Yet, bombarded and assailed day and night, they were beginning to hold out mainly on their hopes of being relieved.

Carlo Orsini and Vitellozzo, who was linked by the Guelph faction to the Orsini, had received money from the King of France to reorganize their companies which had been dispersed in the Kingdom of Naples. They had returned to Italy by sea in the ship sailing from Provence to Leghorn and were preparing to come to the relief of Bracciano. Carlo went to Soriano, where he was collecting former soldiers, friends and partisans of the Orsini. Vitellozzo was doing the same at Città di Castello with his own troops and local recruits; and when he had got together 200 men-at-arms and 1,800 of his infantry, with some artillery carried on wagons in French style, he joined Carlo at Soriano. Because of this the papal captains thought it might be dangerous if they came any nearer to be caught between them and the force in Bracciano; and so as not to have to abandon all the country around, in which they had already sacked some castles, they raised the siege of Bracciano, withdrew the heavy artillery into Anguillara and went to meet the enemy. They met between Soriano and Bassano, and fought fiercely for several hours. Although at the beginning of the fighting Franciotto Orsini was captured by the Colonna, in the end the papal troops were put to flight, their wagons and artillery taken and more than 500 of their men killed or taken prisoner. Among the prisoners were the Duke of Urbino, Giampiero da Gonzaga, Conte di Nugolara and many other nobles. The Duke of Candia was slightly wounded in the face; and with him the apostolic legate and Fabrizio Colonna fled to Ronciglione. The main credit for this victory was due to Vitellozzo because the infantry from Città di Castello, which had formerly been trained by him and his brothers after the ultramontane fashion, was greatly assisted on this day by his efforts. He had armed them with lances an arm's length longer than those in normal use, and they had the advantage when he led them to fight the enemy infantry that, being able to strike without being hit themselves, they easily put them to flight. The honor of this encounter was all the greater because the opposing force had 800 German infantry; and since the invasion of King Charles the Italian infantry had always been terrified of the Germans.

After this battle the victors began to range unhindered over all the territory on this side of the Tiber and then put a part of their troops across the river below Monte Ritondo; and so they were able to use the road which alone had been safe up to then. Because of these dangers the Pope recruited many more soldiers and recalled Gonzalo and Prospero Colonna from the Kingdom of Naples to assist him. Yet, a few days later, when the Venetian envoys intervened diligently on behalf of the Orsini, and the Spanish ambassador too out of fear that the present dissension might lead to greater troubles within the league, peace was made. The Pope was very ready to do so, as he was by nature averse to spending money, and so too were the Orsini; for being without money and abandoned by all, they knew they must in the end succumb to the power of the Pope. Briefly the terms of the pact were these: the Orsini were to be allowed to finish their contract in the service of the King of France, in which it was stated that they would not have to take arms against the Church. They were to have back all their territory lost in this war on payment to the Pope of 50,000 ducats, 30,000 as soon as Federigo freed Giangiordano and Paolo Orsini (as Virginio had died shortly before in Castel dell' Uovo either of fever or, as some believed, of poison), and the other 20,000 within eight months, during which time Aguillara and Cervetri were to be placed in the hands of Cardinals Ascanio and Sanseverino as a guarantee of payment. They were to free the prisoners taken at the battle of Soriano, except the Duke of Urbino. The Pope did not insist on his being freed, although the envoys of the league pressed his case, because he knew the Orsini had no way of getting the money they were agreeing to pay him except by the Duke's ransom. This was soon after agreed at 40,000 ducats; and it was stipulated that, as soon as he was freed, Paolo Vitelli, who had fallen into the hands of the Marquis of Mantua when Atella surrendered, would regain his freedom without paying anything.

Once the Pope had concluded his war against the Orsini without much honor, he gave money to the troops led by Gonzalo; and adding them to his own forces, he sent him to take Ostia which was still held for the Cardinal of San Piero in Vincoli. Hardly had the artillery been placed in position than the warden surrendered unconditionally to Gonzalo. After taking Ostia, Gonzalo entered Rome almost in triumph with 100 men-at-arms, 200 light horse and 1,500 foot soldiers—all Spanish—bringing the warden of Ostia with him as prisoner, though he freed him shortly after. He was met by a great number of prelates, the Pope's household and all the cardinals, all the people and the court crowding to see a captain whose name rang gloriously throughout Italy. He was then escorted to the Pope sitting in consistory. The latter received him with great honors, giving him the rose, which the Popes give each year, in recognition of his valor. He then went back to join Federigo, who had attacked the states of the Prefect of Rome and had recaptured all the territories which had been given to the Prefect by the King of France when they were taken from the Marquis of Pescara during his conquest of the kingdom. He took Sora and Arci, but not the forts, and was besieging Rocca Guglielma, having already taken by treaty the estates of the Conte d'Uliveto, who had been Duke of Sora before he sold his duchy to the Prefect. Nevertheless, amid all this good fortune Federigo had many troubles arising not only from his friends—for Gonzalo was holding part of Calabria in the name of the Spanish monarchs—but also from his reconciled enemies. For one evening, when leaving Castelnuovo in Naples, the Prince of Bisignano was gravely wounded by a certain Greek, and the Prince of Salerno was so terrified that this had been done on the King's orders in revenge for their past offenses, that he fled at once from Naples to Salerno without concealing the cause of his fears. The King, in order to justify himself, sent the Greek, who had been imprisoned, to the Prince, to say that he had wounded him because of an injury the Prince of Bisignano had caused him many years before in the person of his wife (which was perfectly true). Nevertheless, as in deep and long-standing enmity it is difficult to establish true reconciliation (because it is hampered by fear of or desire for revenge), the Prince could never bring himself to trust the King again. This gave the French hopes of further upheavals in the Kingdom of Naples; and as they still held the Monte di Sant' Angelo and a few other strongholds, it led them to persevere more constantly in their defense.

Chapter XII

[*Charles VIII negotiates a truce with the King of Spain and sends troops against Genoa and the Duchy of Milan, occupying some towns. Failure of the enterprise and probable reasons for its failure. Terms of the truce between the King of*

347

*France and the Spanish monarchs. The French
lose in Italy nearly all the towns recently occupied. The Florentines busy with the reconquest
of Pisa accept the truce unwillingly.*]

A situation of greater danger now arose in Lombardy
because of the movements of the French, freed for the
time being from the threat of the Spanish. There had
been minor incidents between them and shows of war
rather than anything of importance, except that the
French had rapidly taken and burnt the town of Salses;
and now the monarchs had begun negotiations for an
agreement. In order to facilitate this they had declared a
truce for two months. Charles was thus enabled to deal
more easily with the affairs of Genoa and Savona; and
having sent to Asti as many as 1,000 lances, 3,000 Swiss
and an equal number of Gascons, he charged Trivulzio,
his lieutenant in Italy, to go to the assistance of Batistino
and Vincoli. He further planned to send the Duke of
Orléans with a large army to conquer the Duchy of
Milan on his own account. To assist the campaign
against Genoa he sent Ottaviano Fregoso to the Florentines to ask them to attack Lunigiana and the eastern
Riviera simultaneously, and he ordered Pol Batista Fregoso to attack the western Riviera with six galleys.

These movements greatly alarmed the Duke of Milan
who was not yet himself sufficiently prepared to meet
them and had not yet received the assistance promised
him by the Venetians. If they had gone ahead as they
should have done they would have had some important
result—probably more so in the Duchy than in Genoa
where Gianluigi dal Fiesco and the Adorni had become
reconciled through Lodovico and where they had recruited
a large body of infantry and collected a fleet at the joint
expense of Lodovico and the Venetians. To this were
added six galleys sent by Federigo. The Pope, whose
membership in the league was confined to its decisions
and formalities rather than its practical actions, would
not incur any expense in this emergency either for land
or sea forces. The campaign proceeded as follows: Batistino and Trivulzio went together to Novi where Batis-

tino held the fortress, though the town had been taken from him by the Duke of Milan. Learning of their coming the Count of Gaiazzo who was garrisoning the town with 60 men-at-arms, 200 light horse and 500 foot soldiers, feared he could not defend it and retired to Serravalle. The taking of Novi increased the reputation of the exiles considerably, because the town bars the road from Milan to Genoa, besides being capable of sustaining a large population; and its position is very convenient for launching attacks on the surrounding places. Batistino subsequently occupied other places near Novi; and at the same time the Cardinal with 200 lances and 3,000 foot soldiers took Ventimiglia and moved up to Savona. But as those within made no move and he heard that Giovanni Adorno was approaching with a large body of infantry, he withdrew to Altare, a place belonging to the Marquis of Monferrato eight miles from Savona.

Trivulzio's moves were of greater importance. He was anxious to begin operations of war in the Duchy of Milan, though the King's instructions were to deal first with Genoa and Savona. He took Bosco, an important castle in the territory around Alessandria, on the pretext that it was necessary, for the safety of the force which had gone to the coast, to prevent the Duke of Milan's troops from moving from Alessandria to Genoa. Nevertheless, so as not to openly disobey the King's orders, he went no farther, thus losing a great opportunity; for the surrounding country was in great disorder through the taking of Bosco, some out of fear, others eager for change —and the Duke had only 500 men-at-arms and 6,000 foot soldiers in that area. Indeed Galeazzo Sanseverino, who was in Alessandria, where the Count of Gaiazzo also withdrew, was beginning to fear he could not defend it without a larger force. Lodovico, no less timid in this adversity than he was by nature in all the others, was asking the Duke of Ferrara to intervene between himself and the King of France to make peace. But Trivulzio's stopping between Bosco and Novi gave Lodovico time to make preparations and gave the Venetians, who had come quickly to his aid by sending 1,500 foot soldiers to Genoa, time to dispatch many men-at-arms and light horse to Alessandria. Finally they ordered the Count of Pitigliano, the leader of their army since the Marquis of Mantua had left the service of the Venetians, to go to the assistance of that state with most of his troops.

Thus what had begun with great expectations faded away. Batistino had no success at Genoa because the city remained quiet as a result of the precautions taken; and so he returned to join Trivulzio, saying that his plan had failed because the Florentines had not attacked the eastern Riviera. They had not thought it wise to involve themselves in the war before the efforts of the French showed themselves more vigorous and successful. Vincoli also went to join Trivulzio, having taken only a few places belonging to the Marchese del Finale, who had come out in defense of Savona. With the French forces collected together they made some sorties toward Castellaccio, a fortress near Bosco which had been fortified by the Duke's captains. But as the army of the league was constantly increasing and massing around Alessandria—while the French were beginning to be short of food and money, and the other captains were not very willing to obey Trivulzio—he was forced to withdraw his army near Asti, leaving garrisons behind in Novi and Bosco.

It is believed that this expedition was impeded, as often happens, by the division of the army into several parts, and that if at the beginning they had all gone to Genoa, they might have been more successful. Besides the feelings among the factions and the indignation the Genoese felt over Pietrasanta, part of the German cavalry and infantry sent there by the Duke remained only a few days and then suddenly returned to Germany. It may also be that the same ministers, who the year before had hindered the King's entry into Italy and the relief of the Kingdom of Naples, again used their cunning to impede this expedition by holding up supplies. The more so as it was said that the Duke of Milan, who placed heavy taxes on his subjects, gave a lot of money to the Duke of Bourbon and others who had influence with the King; and this evil rumor also included the Cardinal of St. Malo. However that may be, it is certain that the Duke of Orléans who was to go to Asti and was being urged to hasten by the King, made all the necessary preparations for going but delayed his departure, either because he was not satisfied with the arrangements which were being made, or because, as many believed, he was unwilling to leave France—as the King was constantly unwell; and if he should die without sons, the Duke was heir to the throne.

The King, having failed to bring about a change in government in Genoa and Savona, strove to bring to conclusion the negotiations with the King of Spain, which had been held up by one particular difficulty: the King of France, who wished to have his hands free for his enterprises on this side of the Alps, refused to have the affairs of Italy included in the terms of the truce. The King of Spain, showing that it was only for the sake of his own honor that he made difficulties about agreeing to this, insisted that they should be included. For, as it was their mutual intention to have a truce in order to negotiate a peace more easily, it would then be easier for them decently to abandon their alliance with the Italians. After ambassadors from both sides had gone to and fro several times, Spanish guile in the end prevailed—as it nearly always does. They signed a truce for themselves, their subjects and dependents, and also for anyone else either side might name. This truce was to come into force for themselves on March 5th and for their nominees fifty days later, and was to last until the end of the following October. Each nominated those Italian rulers and states which were their allies and supporters; the King of Spain in addition nominated King Federigo and the Pisans. They further agreed to send representatives to Montpelier to negotiate the peace treaty, where envoys of the other allies might participate. The Spanish monarchs held out hopes that they might then find some opportunity to ally themselves with the King of France against the Italians, proposing, even then, the idea of dividing the Kingdom of Naples between them. Although this truce was made without the participation of the Italian allies, it was nevertheless welcome to all and particularly the Duke of Milan who was most anxious for the war to move away from his territory.

But as they were free in Italy to attack one another up to April 25th, Trivulzio and Batistino, and with them Serenon, returned with 5,000 men to the western Riviera and attacked Albinga. Although they occupied almost the whole town at the first assault, they broke their ranks on entering and were driven out by a small number of the enemy. Then they entered the territory of the Marchese del Finale, hoping the Italian army would come to his assistance, and they could force it to a battle. When this failed, they did nothing further of importance, particularly as the disagreements among the captains had increased and payments were daily becoming scarcer on account of the truce. Meanwhile the league had recovered the places they had lost except for Novi; and this they finally gained by treaty, though the Count of Gaiazzo had been repulsed when he laid siege to it. Of the places they had taken there remained only a few small towns in the Marchesato del Finale in the hands of the French. Amid these troubles the Duke of Savoy, pursued with great offers by both sides, and the Marquis of Monferrato, whose tutelage had been adjudicated by the King of the Romans to Constantine of Macedonia, declared themselves neither for the King of France nor for the confederates.

During this year nothing of importance had occurred between the Florentines and the Pisans, although the war was still being carried on. Except that the Pisans under Giampaolo Manfrone went with 400 light horse and 1,500 foot soldiers to retake the bastion they had built at Ponte a Stagno, which they had lost when Maximilian left Leghorn. Conte Renuccio heard of this and went to relieve it with a large body of cavalry by the Leghorn road—while the Pisans did not think they might be attacked except by the Pontedera road. He arrived just as they were attacking the bastion and easily put them to flight, taking many prisoners. However both sides laid down their arms because of the truce, though the Florentines accepted this unwillingly because they thought it to their disadvantage to give the Pisans time to breathe. Also, in spite of the truce, they were forced to go· on

incurring the same expenses out of fear of Piero de'
Medici who was constantly plotting against them, and
also out of fear of the Venetian troops in Pisa.

Chapter XIII

[*The Duke of Milan proposes to the league to
hand over Pisa to the Florentines in order to draw
them away from the French alliance. The proposal
fails. Internal conditions in Florence. Piero de'
Medici's unsuccessful attempt to return to Florence. Wickedness and tragedy in the Pope's
family. Execution of those involved in Piero de'
Medici's plot.*]

Thus, as hostilities had ended everywhere or were
about to end, the Duke of Milan—though when danger
was imminent he had shown extreme gratitude to the
Venetian senate for the prompt assistance he had received, publicly praising with generous words the power
and glory of Venice and commending the foresight of
Giovan Galeazzo first Duke of Milan for having committed to the senate the execution of his will—could not
endure to see Pisa, which he had expended so much
effort and cunning to secure, fall into their hands, as
now seemed inevitable. So, endeavoring to attain by
cunning what he could not acquire by force, he arranged
for the Pope and the ambassadors of the King of Spain,
who objected to this increase in the power of the Venetians, to propose that, in order to remove all support in
Italy from the French and bring the whole nation into
harmony, it was necessary to persuade the Florentines
to join the league by restoring Pisa to them, there being
no other way of inducing them to do so. While they stood
apart from the rest, they were continually urging the
King of France to invade Italy; and if he did, they could
make quite a difference, with their troops and money,
placed as they were in the center of Italy. This proposal
was opposed by the Venetian ambassador as very harmful to the common good: he said that the Florentine

353

loyalty to the King of France was such that, even if this
benefit were conferred, they could not be trusted unless
they gave an adequate guarantee that they would observe
their promises; and in matters of such moment the only
security strong enough would be the depositing of Leghorn in the hands of the league. This was a cunning
suggestion, as he knew they would never consent to
pledge a city so important to their state; and so he had
ample opportunity to go on objecting. When this turned
out as he hoped, he objected so strongly that the Pope
and the Duke of Milan's representative were afraid to
oppose him so as not to drive him away from their alliance, and the proposal was dropped. The Pope and the
Venetians now conceived another plan to separate the
Florentines from the French alliance by force. The poor
state of Florence at that time gave encouragement to
anyone planning to attack the city, for there were great
divisions among the citizens over the present form of
her government.

At first when the popular government was set up, it
was not given those safeguards which, while ensuring
proper guarantees of freedom, would prevent the Republic from being disorganized by the inexperience and
license of the masses. In consequence there was great
confusion in the administration of the Republic: the
citizens of greater worth were too little regarded and
their ambitions suspected by the people; many men who
were not well qualified often had a hand in important
decisions, and the officers of the highest magistrature to
which the most important matters were referred were
changed every two months. There was also the great influence of Savonarola, whose followers had joined together almost in a tacit society; and as many of them
were eminent and respected citizens and they were more
numerous than the opposition, it seemed as though offices
and public honors were distributed more among his followers than among the others. For this reason the city
was openly divided, both sides coming into conflict in
public councils; and men did not mind, as generally
happens in divided cities, hindering the common good in
order to damage the reputation of their opponents.

What made these dissensions more serious was that in addition to the long hardships and heavy expense suffered by the city, there was a great shortage of food that year which led one to suppose that the hungry populace would seek some drastic change.

This state of affairs gave Piero de' Medici hopes of attaining his objects easily; and in this he was also encouraged by certain citizens. So, taking counsel with Federigo Cardinal of Sanseverino, an old friend of his, and with Alviano, and secretly urged on by the Venetians who hoped to settle the Pisan situation as a result of the troubles of the Florentines, Piero planned to enter Florence by treachery—the more so when he heard that the newly elected Gonfalonier of Justice, the head of the supreme magistrature, was Bernardo del Nero, a man of great gravity and authority who had long been his father's friend and his own. Moreover certain others had been elected to the same body who he believed might support him on account of their former allegiance. The Pope agreed to this plan, wishing as he did to separate the Florentines from the King of France by force since he had been prevented from doing so by means of generous offers. The Duke of Milan did not object either, as he did not think any stable agreement or firm basis could be reached with that city because of the disorganized condition of her government—though on the other hand he did not welcome the return of Piero de' Medici, both because of the harm he had done him and because he feared Piero might be too dependent on the Venetians.

When, therefore, Piero had collected what money he could on his own and with the help of friends (and it was believed a small quantity was given him by the Venetians), he went to Siena followed by Alviano with the cavalry and infantry, always traveling by night and across country so that his movements would not be known to the Florentines. At Siena, thanks to Jacopo and Pandolfo Petrucci, principal citizens of that state and friends of his and of his father, he secretly obtained further troops. So with 600 horse and 400 picked infantry he left for Florence two days after the beginning of the truce, in which the Sienese had not been included;

and he hoped that if he arrived by surprise at dawn, he would easily get in through some tumult or disorder which he expected to arise on his behalf. This plan might not have failed if luck had not favored his neglectful opponents; for when he had stopped early in the evening at Tavernelle—a group of houses on the main road— intending to ride on for most of the night, rain fell so heavily that he was held up and could not reach Florence until several hours after sunrise. This delay gave time to those who professed to be his particular enemies— because the populace and nearly all the rest of the citizens were waiting quietly for the outcome of the affair— to take up arms with their friends and followers and arrange for the suspected citizens to be summoned by the magistrates and detained in the palace, and to gather in strength at the gate opening onto the road to Siena. At their request Paolo Vitelli also went there, having arrived in Florence by chance the previous evening on his way back from Mantua. Therefore, as all the city was quiet and Piero was not strong enough to force the gate to which he had approached within a bowshot, after remaining there for four hours and beginning to fear that he might be in danger from the Florentine troops whom he correctly surmised had been sent for from Pisa, he went back to Siena and, having been let into Todi by the Guelphs, sacked nearly all the houses of the Ghibellines, killing 53 leading citizens of that party. Following his example Antonello Savelli entered Terni, and the Gatteschi entered Viterbo with the support of the Colonna faction and committed similar atrocities against the Guelphs in both towns and in the surrounding country. The Pope did nothing to prevent such disorders in the papal states, as he hated spending money on such things. And being by nature little troubled by the calamities of others, he was not disturbed by those things which offended his honor as long as his profit or pleasure was not interfered with.

However he could not escape family misfortunes which disturbed his house with tragic events—and with lechery and cruelty which would be horrible even in any barbarian country. From the beginning of his papacy he had planned to confer all his temporal power on his eldest son, the Duke of Gandia; but the Cardinal of Valencia (Cesare Borgia), whose temperament was totally unsuited to the priesthood, aspired to a military career, and could not bear to see this position occupied by his brother, of whom he was also jealous because he had a greater share in the love of their sister Madonna Lucrezia. So, spurred on by lechery and ambition (powerful agents of all great deeds of wickedness), he had him assassinated one night when he was riding alone through Rome and his body secretly thrown into the Tiber. It was also said (if such an enormity is to be believed) that not only the two brothers were rivals for the love of Madonna Lucrezia but their father as well. When he became Pope he had removed her from her first husband as a person now inferior to her station, and married her to Giovanni Sforza Lord of Pesaro. Then, unable to bear having her husband as his rival, he dissolved the marriage which had already been consummated, and had it proved by false witnesses before judges appointed by himself, who confirmed it in their findings that Giovanni was by nature frigid and impotent.

The death of the Duke of Gandia grieved the Pope beyond measure, for no father loved his children more passionately. And he was not used to the blows of fate, as from childhood until that time he had always been most fortunate in everything. He was so upset that in the consistory, after lamenting his sorrow with deep emotion and tears, and blaming many of his own actions and his way of living up to that time, he earnestly declared his wish to behave in the future with quite different intentions and habits, and he charged some of the cardinals with helping him to reform the habits and manners of the court. He pursued this course for several days, and as it began to be clear who was his son's assassin—at first it had been thought to be the work of Cardinal Ascanio or the Orsini—he gave up his good intentions and his tears and returned more immoderately than ever to those thoughts and actions in which he had spent all his life until then.

357

At this time new troubles arose in Florence as a result of Piero's action, because soon afterward the understanding he had with people in the city became known and many noble citizens were imprisoned while others fled. And when the conspiracy was verified by legal processes, there were condemned to death not only Niccolò Ridolfi, Lorenzo Tornabuoni, Giannozzo Pucci, and Giovanni Cambi, who had asked Piero to come, together with Lorenzo who had provided him with money for the purpose, but also Bernardo del Nero, who was charged with having known of the plot and not revealed it. This fault, which is punishable by death according to the Florentine statutes and also to the interpretation most lawyers place on the common law, was rendered more serious in his case by his being gonfalonier when Piero came to Florence. He had therefore a greater obligation to act as a public figure rather than as a private person. When the relatives of those condemned appealed the sentence to the great council of the people in virtue of a law which had been made when the popular government was first instituted, those who were responsible for the sentence got together, fearing lest compassion for their age and nobility and the great number of their relatives might soften the severity of the sentence in the hearts of the populace. They arranged that a small number of citizens should decide whether the appeal should be allowed to go forward or not. Among these there was a majority which said that it was dangerous and might engender sedition and that the laws themselves allowed laws to be set aside in such circumstances in order to avoid disorder. Some of those who sat in the supreme magistrature were forced to agree, almost with violence and threats, that the executions should be carried out that same night notwithstanding the appeal which had been lodged. The supporters of Savonarola were the most vehement on this point, and it was not to his credit not to have dissuaded at least his own followers from violating a law which had been proposed by him a few years before as very salutary, and virtually essential to the preservation of freedom.

Chapter XIV

[Federigo wins back more towns. Conclusion of a truce between Charles VIII and the King of Spain. Death of the Duke of Savoy. The Duke of Ferrara hands over the castle at Genoa to Lodovico Sforza. Further doubts and carelessness of the King of France, and their consequences for the affairs of Italy. The Italian allies again discuss the advisability of ceding Pisa to the Florentines. Opposition and objections of the Venetians.]

In this same year King Federigo of Naples obtained the investiture of his kingdom from the Pope and was ceremoniously crowned. He regained by agreement Monte Sant' Angelo which had been bravely defended by Don Julien de Lorraine, who had been left there by the King of France; also Civita and some other places held by Charles de Sanguine. As soon as the truce was over, he drove the Prefect of Rome from his kingdom and turned to do likewise with the Prince of Salerno, who, finally besieged in the fortress of Diano and abandoned by all, was given the chance to leave under safe-conduct with all his possessions. He left that part of his territory which he still held in the hands of the Prince of Bisignano with orders that he was to hand it over to Federigo as soon as he heard of his safe arrival at Sinigaglia.

At the end of this year, the Diet which had been transferred from Montpelier to Narbonne having been broken off owing to the exorbitant demands of the King of Spain, negotiations began again between the two monarchs. The same difficulties still existed: the King of France was determined not to make any further agreement which included Italy, and the Spanish monarchs thought it dangerous to leave him free to conquer Italy, while unwilling to have to fight him on his own soil in a war which would be very troublesome to them and of little profit. Finally a truce was concluded between them which was to last until denounced two months afterward; and none

of the Italian powers were included in it. The Spanish
monarchs informed them of the truce when it was concluded, saying that they were justified in making it
without the knowledge of the allies, just as the Duke of
Milan had been in concluding the Treaty of Vercelli
without their knowledge; and further, that as they had
declared war on France when the league was made and
continued it for several months while the money they
had been promised by the allies had not been paid—
though they had just cause to give up helping those who
had failed them—they had nevertheless said repeatedly
that, if they were paid 150,000 ducats owed to them for
expenses of the war so far, they were willing to accept
the money on account for their future efforts and to
enter France with a very powerful army. However (they
went on) as the allies had not replied to these demands,
failing both in their faith and their common interests,
and seeing that the league set up for the freedom of
Italy was now being used to usurp and oppress freedom,
since the Venetians, not content with having acquired
many ports of the Kingdom of Naples had without cause
occupied Pisa, it had seemed reasonable to them, since
others were already working against their common interest, to provide for their own with a truce. This had,
however, been made in such a way that it could be regarded rather as a warning than a desire to abandon the
league—as they could always terminate it by denouncing
it. They would denounce it when they saw the Italian
powers change their intentions and actions to the common good. However the Spanish monarchs were not able
to taste the joys of peace, because of the death of Juan,
Prince of Spain, their only son.

At this same time Philippe Duke of Savoy died leaving
a young son. After long hesitation he had seemed to be
inclining toward the league, which had promised to give
him 20,000 ducats a year. Yet he was so little trusted
that they did not place any great hopes on him should
the King of France invade in force.

At the end of the same year the Duke of Ferrara, who
had held the castle of Genoa in pledge for two years,
returned it to his son-in-law, Lodovico, having first asked

the King of France to make good half the expenses incurred in his guardianship—as had been agreed at Vercelli. The King said he would pay if the castle were
handed over to him, as he said the Duke was bound to do
because of the Duke of Milan's failure to honor the terms
of the treaty. When the Duke replied that this was not
proved and that to establish the contumacy of the Duke of
Milan it would be necessary to make a formal complaint,
the King offered to deposit the money, so that before the
payment was made it could be examined whether he was
in law bound to hand it over. But the pressing demands
to the contrary made by the Venetians and his son-in-law
weighed more on Ercole, who was influenced not only by
the instances and favors of Lodovico, who a few days
before had given the Archbishopric of Milan to Cardinal
Ippolito his son, but much more by the dangers of provoking the enmity of such powerful neighbors at a time
when the French invasions seemed less and less likely.
Therefore he recalled his son Ferrando from the French
court and returned the castle to Lodovico, who repaid
him his expenses in keeping it—even the portion which
the King should have paid. The Venetians, in order to
show their gratitude, commissioned his son Don Ferrando
with 100 men-at-arms.

This restitution which was done with very little justification—though it was very much to the detriment of
the King's prestige in Italy—did not seem to anger him
very much. In fact, when Ercole sent him an ambassador
to justify his action saying that, as his state was hemmed
in by the Venetians and the Duke of Milan who had
virtually threatened him with war, he had been forced to
comply, the King heard him with the same lack of interest as though it were a matter of little importance; and
it appeared that, in addition to his characteristic hap-
hazard behavior in all matters, he was still in his usual
straits and difficulties. For he was eager as ever to enter
Italy and now had even more powerful reasons for doing
so. There was his truce with Spain; the Swiss had recently confirmed their alliance with him, and many causes of
disunity had arisen among the members of the league.
However most of those around him were preventing him

from doing so by a variety of means. Some suggested new pleasures; others, while encouraging him to undertake the expedition, said he should go with such a powerful force by land and sea and with so great a fund of money that it would take a very long time to prepare; others took advantage of every opportunity and difficulty, while the Cardinal of St. Malo did not fail to make the usual delays in the financial provisions. Thus not only was the date when they were to enter Italy made more uncertain than ever, but the preparations that were almost completed were also dropped.

The Florentines, who were constantly urging him to come, had agreed that as soon as he had begun the war they would attack with their army in another quarter; and that Aubigny with 150 French lances, 100 paid for by the King and 50 by them, should come to Tuscany by sea to lead their army. The Marquis of Mantua, who had been dishonorably removed from his command with the Venetians when he returned victorious from the Kingdom of Naples—as he was suspected of planning to enter the service of the King of France—now really was seeking to be employed by him; and the new Duke of Savoy had confirmed his alliance with the French. Bentivoglio also promised to follow his orders when he entered Italy; and the Pope, who would not say whether or not he would contract an alliance, though the matter was continually under discussion, had decided that he would not at any rate oppose him. However, the King's delays and inattention damped everyone's enthusiasm because the troops he had promised were not entering Italy to mass at Asti, Aubigny's commission was not being arranged and he was not sending money to pay the Orsini and the Vitelli who were in his service; and this was a matter of some importance if there was going to be a war. Hence, when the Vitelli were about to take service with the Venetians, the Florentines, having no time to advise the King, commissioned them for one year jointly at the King's expense and theirs. This was applauded by him, but he never ratified the arrangement or paid his share. On the contrary he sent Gemel to ask them to lend him 150,000 ducats for the expedition. In the end, adopting other people's wishes as his own, as he so often did, he suddenly left Lyons and went to Tours and then to Amboise, making the usual promises to return soon to Lyons. Hence all those who supported him in Italy lost hope and Batistino Fregoso was reconciled with the Duke of Milan.

The Duke, taking courage from these events, made more and more clear his opposition to the Venetians over Pisa. He urged the Pope and the King of Spain to bring up again and more effectively the question of restoring the city to the Florentines. For this purpose the Florentines—at the instigation of the Duke—sent an ambassador to Rome early in 1498 with instructions to proceed very cautiously so as to convey to the Pope and the others that if Pisa were returned, they would join in the defense of Italy against the French, but with the proviso that, if nothing came of it, the King of France would not have cause to suspect them. These discussions went on in Rome for many days. The Pope, the Spanish ambassadors and those of the Duke of Milan, and the King of Naples openly urged on the Venetian ambassador that it was necessary for their mutual safety to bring in the Florentines against the French by this means and that the senate should agree with the rest; so that by destroying the cause of dissension, no one should remain in Italy with any reason to call in the foreigner. If unity were prevented on this account, it might cause the others to think again; and some major upheaval might result to the detriment of all. However the argument of the Venetian senate was quite different. Offering various pretexts for their greed and realizing who was principally responsible for this demand, they replied through their ambassador, protesting vigorously that the proposal did not arise from considerations of common benefit but from the ill will borne them by one of the members of the league; for as the Florentines had very close ties with the French and hoped, on their return, to be able to occupy most of Tuscany, there was no doubt that it would not be enough to return Pisa to them to wean them from this alliance. Rather would it be very dangerous to give it back to them, as the stronger they were, the more they would harm the security of Italy. In this restitution there was at stake the honor and good faith of all, but principally of their own Republic. For as the allies had all agreed to guarantee the freedom of the Pisans and then, as none was anxious to spend money on the common good, had left the expense to them while they had shirked no trouble or expense, it would be too dishonorable for them to abandon it and break their word. Because if others did not value theirs, they had always been accustomed to keep it and would under no circumstances dishonor it. The Venetian senate was extremely annoyed (they said) that others attacked them without any consideration for what they had begun with the consent of all and continued in their common interest, and that their good works were complained of with such ingratitude. The unbearably heavy expenses they had borne in this enterprise and in so many others and the hardships and dangers they had undergone since the league was formed did not deserve such a reward. These efforts had been such that they could boldly claim that Italy had been saved by them—for their arms alone had fought on the Taro, and their arms had recaptured the Kingdom of Naples. Whose army had forced Novara to surrender? Whose army had forced the King of France to leave the country? Whose forces had faced him in Piedmont whenever he showed signs of wanting to return? It could not be denied that these actions were largely inspired by their desire for the welfare of Italy, for they had never been the most exposed to danger nor had they been the cause of disturbances which they felt they ought to remedy. They had not called the King of France into Italy or helped him after he had crossed the Alps, or allowed the common good to fall into decay to save their own money. On the contrary the Venetian senate had often been forced to remedy the disturbances caused by others to the detriment of all. If these efforts of theirs were not appreciated or were so soon forgotten, they were not willing on that account to follow the dubious example of others and sully the faith and dignity of their Republic—particularly as the safety and well-being of all Italy was bound up with the preservation of the freedom of the Pisans.

364

Chapter XV

*[Death of Charles VIII and its consequences. De-
cline of Savonarola's authority in Florence. His
conflict with the Pope. His execution.]*

While these discussions were proceeding among the
allies with unconcealed disagreement, an event occurred
which had unexpected results. On the night of April 7th
King Charles died at Amboise from an attack of what the
doctors call apoplexy. It happened while he was watching
a game of tennis and it was so violent that he died within
a few hours without being moved. In his life he had set
the world in turmoil with more temerity than courage
and there was the danger that he would do so again.
Many believed that his strong desire to return to Italy
would have led him—either of his own accord or by the
influence of those who were jealous of the power of the
Cardinal of St. Malo—to overcome the obstacles which
had been placed in his way. Thus, though his invasion
seemed now more, now less likely in Italy, according to
his changes of mood, it kept everyone in continual suspense. Hence the Pope, moved by his ambition to promote
the power of his sons, had already begun to negotiate
secretly with him; and it was later said—whether true or
false—that the Duke of Milan, so as not to be in perpetual fear, had done likewise.

As Charles died without a son the Kingdom of France
passed to Louis Duke of Orléans, who was more nearly
related to him in the male line than anyone else. When
the King was dead, the royal guard and all the court
hastened to him at Blois; and then one by one came all
the princes of the kingdom, to pay their respects and
recognize him as king—though some secretly complained
that he had become ineligible for the crown, against
which he had taken up arms in the war in Brittany.

The day after Charles' death—which was Palm Sunday
—Savonarola's authority in Florence also ended. Some
time before he had been denounced to the Pope for

preaching scandalously against the behavior of the clergy and the court of Rome, for nourishing discord in Florence and for holding doctrines not wholly Catholic; and for this reason he had been summoned to Rome by several apostolic letters. He had offered various excuses for not going and finally, the year before, the Pope had excommunicated him from the Church. He had therefore stopped preaching for a few months and if he had abstained a little longer he would have obtained his absolution without much difficulty, because the Pope held him of small account and had proceeded against him more as a result of the influence and pressure of his enemies than for any other reason. But Savonarola felt his influence declining if he remained silent—or that his objectives would be harmed, as they had largely been promoted by the power of his preaching; so, flouting the Pope's commands, he again began to preach in public. He asserted that the censures on him were contrary to God's will and harmful to the common good and so were unjust and invalid; and he attacked the Pope and all his court with extreme vehemence.

This gave rise to serious disturbances because his opponents, whose influence with the people was increasing all the time, objected to his disobedience and complained that his temerity would anger the Pope at the very moment when the restitution of Pisa was being discussed by him and the league, and they ought to make every effort to encourage the Pope in this intention. On the other hand he was defended by his supporters, who said that the work of God ought not to be disturbed by worldly concerns, and they ought not to allow the Pope to interfere in the affairs of their Republic under such a pretext. This dispute went on for many days. And in the end the Pope became exceedingly angry and fulminated with still more letters and threats of excommunication against the whole city. So the magistrates forbade Savonarola to preach. Though he obeyed, many of his friars went on preaching in a number of churches. As the divisions between the priests were no less than those among laymen, the friars of other orders constantly and passionately preached against them. Finally their outbursts became so violent that one of Savonarola's friars and one of the Minorites agreed to walk through fire before the whole assembled population—so that according to whether Savonarola's friar was burnt or not everyone would know for certain whether he was a true prophet or a fraud. For he had often said in the past in his sermons that as a sign of the truth of his preaching he would, if need be, obtain God's grace to pass unharmed through fire. Nevertheless, he was not pleased that the question of trying the ordeal now had been raised without his knowledge and he attempted with some skill to prevent it; but as the affair had gone very far of its own accord and was encouraged by some citizens who wished to see the city freed from these dissensions, in the end they were forced to go on with it.

On the appointed day the two friars, followed by all the members of their orders, came into the square before the palace, where there had gathered not only the Florentines but many people from the surrounding towns. Then the Minor friars heard that Savonarola had instructed his friar to bear the Sacrament in his hands when he entered the fire. They objected to this, maintaining that the authority of the Christian faith was being placed in jeopardy, and would lose much of its power if the Host were burned. As Savonarola, who was present, persisted in his decision, they began to quarrel and the ordeal was abandoned. Because of this his credit declined so much that the following day when a riot occurred for some reason, his enemies took arms and with the authority of the chief magistrates stormed the monastery of San Marco where he lived. They dragged him with two of his friars to the common jail. In this upheaval the kinsmen of those who had been beheaded the year before assassinated Francesco Valori, a very great citizen and chief among Savonarola's supporters. This was done because it had been largely his authority which had deprived them of the right to appeal to the people's council.

Afterward Savonarola was examined under torture, though not very severe, and a report was published based on this examination. This contained none of the calumnies that had been uttered against him, of avarice or

367

wicked practices, or of having had secret negotiations with foreign princes. It said simply that the things he had predicted were not divine revelations but his own views based on doctrine and the study of Holy Scripture; that he had not been moved by any wicked purpose or by ambition to gain ecclesiastical preferment, but had wished to bring about a general council in which the corrupt lives of the clergy would be reformed and the state of God's Church, which was so depraved, would be made as like as possible to that of apostolic times. He had prized this glory of achieving so great and worthy a purpose far more than obtaining the papacy for himself; because the former could only be brought about by most excellent doctrine and virtue and by the high respect of all men, but the papacy was often obtained by evil arts or good fortune.

As a result of this report—which he agreed to in the presence of many priests, including some of his own order, though he did so (if what his followers later said is true) in a few words which could be interpreted in various ways—he was sentenced along with the other two friars by order of the General of the Dominicans and Bishop Romolino, who later became Cardinal of Sorrento, commissioners appointed by the Pope, to be stripped of his Holy Orders with the ceremonies prescribed by the Roman Church, and given into the hands of the secular court.

They were then hanged and burned at the stake. A crowd came to see his degradation and execution, just as large as the one which had gathered on the same spot on the day appointed for the ordeal by fire in the hopes of seeing the miracle he had promised. His death, which was suffered with constancy but without a word expressing either innocence or guilt, did not put an end to the variety of men's judgments on him or their passions. Many thought him a charlatan; many on the other hand believed either that the confession which was published had been falsely invented or that torture had greater power over his frail constitution than truth. They excused this weakness with the example of the Prince of Apostles who, neither imprisoned nor forced by torture or any other compulsion but simply at the words of maids and servants, denied that he was the disciple of the Master whose many holy teachings and miracles he had witnessed.

Hugh R. Trevor-Roper, general editor of *The Great Histories Series*, is the distinguished Regius Professor of Modern History at Oxford University. He is probably most well known to American readers for his book *The Last Days of Hitler*, which is a classic in the field of modern German history and was the result of official investigations carried out by Professor Trevor-Roper at the behest of British Intelligence in an attempt to unshroud the mystery surrounding the dictator's fate. The book has already been translated into nineteen foreign languages. Professor Trevor-Roper is a specialist in sixteenth- and seventeenth-century history and has published several other notable works: *Archbishop Laud, Man and Events*. He has contributed numerous articles on political and historical subjects to the journals and is familiar to American readers of *The New York Times Magazine* and *Horizon*.

John R. Hale, editor of this volume, received his M.A. at Oxford in 1948 and since 1949 has been a Fellow and Tutor of Jesus College, Oxford University. In 1959-60 he was a Visiting Associate Professor at Cornell University. A distinguished scholar and lecturer, Professor Hale has published numerous works in his special field of Renaissance history. Among his books are ENGLAND AND THE ITALIAN RENAISSANCE, MACHIAVELLI AND RENAISSANCE ITALY, and THE LITERARY WORKS OF MACHIAVELLI. He has contributed to Volumes I and II of THE NEW CAMBRIDGE MODERN HISTORY and to such eminent journals as *Italian Studies, Past and Present, The Huntington Library Quarterly,* and *The Newberry Library Bulletin.*

NOTES ON THE TEXT

1. In 1482 Florence intervened to protect Ferrara from Venice, and in 1485 assisted Ferdinand of Naples against a rising of discontented barons. Later in this narrative, and in the *History of Italy*, the form "Ferrando" is used for Ferdinand II of Naples, to distinguish him from Ferdinand I (mentioned here) of Naples, his grandfather, and from Ferdinand of Aragon.

2. Blank in ms. Actually April 8th.

3. The cathedral.

4. In 1478 Lorenzo escaped with renewed security and prestige from the assassination plot known as the Pazzi Conspiracy; in 1479 he went to Naples and succeeded, at great personal risk, in detaching Ferdinand from his anti-Florentine alliance with Pope Sixtus IV.

5. Lorenzo's father; Cosimo was his grandfather.

6. July 25th. Borgia took the name Alexander VI.

7. Actually January 25, 1494; but Guicciardini is using the Florentine year which ended on March 24th, not December 31st.

8. The chief officers of state.

9. Of the Palazzo Vecchio, then called Palazzo della Signoria.

10. A *quattrino* introduced in 1490 which had the effect of devaluing the old copper *quattrino*. Taxes were commonly paid in these copper coins, and thus became more burdensome. It was one of the most unpopular innovations of Lorenzo's regime.

11. The Council of Seventy elected the Signoria; the Eight looked after external affairs. Both were creations of Lorenzo and were used to buttress his power.

12. November 17, 1494.

13. Until November 28th.

14. In fact, November 25th.

15. The *parlamento* was an open meeting of the people as a whole.

16. Council of Ten, in charge of military operations.

17. In charge of the administration of justice.

18. The chief financial organ of the state.

19. The council in charge of commerce and finance.

20. The Signoria, the 12 and the 16 Gonfaloniers of companies.

21. i.e., two thirds majority.

22. The title given the German Emperor when he had not yet been formally crowned by the Pope.

23. A white bean was an adverse vote.

24. *Pratica;* an *ad hoc* body called to discuss a specific problem.

25. April 7th.

26. Maruffi.

27. May 23rd.

28. Not to be confused with his contemporary, Ferdinand King of Aragon, husband of Isabella, Queen of Castille.

29. This was early in 1492.

30. In fact it was Louis de Graville.

31. Each "lance" consisted of a mounted man-at-arms and his entourage, which might include three fighting men.

32. Treaty of Barcelona, January 19, 1493.

33. Treaty of Senlis, May 3, 1493.

34. Alexander VI's son. Don Gioffredo, mentioned a few lines later, was the Pope's youngest son.

35. The Pazzi Conspiracy of 1478.

36. Louis XI, Charles VIII's father.

37. Alfonso's brother.

38. He became Pope Julius II.

39. Walter of Brienne, brought in to settle civic factions in 1342 and expelled in the following year.

40. The League of Venice, March 31, 1495.

41. Balkan light cavalry.

42. This theory as to the introduction of syphilis still has wide support.

GUICCIARDINI: SOME DATES

1483	Born, March 6th
1508-9	Writes *History of Florence*
1511	Chosen ambassador to Spain
1516	Governor of Modena
1517	Governor of Reggio
1521	Governor of Parma
1524	President of the Romagna
1526	Lieutenant General of papal armies
1527	Returns to Florence after the sack of Rome
1527-8	Begins the *Florentine Affairs*
1536	Begins the *History of Italy*
1540	Dies, May 22nd

Index